Boricua Power

Boricua Power

A Political History of Puerto Ricans in the United States

José Ramón Sánchez

NEW YORK UNIVERSITY PRESS
New York and London

NEW YORK UNIVERSITY PRESS
New York and London
www.nyupress.org

Library of Congress Cataloging-in-Publication Data
Sánchez, José Ramón.
Boricua power : a political history of Puerto Ricans in the United
States / José Ramón Sánchez.
p.   cm.
Includes bibliographical references and index.
ISBN-13: 978-0-8147-9847-8 (cloth : alk. paper)
ISBN-10: 0-8147-9847-0 (cloth : alk. paper)
ISBN-13: 978-0-8147-9848-5 (pbk. : alk. paper)
ISBN-10: 0-8147-9848-9 (pbk. : alk. paper)
   1. Puerto Ricans—United States—Politics and government. 2. Puerto
Ricans—United States—Social conditions. 3. Power (Social sciences)—
United States—History. 4. Political participation—United States—
History. 5. Community life—United States—History. 6. United States
—Ethnic relations—Political aspects.   I. Title.
E184.P85S255 2007
305.868'7295—dc22   2006032855

New York University Press books are printed on acid-free paper,
and their binding materials are chosen for strength and durability.

Manufactured in the United States of America

c 10 9 8 7 6 5 4 3 2 1
p 10 9 8 7 6 5 4 3 2 1

Contents

Acknowledgments

Projects that last as long as this one don't get done without the visible and invisible help of tons of people. A limitation of space prevents me from trying to list them all. I have an obligation, however, to thank those people who I think have given me direct support and assistance. Some will be surprised but, hopefully, not offended at being so recognized.

Families are usually left for last in these matters. Mine won't be. They are vital to who I am and what I have been able to achieve. Their impact has been both positive and twisted, an album of pains and joys that form the fabric that is my life. First, there's Mami. Obviously, without her I would not be around to write this. More important, she taught me the only lesson I needed to survive and advance in this world. She never let our desperation and poverty get in the way of dreaming and striving for something better, even if it was only another apartment in the same building.

If I took that lesson to heart, it was my wife, Luchi, who showed me so much about how to dream as well as to always enjoy the journey towards those dreams. Luchi, you have always believed in me and supported my efforts in ways that I thought were not humanly possible. You nourished my thoughts, my soul, and my stomach. Your *adobo* has inspired and reminded me of what true perfection tastes like. You showed enormous patience and endured enormous deprivations in the course of this work. You have been my true dance partner in life and on the dance floor. After all these years, you still move me.

I thank my children for pushing me to grow up and for keeping me young. Leina, I marvel at your quiet introspection, your calm, and your creativity. You are right. It is usually better to say too little than to say too much. Hope I didn't disappoint you in this book. Desi, I borrowed some of your energy but not many of your brain cells. If I achieved some balance between substance and style, between breadth and depth, between seriousness and levity, I owe it to you, Hannah. Carlo, what you build is always strong, beautiful, and, for that reason, an everlasting model for me. Jam, your smile always makes me smile. And then there is Alex. Your questions about this book at eight years old not only amused me but they forced me, hopefully, to articulate the main ideas better.

I've been blessed to enjoy the friendship of truly amazing, intelligent, and beautiful people. Compadre Angelo Falcon, you didn't always agree with the ideas in this book. What you had to say, however, was always important and critical to my thinking, even if I didn't always follow your advice. More important, these intellectual disagreements never got in the way of a friendship that has been so critical to my development as a person and to the fight for justice we continue to wage. Iris Lopez, you understood many of the obstacles I had to overcome and helped me to get over them. Your advice was critical to getting this project off the ground. I only hope I can repay your wisdom and kindness some day. Hermano Rudy Rosales, you live far from me but you are the closest to where I reside intellectually. You provided important feedback in earlier drafts and many, always enjoyable, *charlas* on so many political and theoretical issues. Marcos Pelaez and Amadio Medina, you kept the pressure on by asking about my writing progress every time I saw you. Hard physical labor did not prevent you guys from offering me persistent and critical encouragement towards the completion of this book.

I owe huge debts to my place of work, the Brooklyn Campus of Long Island University, and the wonderful colleagues and staff who believed in me and had great patience in helping me complete this project. John Ehrenberg has always been a shining example of Gramsci's organic intellectual, a terrific colleague, and a supportive friend. Gladys Schrynemakers, Al DiMaio, Patrice McSherry, JoAnn Faraci, and Minna Pacheco also provided encouragement, support, occasional chuckles, and more kindness than I ever deserved. My students were always a source of wonder and the hapless guinea pigs on which I foisted my shapeless ideas. They deserve more credit than they will ever know for helping me hone my ideas and none of the blame for my failures in presenting them.

The editors and managers at New York University Press have made a tremendous contribution to this book. Salwa Jabado was a great babysitter. She provided encouragement and just the right amount of pressure combined with freedom. Managing editor Despina Papazoglou Gimbel did magical work in cleaning and improving the language of this book. Any remaining weaknesses are, of course, due to my own stubbornness.

My last thanks are to the Puerto Rican people. You've welcomed me into your arms in so many ways, and I've always felt so comfortable there. I was born in Jarabacoa, the Dominican Republic. My direct Puerto Rican ancestry is thin and remote, a grandfather on my mother's side. My connection to the Puerto Rican people was and is, however, forged in steel, hammered into being by the *jibaro* guitars I heard growing up on 133rd Street, Puerto Rican *ay benditos!, arroz y gandules* on Sundays, and a long history of struggle to achieve justice and equality together in this country. Power was always part of that consciousness. It was always hard to understand, let alone reconcile, the vibrancy, resilience, and blunt impact of Puerto Rican culture, life, and people with the persistent inability of this community to seriously shape the life of others in this society. Something was missing. Most of the popular explanations and theories about power could not explain what went wrong. I found some answers, however, with my students in introductory political science classes.

Some of the most important ideas about power I discovered in the classroom. The recent tradition in political science has been to simply ignore the basic question of where power comes from and how it disappears because these questions are just not amenable to quantification. Teaching interdisciplinary courses made it possible for me to discover a useful research literature in social exchange theory that political science had completely ignored. That literature opened new theoretical possibilities. More important was the teaching process itself.

There was complex power in my exchanges with students. Not just mine but theirs. Teachers have to rely on more than their position of authority in order to get students to pay attention, to learn, and to pursue knowledge on their own. The power we have over students, even the authoritative kind, is more than relative and variable. It is deeply dependent on them. The lines of dependence and influence cross each other and originate in both partners. This interaction resembles a kind of social dance, with an ebb and flow of influence that is more mutual than it might appear. My students can ruin my evenings as much as I can ruin theirs. I began to see power as generated by critical levels of dependence, desire, needs, and wants in each partner. From that point on, I pursued the theoretical outlines of this idea and the empirical test in Puerto Rican community history that could give it validity. In fundamental ways, then, this book was born in my experiences with my students in the classroom. I will forever owe you guys. Thanks.

Introduction

Every social act is an exercise of power, every social relationship is a power equation, and every social group or system is an organization of power.[1]

Power here. Power there. Power is everywhere (Boulding 1990, 131). Power exists as much in the way that lovers relate to each other as in electoral contests for political office.[2] We've learned that power can be conveyed and shaped by conversation and by the way we organize the space in which we live and work (Korda 1975; Goodsell 1988). However, though it seems as though we know more now about the many places where power can be found, we don't know much about how power grows or is lost.

Existing theories of power avoid or fail to adequately explain how power gets created and destroyed. In most cases, the reason for this failure is simply that these theories insist on treating power as if it were an object. Power is viewed as an instrument, a structure, a possession, a finite object like gold that can be held, lost, or taken from others. Power, in this sense, is never destroyed or created. It is simply hoarded, taken or passed from one person, institution, or state to another. But power, this study argues, is not object but movement. It is not fixed but dynamic. It is not dead but alive. It is always either building up or breaking down. Power is always a movement initiated not by solitary individuals but between couples, groups, and communities. Because it is something we set in motion, power is in fact a dance.[3]

The deficiencies of the thing-like approach to power become clear in popular language, current debates, and history. During the last fifteen years, for example, analysts and pundits have made extravagant claims about the emerging power of the Puerto Rican and Latino community in the United States based simply on the expectation of growing population size. The "Year of the Hispanic" quickly turned into the "Decade of the

Hispanic." The reality is that though Puerto Ricans and Latinos now have more people, they are not, by most people's estimates, any more powerful. None of the predictions considered whether having more people would really allow Latinos to make more policy decisions, set more political agendas, or influence and manipulate the self-interest of others (see Sanchez 1994). The reason is that these predictions assume, with many other theoretical approaches, that power is thing-like, something that can be amassed by pure addition, piece by piece or person by person. Power is not, in reality, anything like that.

The analysis in this study of Puerto Rican community history demonstrates that, frequently, power is amassed according to processes that are exactly at odds with the thing-like approach. In fact, being small in numbers, having little money, and controlling few votes did not prevent Puerto Ricans from gaining power during the early part of the twentieth century. That story of a powerful, yet small Puerto Rican community in the early twentieth century has much to teach us about the nature of power and how Latinos or any group can acquire it.

Contrary to the predictions of Latino emergence, Puerto Ricans today have very little power. They lack what Isaac has called the "enduring capacity to act" in society (1987, 142). In simplistic and crude terms, Puerto Ricans are acted upon. And yet we know that Puerto Ricans do, of course, act. Is it that when they do so, they leave no real mark? The broad scholarly and popular consensus seems to be that when Puerto Ricans act, the tracks and imprints of their impact quickly disappear. The social landscape and its inhabitants remain relatively unchanged by their presence. It is as if Puerto Ricans walk perpetually on wet sand. This conclusion is a common and popular one, even among Puerto Ricans, and yet, basically, it is not true. Puerto Ricans are generally not that powerful a group. However, in different historical periods, Puerto Ricans have increased their power as well as lost it.

How did the Puerto Rican community get and then lose power? The existing theoretical approaches to explaining power offer little help. The main reason is that most cannot explain what makes power possible. In some theories, power is reduced to the making of decisions (Dahl 1957). But power is, as Dahl's critics have aptly pointed out, not simply the making of decisions. It is more like an assurance that decisions made are likely to be enforced, obeyed, and followed. Decision-making theories can't explain that. In response to these deficiencies, other theories point to agenda setting and the manipulation of interests to explain who has power. This approach doesn't explain, however, how and why some people get to such lofty, commanding positions with regards to others in the first place (Bachrach and Baratz 1962; Lukes 1974). What, for instance, gives someone, some groups, some institutions, or some class the ability to set agendas and shape self-interest?

More recent, "postmodern" theories have avoided the issue of the origins of power entirely by claiming that power comes into existence on its own as an almost primordial and ghostly entity (Foucault and Gordon 1980). This approach never attempts to answer the question of where power comes from. Power, in this perspective, is everywhere and has always existed.

If, as some have said, power is the core concept in the social sciences, it has, nonetheless, proven impossible to conceptualize and measure accurately. The problem in understanding power is not really about measurement. It is, actually, that we don't really probe where power comes from and how and why it disappears. We assume and thus look for resources, weapons, soldiers, and in general for hard, fixed bodies that contain the force necessary to overcome the resistance of those bereft of will and of similar "things with power." This study argues for the idea that power emerges, instead, from the "dance" between agents driven by interests and passions to engage and put themselves into another's hands.

We know that Puerto Ricans today do not make an enduring impact on the social sphere that makes their lives possible. As Puerto Rican government official Manny Diaz once put it, Puerto Ricans do "not own banks, buy and sell the corporate stocks, deal in the real estate of whole neighborhoods, or control jobs the way an industrialist does" (Steiner 1974, 370). However, while the possession of these "things" certainly makes some people powerful, it does so only because other people need and desire those things. Money possesses an enormous amount of power in capitalist society precisely because life is made almost impossible for any of its members who don't have much of it. Knowing that, members of capitalist society develop heightened levels of need and desire for money. That desire and need is what gives money such tremendous influence over their lives.

The key to power, then, lies not in the "things" themselves but in the degree to which people need, want, and desire them. It is that intersection of desires and needs for particular "values" (like money but also sex or music or anything else) between different groups that determines which groups develop more power. Put simply, groups have power to the extent that they control values that others need, want, or desire. Power is, as a consequence, dynamic and fluid. It grows and shrinks as interests and values rise and fall. It is a dance of attraction and repulsion, a movement towards and away, that transfers and delivers power with each swing. The power of Puerto Ricans, when they had much and when they had less of it, is thus best studied through an examination of the nature, direction, and intensity of the needs, wants, and desires between Puerto Ricans and other groups. It is these movements to and fro, these stirrings of passions and interests, as theorists have long called them, that create and destroy power.

The main assumption of the dance model is, thus, that we gain power as a result of the interests and passions we have in the values possessed by others. We seek rewards from others, avoid punishment from some, and meet our needs for affection, sustenance, and gain from an assortment of other people. What we seek and how we define these relationships gives others the ability to influence us, to change us, even if only temporarily. That's power. This idea of power is brought beautifully to life in Julia Alvarez's fictionalized account of a young Dominican woman's dance with the Dominican dictator Trujillo from her book *In the Time of the Butterflies*. Alvarez writes, from the young woman's perspective,

His hold is proprietary and masculine, but he is not a good dancer. All firmness, and too many flourishes. A couple of times, he steps on my foot, but he does not excuse himself. "You dance very well," he says gallantly. "But then women from El Cibao make the best dancers and the best lovers," he whispers, tightening his hold. I can feel the moisture of his breath on my ear.

"And your last partner, was she from El Cibao?" I ask, encouraging conversation so he has to draw back a little. I have to check myself from saying, A visit is not a long stay, you know.

He holds me out in his arms, his eyes moving over my body, exploring it rudely with his glances. "I am speaking of the national treasure in my arms," he says, smiling.

I laugh out loud, my fear dissipating, a dangerous sense of my own power growing. "I don't feel very much like a national treasure."

"And why not, a jewel like you?" His eyes sparkled with interest.

"I feel like I'm wasting my life in Ojo de Agua."

"Perhaps we can bring you down to the capital," he says archly.

"That's exactly what I'm trying to convince Papa to do. I want to go to the university," I confess, playing this man against my own father. If El Jefe says he wants me to study, Papa will have to let me. "I've always wanted to study law."

He gives me the indulgent smile of an adult hearing an outrageous claim from a child. "A woman like you, a lawyer?"

I play on his vanity, and so, perhaps, become his creature like all the others. "You gave the women the vote in '42. You encouraged the founding of the women's branch of the Dominican party. You've always been an advocate for women."

"That I have." He grins a naughty grin. "A woman with a mind of her own. So you want to study in the capital, eh?"

I nod decisively, at the last minute softening the gesture with a tilt of my head.

"I could see our national treasure then on a regular basis. Perhaps, I could conquer this jewel as El Conquistado conquered our island."

The game has gone too far. "I'm afraid I'm not for conquest."

"You already have a novio?" This can be the only explanation. Even so, engagement, marriage—such things make a conquest more interesting. "A woman like you should have many admirers."

"I'm not interested in admirers until I have my law degree."

A look of impatience crosses his face. Our tête-à-tête is not following its usual course. "The university is no place for a woman these days."

"Why not, Jefe?"

He seems pleased by my referring to him by his affectionate title of Chief. By now, we are so immersed in conversation we are barely dancing. I can feel the crowd watching us.

"It's full of communists and agitators, who want to bring down the government. That Luperon mess, they were in back of it." His look is fierce—as if the mere mention had summoned his enemies before him. "But we've been teaching those teachers their lessons all right!"

They must have caught him! "Virgilio Morales?" I blurt out. I can't believe my own ears. His face hardens, suspicion clouds the gaze. "You know Virgilio Morales?"

What a complete idiot I am! How can I now protect him and myself? "His family is from El Cibao, too," I say, choosing my words carefully. "I know the son teaches at the university."

El Jefe's gaze is withdrawing further and further into some back room of his mind where he tortures meaning out of the words he hears. He can tell I'm stalling. "So, you do know him?"

"Not personally, no," I say in a little voice. Instantly, I feel ashamed of myself. I see now how easily it happens. You give in on little things, and soon you're serving in his government, marching in his parades, sleeping in his bed. (Alvarez 1994, 98–99)

This passage provides a marvelous example of how power can be generated from the passions and interests evoked and expressed in relationships like the one between the young woman and the dictator Trujillo. The young woman tries to take advantage of the power she is momentarily given as a result of El Jefe's lust for her. She wants to become a lawyer in a male-dominated society and Trujillo can make it possible. At that moment, because of his lust, she has him in her hands. She can use El Jefe against her father. That power dissipates when she carelessly admits to knowing the dissident/agitator Virgilio Morales. At that moment, Trujillo pushes aside his lust and lets his dictator's fear of being overthrown occupy a primary position in his mind and feelings. The lust for her gone, so is whatever little and temporary power she had acquired over El Jefe.

The dance floor, whether peopled by dictators or high school students, is fraught with lessons in power. We hope and try to engage others who can satisfy some of our needs and desires. We look, admire, envy, covet, and perhaps even believe that we have what it takes to dance with a special someone. The key is that it is by having those interests, expressing them, and acting upon them that we give others, even if they don't know it, some power over us. They may bask in our adoration, become arrogant and smug, or act happily and humbly surprised. But to a great extent, they derive their power from us. Those others can take knowledge of our interest and treat us kindly (return a smile) or patronizingly (agree to a dance) or manipulatively ("buy me a drink first!").

In turn, the power created this way makes possible three basic strategies for the less powerful. One response is to agree, tolerate, or simply accept the power they have given others. A second possible response is to regain some or all of that power for themselves by reducing how much they need, want, or desire that particular dance partner. They can act as if they no longer want to dance. A final strategy is to gain some power for themselves and against others by increasing the interest others have in dancing with them. Some of these three strategies of power are harder to realize for some people and groups than for others. They are, nonetheless, the basic elements of the dance of power in any context.

Why Puerto Ricans?

Puerto Ricans are one of the poorest groups in the United States. They are, arguably, also one of the least powerful. They do not lack power because they are small in numbers or very poor. Other ethnic-racial groups, like Italians and Jews, have increased their social power despite their poverty and small population. Nor can the explanation simply be that Puerto Ricans face racial discrimination. Yes, Puerto Ricans do live in the "belly of the monster," as Jose Marti once said of life in the United States. They do face racism and exploitation. But any explanation that relies on these categories succeeds only in making Puerto Ricans into victims, objects, and pawns of larger forces, like the racist American capitalist society.

The dance model argues that the story of power for Puerto Ricans has more to do with dancing than carnage. This means that though Puerto Ricans were and are "consumed" by the monster, this is the case not simply because the monster is strong and has sharp teeth. Puerto Ricans are devoured and weakened by the monster only because they want to and sometimes become its dance partner. Puerto Ricans, as Marx once wrote about money, "give their power and strength unto the beast."[4]

This study examines how and to what extent Puerto Ricans lost and gained power by "dancing." To a large extent, Puerto Rican attempts to satisfy their own needs and desires placed them in the hands of landlords, employers, politicians, and many others. But how much "choice" did they have? How many options did they have as they placed themselves in the hands of others? Also, were they acting in response to needs or desires? Could Puerto Ricans have danced differently, with different partners? What did they accept? What did they reject? Upon landing in America, how eager and willing were Puerto Ricans to dance on a "dance floor" and with "dance steps" that were "written by usually nameless others, past, present, or future"—that is, how eager were they to act within existing social structures (Berger 1995, 4)?

The general answer to these questions is that Puerto Ricans, like any other group, gained and lost power by taking steps, making advances, engaging others, and, in general, by becoming active partners in the many sets of relationships they faced in America. Usually, decisions made by them and others, paths laid down in the past, shaped how and with whom they could dance. This process of approach and engagement is necessary for power to exist between individuals, between groups, and between nation states. This is clearly evident in the international political system. John M. Rothgeb, for example, states that "if one country seeks to control the behavior of another, then at a minimum it must have some degree of contact with the entity it wishes to control" (Rothgeb 1993, 27). The big question for the dance model is this: if the dance model of power is true, why would Puerto Ricans, or any group or state, continue to dance if they get weaker by doing so?

Puerto Ricans did act, did dance even when dancing made them weak. And dancing made them weak more often than not. For example, Puerto Ricans were among the thirty thousand cigar workers who went on strike in 1919 and brought the tobacco industry in New York City to a halt. They found themselves out of work a few short years later, however, when cigar manufacturers switched to machines and reduced their dependence on cigar makers. Despite such disappointment, Puerto Ricans did not hesitate, later, to continue moving and dancing. They had too many needs, too many desires, and few ways to satisfy them. They sought power where they could and thought they could get more of it that way. The impetus to act or dance is conscious and unconscious, intentional and unintentional, as well as individual and social. The more important observation is that power can only come from dancing, by engaging others, by getting others to seek and value Puerto Ricans.

That, in general, is why Puerto Ricans continued to move, though in the long run doing so made them weak. At times, their hopes for more power were misplaced or mistaken. They chose the wrong partner. Migrating to the United States to take jobs in a declining manufacturing sector is one example. The "music" was sometimes wrong and unfamiliar. They lacked skills to dance well in the jobs and cities they found in the United States. Their movements sometimes broke them down. The ironic, debilitating consequence of successful class struggle in the tobacco industry is one example.

Then, there were times when dancing did bring Puerto Ricans more power. But that power often proved fleeting or temporary. An example is the economic and political interest by New York City business and political leaders in bringing Puerto Rican labor to work in New York in the early 1950s. The music sometimes changed. Cheaper, more compliant labor was found to replace Puerto Ricans. Dance styles evolved and Puerto Ricans did not. Their partners became better or worse dancers. In any number of different ways, then, Puerto Ricans moved or danced to gain power, sometimes got it, but lost it later.

Puerto Rican losses have been great. Taken as a whole, studies of Puerto Rican community history in New York City suggest that their social power has steadily declined over the last fifty years. We know that Puerto Ricans have lived in the United States since the nineteenth century. They've worked hard since that time to earn a living and establish homes and communities, and, in general, they've learned how to live in the United States. Though these efforts have not always been successful, Puerto Ricans can now be found in almost every state of the union and in most occupations, from the sciences to the arts.

Thousands of organizations represent Puerto Rican economic, political, or cultural interests. Puerto Ricans are also one of the most decorated groups in recent U.S. military history. They have received more medals for more deaths than any other group. As heroic and glorious as Puerto Ricans must have been to receive them, it's also true that Puerto Ricans have received little else but medals. They got medals but not real public honor and recognition. Puerto Ricans have found more failure and degradation than glory in the United States.

Puerto Ricans have not only become poorer in the last three decades; they've also remained largely invisible in the political and cultural life of the nation (Torres 1995; Lemann 1991, 15). Olga Mendez, long-term

Puerto Rican assemblywoman from the East Harlem district, stated in 1986 that the power of the Puerto Rican community had eroded since it had "less political influence than it had 10 years ago" (Chavez 1986). Indeed, the temptation is to conclude that Puerto Ricans, as Iris Marion Young has observed in another context, have become so powerless because they "have little or no work autonomy, exercise little creativity or judgment in their work, have no technical expertise or authority, express themselves awkwardly, especially in public or bureaucratic settings, and do not command respect" (Wartenberg 1992, 189). Young's explanation for Puerto Rican powerlessness certainly resonates with what a critical mass of observers assert about the Puerto Rican experience in U.S. society. It is an explanation, however, that wrongly makes Puerto Ricans victims and pawns as well as misconstrues the nature of power.

The temptation to cast Puerto Ricans as victims often springs from dire economic and social data. There are almost three million Puerto Ricans living in the United States, apart from those living in Puerto Rico itself.[5] Only about 60 percent of U.S. Puerto Ricans have graduated from high school. This rate is not only lower than that of non-Latino whites (85 percent); it is lower than that of non-Latino blacks (at 73 percent). The same dismal picture is true in employment. Only about 54 percent of Puerto Ricans participate in the labor force. This compares to about 65 percent for all Latinos, 66 percent for non-Latino whites, and 62 percent for non-Latino blacks. Puerto Ricans are, not surprisingly, one of the poorest groups in the United States. Almost 39 percent of all Puerto Ricans live in poverty, compared to 31 percent for all Latinos, 10 percent for non-Latino whites, and 33 percent for non-Latino blacks. Most shocking, this dismal economic picture reflects a thirty-year decline. The economic and social picture for Puerto Ricans was actually better in the 1950s than it is now.

Political information creates a slightly more positive picture, revealing a geometric increase in the number of elected officials of Puerto Rican descent. Puerto Ricans can now boast that they have three of their own in the U.S. House of Representatives, whereas twenty years ago they had only one. There are many more Puerto Ricans in local and state legislatures as well. In New York City, for example, there is a Puerto Rican borough president in the Bronx, eight city council members, seven state assemblymen, and four state senators (IPR 1995, 1). But these numbers seem to mean little. Poverty, a lack of educational opportunity, and joblessness remains unabated for Puerto Ricans.

More important, in some ways, is the question of Puerto Rican visibility. For the general public, Puerto Ricans are an invisible and weak community. Nicholas Lemann writes in *The Atlantic Monthly* that "black politicians are more powerful than Puerto Rican politicians in all cities with big Puerto Rican populations; and there is a feeling that blacks have America's attention, whereas Puerto Ricans, after a brief flurry of publicity back in *West Side Story* days, have become invisible" (1991, 15). Even when Puerto Ricans commit notorious crimes, the public hardly seems to notice. Hunter and Bainbridge argue that the 1950 attempted assassination of President Truman by Puerto Rican nationalists was "gigantic news—for about a week" only (3). The attempted assassination was a big story for only a few days; then "it quickly went away" (Hunter and Bainbridge 2005, 3). The 1950 attempted assassination even got confused or "melded in the U.S. folk imagination" with the later 1954 Puerto Rican assault on the Congress.

The September 1995 issue of *Vibe* magazine, devoted to a discussion of who or what has "juice" or power in American society, could identify only one Latino—the actress Rosie Perez. Actually, they chose Rosie's bra rather than Rosie herself. Even Hispanic magazines can't seem to find enough powerful Latinos, let alone powerful Puerto Ricans. The July 1995 issue of *Hispanic Business* lists the top Latino entertainers in earned income. But of the top ten, only four are actually Latino and only one and a half (e.g., Geraldo Rivera) are Puerto Ricans. The rest are all Spaniards. Puerto Ricans are thus invisible even to the Latino community. Antonia Pantoja, one of the most respected Puerto Rican leaders of the last forty years, lamented once that "today, many Puerto Ricans feel powerless and, indeed, are powerless. Many consider themselves ineffective in their personal life and in the struggles of their community and of the society at large" (Pantoja 1989, 23). And Puerto Ricans have become increasingly aware of their powerlessness and invisibility. A coalition of Puerto Rican organizations got together a few years ago to establish Boricua First, an organization "created with the goal of unifying Puerto Ricans on issues critical to their development and survival, and transforming the Puerto Rican community from one that has been invisible at the national level to a community that plays an integral part in national policy debates."[6] Gaining visibility will probably require that Puerto Ricans do more than have press conferences, plan demonstrations, and schedule lobbying days in Washington, D.C.

Puerto Ricans seem to know that while the path to power may require greater visibility, images that spin out of control can hurt also. Recent examples include the flagrant pot shots taken at Puerto Ricans by politicians and reporters hardened by the knowledge that Puerto Ricans are too powerless to fight back. One writer for a British journal, for example, called Puerto Ricans "fat, squat, ugly, dusky, and unbelievably loud" because the Puerto Rican Day Parade had spoiled his weekend in New York City

(Taki 1997). His reaction was not just visceral, hateful, and self-absorbed. It was also arrogant and smug. He also claimed knowledge of the place of Puerto Ricans in American civilization. Thus, he declared that "there has never been—nor will there ever be—a single positive contribution by a Puerto Rican outside of receiving American welfare and beating the system."

Explanations

Puerto Ricans, as remarked earlier, dance but get weaker. Each attempt by Puerto Ricans to either perform according to socially established roles and functions or reject them in pursuit of elicit, defiant, or socially prescribed alternatives leaves them exactly where they started or worse. Working places them in a job requiring few skills, with no future and with small wages. Not working means subsisting on a below-poverty income through public assistance or succumbing to the vagaries of the underground and illegal economies. The results are deprivation, jail, or death. Puerto Ricans, according to the poet Pedro Pietri, "must work until they have saved enough money for a good down payment on a semi-decent credit card funeral."[7] Puerto Ricans, thus, lose social power almost every time they choose to act. They become less powerful by most of the decisions they make and by most of the actions they take. The reason they become less powerful is that they make no enduring impact on the way others in society go about doing their everyday business. Nobody wants to dance.

Puerto Ricans don't seek powerlessness. Most of the people they confront probably don't aim for this either. But, as for many people, powerlessness just seems to seep through defensive barriers and weigh down their every vehicle of change. It comes as "a kind of unintended consequence of intentional action" (Digeser 1992, 984). It is not an attribute of individual Puerto Ricans or caused by cultural deficiencies. It is not the product of Puerto Rican individual or family pathology (Jennings 1999).

The argument that Puerto Rican poverty and powerlessness spring from the unintended consequences of everyday actions is not a pessimistic view of the Puerto Rican potential for power. It is, actually, a recognition of the reality that power is created and destroyed in deep, obscure, tangled layers of social action and experience. These processes create structures and institutions. Interests and passions reside there and encode behavior. Efforts to amass power that ignore this fact succeed, in general, by accident. By illuminating those deep layers with the dance model of power, we gain a better understanding of how Puerto Ricans became both less and more powerful as well as what needs to change in order to enhance their chances for greater power.

Power is the ability to get others to move, the ability to change the way people think, feel, and act. What gets others to move and how they move springs from diverse social relations. Cultural and political relations are as important as economic ones in that regard. Economic decisions are often shaped by cultural perceptions (as when employers don't hire from particular groups because they are perceived to be lazy). Political advances are often made possible by economic prosperity or decline. The New Deal policies of FDR and the Great Society policies of LBJ are good examples.

Puerto Ricans are, for all these reasons, a good test of the thesis that power originates in the passions and interests of social interaction. Because they present an extreme case of both power and powerlessness, Puerto Ricans provide a good test of the dance model's simple proposition. It is in the relationships created by passions and interests that one partner becomes stronger while the other becomes weaker. If the dance model of power is true, Puerto Ricans will have less power when they have greater levels of passion and interest in their partners than their partners have in them. They will have more power when the reverse is true. In general, this study found support for this thesis.

The concept of power as dance is more than a heuristic device. Dance doesn't just explain in a more graphic way how power changes. It explains why. The point is not simply that power is something fluid. Power originates as a product of actors pursuing interests and acting on their passions with each other. The origins of power cannot be accounted for by any other theoretical proposition. It is also not an original idea. I have merely collected a few stray pieces from various theories to make this a coherent theoretical argument.

The dance model invites comparison with conservative explanations of minority poverty and helplessness. Many conservative approaches are quick to blame poverty on the poor themselves. They accuse the poor of making bad choices, being lazy, or possessing the wrong moral values. Conservatives claim that they are simply holding individuals accountable for the decisions they've made. They are only partially right about this, however. The problem with the conservative position is that some individuals make more important decisions than others. More importantly, decisions made in the recent and distant past get institutionalized and coded into practice in the present.

Some people have more choices and have more options in making them. This reality is generally due to the nature of people's needs, wants, and desires in society. Poor people find themselves swept up by the demands of a society where money determines so much of life's possibilities.

Yes, they do go along with the music. They dance to its rhythms and help to keep the whole thing going. It's not their dance floor or music, however. They belong to those who set things in motion in earlier times and to those who are given authority to keep them going in the present because they know more about the music and how to dance to it. We can call these people elites, upper classes, or capitalists. The point is that these advantages suggest that the problems of the poor exist not just because of the decisions the poor have made. The problem for the poor is that the social roles and interests they move in are not completely theirs. Groups like Puerto Ricans also often refuse to participate in some activities (like education or wage labor) because they feel out of place in those venues, alienated, or rejected. They do so to gain short-term power even as they lose power in the long run. It's hard to blame them for doing so.

The dance model assumes the presence of active agents. It doesn't assume that those agents are always capable of moving the way they want. While improvisation within a dance and the invention of new dances are always possible, they are not easy to do. Most of the time, dancers have to dance the dance the way everyone else does it.

1

Dance
A Theory of Power

It is easy to mistake what's on the surface for what is really going on beneath. It is easy to think that what can be touched exhausts all that is real. Weapons, money, and position provide those who possess them with a clear advantage in what most people conceive as power; getting others to do what they otherwise would not do. The mere possession of those things doesn't explain, however, why that advantage exists. Similarly, it doesn't explain why having those things does not prevent the loss of power. It can't explain why it is that babies and others, like Puerto Ricans, usually considered weak in society are sometimes able to get their way, to get power, despite possessing few of those things.

The dance model can explain the origins and loss of power because it calls attention to agents and social relations rather than things. It gives importance to the role of the agent, both individual and social, in the constitution of society. More specifically, the dance model focuses on the social interests, passions, and habits that set people in motion, usually towards and with each other, and that form the foundation for the exchanges that take place between people while in motion. It is economic, political, and social interests, thus, that send people in motion into each other's arms, that keep them going as social relations, and that often bring those partnerships to an end.

Power rises and falls with social interests and the movements they inspire. Power, for that reason, is more than things. Money, weapons, and position deliver power only to the extent that others desire money, fear getting hurt, and respect authorities. Power, in that sense, gets going and is kept going because some possess values and others have interests and passions. Agents with values meet or are simply born together with agents with interests. Agents with needs, wants, or desires respond to and can be influenced by agents with the values they seek.

Power is generated in this basic two-way interaction involving agents and interests. Power is generated and is lost in repeated interactions like this and in more complex ones involving many other agents. It is, as a result, something fluid, variable, and dialectical. Agents make the rules that inform such interactions, usually not consciously, not directly, and not in their own time. Agents are usually happy to know those rules, accept their constraints, and perpetuate them. These rules make things happen, make life happen. Agents sometimes attempt to resist the rules but can't find enough others to join them in casting them aside or bending them their way, and thus resign themselves and continue to perform them (Irvine 2006, 221). In most cases, social agents simply act and carry forward the rules that guide their actions. Power is created and lost in processes that look, thus, a lot like dance.

There are alternative and good ways of depicting and explaining power. The dance model is better than the models based on chess, game theory, or the simple possession of things. It is better because power, like dance, is variable, interactive, and social. Power is not a solid, an eternal status, or an independent force. Dance also better represents the way that people provoke power while in pursuit of something. Admittedly, people also play games like chess for many reasons. Chess is also interactive. Chess is not, however, a good model for power. While people enter chess games for lots of reasons, playing chess requires that each side use logic and reason, and playing it is basically a limited two-party exchange.[1]

Chess can't be played by drunk, dreamy, distracted, or irrational people. Dance can. Also unlike chess, people dance in search of freedom, escape, security, happiness, self-expression, and much more. They also dance, of course, in search of power. More importantly, dancing can result from and invoke any number of human senses—from reason to habit to hedonistic pleasure. Whatever agents' motivations or states, it is their interests that launch them into an engagement with other agents and that offer the possibility of greater or lesser power. As we often discover, "desires bubble up from deep within us" (Irvine 2006, 218).

The theoretical lineage of this dance model can be found in the social power theory of the 1960s (Emerson 1993; French and Raven 1959), Marxism, social network analysis, Bourdieu, and the postmodern theories of Baudrillard and Foucault. The dance model of power presented here shares some elements of those theories. Power, for instance, appears as a relational phenomenon in many postmodern theories, and yet those theories pay very little attention to what gets power going. Early in the 1960s, the social power movement of Emerson and Raven did pull many of the necessary pieces together for a theory of power that could explain its origins. Power was relational for these theorists and sprang from the complex interaction of interests. The theoretical focus on individuals, however, limited its ability to explain the power of groups, institutions, and society. Marxist theory provides a dialectical method that does a good job of capturing the complex interaction of interests and social groups in the construction of social power. Marxist theory, however, reifies economic structures as well as ignores political and cultural power.

The dance model doesn't just correct each of these theoretical deficiencies. It does so as a coherent model that validates the role of both social agents and social structures in a complex dialectic that reveals how power emerges, changes, and disappears. It does so by a focus on interests, structures, and the consensus and agreement between partners involved in a dance whose outline often gets exposed at particular junctures. That ebb and flow of power can be seen in the historical experience of the Puerto Rican community in the United States. Surface experiences often hide a deeper, unrecognized reality. They are not, however, irrelevant to that deeper reality. The social interaction that is the dance of power has both a surface and an inner dimension.

Real and Theoretical Origins of Power as Dance

The idea that power originates in a dance of mutual accommodation between partners is not a completely new one. It can be found in a number of classical and modern theories as well as in many everyday examples of power. Hobbes's atomistic individuals, for example, created society or "commonwealth" out of an active and knowing mutual consent and agreement, a "covenant of every man with every man" (Hobbes 1986, 227). More recently, Marta E. Savigliano has observed that tango is like politics and power because "tango is a practice already ready for struggle. It knows about taking sides, positions, risks. It has the experience of domination/resistance from within" (Savigliano 1995, 17).

The erotic and social tension of interests in the constitution of power as a dialectic internal to social relations, as dance, can be found in a diverse number of everyday and theoretical examples. The power of babies, teachers, spouses, congressional aides, and Machiavelli's royal prince all result from the interest in values that can only be achieved by dancing with others. Each of the examples discussed below demonstrates the ubiquity of dance-like qualities in the constitution of power.

Parents know that babies are some of the most powerful people on earth. Babies can't talk, walk, or see very clearly. They are a drain on the economic, social, and attentive resources of a family. Despite all this, parents and others make tremendous sacrifices to respond to the immediate and long-term needs of babies. *They don't have to.* They could easily refuse to respond or even retaliate against a crying, demanding child by inflicting injury or death. That rarely happens, but certainly not because of anything that a baby can do to prevent it.

We take care of babies because of what babies inspire in us. A baby gets us to move towards it and serve its needs because it has "the capacity to call forth feelings of love and duty on the part of those around it" (Boulding 1990, 125). It doesn't matter why we have that reaction. It could be the product of biology or socialization. What is clear is that, like an expert, but in this case unknowing, dancer, babies have a special way of getting us to move towards and for them by stimulating the deep, hidden desires and the interest *we have* in securing their continued survival.[2]

Similar deep emotional bonds create power in romantic relationships between adults. Individuals often sacrifice everything, even their very lives, in an attempt to please, keep, or mourn the loss of a lover. In fact, as Dennis Wrong has argued, "the power of the loved one over the lover in a passionate, 'romantic' love-relationship represents the most narrowly extensive and highly individualized form of power relation" (1993, 16). The loved one can cause tremendous physical and emotional changes in a lover, even if that lover has kept the knowledge of these feelings of attraction to him- or herself.

In general, partners in romantic relationships find that the power each has follows an ebb and flow determined by the level of attention, interest, and love that exists in the other. As Peter M. Blau has observed, "the individual whose spontaneous affection for the other is stronger must accede to the other's wishes and make special efforts to please the other" (1996, 78). For that reason, Michael Korda argues that the most dangerous moment in a romantic relationship occurs "when one person's need for the other becomes strong enough to shift the balance of power" in favor of the other (1975, 5). The person who needs the other, who *can't live without* the other, becomes weak and vulnerable before that person. When a lover needs another, the need causes the lover to dance, to draw near, to gaze lovingly, and to display feelings of uncontrolled joy. It also causes power to "boil up in unexpected places" in the beloved (Janeway 1980, 3).

New teachers are often similarly surprised and bemused by their own power over students. While it is certainly not perfect or consistent, teachers do have considerable power over students. Students may not do the reading and other assignments, yet they usually give teachers at least a modicum of grudging respect and attention. Most explanations of a teacher's power, however, center on the grading. Students respond to teachers, the argument goes, because they are afraid of low grades. Teachers thus have power because of the potential harm they can do to students. Wartenberg modifies this argument to say that the harm to the student is not intrinsic to the relation between student and teacher. The harm, he says, is due to social structures. Bad grades hurt because of "the mediation of human beings situated outside the classroom," people who are capable of denying the student opportunities for employment or further education (1990, 145).

Though true, this characterization of a teacher's power ignores a more basic dimension. None of it much matters if the students don't like or want anything (grades, knowledge, attention) from the teacher. Those "outside" structures shape the motivations of students to the extent that students internalize those rules and pressures. Those teachers who work in classrooms where student motivation can't be taken for granted know that a teacher's power in the classroom requires a subtle dance of seduction with the students.[3] A teacher must get students interested and/or passionate about the material, grades, or teacher. Sometimes this happens with humor, compassion, discipline, positive incentives, or any number of different techniques. bell hooks says as much when she proposes that to "restore passion to the classroom or to excite it in classrooms where it has never been, we must find again the place of eros within ourselves and together allow the mind and body to feel and know and desire" (hooks 1994, in Giroux and McLaren, 118). A teacher's power is thus built on a seductive engagement, a dance, with students.

The idea that social interests and social relations, rather than social position, generate power is true not only for teachers. Congressmen and senators, or any elected officials, presumably have power and authority generated by the fact that they are the official government representatives for districts or states. Students of American government, however, have found recently that the power of elected officials in Congress often pales beside the power of their staff employees. Legislative aides are hired by legislators to keep them informed about important policy issues, write legislation, negotiate with the staff of other elected officials, and keep in touch with important constituents. They form a kind of "shadow congress," with most aides wielding an "impressive influence" that is often greater than that of the elected officials they serve.[4] Sometimes, an aide's power can oppose that of his or her boss. Analysts suggest that some senators have been reduced to mere talking "dummies" before their "ventriloquist" chiefs of staff.[5]

The more than twenty thousand aides serving legislators in Congress are often the crucial forces in the defeat and success of particular legislation. Despite this impressive influence, their power is fully given to them by elected officials who find the current quantity and complexity of their legislative business daunting and overwhelming. Like novice dancers before a skilled dance instructor, elected officials are seduced by and become dependent on the expertise of aides. They thus willingly give aides much of their power, as Democratic congressman Thomas J. Downey stated, "to formulate and refine ideas" (Tolchin 1991). Senators and congressmen deliver power to their aides because without them they could not conduct their business as legislators.

Senators are, of course, not the first to find that realities of office can force rulers to give others some of their power. Niccolo Machiavelli's *Prince* understood the dance of power. That book is not simply, as it is often depicted, a manual for teaching the prince how to rule. It is also a treatise on how those who are ruled affect the power of the prince. One of the most repeated of Machiavelli's instructions to the prince was that "one ought to be both feared and loved, but as it is difficult for the two to go together, it is much safer to be feared than loved" (Machiavelli 1950, 61). Machiavelli argues that this is necessary given the natural character of men whom he views as "ungrateful, voluble, dissemblers, anxious to avoid danger, and covetous of gain" (61).

Machiavelli's conclusions are, actually, based on what is most efficient given the complex interaction between the prince and the ruled. Later on, Machiavelli explained his reasoning. The prince should rely on fear because "men love at their own free will, but fear at the will of the prince" (63). What exactly the prince can do to inspire love in followers is complex, varied, and hopelessly unpredictable. Splendid oratory may do it one time, but bravery in battle may be what is needed next. The people's heart is too whimsical and fickle. Fear, however, is easier for the prince to create and control in the people.

Fear is a tool for power that is easier for the prince to harness. The prince's ability to gain and maintain power thus requires that he present his partners, the ruled, with something they cannot avoid or control—their own fear. The prince's power is secured by establishing control of what the ruled cherish above everything else—their lives. That coercive power is easy to attain yet fleeting. Machiavelli's main point is, however, about knowing your partner. In social dancing, good leads know that their ability to guide, and influence, the movements of their partners is, in large measure, determined by their giving clear signals about where to move and when. The leader can also use manipulation and propaganda. What is important for the leader is knowing what partners need, want, desire, and, most of all, fear.

Dancers gently push and pull each other across the dance floor. At times, they appear almost as one being. At other times, a partner makes radical independent movements that are only possible because of the connection of one to the other. Nothing captures this complex exchange better than the idea of dialectical movement developed by Hegel and

Marx. Hegel's ideas about the master-slave relation constitute a good example.

The slave master, we naturally expect, has an incredible amount of power over the slave. Hegel, however, demonstrated that the master is, in some ways, actually weak before the slave. The master can only achieve his independent power as an agent through someone who has a reduced status as the "other"—the slave. As Hegel states, "the master gets his recognition through an other consciousness . . . by the fact of being dependent on a determinate existence" (Hegel 1967, 236). In a similar way, social dancers can demonstrate their skill and energy only with and through their partners.[6] Social dancing shackles one dancer to another, good and bad. It also makes possible movements and freedom that could not be imagined otherwise.

Marx turned Hegel back on his feet. He showed how, in capitalist society, it is labor that is realized through capital. As Marx stated in the *Communist Manifesto*, "in proportion as the bourgeoisie, i.e. capital, is developed, in the same proportion is the proletariate, the modern working class, developed—a class of labourers, who live only so long as they find work, and who find work only so long as their labour increases capital" (Tucker 1972, 340). Both Hegel and Marx argue, then, that one class's capacity and power to perform is realized through the other. The dance notion is, in this way, a metaphorical restatement of Hegel and Marx's dialectics of social change. Dialectics focuses on the complex inner dependence and exchange that Marx found in the class relations of capitalism. The dance model extends the dialectic. It explains how and why one party or class appears to gain power, in more than the productive sphere, to turn things and the table its way.

The previous examples demonstrated how power gets created in social relations. What's important is not only that social agents interact and get created by that interaction, or even that those relations are objective features of the social structure. What's important is the role of social interests, passions, and habits. It is these features of the dance model that permit us to overcome the continuing dichotomies in social theory between agency and structure, power and powerlessness, as well as permanence and change.

Social dancing requires passionate, interested, cooperative, and compliant partners. Power emerges from the collective contribution of active, collective subjects. It is the elemental product of each partner's actions. As Richard Schmitt argued, "power is not owned by individuals but is rather a collective product" (1995, 153). Dance reminds us that power is an unstable combination of structure and energy between passionate, interested partners.

Power as Dance

Power is the ability to shape the way others think, feel, and act. The dance model explains how people get and lose that ability. If we assume, instead, that power is thing-like (money, arms, bodies), we could not explain how people get the ability to shape others. Money can influence some people and not others. People, in capitalist societies, usually desire money, but not always. Guns can force some people to do what they otherwise would not, but not always. There are people who are not easily stopped by guns. These people are often heralded for their bravery and heroism. The key point is that having money or a weapon is not, by itself, enough to create power. Other parties also play a role.[7] It is not enough to claim, as many recent theories do, that power is relational, that it flows in two directions and that both parties in a power relation have some. That merely gets at the operational dimensions of power. The key is explaining how that capacity gets created for either side.

Voluntarist and structuralist explanations are inadequate. They assume too much about the effectiveness either of individual will or of structural constraint. The first assumes that humans are pure agents with their own intrinsic and efficacious desires, interests, and will (Dahl 1957; Bachrach and Baratz 1962). The second assumes that they are not (Isaac 1987). The problem has been reconciling the idea that humans are agents with choices and the realization that they are also not able to choose freely, consciously, or with the results they intend. Social structures, social roles, even power itself obviously play strong roles in shaping social reality. The power of social structures comes from the fact that they are "relatively enduring." That admission, however, simply begs the question. If social agents carry their social roles and structures, no matter how limiting or destructive, with them, what keeps those alive?

One answer is that social agents are dupes. They are weak, manipulated, ignorant bearers of their own false consciousness. They are ruled and shaped by social structures. If this were true, they would never be able to amass their own defense, to resist, or even to capture any power for themselves. And yet they do.

Another answer is to view power as residing, for the most part, in social roles and structures, yet being subject to constant assault and potential transformation by the combined actions of all social agents. Social interests, habit, and passions set certain social agents and relations in motion or simply keep them going. The process is complex, a kind of dance. Yet, it is these interests that make possible relatively enduring possibilities for power.

Desire is, as Irvine states, what "animates the world" (Irvine 2006, 2).

It is also what creates power in that world. Passions and intellect generate desires and wants. Very often, we find that desires "pop into our heads, uninvited and unannounced" (ibid., 11). Without desires, needs, or wants, however, there is nothing to motivate us, set us in motion, or give meaning and importance to what we do. When we lack desires, needs, and wants, others have no chance of gaining power over us. Some of this can be seen in the transactions that happen behind the use of coercive power.

It is natural and easy to assume that it is the gun or knife that provides the "power" necessary to force someone to do what he or she would otherwise not do. Even in coercive situations, however, power does not come purely from the weapon. In many ways, it comes from the victim.

A weapon exacts compliance because the vast majority of people are afraid to get hurt or killed. The weapon actually hides the relational nature of the transaction that delivers power to its owner. The victim complies with the demand to hand over goods, lie on the floor, or dance a jig because the victim values his or her health and safety. The key is that a weapon's "power" depends on the reasonable expectation that most victims have those interests. Where that is not true, no weapon can make a victim do anything. Suicidal bombers, kamikaze pilots, and war heroes counter the common assumption that weapons create power. Their actions against weapons, against greater coercive force, indicate that they are not afraid to get hurt or die or simply that they value other things (national defense, religious glory, etc.) more. By rejecting the threat posed by the weapon, they impede the delivery of power to its owner. A gun in itself, therefore, possesses little intrinsic power. It simply makes transparent that its owner is in a position to take away something that most victims hold most dear—their health and life. Its power is, to a large extent, generated by what's in the mind and heart of the victim.

This suggests that individual agents help to make themselves weaker, followers, and subordinates by permitting the interest and passion they have in others to push them into an other's arms.[8] The targeted individual, the eventual leader or superior, also has choices. That agent can ignore or can attempt to harness for his or her own purposes the interest and passions he or she inspires or finds in others. That second choice makes real what had been merely a potential.

Power emerges from this complex initial reading, response, and accommodation of one to another.[9] Power emerges also from more subtle and indirect shades of accommodation between individual agents as they move towards each other and once they're together. This dance view of power, in this way, asserts something more than the postmodern notion that power is a relational phenomenon (Bourdieu and Wacquant 1992). It points to the complex interaction between agents in a social relation and to the social interests, habits, and passions that drive those interactions. Its value is particularly clear in explaining situations when the "weak" become powerful.

Powers of the Weak

Most modern and postmodern theories of power admit the possibility that the weak can resist or even end the powers of the strong. Some recent theorists have moved beyond the (voluntarist?) idea that power necessarily rests in agents, whether they are strong or weak. These arguments have begun to locate power in "fields" and "matrices" that enable and create boundaries to action (Bourdeiu and Wacquant 1992; Hayward 2000). These theoretical formulations make it possible to avoid intentionalist arguments about power. They also help to better explain the reality that power often operates "at a distance." These theories, however, still have problems accounting for the powers of the weak. The problem is precisely those theoretical innovations.

In these theories, fields act on both the strong and the weak. The argument is that there is a "network of social boundaries that delimits, for all, fields of possible action" (Hayward 2000, 27). As a feature of the social landscape, however, fields can't explain how the weak ever gain power if they are operating in a field that gives power to the strong most of the time. If the response is that the "field" changes, the theories can't explain why and how the field of power changes.

There are no easy answers to such questions. The temptation is to give those fields an independence that jeopardizes the role of social agents. Adam Smith did just that with his theory of an "invisible hand" that shapes what happens in a market place full of active, self-interested traders. The combined, unintended effects of the uncoordinated actions of self-interested agents are outcomes that often benefit society, almost as if the hand of a greater intelligence was at work.[10] For Smith, the invisible hand was ultimately God's. This attribution was more than simply a bow to religious orthodoxy. It was a weak theoretical fix.

There are serious problems for any social theory that relies on mysterious extra-agent mechanisms to explain the creation of spontaneous order. Such theories can't explain why particular orders with class, racial, and other forms of domination and exploitation appear and endure. They can't explain, for that reason, the historical experience of Puerto Ricans in the United States. Often mediating principles (survival of the fittest in evolutionary biology or maximizing rationality in rational choice theory) are introduced to provide the organizing and catalytic mechanisms that bring order to the chaotic actions of agents. This solution, though powerful in some instances, homogenizes the range of human motivations at work at any given moment and, more seriously, limits the ability to understand the nature of power and social order.

We can speak about structural forces as if they are "external" to social agents. However, the reality is that the constraints and possibilities made possible by social structures are really in the agent. They are present as rules, habits, dispositions, and projects in the agent. It is for that reason that, Bourdieu argues, "social agents are determined to the extent that they determine themselves" (Bourdieu and Wacquant 1992, 136). There is no ontological alternative to social agents, and their relations with each other, as a source of social reality and change.

The theoretical problem continues to be to determine how social agents create social structures and how social structures, residing within these same agents, affect their actions. The solution has been elusive because theorists have not distinguished what it is in social agents that produces strategies "or practices conforming to structural domination" or the resistance to it (Rothenberg 2004, 737). The attributes of the social agent that prove, after the fact, effective in altering social structures are enormously varied, even confounding. In some cases, "even so-called complicitous actions can have transformative and progressive social effects" (742).

This suggests that while the locus of change is in social agents and relations, what produces transformative moments is different or varies between agents. The dance model of power presented in this study argues that the mechanism at work is the interaction between agents with values and agents with interests, passions, and habits. This can be illustrated by the process of "taking into account" that occurs in most human interactions. This assessment occurs in most social relationships, even those that occur at a distance or that are defined as a structural role.

All social power, like all social dancing, is about partnerships and relationships. Whether agents know and are close to each other or are passive with others, they move towards, around, and with each other by an assessment of who is around them and what it is they present. Thus an agent cannot influence or dominate others "without taking his partner's reactions into account" (Jonas 1992, 124).

Apart from anything a potential partner may do, in order to make good dancing, the agent seeking to lead on the dance floor must take into account another agent's skill level, experience, and physical abilities. The requirements for the lead dancer, according to dance manuals, include "experimentally determining the follower's vocabulary and picking out from the subset of your possible leads the ones that you determine she's likely to be able to follow" (Balzer 2005, 8.10). Lead dancers must "size up" potential partners.

Likewise, a potential follower also responds to signals of interest and influence coming from a leader, complying and resisting to different degrees at different moments. The follower may look interested at one moment and not at another—may display the full range of his or her abilities to dance on the floor or not. Clearly, though both types of agents take the other "into account," they do so in different ways.

Each social actor offers and presents different aspects of himself or herself to others. The mix at any given moment gets shaped by social structural roles and by the agent. Those agents who can satisfy their needs and interests with little effort or expense have more power than those who can't. They have more options in satisfying their pursuit of particular values. Much of what they pursue is, as Bourdieu claims, however, given by social structures. Even if social agents are "socialized," "trained," or "manipulated" into desiring and pursuing certain values, they must still recognize what they value, locate that value in others, and decide whether it is possible to pursue and attain it.

It is that "taking into account," by the strong and the weak, that delivers power. It also affords even weaker partners some room to maneuver and negotiate as well as to bracket the dominant other's influence. That process of "taking into account" is variable, unpredictable, and critical to determining the social power of agents. *What* is taken into account is just as important.

Social agents act in the context of trying to achieve their own and social interests, because of habit, as a passionate response to others, or in accordance with idiosyncratic purposes. Relatively enduring habits, passions, and interests tend to produce relatively enduring social roles, structures, and power. It is the "taking into account" that makes these structures relative rather than permanent. Social agents know and don't know, act and don't act, and perform exactly or approximately. Most of the time, enough social agents are close enough in their assessment of what "to do" that they perpetuate existing social roles and structures. In the gaps, when agents fall short of full replication, social structures drift, shake, and get transformed.

That limit on what leaders or the powerful can do means that subordinates to power are never completely powerless, even in relations of apparent domination. Very often, as for the weaker Julia in the movie *Danzon,* the follower finds subtle ways of asserting a bracketed yet real power. In *Danzon,* the timid character Julia has learned to dance danzon with the erotic hip movements of a rumba. Julia sees rumba as a vehicle to express her passion and independence. As a result, at the conclusion of the movie,

Julia's ability to graft a rumba onto a danzon gives her greater opportunities to influence her dance partner, Carmelo. During the dance, we find that the macho Carmelo can "still 'lead' the dance, but Julia has discovered a way to assert her own position, her 'certain way' of doing things" (Lopez 1997, 339).

In general, like followers in social dancing, subordinates take an active part in making another's power over them possible. They must listen, act responsive, learn, desire, and, in general, accept the influence of those seeking power. As Balzer states, "a good follower will complement the dance style of the leader she is dancing with" (2005, 2.10). This makes the follower an active partner who complies with domination.

Followers are always active in power relations at those times when they *resist* and, occasionally, overthrow power, as James Scott and others have established. They are also active when they don't. Ultimately, social actors determine who and how much power others will have over them. They become subject to power because they seek and pursue something of value in others. As Parenti stated, "The threat to withdraw affection or fire one from a job or fling one into prison or take one's life are effective constraints only if one is interested in maintaining oneself as an object of affection, holding one's job, or preserving one's freedom, health, or life" (Parenti 1978, 8).

Bosses, cops, and robbers have power because we do value, often very highly, what they control. We find them and the values (like wages, life, or freedom) they control so attractive and necessary that we succumb to the way they want us to move. Having delivered ourselves into the arms of others, we could respond to their power by basic acts of passive resistance or noncooperation. In many cases, the weak respond to power with "sullenness, failing to carry out what is required, silence, total zaniness" (Rorty 1992, 9). This is the dance-floor equivalent of dragging one's feet. Dropping out of school and turning to drugs and crime are two destructive examples of this tactic in the Puerto Rican and other minority communities.

The weak can also tip power toward themselves by a total rejection of the values controlled by those on top, by becoming free of their own apparently insatiable desires, by "either nihilistic, inventive destruction or Stoicism" (ibid.). The weak can become stronger, thus, by reducing or denying the passion and interests *they have* in others, by a "renunciation of desire" (Irvine 2006, 186). Puerto Ricans kept their culture alive in the United States and demand bilingual education for this reason. It's an attempt to reject English and the Americans who speak it. Power returns to those who change themselves rather than the world. It returns to those, like Buddhists, Old Order Amish, and the Stoics, who realize that they can be happy and keep more power for themselves by desiring less, by being happy with what they already have (ibid.).

The Foundations of Social Power as Dance

The theory of power as dance developed in this study has its roots in the "social power" movement that had brief popularity in sociology during the early 1960s and that was fueled by the research of J. R. P. French and B. H. Raven, Marvin Olsen, and Richard M. Emerson (French and Raven 1959; Olsen 1970; Emerson 1993).[11] The early social power theorists actually anticipated much of Foucault's thinking on power. Olsen wrote, for instance, that "power does not exist until social actors begin relating to one another in some manner" (1970, 2). Etzioni put it more bluntly: "an actor by himself is not powerful or weak" (1993, 18).

Power, for social power theorists, is not only relational but is also, in part, the consequence of social aims and organization. Like Foucault, thus, social power theorists argue that power "is created through social interaction and relationships, as an outgrowth of social ordering" (Olsen 1970, 2). Social power theorists, similar to Foucault, also make no distinction between the macro and the micro universes of power. Social power theory, unlike Foucault, however, is not limited to discourse. Thus, for social power theory, a social actor can exert power to the extent that he or she is in a relationship that provides access to resources such as "money, land, material possessions, and organizational members, or relatively intangible assets such as knowledge, skills, legitimacy, and organizational unity" (Olsen 1970, 4).

The most important contribution of social power theory was the idea that it is people that can make others move across the dance floor or the battlefield because they have something that others desire or need. Emerson said as much when he wrote that "the power to control or influence the other resides in control over the things he values" (1993, 49). These values, he stated, can range "all the way from oil resources to ego-support, depending upon the relation in question" (49). Steward Clegg added that "there is little point in constructing a priori abstract lists of specific resources as power resources" because "whether they, whatever they are, are power resources depends entirely on how they are positioned and fixed by the players, the rules, and the game" (1989, 209). That much Foucault also understood. Power gets created, according to Foucault, by "a multiplicity of organisms, forces, energies, materials, desires, thoughts, etc." (Foucault and Gordon 1980, 47). But social power theory argued that actions, goals, interests, and knowledge create power for some to the extent that others depend on what they control. Power, thus, is created by social agents and by their interests.

Relations of power, in this sense, are a kind of exchange. Control and influence flow in one direction to the extent that dependence flows in the other. Emerson gives a more precise formulation: "the power of A over B is equal to, and based upon the dependence of B upon A" (1993, 50). It is what we seek and pursue that gives others power over us. What we seek and pursue is the result of passion (therefore blind and often arbitrary) or interests (which can be subjective, objective, or real). This view of power has been called Exchange Theory.

The dance model in this study departs from this forgotten but fruitful approach to power by insisting on the reality of intersubjective and collective subjects rather than solitary individuals as well as by reclaiming the significance of objective, subjective, and real interests in motion. Collective social agents are both free and not free to act. They are "embedded in a complex evolving structure of rules, roles, relations, and meanings that must be collectively reproduced in daily life" (Lloyd 1993, 127).

Social power theory has been mostly ignored by social science. It remains a key contributor to network and exchange theory as well as to leadership training practices in business.[12] Modern and postmodern theories of power have been shortsighted to ignore it, however. Social power theory helps explain the strategies that make power possible between people. It helps explain why and how someone like Vice President Cheney has been able to overcome the traditional weaknesses inherent in the office of the vice president.[13] It helps to explain how particular groups like Puerto Ricans or, in Bourdieu's terms, "arbitrarily defined populations," are able to gain power on occasion (Bourdieu and Wacquant 1992, 229).

The Missing Element in Contemporary Theories of Power

As the examples above showed, agents give others power by placing themselves in their arms. Their interests drove them there, and as they "accommodated" to each other, they established and managed power between them.[14] This is summarized in Michael Parenti's statement that "what makes one person so much more powerful than others are those very others who give him or her their empowering responses" (1978, 7). Although many contemporary theories of power focus on social relations, they avoid social interests and are thus unable to account for how those social relations change and create power.

The dance approach to power has notable benefits. First, it is a relatively simple model that accounts for both the role of agents and the role of structures. Second, it accounts for changes that occur in power between agents and over time. And third, it offers a nondeterminist explanation of the origins of power. Many of the postmodernist theories have avoided determinism only by making the social agent disappear altogether. They have sought to avoid both reified structures and the complicated problems created by assuming that individual intentions have a role in constituting the social world. Other theories have explained power as a social relation, created in the interaction between agents. They can't explain, however, what is at stake in the interaction between these agents that produces changes in the relation.

Pierre Bourdieu comes the closest to a dance-like theory of power, particularly in the concept of habitus. Bourdieu explains habitus as the set of "durable and transposable dispositions" that internalize, in the agent, the rules and constraints of social structure (Bourdieu 1992, 13). Fields are Bourdieu's way of explaining the various social structures that exist in any particular society and that compete and struggle to achieve dominance. Together, these two concepts do a fairly good job of explaining the variation and differences in societies that are often characterized as seamless entities, such as "modern," "industrial," or "capitalist."

Social agents play in the various fields of social life, sometimes modify them, and are in turn changed by those fields. In this way, Bourdieu allows for the creative, unpredictable nature of social life while accounting for the fact that it is also largely stable and relatively permanent. This allows for the historical constitution of social structure while including the idea that social agents "are acting and efficacious" (ibid., 19). What's missing is an explanation about what is in the agent's habitus and in the social fields that produces more of the same or something different.

The reproduction of social structures or their modification, in Bourdieu's theory, happen to social agents rather than spring from them. The "social field" is, according to Bourdieu, a "site of struggle with its boundaries an empirically open question" (ibid., 101). Social fields are historically contingent. They are subject to free play and are always a set of possibilities. They produce social agents and are changed by them. As Bourdieu states, "social agents are determined only to the extent that they determine themselves" (136). The problem is determining when and how the structures or the agents change.

Early in his theorizing, Bourdieu did make use of interests to explain the social agent's desire to "play" and to "pursue goals." However, he largely abandoned the notion of interests later in exchange for the concepts of "illusio" and "libido," which serve to devalue their import (25). Interests, he claimed, are too instrumental and normative. They do not help us to understand how "habitus sensitizes and mobilizes [agents] to perceive and pursue" interests (26). Bourdieu is right to avoid the instrumentalist and normative limitations of the concept of interest. Not everything people do is aimed at satisfying an interest. It is also true that establishing social and group interests is a cumbersome and difficult project. By throwing out interests altogether, however, he creates the scenario he sought to avoid where social agents appear to be "pushed and pulled about by external forces" (108).

Social agents are essentially inert, for Bourdieu. They are basically "disinterested" until they are made interested by the influence of social fields (26). This is a serious shortcoming. Bourdieu has made social agents into neutral and inert vessels. In his attempt to account for the complex and dialectical contributions to power by both agents and structures, he has robbed agents of their life and movement. He does so by focusing on the mediating processes between agents. He has forgotten that humans must act, must move.

Bourdieu no longer sees interests as the springs of human action. There is, however, no alternative to interests, habits, and passions as the stimuli that sensitize and mobilize social agents to commit, move, and pursue particular goals. Social agents don't have to be conscious of their interests. Nor do those interests have to be good for agents.

Bourdieu is right in one sense. Structural fields shape interests and yet they do not do so completely or cleanly. As he admits, "social agents construct social reality" (10). He goes wrong in placing the source of that agency in habitus and fields. In his theory, these are mediating processes that produce social reality and often attain a "life of their own." This "generative matrix," of social field–habitus–social structure, however, can't exclude the causal role of the social agent completely.

For Bourdieu, social agents become efficacious to the extent that they can reflect on what determines them, reflect on their own dispositions (137). How and why that happens is left unexplained. Indeed, habitus works to reproduce structures precisely because social agents are mostly unconscious, inert, and unreflective. That view, however, mystifies the question of how social agents ever become creative improvisers, able to modify social structures.

In some ways, Bourdieu recognizes the paradox of domination. The weak, the dominated, "always contribute to their own domination" (24). He goes on, however, to explain this complicity as a function of a habitus that is also the "effect, embodied, of domination" (ibid.). Is habitus always the effect of social structures, however? How long does the effect last? The answer can't be known. The processes are, in fact, too dialectical. Bourdieu admits as much when he states that it's too hard to unravel these processes since it is often true that "resistance can be alienating and submission can be liberating" (ibid.).

It's not enough to declare that social agents are "born in a social world" and that they "accept a whole range of postulates, axioms, which go without saying and require no inculcating" (168). Bourdieu doesn't recognize that social agents choose at every moment and accept those "axioms" at every turn. Social agents modify the social field with every act. They just cannot do it consistently, with enough others, with enough purpose, or with enough consciousness to have a lasting impact. What they do at each moment is, however, to act, largely in accordance with their interests and the values they encounter in those "fields."

Most of the time, social agents choose (however imperfectly, unconsciously, conflictedly, or painfully) to be a part of some of the groups around them. They know that there is no "doing" outside of social agents and social relations. The outcomes are complex, dialectical, even confounding. Yet interests, dancing and power all take place with and in social agents. The truth is that "we find it hard to live with other people, and we find it even harder to live without them" (Irvine 2006, 43). What's important is figuring out what interests and what values in social agents and in social structures contribute to producing social reality and power. There is no straight or absolute answer. Yet only these factors provide any clue about which social agents and relations will gain power.

Interests are, thus, integral to the question of power. An individual or group has an interest when it has a stake in something or is affected by it.[15] Therefore individuals and groups are key components in the theoretical explanation of human actions (Heller 1974, 58). The fact that interests don't always coincide with results or power does not diminish their importance. Interests are a key feature of social life whether or not social agents are in control of them. They orient social agents and, in fact, make them what they are. Capitalists, in this sense, have an interest in making profit because without it they cease being capitalists. It is interests, both long-term and short-term, that shape what social agents do and, thus, what power they have.

Interests are not the same as preferences, which are subjective and explicit for a subject. In this I agree with Jeffrey C. Isaac, who distinguished *real* interests not only from *subjective* preferences but also from *objective* interests. The latter spring from social structural class positions and roles that affect what social agents do. Real interests, on the other hand, are equally causal to social agents "even if they are not avowed by social agents, and . . . these interests shape and limit (though they do not unequivocally determine) the development of subjective interests" (1987,

98). Real interests, however, are implicit in social practice. They are not the interests agents *should* have or the preferences they actually do express. Real interests are revealed in dancing, in the habitual practices with "rules . . . and expectations . . . that govern their conduct" (Isaac 1987, 99).

Karl Marx once said that "men make their own history, but they do not make it just as they please; they do not make it under circumstances chosen by themselves, but under circumstances directly found, given and transmitted from the past" (in Tucker 1972, 437). As overused as this quotation might be, nothing else in social theory comes as close to capturing the intimate, complex, and "dialectical" relationship between human agency and structural determination. Individuals act and choose, but not freely. The decisions and actions of previous generations tend to crystallize into structures and rules that "weighs like a nightmare on the brain of the living" (ibid.). When previous generations organize property and production into a system that extracts surplus from wage labor, a class society is created that Marx called capitalism. That is the essence of Marx's social theory.

Much of Marx's writings were devoted to working out the logic and processes through which the individual actions of labor and owners of capital [turn] "accumulated labour into capital" (Tucker 1972, 178). Individuals and groups, for Marx, don't ever cease being active and creative. But they often find their actions turned against them. Workers labor and contribute to the growth of capital, which confronts them "as an alien power" that increasingly exploits and limits them, as "social structures" of "fixed, fast-frozen relations" (Tucker 1972, 63, 338). The dance model of power captures that dynamic of power not only in class relations but also in political and cultural relations.

As against Foucault, dancer-agents have not disappeared in contemporary capitalism. Workers are no less active as subjects because we give more attention to what is consumed than what is produced in advanced capitalist nations. The fact is that workers have not ceased needing to work to live. Apart from that, consumers, as individuals and groups, do more than receive and take what is produced. They also transform the meaning of the goods they acquire (Ashley 1997: 215). Very often the managers of capitalist commodification get their clues about what to colonize in the culture by acting as good observers and social scientists and figuring out what "consumers" are up to.

In addition, consumer culture is not quite the monolith around the world it is perceived to be. First, there still exist plenty of uncolonized or semicolonized places both in the developing and in the developed world.

It's true that these places are likely to be eventually incorporated into consumer culture. Certainly, the recent arrival of television to the remote and isolated nation of Bhutan in the Himalayan highlands is just the most recent example of capitalism's inexorable push to commodify and absorb all to the capitalist orbit.[16]

Second, even within the developed countries there are many non- or decommodified places and groups, not fully incorporated into capitalist work and culture. Many minority groups, like Puerto Ricans, have large portions of their population that are not working, not interested in getting work, or engaged in economic activities that are either illegal or outside regular capitalist market processes. They are not, as a result, simply untapped, fertile sites for future commodification and colonization by capital. They may prove that in the future. Though they may be excluded from capitalist productive activity, they may often be active and resistant reformulators of the dominant cultural currents. They may create substitute and oppositional spaces that give some groups the opportunity to move within, exchange, and establish cultural values that are independent of the culture that is traded in the capitalist market. Such independent cultural places create opportunities for power that lasts until the larger capitalist society notices them, observes how they dance, and moves in with hopes of capitalizing on these new cultural ideas and styles.

Denied good housing, Puerto Ricans, for example, have alternatively protested the inequity, built themselves housing, or bemoaned their bad fortune. More interesting is that Puerto Ricans in the South Bronx and East Harlem have taken empty lots, cleaned them of garbage, landscaped them, and constructed "casitas" or small shacks, replicas of traditional peasant housing in nineteenth-century Puerto Rico. They use these casitas along with the lot, over the last thirty years, as a social and cultural gathering place in the midst of the world capitalist city of New York but outside it.

Puerto Ricans build casitas to reclaim abandoned territory as an uncommodified social space that represents nineteenth-century Puerto Rican peasant culture. Casitas impart "identity to the urban landscape by rescuing images, *rescatando imagines,* by alluding to the power of places everybody recognizes, feels good about, and can identity with" (Aponte-Pares 1994,14). In this way, Puerto Ricans continue to remind us of their status as historical agents resisting capitalist forces. They remind us also through a continuing pattern of circular migration between Puerto Rico and the United States as well as through their attachment to musical idioms like Salsa.

The Dance of Power

At bottom, dance is important because it encapsulates, in so many ways, the complex actions that produce power. The dance metaphor reminds us to focus on the relations between actors, on their actions, rather than the rules and structures that guide their moves at any particular moment. It reminds us to focus on the energies and goals that precede movement. This not-new idea suggests that power rests on the active and mutual accommodation of the weak as well as the strong and the follower as well as the leader.

Dance, like all movement, helps to create a sense of freedom and space. Movement through space defines much of what we mean by freedom (Tuan 1977, 52). We are free to the extent that we can move easily and without constraint. Freedom is, in turn, connected to power. The ability to move without obstacles, in fact, provides a unique sense of what we mean by power. This element of power is felt most deeply at the micro level with the strategic maneuvers of social actors trying to gain advantages. This study of Puerto Rican community power is at this level. Actions at this level may not change the macro level of social structures, but they are significant nonetheless to social agents and, in some cases, to those social structures as well.

Dance can set us free. The ability to kick our feet into the air allows us to escape the bounds of gravity. That freedom is, in many ways, negative. It is achieved at the expense of other agents, other things, and external forces (gravity). Freedom is also positive, however. Dancing with others, with a partner, means both less and more freedom and power. We cannot kick our feet exactly as we please, and yet that partner can swing us in ways we could not swing alone.

Dancing with others produces a kind of freedom and power we could not have by ourselves. The dance metaphor reminds us that partnering with others, even with monsters, on the dance floor creates the potential for more power. It reminds us of the power that people seek when they enter a dance space and engage others. It reminds of the power that is created in the interaction of interested partners. Power is dance-like because, in the pursuit of certain goals, interests, and power, people place themselves in the arms of others. By doing so, we achieve a greater or lesser ability to move.

Passions and interests bring people together and push them apart. They produce action and interaction. They create social relations and bonds. The patterns of transactions that results from the interaction of social agents often "clump into social ties, social ties consternate into networks" (Tilly 1999, 21). Social structures emerge from such interactions, much as dance styles emerge from innovations and mistakes on the dance floor. As Barth, Tilly, and others have noted, social structures are the "variable by-products of . . . the actions and interactions" of individuals (Tilly 1999, 48).

Social action is also shaped, limited, and encouraged by these structures. Without getting into a chicken-and-egg problem, we can say that a social structure cannot exist without the social action that got it started and that keeps it going. Actions set in motion by passions and interests, some initiated by structures and others by agents, feed social structures and/or transform them.[17] Social interest, like desire, "animates the world" (Irvine 2006, 2). The key is that change (in power, in freedom) happens within or transforms the context of continuous exchange and negotiation established by social relations.

Social structures clearly also create interests and power. They limit some action and make other action possible. They are like the rules dancers follow. Particular dance styles, like particular structures, encourage and limit different movements. Those rules or structures of dance become evident, to participants and observers alike, in the dance itself. Social structures get perpetuated, like the rules for particular dances, by movement and yet are continually threatened by the random errors or the improvisation of the dancers.[18] Separating the independent role of agency from social structure is difficult (Brettell 2002; Rothenberg 2004).

Agents usually carry forward and perpetuate social structures through their actions. Social structures represent and incorporate the old and new actions, goals, and passions of agents as well. The best moments for assessing the relative contribution of each to social change is at those singular, disruptive moments when shifts occur in the way people interact with each other. The key is to focus on those moments when new and old rules of engagement, for dancing, reach heightened levels of struggle, when social agents discover either success or failure against the weight of social structures that they carry and perform. Those moments reveal the nature of the interests that prevail for different groups, their conflict, and their ability to insert themselves as new social structures of power.[19]

Limits of Power as Dance

It is by moving and performing that the three types of interest reveal themselves. Observers can often note the difference between what agents may prefer to do, what the social roles they are trying to perform "objectively" require of them, and what their actual movements ultimately confirm as a constitutive (or real) compromise (Ball 1992, 29). Individuals and groups must draw upon preexisting social structural roles in order to engage in purposeful activities like dance. The main questions that can be raised about the dance model concern the role of structures, the definition of agency, and the relationship among economic, political, and cultural forms of power.

Each dance style specifies particular steps and movements that objectively define what it means to dance in that style.[20] Individuals and couples cannot dance successfully, especially with each other, without trying to follow those rules. Dancers often prefer to change the style. In most cases, however, the dancers merely reproduce the style because the music, the other dancers, or their own trepidation and skill level permit them very little choice. The resulting performance is neither what the dancers may subjectively prefer nor exactly what that particular dance style objectively demands. That is what Isaac defined as real interest (1987, 98).

An additional question about the dance model has to do with the idea of action. The idea that power centers on and springs from action appears to set us back to all of the theoretical problems associated with Dahl's behavioralist model. This would force out of consideration the study of agenda setting, the manipulation of interests, and the formation of social subjects that result in giving some people more power than others. All of these nonactions and covert strategies would not count then as power. Most analysts agree, however, that power is not the same as the use or exercise of power. Power is dispositional, latent, a capacity "to perform intentional activities and to engage in normatively constituted practices" (Isaac 1987, 76). The dance model, however, does appear to favor actions over nonactions. Dance is action, after all. The dance metaphor, however, is still useful. The phenomena that define movement or dancing must be expanded.

Much goes on in a dance hall beyond the actual movement of bodies on the floor that involves dancing and power. Who gets asked and when involves a complex process involving a "mobilization of bias" that typically centers on prevailing standards of beauty, dance skill, and personal and peer preferences. One study described how some participants at singles dances improve their status by rejecting all advances others make to dance with them. These individuals often don't even acknowledge a request to dance. This personal tactic of inaccessibility is but one of over a score of tactics that participants use in dance halls to increase their power and status.

Some participants at dances minimized their weakness by complete inaccessibility. They often locate themselves "behind a door, in a dark corner, or wedged behind a group of tables" to dramatize their indifference to others and whatever values for dancing they may offer. Such participants locate themselves far from the dance floor, physically doing nothing. These actions are a kind of dance, however. Some of the strategies are aimed "toward enhancing the subject's identity, others toward reducing the status of other participants, and still others to changing the definition of the situation, or withdrawing from the social field."[21] Not dancing is an act of agency—a symbolic and emotional one. Sitting still, in a corner, often requires tremendous effort, is directed at others, and has consequences for power. These "nonactions" are, thus, part of what we call the dance-like processes that produce power.

These tactics of indifference resemble Albert O. Hirschman's concept of exit (Hirschman 1970). Hirschman posits that every form of human enterprise that offers a product or service can be punished and compelled to change by the ability of consumers to exit. Individual consumers have the option to exit, or to act by not buying a product or service as well as by abandoning the provider completely. In a competitive environment, institutions that experience too many exiting consumers will undergo pressure to correct their deficiencies or lose to other providers. The Hirschman model has great explanatory power. It goes considerably beyond traditional supply and demand models to include the strategic actions of consumers to not buy. Its problems lie basically in its assumptions.

Hirschman can be criticized for not imagining the possibility of "inelastic conditions." A monopoly creates conditions where the consumer or voter is "captive" with "nowhere else to go" (Hirschman 1970, 70). Hirschman claims that consumers facing monopolies still have "considerable influence *via voice*" (ibid.). Protest and discontent, he argues, can "force the firm or the party" to change. Such corrective behavior in firms or parties, however, is unlikely if consumers simply boycott and become indifferent.

Hirschman's problem is that he assumes that the firm or party has a single business goal—to acquire more money or votes no matter from whom. This market assumption doesn't work well outside and even, in some cases, inside the market place. Firms and parties don't have singular interests in money or votes alone. Who they get money or votes from can also be important. While rational choice theory suggests that most firms and parties will "sell" to whomever buys, nonresponsive consumers are usually avoided. This kind of behavior is important for the dance model of power.

Indifference on the dance floor, like the kind discussed above, often causes firms and parties to stop making any more offers to dance. Firms and parties that get little response from particular consumers and voters will go elsewhere. Indifference is thus a sign of pain and rejection in consumers and voters that produces no corresponding pain-reducing responses from firms or parties. It is also an attempt by the spurned to recapture some power away from those who have rejected them in the past. The point is that indifference is already about power even when there are no corresponding corrective behaviors in those who delivered pain. Hirschman assumes singular interests and underestimates the role of symbolic actions, like indifference.

The role of politics, especially with regards to state actions, in the constitution of social power for classes and groups is no longer controversial. The idea of interaction between politics and economics is, in fact, a respected and enduring subfield within each discipline at least since Adam Smith. Some theorists have gone as far as C. Wright Mills, who declared that "we must speak of the political and the economic in one breath, of a *political economy*" (1967, 185). The role of culture, however, is more problematic. Its impact is less clearly understood. Its causal mechanisms are harder to detect.

Postmodern theory has placed culture in the foreground of social research. It claims that discourse, colonized desire, mass media, and new technologies of communication are irreducible to the processes of economic production or state politics and policies. That may be true. Culture cannot be reduced to economics or politics. But that certainly cannot mean that culture shares nothing, has no interaction, or is not shaped at all by economic and political processes.

Marx was correct to insist that class carries long-term causal significance. Political and cultural relations, like racism, in this sense, do not lie outside of class. Racism, for example, is not an *additional,* irreducible social cleavage, factor, or force. To a great extent, racism exists as a different but complementary set of relations within the capitalist orbit. Racism endures and creates a social order that often hurts, confounds, separates, violates, and assaults most of what it touches. Racism also has a life span that predates the birth of capitalism and may outlast its death.

At the same time, the signs and discourses that transmit this racial order cannot be viewed in postmodern terms as dematerialized, abstract, ghostly entities. Desire may be a principle medium for depositing unconscious investments that tie individuals to "powerful and destructive emotional sources or symbols, or demagogic leaders" (Best and Kellner 1991, 4). But that does not mean that the cultural process of racism, to desire/oppose the other, rests and survives on its own, without the help of class and the capitalist order.

The reality is that racism creates an order that contributes, benefits, hurts, or undermines some classes and not others. Capitalist class relations are etched deeper in the social structure. The relations of class run like the energy and water circuits in a house, providing most of the energy, fuel, and sustenance to its occupants. Those occupants can also make use of racial or political processes. To the extent that they find increasing validation and sustenance in those alternatives, capitalist class relations lose some of their strength. Before reaching the critical level where racism or some other alternative social relation threatens the perpetuation of capitalism, there is coexistence.

Class relations do not have any stronger grip on social life than racism or state power. As the social relation defining capitalism, however, class is necessary to social reproduction in a way that is not true of racism or state power (Lemert 1997, 127). Capitalist class relations, in this formulation, rule but do not govern. They give life, character, logic, and limits to other social, political, cultural, and economic relations. Capitalist class relations create the stage upon which other social relations improvise their own dances, even some, like racism, inherited from a time before capitalism. R. Marsden and B. Townley have suggested that "capital is analogous to DNA because it is the primary, self-replicating genetic material from which action is produced" (Marsden and Townley 1995, 16). Heilbroner sees it in similar terms. As he once said, "the influence of the economic realm on its intertwined political and social realms does not therefore involve any mechanical dependency or slavish passivity of the latter but only their congruence with, and complementarity to, the operating relationships of capital" (Heilbroner 1985, 84).

Political and cultural power intertwine with class. This means that class power is not simply material but political and cultural. Property, for example, rests on legal and state power. Property also has a cultural dimension that exists not only in the form of ideological processes of legitimation. Cultural relations establish the symbolic basis to make capitalist exploitation and exchange possible. This is apparent in the evolution of concepts like privacy and atomistic notions of the self. At the same time, it is also true that political and cultural relations include a lot more that has no direct, and sometimes has an oppositional, relationship to material production and class power. Racist practices, for example, can either facilitate or impede the exploitation of labor and the accumulation of capital. This is also true of other forms of cultural and political power.

Recent research on the "social construction of target populations" has disclosed the important impact of cultural capital or status on the design of public policy.[22] Some groups are "constructed" as, among other things, "deserving" or "undeserving" and receive either benefits or costs from the policy design that results. Social constructions, in this view, are not derived from economic or class position. They are, in fact, "created by politics, media, literature, culture, socialization, history, religion" (Schneider and Ingram 1995, 443). Politics and culture, thus, can have their own independent impact on policy making, social status, consumption, and productive processes. This makes political and cultural values as attractive and compelling to social agents, to aspiring dancers seeking power as economic values.

In the short run, social agents can dance and acquire social power as easily by controlling cultural and political values as by controlling economic values. The key to getting power is to get to dance, to engage others in social relations embedded with interests and the possibilities of exchange. Whatever inspires invitations to dance creates power. Different interests determine how long the dancing lasts. Also, the more opportunities an agent has to dance, the greater the social power. Culture, politics, and economics are each, in that sense, as important as the others.

In the long run, economic power has a bigger impact than politics and culture. It is the DNA and inner logic of capitalist societies because it forms the most consistent and pervasive social relation able to create and bind social agents and social power. In the short run, economic power is "relative." Ann Douglas points to how easy it is sometimes for agents to get too distracted, misled, confused, and eager to see the limits of some kinds of dancing. She points, for instance, to the long-term limits of cultural power in her account of the Harlem Renaissance during the 1920s when "New Negroes" decided "to work through culture, not politics" (Douglas 1995, 323). They had, she argued, "fallen prey to the weakness inherent in using culture as a substitute for the economic and political arena" (ibid.). The New Negro's dance for power was based principally on cultural values because they had, otherwise, "few claims on mainline America's attention, interest, or sympathy" (ibid.).

Studying the Dance of Power

Group interests and exchange are at the core of the dance model of power. Interests and passions affect the actions of individuals and groups, resulting in a grant of power to others. Social agents attempt to satisfy needs and desires for particular values controlled by others. When those values are rare or not given easily, interests result in dependence and subjugation. Power, thus, amounts to a dance that swells, falls, and changes directions with the fluctuations, in either partner, of those interests, needs, and desires. This is the theoretical basis of the dance model. The dance model is applied and tested in a historical case study of Puerto Ricans in the United States. More specifically, this case study makes use of "process tracing." Changes in interests and passions produced a "sequence and structure of

	A's INTERESTS:	
	HIGH INTEREST IN B	LOW INTEREST IN B
B's INTERESTS: HIGH INTEREST IN A	High Equilibrium Power Betw. A and B ↓	A has more power ↑
LOW INTEREST IN A	B has more power	Low Equilibrium Power Betw. A and B

Figure 1.1. Power in Relation to Interests

events" that resulted in a change in power for Puerto Ricans (Van Evera 1997, 65).

A number of methodological problems exist with the use of concepts like interest and power. Interests and their connection to action are defined here in collective and empirical terms. The focus is on the collective and real interests of Puerto Ricans over time rather than the essentially deductive conception of objective interests found in rational choice theory and Marxism. That makes the identification of interests harder to fix. Collective interests were mostly identified by relying on Victor Turner's "drama" model of interpretation as well as the use of nonobtrusive measurements of interests. This issue will be discussed later.

A more difficult problem was the assessment of power.[23] As in a dance, each partner's power is in constant flux. The assumption of a cooperative and joint contribution by each partner to the movements of the couple, moreover, makes it difficult to determine how much power each possesses at a given moment. It is the political science equivalent of the Heisenberg paradox in quantum physics—one can establish the location or the velocity of quantum particles, but not both at the same time. This study establishes the level of power for Puerto Ricans by assessing a number of empirical measures, establishing structural position, and utilizing multiple historical accounts.

The dance model of power is complex. It is founded on certain simple and specific causal rules, however. Figure 1.1, for example, outlines the possible power resulting from varying interests between social agents A and B. Thus, when B has very high interest in values controlled by A, but A has very little interest in values controlled by B, then A will have greater power over B. When both A and B have high interest in the values controlled by the other, as existed during the Cold War period between the United States and the U.S.S.R, the result is an equilibrium of great power between A and B. The impact of interests on power, at this level of abstraction, is thus causal and direct.

Power is a function of varying interests. This is also illustrated in figure 1.1. Each row and column in figure 1.1 represents an evolving historical relationship between levels of interest and the power of A and B. Though an exact quantitative measurement of interests and power may be impossible, this study does examine the broad structural relation using historical and empirical evidence.

The major theoretical claim in this study is that a social agent's actions and relations with others create and destroy power. Those actions result in and are driven by passions, habits, and interests. As figure 1.1 makes clear, it is because B has a stake in or simply desires being close to A that A acquires power over B. The problem comes, however, in determining B's interests and passions. The discussion on interests in the pages above established that these must be understood as more than an individual quality. Objective interests, for example, are those things that are really "in the interest, or good, of an agent whether he thinks so or not" (Isaac 1992, 50). These objective interests arise from what is enabled and constrained by an agent's place in social relations and the social structure. Objective interests are thus social and collective.

Social agents may or may not want to do something about their objective interests. The positions they take on what is objectively good for them are what we call subjective interests. Surveys and polls can often be used to describe them. Real interests, on the other hand, are "the practical norms that justify and legitimate power relations" (Isaac 1992, 51). These interests represent what social agents do and believe apart from and sometimes against their objective and their subjectively perceived interests. Real interests are "implicit in the practice of social life" (Isaac 1992, 50). In one example, Isaac writes that "while the proletarian may prefer to make more money and may have an objective interest in the transformation of capitalism into socialism, he has, in a capitalist society, a real interest in finding and keeping a job" (Isaac 1992, 51).

Objective and real interests cannot be drawn directly from surveys and interviews. Most theories that resort to them discover objective interests with deductive methods. Rational choice theory, for example, assumes that only individuals have interests and that these are the product of that individual's rational calculation, based, in most cases, on a principle of maximizing benefits. An individual's objective self-interest is thus determined by formal, analytical modeling of particular situations. The results are simple and elegant, but often wrong or tautological (Hirsch et al. 1990, 52). As Green and Shapiro argue, "rational choice theory has yet to deliver on its promise to advance the empirical study of politics" (1994, 7). They also leave out habits and emotional motivations.[24]

Marxism, in some sense, also makes a deductive derivation of interests.

The interests of capital and labor are determined by the (dialectical) logic of their interdependent relation. The interests of capital and labor are classwide, not individual. Capital's interest to produce surplus, to accumulate capital by hiring and exploiting labor, is derived from capital's and labor's conjoined historical evolution. The objective interests of labor, on the other hand, do not exist under capitalism. What labor expresses as a class interest is usually subjective or, following Isaac, a real, practical accommodation to capitalism. In fact, as Marx stated, to say that "the interests of capital and those of the workers are one and the same is only to say that capital and wage labour are two sides of one and the same relationship. The one determines the other, as usurer and squanderer reciprocally condition the existence of each other" (Tucker 1972, 180). Labor has no objective interests, then, except for the overthrow of capitalism because of the connection, which Marx makes, between needs and interests.

Capital cannot exist without accumulation. Since only labor can produce surplus, capital must, or needs to, exploit labor. However, under capitalism, the laborer is "deprived of every need in order to be able to satisfy one need only, that is, the need to keep himself alive" (Heller 1974, 57). That need, to keep themselves alive, makes workers sell their labor and collapse their interests into those of capital. Interests for Marxism are thus derived analytically from the structural properties of the interdependent and historical relation between capital and labor. These interests are an "objective" statement of how capital treats labor as well as what labor can realize under capitalism. As a statement of what actually motivates labor or capital, however, it hardly captures the full range of interests that encourages the actions of these social agents. Subjective and real interests, as discussed above, also play a critical role.

Objective interests can, nevertheless, be confidently presented as good explanations of social processes since they originate as a logical derivation from a coherent, well-argued theory about the nature of relatively enduring social class relations. Objective interests are deeply connected to power. Structural position establishes objective interests that constrain and enable social actions. Objective interests are like a mean around which real and subjective interests fluctuate. Objective interests are, thus, important to the assessment of power. Real interests are, in some ways, more important indicators of the actual practice and experience between social groups. Real interests point to what groups want and desire from each other. These may only partially reflect their structural position.

This study focuses primarily on the real interests of Puerto Ricans, those formed by the norms and practices that "justify and legitimate power relations" for this group (Isaac 1987, 98). Puerto Ricans have real interests even if they are not aware of, or even prefer, them. Real interests, thus, are contingent dispositions that emerge in the historical unfolding and perpetuation of structural social relations. Real interests cannot be analytically derived from objective interests even if they often help to sustain them. Real interests are fluid, open, and nonfixed (Isaac 1987, 103). How do we know them?

We examine what Puerto Ricans do. This means, for example, finding out why Puerto Ricans, as a predominantly working-class group, joined and organized themselves into labor unions rather than ethnic fraternal organizations during the early twentieth century. Such class organizations were an appropriate, objective response by Puerto Ricans to their structural position. After an initial period of serious exploration and organizing around their objective class interests, however, Puerto Ricans, by the late 1920s began to organize themselves into a racial minority.

Explaining these changes is a historical and interpretative research task. The goal is to understand not just what Puerto Ricans did. The need is to understand the subjective and real meanings they gave those actions and practices (Little 1991, 76). The methodological task is to fashion some answer to the question posed by Jerry Lembcke: "what are the empirical referents for collectivity?" (Lembcke 1991, 88).

There are no universally accepted or foolproof methods of making these interpretations in social science.[25] Among the accepted methods in historical interpretation are Clifford Geertz's focus on rule-guided "rituals," Victor Turner's model of extended social interaction suggesting a "drama," or Pierre Bourdieu's notion of habitus, which encompass both rule-guided behavior and deliberate human action (Little 1991, 77–79). The historical nature of this study favored the use of Turner's method. This study is about the past rather than the present. It is also, partly for that reason, dependent on published and archival materials rather than ethnographic materials. This makes Turner's model more useful.

Turner's model focuses on the meanings of a sequence of events, especially how the interaction of "interests, concerns, and intentions" between participants over time shape those meanings. Dramatic moments or episodes are like "windows of structuring . . . through which the structuring process in general can be grasped better" (Lloyd 1993, 101). The focus on dramatic moments provides good opportunities for interpretation, much as the act of learning a new dance exposes for all to see the coded, not immediately apparent, rituals and rules that constitute a dance style. Such indirect and opportunistic methods are not unknown in natural science. Astronomers wait for rare lunar eclipses to study solar phenomena because more is revealed during those unusual celestial moments than under the sun's normal glare. In a similar way, physicists Bombard nuclear particles with other particles traveling at high speeds to create special conditions that allow them to pry out information about nuclear structures they ordinarily could not see.[26]

Turner's drama model is a useful tool for historical interpretation but is less useful than the dance model for understanding the transactions that create power. Drama, like dance, represents social interaction as a performance. Turner's social dramas are, in fact, eruptions, crises, and breaks in the everyday interactions of social agents. He defines them as a "breach of regular norm-governed social relations, signaled by the infraction of a law, a rule, a contract, a code of etiquette, in fact, any regulation for action authorized by the group or community" (Turner 1985, 215). Social dramas are, thus, moments of deep alterations in existing relations of power.

As a model of social relations, therefore, social dramas are useful for identifying and explaining periods of crisis but not periods of harmonic continuity. The social drama model is an excellent method for probing moments of liminal transition, those times when we can more easily "observe the crucial principles of the social structure in their operation" (Turner 1985, 199). The dance model's focus on group interests, however, provides a better way of capturing how and why structures of power between social agents emerge, continue, and disappear.

Turner's interpretative model does make it possible to identify and explore three critical historical "dramas," moments when Puerto Ricans in New York City engaged in economic, cultural, or political relations that had a profound impact on their power. One of these, the 1919 cigar maker's strike, was a brash and briefly successful attempt by a young Puerto Rican community to enhance its power. A second critical moment was the 1949 creation of the Mayor's Committee for Puerto Rican Affairs. Puerto Ricans rode a crest of intense political and economic interest in them as cheap labor during the early 1950s, an interest, however, that they could not ultimately leverage into greater power. A third moment is the period of radical political activity in the Puerto Rican community during the 1960s and '70s. Puerto Ricans gained some temporary and limited power by their rejection of dominant political and cultural values. Each of these periods represented a defining moment in Puerto Rican community history with decisive impact on Puerto Ricans' power as a community. How were they identified?

Except for the third 1960s moment, most historical studies of Puerto Rican community history have paid little attention to the two other dramatic moments selected in this study (see Torres and Velazquez 1998). All three moments, however, meet the criteria as dramatic periods when deep violations occurred in the norm-governed relations between Puerto Ricans and other social agents in the United States. Evidence for the existence of such violations during the selected periods can be found in many published historical accounts, where they remain unanalyzed by the authors.

The subjective and real interests of the public can't be identified by interviews and questionnaires. Nevertheless, it is valid to propose that there is a public interest or perhaps a publics' interest comprised of a variety of different class, social, and political groups. These groups often become aware of the presence of Puerto Ricans and develop an interest in what they have to offer economically (as workers, consumers, professionals, merchants, etc.), politically (as voters, activists, campaign contributors, elected officials, etc.) or culturally (as musicians, dancers, artists, Spanish speakers, writers, cooks, etc.). These group and public interests can be gauged indirectly only. Except for rare moments of candid self-reflection, most groups make no public declaration of their interests. Instead, these interests are identified, in later chapters, by examining the tracks and tracings left behind as these groups move in pursuit of them.

The "tracings" used in this study include obituary notices, the record of ethnic and racial group inclusion on U.S. postage stamps, music award lists, leadership and power media polls, as well as congressional and presidential recognition awards. The premise in using these measures is that any recognition and interest in a group like Puerto Ricans is likely to become registered in such public records of collective tastes and preferences. Latin music, for example, has been part of the music scene in the United States since at least the beginning of the twentieth century. It has even made strong contributions to the development of American jazz (Roberts 1999). Despite this presence and contribution, and except for a period in the 1940s and more recently in the late 1990s, Latinos have long felt that Latin music is effectively ignored by mainstream Americans. The music award lists provide a good indicator of this intuitive suspicion about the mainstream public response to Latin music. Award lists reflect the upward and downward movement of public taste, or at least a portion of the public's taste.

Obituary notices are another useful tool for measuring public attentiveness and recognition. Whose death gets noticed and remembered reveals a great deal about which groups are exposed to public radar, are engaged with mainstream social life, and receive public validation.[27] Obituary notices are, for that reason, a good indicator of a group's status in society.

These and other measures are imperfect but valuable instruments for probing the historical evolution of public interest in values controlled by Puerto Ricans. The analysis, in this study, of music consumption practices as revealed by hit parade listings, for example, permitted an uncovering, at "a distance," of how negligible has been the real public interest in Puerto Rican cultural values (Holsti 1969, 685). The analysis of organizational history combined with an analysis of political, economic, and cultural practices provides a mechanism for data triangulation that helps to validate the interpretation of interests.[28]

In general, the Puerto Rican story with power has been largely shaped by decline rather than success. This is hardly what was expected of them by most social scientists. What went wrong is revealed by a close examination of these three critical periods in their history. The analysis of these three historical moments casts light on the Puerto Rican ability, in social relations with others, to amass power both when conditions were good and when they were bad.

The dialectical, interdependent nature of power in the dance model can make efforts to measure it a mere tautological exercise. A's power is the result both of values that A controls and B's interest in those values. That problem is compounded by the multiple dimensions or "faces" of power. Much of what we call power operates invisibly and remotely. This makes it hard to measure. Bachrach and Baratz could not avoid this measurement problem when they tried to find empirical proof for their theoretical critique of Dahl's behavioral view of power. Their concept of a "mobilization of bias," for instance, is an empirical issue that is studied by looking for "covert instances of suppression" (Isaac 1992, 38). Their concept of "non–decision making," however, involves, by definition, no action. Like social structures, nondecisions are not very amenable to empirical study.

It's true that in any attempt to measure a complex concept like power, as with most social science concepts, researchers find that their measurements "correspond only indirectly to our mental constructs" (Shively 1998, 37). The solution in political science has been to concentrate on topics like voting that are easy to measure directly. It's like the old joke about a drunk who looks for his lost keys by the lamppost because that is where the light is. Bachrach and Baratz could not avoid a similar problem in their empirical studies. Because measuring it was too difficult, their solution was to ignore "non–decision making." They instead settled for testing the "mobilization of bias." This, of course, is not a viable solution. By caving in, they limited the potential advance in the understanding of power suggested by their theory.[29]

In recognition of these problems, this study utilizes a number of mechanisms to minimize the problems with trying to assess Puerto Rican power. These include empirical indicators, interpretative studies of structural roles, and the assessment of other research studies. This combination of methods creates the best chance for a reliable and valid assessment of power. It would have been relatively easy to measure power by the possession of money or weapons.[30] This, however, would not have provided a true indication of the ability of the Puerto Rican community to shape the way other groups and society as a whole think, act, and feel.

The concept of needs is also very complex. It has a physical component. Humans, for example, cannot survive without air or water. But needs are also social. Each society has a particular level of development in which certain goods and levels of consumption become a prerequisite for the sound reproduction of its people. Indoor plumbing, for example, is a social rather than an absolute physical necessity for people in advanced capitalist countries. Social need, then, as Marx once said, "regulates the principle of demand [and] is essentially conditioned on the mutual relations of the different economic classes and their relative economic positions" (Engels 1909, 214).

This suggests, therefore, that the social needs and structural roles of Puerto Ricans can be indirectly represented by economic and socioeconomic measurements of social needs like income, poverty rate, and unemployment data. Where possible, actual observations of Puerto Rican power were utilized. The fluctuation of these needs, as represented by these data, provides a rough approximation of the level of Puerto Rican social power at any given moment, compared to other groups. The use of these data to discern Puerto Rican power also helps in avoiding the tautological problems of relying on measurements of need to establish both interests and power.

The periods identified earlier presented Puerto Ricans with unusual opportunities for altering or solidifying their structural position. The 1919 cigar maker's strike, one of three historical "dramas," signaled the first major challenge to the structural position that Puerto Ricans then occupied. This transitional period exposed the Puerto Rican structural position precisely by calling it into question. What Puerto Ricans could do and demand as well as how they saw themselves was forever shaped by that strike and the response of the cigar industry. The structural changes that occurred varied by social dimension. The political and cultural impact of that 1919 strike, for example, came later than the economic. The key is that the focus on such transitional, dramatic moments exposes the Puerto Rican social structural position, their objective interests, and, thus, their structural power.

A third approach used to assess Puerto Rican social power is the critical review of work by other researchers. Virginia E. Sanchez-Korral, for example, suggested in her book *From Colonia to Community: The History of Puerto Ricans in New York City*, that Puerto Ricans had little political power during the pre-1930s period. Sanchez-Korral argued that Puerto Ricans had little power because they were treated by elected officials as no more than a passive voting bloc (1983, 178). In addition, the

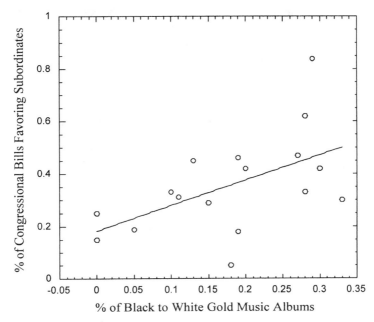

Figure 1.2. Cultural Capital's Impact on Political Power: Correlation of Black Gold Music Albums to Congressional Bills Favoring Subordinates, 1955 to 1988. *Note*: Gold = 500,000 Albums Sold. *Sources*: Joel Whitburn (1985), *Joel Whitburn's Top Pop Albums, 1955–1985*, Menomonee Falls, WI: Record Research; Adam White (1990), *The Billboard Book of Gold and Platinum Records*, New York: Billboard Publications; U.S. House, *Journal*, Washington, D.C.: Govt. Printing Office, 1889–1993.

works of Carlos Sanabria, Bernardo Vega, Jesus Colon, and others provide alternative and comparative perspectives on the level of social power for Puerto Ricans in that period. Assessments of the power of the Puerto Rican community by other scholars and analysts are also examined for the other two historical periods.

The methods used in this study are similar to the approach used by Richard M. Merelman in his book *Representing Black Culture*. Merelman measures the projection of black cultural capital into the wider U.S. society. His major premise is that "the more cultural capital a group controls, the greater are its resources for wielding power" (Merelman 1995, 29). Merelman presents a variety of empirical evidence as proof. This includes the projection of black cultural capital in the form of black music and success in the enactment of cultural legislation favoring blacks by Congress. I have collected and plotted data, like the kind Merelman used, in figure 1.2.

While this is not the place to analyze the results in detail, it's clear that a positive relationship exists between these variables.

These results provide some validation of the methods used to test the basic hypothesis in Merelman's study: an increase in white America's interest in African American culture does appear to confer political power on the African American community. Presumably, as white America became better acquainted with and enjoyed black culture, black congressmen found that their legislation got better reception. A similar relationship can be assumed with other symbolic representations and projections for particular groups. Postage stamps, music consumption, and TV programs can set in motion or freeze images that represent or project particular groups into the wider society. The result of those projections is that the images may provide or limit real opportunities "to improve [group] social, political, and economic positions" (ibid. 4).

Hypothesis and the Story of Power

The general hypothesis in this study is that the decline in Puerto Rican community power can be attributed to the extensive degree of Puerto Rican dependence, compared to other groups, on the values controlled by others in the larger society. As Amelie Oksenberg Rorty has argued, "power and powerlessness are always a function of desire—desire for some apparent good and the ability or inability to satisfy it" (Rorty 1992, 9). The greater the interest an agent has in dancing with another, the greater the vulnerability of that agent.

Increasingly, during the 1960s, however, Puerto Ricans loosened the ties of dependence to the larger society, seeking to empower themselves by a stoic disavowal of things *Americano*. Puerto Rican nationalist and radical movements, for example, increased dramatically during this period. During that time, however, Puerto Ricans also lost power since the larger society had already begun to reduce its interest and investment in goals mediated by Puerto Ricans.

A second general hypothesis is that from the mid-1950s on, Puerto Ricans controlled few values pursued by others in the larger society. Social interest in values controlled by Puerto Ricans varied temporally as well as by area. Thus, though interest in Puerto Ricans as a group with productive economic value generally declined, interest in Puerto Ricans as a community controlling political values (e.g., votes) increased during the 1960s.

In addition, while economic interest in Puerto Ricans as cheap labor declined in New York City during the 1950s, it grew in places like Hartford, Connecticut, and Gary, Indiana. These different responses to Puerto Ricans reflected the heterogeneity of economic conditions in the United States, a growth in the Puerto Rican population, and differential assertion of their status as a minority. They were able to capture some political power. Puerto Rican culture, on the other hand, has barely penetrated or been readily and openly adopted by the rest of U.S. society. In general, however, Puerto Ricans could not salvage power in the economic realm.

These two general hypotheses provide a general orientation for research. They are tested with a variety of information, from texts to statutes to speeches to surveys and censuses. Out of this data comes a surprising picture of the social construction of Puerto Ricans as a racial group and as a group with power. As they developed the cadences, posture, look, and skill of racial minorities, Puerto Ricans discovered that some opportunities for dancing disappeared on them even while others opened up. The "full description" of the Puerto Rican experience that emerges provides a good proof of the two general hypotheses of power described above.

The major achievement of this study is to correct some of the principle flaws in social-science and popular explanations of Puerto Rican poverty and powerlessness. Most portray Puerto Ricans as victims of economic processes, of fate, of racism, of political persecution or neglect, of poor education, of a peculiar, self-destructive cultural taste for migration, etc. Each, no doubt, has an impact that is usually revealed in correlation and regression analyses of aggregate Puerto Rican individuals. But the picture of Puerto Ricans that emerges from such statistical analysis gives little weight to interests and mutual interaction, to the fluid elusion of subjects in motion. Governed by external forces, power, according to that statistical paradigm, becomes something that happens to Puerto Ricans rather than something they themselves seek, engage, grasp, and let go. The statistical and individual approach can explain neither the movements nor the origins of power for Puerto Ricans as a group.

The analysis presented in this study shows that Puerto Ricans were not just the objects of external forces and structures. They were also intimate, though not always conscious, collaborators in the creation and destruction of their own power. Puerto Ricans, in this sense, are not objects or masochists but dancers. Puerto Ricans lost power by moving, by acting in the context of establishing and negotiating relationships to others in society. Puerto Ricans became powerless both because what they wanted and needed were too often values controlled by few others and because they could not provide or assemble a package of values that others (particularly those powerful few controlling critical values in society) might want or need. That is the first major lesson on power to emerge from this study.

The Puerto Rican relationship to power also shifted in historical, temporal, and spatial emphases among the economic, political, and cultural realms. Puerto Ricans were accomplices or dancers in this diverse process too. They always accommodated, negotiated, and resisted dominant powers. By the late 1960s, Puerto Ricans took on the battle for power and dignity in a postmodern political world by pursuing civil rights initiatives (the Puerto Rican Forum) and militancy (the Young Lords). They did so without completely giving up on old class and nationalist ambitions. This both empowered and weakened them.

Puerto Ricans struggled to empower themselves by adopting the racial ethnic identity and competition that had come to characterize late-twentieth-century America. But though they "spoke" this new language with some proficiency, they spoke to others in America who still didn't hear them. They had dressed for this new dance but could find few partners. While they acquired linguistic skill in the new politics, Puerto Ricans did not control enough of the values that the rest of society wanted or needed or desired at the time. Not only had Puerto Ricans become redundant for economic uses and marginal politically; Puerto Ricans remained mostly irrelevant as a culture.

At the moment, in the year 2006, and notwithstanding the rise of ersatz pop idols like Ricky Martin, Puerto Ricans are neither sufficiently desired (as symbolic objects of sex or sport) nor despised (as appear to be African-Americans, who often serve as the declared symbol of public menace and as the bearers of society's guilt and association with problems of poverty, crime, and violence). But it is on the basis of such a scaffolding of multiple and divergent dependencies and rejections that a particular power got built and eroded for Puerto Ricans.

The story of Puerto Ricans since the 1950s can best be characterized as the erosion of key opportunities to dance and a voracious attempt by Puerto Ricans to engage and get power that has only met with partial success. Those mixed and uneven results are one of the major lessons on power to emerge from this study. Dependence was at the bottom of all of this loss of power, as the Jesuit Baltazar Gracian understood and advised his king in seventeenth-century Spain: "More is to be got from dependence than from courtesy. He that has satisfied his thirst turns his back on the well, and the orange once squeezed falls from the golden platter into the waste basket."[31]

2

The Cigar Makers' Strike

An Economic Power Goes Up in Smoke, 1919 to 1945

As a child growing up in Cayey, Puerto Rico, Jesus Colon used to hear a clear, strong voice coming from a big factory down the street. The voice was that of "El Lector," or the reader. His job was to read from the works of Zola, Balzac, Hugo, or Marx to the rows of cigar makers facing each other as they tenderly rolled fine cigars between their fingers (Colon 1982, 13). Puerto Rican cigar makers brought the tradition of El Lector with them to New York City around the turn of the century. Rolling cigars was not enough for them. Puerto Rican cigar makers also insisted on enlightening themselves about the critical issues rocking the world, enjoying fine literature they might not otherwise read, as well as reminding themselves to "keep on struggling and learning from struggle" (ibid.). What is interesting is not that Puerto Rican cigar makers wanted to work like this but that they could.

The lector symbolized the power of cigar makers and by extension of the Puerto Rican community itself in the pre-1930s period. Though small in numbers and working class, Puerto Ricans were surprisingly successful in pressing their demands both on employers and on government. In their actions and words, cigar makers exhibited pride and confidence that they could generally prevail. The existing literature, however, has generally overlooked this period of relative power for Puerto Ricans. Researchers who have recognized power, on the other hand, explain it as the fortuitous consequence of effective Puerto Rican leadership or of the strategic interests of dominant political party organizations. But the social power of Puerto Ricans in this period was actually the result of the Puerto Rican ability to dance with, even to lead, cigar manufacturers. The evidence suggests clearly that power grew and declined for Puerto Ricans with changes in the capitalist need for their special skill at rolling cigars. The interest in Puerto Ricans was both objective and real.

A perilous, major strike in 1919 by cigar makers exposed the roots of their power. Puerto Rican and other cigar makers held up their special skill at rolling Havana cigars like a sword to cigar manufacturers in that 1919 strike. Cigar makers had a level of workplace freedoms, pension and unemployment benefits, and wages enjoyed by few other unionized workers in the United States. Cigar makers also knew that cigar manufacturers had begun to experiment with mechanization and automation in eager hopes of reducing their dependence on skilled labor. But they went on strike anyway. They never really believed that manufacturers could ever find a way to move forward without them.

It was not just boldness that made cigar makers so confident. They were also the best organized, highest paid, and, before 1925, largest category of labor in the Puerto Rican community. They were vocal, active, political, intelligent, and, most of all, leaders. They helped form numerous political, economic, and cultural organizations, led them effectively, and formed the political and moral backbone of the Puerto Rican community well into the 1940s. Cigar makers thus made it possible for Puerto Ricans to move easily as economic agents. At times, that skill and resource was put to use at fomenting better cultural and political moves. Cigar makers were thus tremendous contributions and extended the Puerto Rican community's social power. All the real and potential social power they helped to generate, however, went up in smoke for Puerto Ricans by 1930.

The decline in power centered on changes in structural and historical interests. At first, cigar manufacturers capitulated totally to the cigar makers' strike demands. Later, they moved quickly to automate and mechanize cigar production while moving consumer tastes towards smoking cigarettes. Second, these capitalist moves meant that though the cigar makers were still radical, independent, and intelligent, the Puerto Rican community's strength was dependent on a cigar-rolling skill that was quickly depreciating in value.

Third, the new incoming wave of Puerto Ricans, who left the island for New York City, came with skills that were not comparable to or in as great demand as cigar making. The critical population mass in the Puerto Rican community was soon dominated by low-wage, unskilled labor employed at the lowest rungs of the job market. And finally, the Puerto Rican cigar makers' experience was part of a much wider movement transforming the post–World War I relationship between labor and capital. This change in production and the use of labor has been called Fordism.

Whatever its name, after World War I, production became centered on less-skilled labor, involved more management control in exchange for relatively higher wages for labor, and was increasingly mechanized and automated. Labor became increasingly organized along industrial rather than craft lines. Puerto Rican cigar makers appeared to be taken by surprise by all of this. They refused to believe that "anything mechanical could actually produce what it had taken [them] years to master—a fine cigar" (Cooper 1992, 310).

The cigar makers' power had originated in the economic value of their special skill. The 1919 strike revealed this. Puerto Rican makers appeared to understand this too. They tried to extract as much benefit as they could from the heavy employer interest in their skill. Puerto Rican and other Latino cigar makers launched numerous walkouts and smaller strikes in the years leading up to 1919, testing the intensity of employer dependence on their skills. They failed to capitalize and eventually lost their economic value. The Puerto Rican community loss was much greater. What fell apart after the 1919 strike wasn't just the economic power generated by cigar makers but the attempt to forge a working-class identity for the Puerto Rican community as a militant and internationalist group. Ironically, the new political and cultural organizations cigar makers helped to create actually accelerated the shift away from a working-class and towards a racial/ethnic identity for Puerto Ricans.

At first glance, it seems absurd to suggest that Puerto Ricans had any power during the pre–World War II period. Most research never gets beyond the quick conclusions that can be gleaned from such prosaic facts as that "the Puerto Ricans in New York have a very low economic status" (Chenault 1970, 61). What power can poor communities have? More than one might think if we understand the powers of the weak argument presented separately by Elizabeth Janeway and James C. Scott.

Puerto Ricans were prolific creators of organizations in the pre–World War II period. They thus built an infrastructure for the use of power. They also developed considerable formal instruments of power by registering to vote in large majorities, by producing Puerto Rican political candidates, and by drawing the significant attention of dominant political institutions and leaders. If power is a dance, the evidence suggests that Puerto Ricans got considerable notice on the dance floor and actually got to dance despite their small numbers and considerable poverty.

In what is a pioneering history of the Puerto Rican community in New York City, Virginia E. Sanchez-Korral expressed surprised at discovering that "the available evidence suggests the Puerto Ricans of the interwar years were far more politicized than previously assumed" (1983, 184). They were also more powerful. Sanchez-Korral herself admits that there was considerable interest by the Democratic "party to court Puerto Rican support" (185). She quotes then-congressman Fiorello La Guardia's 1927 focus on Puerto Rican voters as his attempt to find "the best way of getting Puerto Ricans interested" (184). Puerto Ricans also had considerable success in getting Congress to listen to their calls to resolve the colonial status of Puerto Rico or to address other foreign policy issues. In one example, Bernardo Vega mentions a successful effort by the Alianza Obrera in the late 1920s to get Congressman Fiorello La Guardia to denounce American intervention in Nicaragua (1980, 193).

Puerto Ricans accomplished this much with a population that barely reached forty-six thousand in 1930 (Chenault 1970, 57). In contrast, the African American community, which had been in New York City much longer, achieved some cultural power but a more limited political power. Just over two hundred thousand African Americans made New York City home by 1930. They had elected six members of the state assembly and two city board aldermen (Douglas 1995, 317; Johnson 1988, 282). These were real political gains. The complaint among African Americans was, however, that these African American politicians kept themselves distant from the concerns and needs of their community and, in most cases, showed themselves to be "very much Negro leaders picked by white men" (Douglas 1995, 318). These African American politicians couldn't even get the public jobs that the political machine routinely doled out in exchange for votes. In fact, the "percentage of blacks in New York municipal employment actually declined in the 1910s and 1920s despite the rise in the black population" (319). But at the same time that African Americans found limited opportunities to move and dance politically and economically, they found no shortage of willing partners interested in their culture.

By 1928, Claude McKay became the first African American to write a best-selling book with his *Home to Harlem* (Katz 1997, 148). And much earlier, in 1917, "three different dramas with African Americans opened at the Garden Theater to critical acclaim" (143). These included Eugene O'Neill's *Emperor Jones* and Eubie Blake's *Shuffle Along*. Unlike Puerto Ricans, then, African Americans in New York City during this period attracted dance partners and amassed some power mostly by putting forward what had the most value to others—their culture. African Americans had discovered that culture offered them "the only horse willing to run under their colors" (Douglas 1995, 323).

African Americans had their music, literature, and art. Puerto Ricans had unique abilities to roll fine cigars. Both communities came to dance with a one-dimensional appeal. The Puerto Rican appeal, however, proved to be much more short lived. With the power of cigar makers as a foundation, Puerto Ricans built a social infrastructure of community institutions and political clubs. That infrastructure gave Puerto Ricans viable representation, a voice, a semblance of unity, and a face to offer prospective dance partners. They acquired the instrument and the ability to reward and punish with votes. If only their partners had been more interested. In the long run, that infrastructure was not enough to lift them, to keep them noticed, to continue to attract and to move others.

This was a terrible loss. Things had looked so good at the beginning of this period. Puerto Ricans became cigar makers and danced as cigar makers despite great odds. From the moment the United States captured Puerto Rico in 1898, the economic interest in Puerto Ricans was to fill the role of cheap, disposable labor. Cigar makers were lucky and insistent. They danced as skilled and well-paid labor as long as they could with cigar manufacturers, creating a power for themselves and for Puerto Ricans in general that stood out for this and any historical period. The story of that dance provides confirmation of the role of interests in the creation of power.

Colonialization and Puerto Rican Labor

Puerto Ricans began the twentieth century as an afterthought. The United States acquired Puerto Rico by beating Spain in 1898. The United States wanted Cuba. It got Puerto Rico in the bargain. Until World War I, the United States had little real use for Puerto Rico or Puerto Ricans. It followed "a system of colonial tutelage based on a conservative *laissez-faire* philosophy" towards Puerto Rico (Carrion 1983, 218). Ripples began to appear in that philosophy around 1917 when the United States's Bureau of Insular Affairs issued a memorandum outlining plans for the "excess population in Porto Rico." One proposal was "to bring to the U.S. from 50,000 to 100,000 laboring men to be used on farms as agricultural laborers, for which they are best fitted, or as right-of-way laborers on the railroads or similar work requiring manual labor" (History Task Force 1982, 104).

What ensued was a conflict about the structural uses and nature of Puerto Rican labor. Some Puerto Ricans accepted offers for jobs in the United States only to find that the promises of well-paying, skilled jobs were lies. Many accepted their plight. Others fought back. Cigar makers were fortunate to land skilled jobs in the cigar industry. More importantly, it wasn't often recognized, especially by researchers, that cigar makers became the most powerful sector of the early Puerto Rican *colonia*. The rise and fall in social power of the cigar makers was directly related to the level of employer interest in them as workers.

The year 1917 was not the first time that U.S. government officials attempted to cast the people of Puerto Rico as cheap labor. Almost immediately after acquiring Puerto Rico from Spain in 1898, the United States began to encourage the emigration of Puerto Ricans to places like Cuba,

Santo Domingo, Hawaii, and the United States (Centro 1979). The government perception and public opinion that prevailed then viewed Puerto Ricans as a good source of labor. One 1901 *New York Times* article suggested that Puerto Ricans could "make good workers" but only if they were provided with "a few months of intelligent treatment and a diet of good and nourishing food" (HTF 1982, 34). This relatively positive view of the Puerto Rican physical capacity to do manual labor did not last, however.

Puerto Ricans could work, but they didn't work hard enough or without succumbing to temptation, according to some U.S. government officials. As early as 1903, the commissioner of labor in Hawaii reported, for example, that many Puerto Ricans had "drifted from the plantations into the towns or their immediate vicinity and form a class of malcontents and petty criminals" (HTF 1982, 55). That same official also described Puerto Ricans as "untidy" and unused to hard work. At times, the official classification took a racist form. Thus, the American governor of Puerto Rico stated in 1915 that Puerto Rico was overpopulated because of the Puerto Ricans' "inherited improvidence, their racial characteristics" (ibid., 99). Another official report stated that Hawaiian employers found only about 40 to 60 percent of Puerto Ricans laborers "were reported good" (ibid., 60). It is hard to establish the truth behind these complaints. It may very well be that Puerto Ricans did abandon Hawaiian plantations in exchange for an itinerant, possibly illegal existence in the towns. The reasons why they did so, however, cannot be so easily explained in terms of laziness or bad character.

It's hard to believe that Puerto Ricans would abandon family and a way of life in Puerto Rico, travel thousands of miles, in treacherous and unsafe boats, just to become petty criminals in Hawaii. What the historical record suggests, instead, is that Puerto Ricans were recruited to work in jobs that didn't live up to expectations and promises. When Puerto Ricans resisted the conditions of their new jobs, their bosses balked at their audacity and government officials rushed to enforce the idea that Puerto Ricans must occupy the lowest and most precarious rung of working-class employment. In any case, the process of defining and enshrining Puerto Ricans as a disposable, cheap source of labor (and, thus, with little social power) begins in the pre–World War I period.

By 1929, the New York Hispanic weekly, *El Nuevo Mundo,* described Puerto Rican life in New York City as a "continual stream of Puerto Ricans to this city of the dollar, like a ghost, or like some left-over that's impossible to get rid of" (Flores 1993, 90). Thus, to some extent Puerto Ricans themselves recognized the extent to which, for many in the United States, they had become not a potential dance partner but an unappetizing morsel of food dropped to the floor from an old dinner party, waiting to be swept away.

Losing Economic Value

During World War I, the U.S. government contracted and brought in seventy-five thousand Puerto Rican men "as a source of common-labor supply" and paid them thirty-five cents an hour to work on behalf of the war effort. Many of these Puerto Rican contract workers suffered at the hands of the U. S. government. One telegram to the commissioner of Puerto Rico stated that "workmen brought here from Porto Rico to work for the Government in New Orleans [are] ill treated. They have also been taken out of the city under soldiers guard and knocked with butt-end of guns" (History Task Force 1982, 118). Missing from these official accounts is the extent to which Puerto Ricans opposed the effort to pour them into a disposable labor mold.[1]

Puerto Ricans resisted these attempts to devalue their labor. Sometimes they did so publicly as when organizations like the Puerto Rican Extraordinary Convention of Agricultural and Constructive Trade Laborers Affiliated with the American Federation of Labor passed a resolution in 1918 stating, in part, that "we are the first to protest, as we do protest, against any Porto Rican degrading the name of organized labor in this country by working at a lower price anywhere" (HTF 1982, 122). One group of thirteen thousand Puerto Ricans, brought to various U.S. cities in 1918 to labor for different private contracting companies, fought the U.S. government well into the late 1930s to collect back pay owed to them from the World War I period.[2]

At times, Puerto Ricans took more immediate action to defend their community. One report by the U.S. Bureau of Insular Affairs complained that Puerto Rican contract workers caused lots of "trouble" for their handlers. At one point on their journey to Arizona by boat in 1926, Puerto Ricans protested badly prepared meals. In this incident, "lots of plates, forks and etc. were thrown overboard after their contents had been thrown over the decks and into the first class dining room and saloon" (ibid., 190). U.S. government officials seemed bewildered by this fierce Puerto Rican reaction to degradation.

One Puerto Rican government official actually described feeling "abused" by the Puerto Rican workers he tried to contract. The Puerto Ricans refused to accept less than $2.50 per day for cotton-picking and other labor. But it's hard to see how the Puerto Rican workers would not refuse these terms or how the official would not expect them to do so. The official himself admitted that "this group was made up of men who represented fourteen different crafts and they had never worked in agricultural pursuits in Porto Rico" (ibid., 192). That skilled background made Puerto Ricans unwilling to happily accept unskilled work at very low wages.

Government officials never anticipated Puerto Rican resistance. Most officials bought into the definition of Puerto Ricans as a superfluous and cheap source of labor, no matter what their capacities or interests.[3] Cigar makers briefly shifted the balance of power in this economic and political struggle to define Puerto Ricans as cheap and disposable labor. They were symbols of resistance and advocates for Puerto Rican labor interests.

Cigar Makers

The story of Puerto Rican cigar makers in the United States brings into stark relief the myriad of sometimes conflicting forces working to produce a Puerto Rican work force of superfluous and cheap labor. From the turn of the century till the 1920s, Puerto Rican and other cigar makers grew to become the highest-paid, best-organized, most independent, and most militant sector of labor in the city. Cigar makers became a force both inside and outside the Puerto Rican community. A large part of the power of cigar makers came from the fact that the tobacco industry was so heavily dependent on this highly labor-intensive and skilled work force (Cooper 1992, 11). The tobacco employers' efforts to reduce that dependence, however, accelerated after 1919 and made Puerto Rican and other cigar makers obsolete, unemployed, and poor. The Puerto Rican community lost a symbol, a leadership, and a source of power in the economic sphere that they would not reclaim in the future.

Closed off from other industries by employers and unions, most Puerto Ricans during the first decades of the twentieth century sought employment in cigar firms or started their own (Vega 1980, 139). The International Cigarmakers' Union reported, for instance, that Puerto Ricans comprised four thousand five hundred out of the almost sixteen thousand who were members of the union within New York City in 1919 (Killough 1924, 19). There were another fourteen to fifteen thousand cigar makers not in the union. The U.S. Census reported that there were only 7,364 people of Puerto Rican birth in New York City in 1920. Cigar makers, thus, represented over 61 percent of the total Puerto Rican population and 28 percent of organized cigar makers. Bernardo Vega supports this estimate in his statement that "in 1916 the Puerto Rican colony amounted to about six thousand people, mostly *tabaqueros*" (12). Ironically, there is evidence to show that as the cigar industry and union declined in size and power, the Puerto Rican and Hispanic component declined in number too but didn't quickly disappear. As late as 1945, there existed a United Cigar Workers Union, whose Local Section 273 in East Harlem had about one thousand four hundred mostly Puerto Rican and Hispanic members.[4]

Cigar makers, Puerto Rican and Hispanic in particular, opposed their objectification as labor. This is illustrated by the insistence on readers as well as on the mobility insured by the "traveling system." The key to the cigar makers' militant philosophy can be found on the front page of their *Official Journal*. Prominently displayed on that page were four core philosophical principles: "Better Working and Living Conditions," "Knowledge Is Power," "Organization," and "Justice." Cigar makers placed enormous importance on raising their class consciousness and enhancing their power as labor. Nowhere were the principles of knowledge and organization truer than with Puerto Ricans.

Early on, Puerto Rican and Hispanic cigar makers had won the right to hire someone to read out loud to them while they worked. These lectors read from newspapers as well as from political and literary works (Vega 1980, 60). Discussions usually followed the readings. Debates not settled at the work place were usually pursued in the frequent evening lectures that were presented by invited speakers and held at the *circulos*, or cultural centers instituted by the cigar union for the edification of its workers (Vega and Iglesias 1984, 34). Cigar makers became, as a consequence, what Bernardo Vega called "the most enlightened sector of the working class" (22). They became the "organic intellectuals" of the Puerto Rican working class, trying to understand the world, as Gramsci hoped, from their own class vantage point.

The tradition of lectors entertained and, no doubt, helped to educate cigar makers. Employers, however, didn't like it since readings often delayed production for varying unprofitable periods. By the turn of the century, most employers responded by making the cigar-making process into piecework. The use of piecework shifted much of the cost of political debate in the work place to the worker. But this strategy also made it harder for employers to increase production rates or to introduce more efficient methods or machinery.

The delicate human skill of rolling a fine "Seed and Havana" cigar was itself hard to mechanize (Cooper 1992). That difficulty, coupled with piecework and a rising consumer demand for cigars, made it possible for cigar makers to increase not only their wages but also control of the work place. Cigar makers, for example, determined what hours their factories stayed open, how much work they did, and when they did it. Employers complained that cigar makers would often leave a factory in the middle of the morning to go to a tavern and get drunk (Cooper 1992, 126). This control of the pace of work gave cigar makers increased opportunity to attend political rallies, actively support the strikes of other unions, as well as go on strike themselves when conditions warranted it. But despite or perhaps because of their power, by 1919, cigar makers believed the time had again come for a major strike.

Cigar makers asserted themselves against employers by insisting on readers and by resorting to strikes. But the "traveling system" was also an equally important mechanism of resistance. The Cigar Makers International Union not only permitted its members to travel from shop to shop, from city to city, but it actually encouraged the practice. It provided members with travel loans and supported a workplace culture wherein cigar makers openly welcomed and hosted visiting fellow cigar makers, offering them meals and lodging. Cigar makers traveled for fun, economic opportunity, and education. At bottom, however, traveling was an expression of the cigar makers' power to control their own time. As Cooper explained it, "travel worked as a group strategy to help cigar makers negotiate the limits of their position within the production process which made them so vulnerable to shifts in the economy and the demands and power of employers" (1992, 77).

Racism made it more difficult for Puerto Ricans to fully enjoy the freedom provided by the traveling system. At least one Puerto Rican cigar maker, Jose Santana, however, did travel "extensively throughout the U.S. and Canada between 1909 and 1916" (ibid., 83). The migration of Puerto Ricans from the island to New York City was also facilitated largely by the traveling system. In any case, traveling was essentially another way for cigar makers to assert some power by rejecting particular employers and, even if only temporarily, dancing with another.

Because they were not engaged in an industry necessary for conducting the war, the cigar industry was prohibited from receiving wage increases, a reduction in hours of work, or improved working conditions. As soon as World War I began to draw to a close, however, the Cigarmakers International called "upon all organized labor to give us their moral support in helping the union cigarmakers to maintain and improve present conditions" (CMIU 1919, 2). On July 1, 1919 over thirty thousand cigar workers went on strike in the New York City metropolitan area to protest stagnant wages and the length of the workday ("Record of Strikes" 1919).

The cigar makers' strike was only one of among one hundred strikes in New York City during 1919, as carpenters, milliners, window cleaners, and other workers in "unnecessary industries" unleashed demands held in check during World War I ("New York's Quota" 1919).[5] Cigar makers made more money than workers in other industries, but there had been no increases during the war. In fact, cigar makers had been among the highest-paid workers in the Puerto Rican community at the time. But that didn't stop Puerto Ricans from joining other cigar workers, who usually got paid more, to quickly close down almost every shop in the city and to spread the strike to national levels. Actually, Puerto Ricans, both in New York City and in Puerto Rico, had engaged in militant strike activity numerous times during the first two decades of the twentieth century.

The Cigar Makers International Union specified that there occurred over fourteen separate strike activities in Puerto Rico and thirty-two in New York City from 1912 to 1920 (CMIU 1920, 11). Many of the strikes in New York were the actions of Puerto Rican and Hispanic cigar makers. Very often, Puerto Rican and Hispanic cigar makers struck against the wishes of the union. In fact, the union accused them of acting irrationally for driving the industry out of the city and to the increased use of machines. The union blamed it on "the temperament and traditions of the Latin and Latin-American cigar workers" (CMIU 1920, 16). The 1919 strike was thus in large part driven by Puerto Rican and Hispanic cigar makers. For some CMIU officers, the 1919 strike was "a nightmare" conceived by Puerto Rican and Hispanic cigar makers as "a plan for the disruption of our Intl. Union" (CMIU 1919, 10). Nevertheless, by the end of 1919, cigar company owners capitulated, conceding to all of the workers' demands and resuming production.

Cigar makers got what they wanted in the 1919 strike: a forty-four hour week, a 50 percent increase in wages, the right to organize, and recognition of a grievance committee (Cooper 1992, 286). This was a momentous victory. Few other workers had achieved as much. In fact, steelworkers went on strike that same year, 1919, because their wages were so extremely low and they worked long twelve-hour days. The 1919 cigar makers' success, however, also led to a quick shift in the balance of power.

After the strike, cigar firm owners made their own moves. They began to look more desperately for cheaper, more stable ways of producing cigars (Vega and Iglesias 1984, 115). Workers and cigar-firm owners continued to clash, as a result, throughout the 1920s. Owners tried to reconstitute some power by relocating first from lower to upper Manhattan then, to the outer boroughs, and then to New Jersey and Pennsylvania, where they brought more women into the cigar trade. Of the cigar makers who worked in Manhattan in 1900, for example, 53 percent worked below Fifty-ninth Street. But by 1922, only 27 percent did so (Killough 1924, 25).

The 1919 strike accelerated the shift of factories out of lower Manhattan. The strike convinced employers that "production must be scattered as a matter of insurance against some accident or strike discontinuing the manufacture of the important brands" (ibid. 52). More importantly, cigar company owners also turned to machinery to reduce the power of workers. In 1926, the *New York Times* reported that new, more efficient machines had begun to make cigar makers "as scarce as private glass-blowers or gold-beaters" ("Age of Hand-made" 1926). Indeed, as the *Times* reported in 1926, the decline was considerable, as "less than 5 percent of the country's total cigar production is now made entirely by hand, and 30 percent is exclusively machine made" (ibid.).

The 1919 strike thus accelerated the introduction of cigar-making machines. Cigar makers themselves thought so. One cigar union organizer claimed that "the sudden interest in cigar making machines is due in large measure to the epidemic of strikes with which the trade has been infected during the past year" (CMIU 1920, 16). Prior to 1919, it was the power of the union that kept machines at bay. The cost was declining productivity. From 1914 to 1919, the percent of value of tobacco products in New York City and New Jersey compared to all manufacturing declined from 3.3 to 2.8 (Killough 1924, 19). The 1919 strike simply blew manufacturers over the top.

What happened to cigar making also happened in other industries. In fact, efforts to mechanize work in other industries made the 1920s one of the most productive in U.S. history. Between 1919 and 1929, for example, horse power per wage earner in manufacturing shot up 50 percent, 60 percent in mines and quarries, and 74 percent in steam railroads (Bernstein 1960, 50).

When it seemed they were not going to stop the trend towards mechanization, Puerto Rican cigar makers in many cases started their own small cigar-making workshops in apartments and storefronts, and, eventually, left cigar making entirely to work in other industries (Sanchez-Korral 1983, 141). Bernardo Vega recounts the major dilemma faced by cigar makers at the height of their conflict with employers, a dilemma identical to the one that would confront Puerto Rican clothing workers later in the 1950s. Vega says that he became deeply frustrated in his role as a cigar-union official since he was required to defend "the interests of the workers, without at the same time forcing the factories to move to other cities" (Vega 1980, 116). But there was probably little that Vega or any labor leader could do since employers were determined to turn back the power of skilled labor by introducing machines and by relocating their factories. Even bringing Puerto Rico's premier labor leader, Santiago Iglesias, to catalyze Puerto Rican cigar makers in New York City during 1925 could not reverse the tide ("El Senador" 1925, 6).

Puerto Rican cigar union organizers had to confront not only the employer's will but also that of other workers. A vast river of workers flowed into U.S. cities during the 1920s. About two million workers moved each year from farms to large cities during that decade (Bernstein and Matusow 1969, 158). These black and white workers flooded U.S. cities, joining the millions that had come from other countries. Puerto Rican workers also migrated to New York City in greater numbers in this period. From 1920 to 1930 over thirty-seven thousand Puerto Ricans came to live in New York City (Chenault 1970, 58). This swelling of the working-class population was a real blessing for employers. As Bernstein states, "the resulting surplus of labor gave [employers] little cause to fear turnover, money wages were stable; and unionism was in the doldrums" (1969, 159). It was easy for employers, thus, to make themselves less dependent on and therefore less vulnerable to the cigar makers' skills and organized militancy in the city. In response, Puerto Rican cigar makers organized in 1925 into a Committee for Social and Economic Reconstruction aimed at imposing a uniform wage throughout New York and the rest of the nation. They spoke eloquently and in class terms about how any wage increase represented nothing more than "el fruto de los esfuerzos condensados de estos mismos trabajadores" ("Los tabaqueros" 1925, 6).[6] They spoke defiantly of their strength because "los trabajadores de Nueva York en sus luchas tendrian la ayuda y la solidaridad del movimiento obrero federativos de Nueva York que tiene 700.000 trabajadors organizados actualmente" (ibid.).[7] And they continued to listen to the words spoken by *el lector*, who soothed, educated, inspired, and completed them. But the lector's words did not carry very far. While the lector was real enough, the cigar makers had become eerie, ghostly images of what they once had been.

By the late 1920s, Puerto Ricans had not only lost jobs and power in tobacco. They had lost their place among the elite categories of labor that possessed strong organization and the political poise to make serious demands on social attention and resources. Puerto Rican cigar makers themselves were quick to realize how fast they had fallen from grace. P. Rivera Martinez of the Internacional de Tabaqueros de los Estados Unidos lamented as early as 1925 that

> el elemento tabaquero, nosostros, pretendiento ser el porta-estandarte en las luchas civicas, de caracter social y del trabajo, hemos dado pruebas en contrario en cuanto a nuestra consistencia y manera de crear una base segura y eficiente para la defensa de nuestro oficio. ("Los anos" 1925, 5)[8]

Puerto Ricans thus lost jobs as cigar makers. While they found other jobs, in other industries, these jobs brought with them a decline in overall skills and wages. These jobs were also in weak or unorganized industries. The loss of a strong and militant labor organization as well as stable and high-paying jobs contributed significantly to the long-term historical degradation of Puerto Rican labor.

What happened to cigar makers would happen much later to other Puerto Rican workers in different industries and cities. Jobs and industries would disappear for Puerto Rican garment workers in New York City during the 1950s and for Puerto Rican steel workers in Gary, Indiana. The cigar makers' decline, however, had a direct and critical economic and political impact on the Puerto Rican community. They formed a prosperous, independent, and militant sector of all Puerto Ricans in New York City. What they experienced had immediate repercussion for other Puerto Ricans.

The cigar makers' loss of power eliminated an essential, countervailing force. The ability of the Puerto Rican community to defend itself against unchecked exploitation and abuse was greatly diminished. Puerto Rican workers had lost the prestige, power, and security that resulted from their being anchored to a profitable, growing industry that was in dire need of their unique skills. Instead, they found themselves cast adrift like dandelion spores among a million other spores, searching for a place to take root, for a place where they could make a productive contribution to society.

What the Puerto Rican cigar makers achieved, even in decline, stands in sharp contrast to the pattern of abuse experienced by other Puerto Rican labor at the time in the United States. Published reports documented defeat and abuse in one incident after another. In one report, Puerto Rican contract workers in Arizona complained during 1926 that cotton growers tried to force them to "trabajar bajo el contrato" ("Los Puertorriguenos" 1926).[9] Another reported on Puerto Rican contract workers in Hawaii, Baltimore, and elsewhere who found themselves receiving wages below the contract level as well as experiencing bad living conditions (History Task Force 1982). In Arizona, official reports indicated the severity of their descent: Puerto Rican contract workers were brought in by cotton growers and government agents to replace Mexican workers who were already receiving the lowest wages in that area ("Los Puertorriquenos" 1926).

The vast numbers of Puerto Ricans who began to migrate to New York City during World War II found jobs but essentially as low-skilled and poorly paid labor. Many Puerto Ricans came to New York City because employers sent recruiters to Ponce and Mayaguez with stories of well-paying jobs in garment work. They came because the U.S. government sent agents to Puerto Rico to sign displaced peasants to contract work in the United States. But they came primarily because there were so few jobs in Puerto Rico and no other means of making a living. Between 1941 and

1950, an average of almost nineteen thousand a year came to the United States seeking jobs (Cardona 1987, 39). The vast majority came to work in the garment, restaurant, hotel, and light manufacturing fields.

Puerto Ricans did have great need for New York City jobs. The Depression of the 1930s devastated Puerto Rico's economy. Industrialization also eliminated many opportunities for Puerto Ricans in the countryside. The pressure to leave Puerto Rico became enormous. As early as 1929, Puerto Ricans who migrated made *nine dollars more per week* in their first job *in New York City* as compared to their last job in Puerto Rico (Senior and Watkins 1973, 158). In the 1930s, Puerto Ricans were working primarily as laborers, porters, factory and laundry workers, and as janitors and handymen in buildings and hotels (Sanchez-Korral 1983, 33).

During World War II, the difference in average weekly wages between the first job in New York City and the last job in Puerto Rico amounted to *more than seventeen dollars* (Senior and Watkins 1973, 157). Obviously, Puerto Ricans came to New York looking for these higher incomes. These wages were attached to lower skilled and unstable jobs, as well as carried a host of other problems. Perhaps what is more important is that Puerto Ricans coming to the United States were more economically dependent on employers than had been the case for cigar makers. As Juan Flores writes, cigar makers like Bernardo Vega saw the Puerto Rican community in New York City "as largely self-contained, and to be understood primarily in reference to Puerto Rico" (Colon 1982, xv). The next generation consisted of "Puerto Ricans who were in New York to stay" (ibid.). That subtle change in perspective made Puerto Ricans more vulnerable to the economic insults New York could deliver.

Puerto Ricans got paid more for lower-skilled jobs in New York City. Of all the Puerto Ricans who came to the United States in 1940, only 21 percent had worked in unskilled positions in Puerto Rico, but 46 percent ended up doing so in the United States. Most of the Puerto Ricans in unskilled jobs in the United States had been at least semiskilled workers in Puerto Rico. Over 41 percent worked in semiskilled positions in Puerto Rico compared to the 25 percent of Puerto Ricans in semiskilled positions in the United States (Sandis 1973, 139). As Oscar Handlin states, "even those [Puerto Ricans] who arrived with skills or had training in white collar occupations had to take whatever places were offered to them" (1962, 70). By doing so, Puerto Ricans became dependent primarily on marginal, low-paying, and unstable sectors of the U.S. economy. This represented a loss of power since the Puerto Ricans' economic value became attached to their ability to perform low-wage and irregular work. The loss of power would, moreover, prove enduring and intractable as the weak economic value of Puerto Rican labor declined further, starting in the 1950s, with the departure of more and more industry from New York and the growth of an economy that was centered increasingly on white-collar, "postindustrial" work.

The government's position towards the abuse of Puerto Rican contract workers was largely to ignore it. Puerto Ricans helped to meet the growing economic need for cheap labor caused by the closure of the immigration door with the 1921 national origins quotas. In this sense, it is easy to understand why an official of the Puerto Rican Department of Agriculture sent to investigate complaints by Puerto Rican contract workers could so easily dismiss their exploitation by arguing that

> we ought not to fear for the people that went to Arizona, because there is a labor shortage and plenty of work. Two facts will prove my assertion:—Last year the farmers of Maricopa County could not gather all their cotton crop, because of lack of labor and consequently, lost one and a half million dollars. Second:—I have seen hundreds of laborers go to their private buggies and automobiles. (History Task Force 1982, 192)

From this official's perspective, Puerto Ricans riding automobiles proved that employers were not abusing them. This was, of course, wishful thinking, an attempt to hide the government's complicity in the abuse of labor. The pressure to construct a Puerto Rican work force of cheap and expendable labor had simply gathered its own steam. The limited or ineffective opposition to that pressure reflects the decline in Puerto Rican economic opportunities and power, especially as a result of the problems of cigar makers. What is interesting is that while Puerto Ricans became less valuable as labor in the 1920s, they still possessed some political power, ironically as a residual and indirect product of the economic power they had once built as cigar makers.

The achievements and potential for power of Puerto Rican cigar makers could not be clearer than when compared to the situation of African Americans during the same period. Thousands of African Americans left racist and economically depressed conditions in the southern United States to seek a better life in northern cities like New York during the first decades of the twentieth century. By 1920, over 164,000 African Americans lived in Harlem alone. The combination of racism and intra–working-class conflict kept African Americans, however, in low-wage, unskilled jobs, often serving as strike workers. One 1910 study reported that "colored men are in few skilled trades. There are no machinists, no structural iron workers, no plumbers, no garment workers" (quoted in Katz 1997, 109). African Americans in the 1920s were "paid lower wages and charged higher rents than any other group in New York" (Douglas 1995,

319). African Americans would turn towards culture and, to some extent, to politics to amass more power. But the economic foundation, which had existed briefly for Puerto Ricans, that could catapult them to political power over other ethnic groups, as had occurred with the Jews, was missing for African Americans.

Political Power, 1920–1945

Despite a relatively small population and a mounting everyday experience with racism and the reduction in their value as labor, Puerto Ricans in the pre–World War II period enjoyed some political power. This has surprised a number of researchers of the Puerto Rican experience during the 1920s and 1930s period in New York City (Sanchez-Korral 1983; Jennings 1977; Estades 1978). Politicians as diverse as Fiorello La Guardia and Mayor Jimmy Walker, as well as political parties like the Republican and the Communist parties all pursued, courted, and competed for the attention and votes of the Puerto Rican community.[10] These actions suggest that Puerto Ricans had some political power. This political power, moreover, sprang from a variety of interests.

For one, the United States had a need to stabilize its relationship with the island of Puerto Rico. This made Puerto Ricans in New York City an important sounding board if not a potential instrument of U.S. diplomacy. The emergence of Puerto Rican social, cultural, and political organizations in New York City during the 1920s also made Puerto Ricans a more vocal and politically focused community, able to make itself available, noticed, and attractive to other political actors. Puerto Rican cigar makers considerably enhanced the impact of these factors on political power.[11]

The Puerto Rican voting community of New York City was not large enough during the 1920s period to be of much electoral importance to politicians or political parties. Puerto Rican cigar makers, however, possessed values that drew the respect and attention of non–Puerto Ricans in the city. They were enlightened, militant, and well organized enough to attract the attention of elected officials like Mayor La Guardia, who had little electoral need for the Puerto Rican vote. The political power of the Puerto Rican community didn't simply rub off from the economic status enjoyed by cigar makers. It required the creation of an organizational infrastructure.

As we have seen, cigar makers were largely responsible for the astounding rate at which new political and social organizations were created after 1919 (see table 2.1). The establishment in 1918 of the Spanish-language daily newspaper *La Prensa* helped to document this period of heightened activism. Seven organizations were created in 1922 alone. These ranged from social groups like the Asociacion Puertorriquena to labor organizations like the Alianza Obrera Puertorriquena and political clubs like Club Betances (Sanchez 1994, 7). Bernardo Vega describes the Alianza Puertorriquena, also founded in 1922, as the "primer esfuerzo serio por establecer una agrupacion unitaria de la comunidad" (Vega 1980, 165).[12] In total, between 1922 and 1930, thirty "civic" organizations dedicated to political, social, or cultural goals were created in the Puerto Rican community (Sanchez 1994, 9). This was a remarkable proliferation of organizations, especially when compared to the rest of the city. The 1,177 political clubs that existed in New York City during 1927, for example, meant that there were only one and a half political clubs for every ten thousand New Yorkers (ibid.). In contrast, there was one political club for every three thousand five hundred Puerto Ricans living in the city at the time. Cigar makers played an unrecognized but critical role in this extraordinary record of Puerto Rican civic participation.

The phenomenal record of organizational creation between 1920 and 1930 was never seen again in the Puerto Rican community. It can't be explained solely as a consequence of Puerto Ricans becoming U.S. citizens through the Jones Act of 1917. Literacy tests and other obstacles generally prevented Puerto Ricans from registering and voting at high rates until about the 1960s (Sanchez-Korral 1983, 183). Organizational growth was also not a reflection of any actions by institutions from outside the Puerto Rican community. U.S. political organizations like the Democratic Party basically ignored Puerto Ricans during the 1920s. Bernardo Vega notes that in the early 1920s, "ningunos de los partidos politicos, ni el democrata ni el republicano, se interesaba serialmente por el apoyo de los puertorriquenos" (Vega 1980, 155).[13]

Established political institutions, in fact, did what they could to dissuade Puerto Ricans from registering to vote. They would subject the Puerto Rican "aspirante a un interrogatorio inquisitorial con el proposito de amedrentarlo y hacerlo desistir" (ibid.).[14] U.S. political institutions thus seemed more intent on limiting than encouraging Puerto Rican political participation and organization. The major countervailing force to this was Puerto Rican cigar makers. They provided the necessary resources, political inspiration, training, leadership, and exemplars to organize and enter the dance floor despite apparent rejection.

In her classic study of the early Puerto Rican communities of New York City, Virginia Sanchez-Korral suggests that *boliteros*, or numbers-game operators, were largely responsible for the growth and influence of Puerto Rican political clubs in Brooklyn during the 1920s. First, *boliteros* became immediate leaders because they "symbolized someone who had succeeded, to a degree, in conquering the new environment" (1983, 176). *Boliteros* had cars and telephones when others did not. They also had information, about the Puerto Rican community as well as about the larger city. More importantly, and second, the *boliteros* contributed funds to the Puerto Rican clubs and organizations. In fact, "much of the outside funding for the Brooklyn clubs during the first decades of the century came from the *colonias'* boliteros" (1983, 175). *Boliteros*, thus, were important agents of power for the early Puerto Rican community.

The *boliteros*, like the cigar makers, enhanced the Puerto Rican ability to dance and gain social power. They provided economic resources as well as leadership to the Puerto Rican community. The *boliteros* were most active in the Brooklyn Puerto Rican *colonia*. Cigar makers were instead a city- and nationally recognized group. The *boliteros'* power, moreover, rested on illegal activities. *Boliteros* could contribute money and perhaps bold, tough advocacy. Cigar makers, however, contributed more than money and leadership. They brought the respect of a wider and mainstream element as a result of their productive role in a major U.S. industry. The social power of both declined, however, as the bonds of need and purpose disappeared. The economic depression of the 1930s made numbers running unaffordable to most. *Boliteros* ran out of numbers. But it was the decline of cigar maker's power that was more important and catastrophic for the Puerto Rican community.

Cigar makers were often among the key founders and leaders of Puerto Rican community organizations. Bernardo Vega alone, a long-time cigar maker, was among the leaders of El Circulo de Trabajadores de Brooklyn, mutual help organizations such as La Aurora, La Razon, and El Ejemplo, community organizations such as the Alianza Obrera, as well as political clubs like Club Eugenio Maria de Hostos (Vega 1980; Sanchez-Korral 1983, 213–18). Taught in his youth by *tabaqueros*, Jesus Colon was also a founder of political organizations like Caribe Democratic Club and Liga Puertorriqueno.[15] Both Vega and Colon wrote and edited newspapers. Vega edited *Grafico*, while Colon wrote for *El Machete Criollo, El Nuevo Mundo, Grafico, The Daily Worker, The Worker, Mainstream,* and *Liberacion*. By means of this "very intricate network of progressive organizations" the "cigarmakers [had] begun to forge a political vanguard in the very heart of *El Barrio*" (Ojeda 1986, 46). Thus, Bernardo Vega and Jesus Colon as well as other Puerto Rican *tabaqueros* in New York City, were actively trying to "most effectively [promote] unity among Puerto Ricans in standing up to the rampant discrimination and chronic injustice leveled against them" (Colon 1982, xi). Cigar maker Bernardo Vega claimed that cigar makers were not afraid of being called a "spick." Rather than deny

TABLE 2.1
Puerto Rican and Latino Organizations in New York City

Organization	Created	Purpose
La Prensa	1918	Daily Newspaper
Trabajadores de la Industria del Tabaco	1919	Economic
Asociacion Puertorriquena	1922	PR Social
Alianza Obrera Puertorriquena	1922	PR Economic, Political
Alianza Puertorriquena	1922	PR Social
Ateneo Obrero	1922	Economic, Culture
Club Betances	1922	PR Social
Club Caborrojeno	1922	PR Social
Club Democrata Hispanoamericano	1922	Political, Social
Club Latino-Americano	1923	Social
Club Videro	1923	Social, Political
Puerto Rico Literario	1923	PR Culture, Social
Puerto Rican Democratic Club	1923	PR Political
El Club Hijos de Borinquen	1926	PR Social
Liga Puertorriquena e Hispana	1926	PR Social
El Grafico	1927	Spanish Newspaper
El Machete Criolla	1927	Spanish Newspaper
Fed. of Porto Rican Democratic Clubs of NY	1927	Political
Liberty Democratic Club	1927	Political
Metropolis	1927	Spanish Newspaper
The Puerto Rican Brotherhood of America	1927	PR Social, Political
Porto Rican Chelsea Democratic Clubs	1927	PR Political
Porto Rican Political Club	1928	PR Political
Comite de Defensa de Puerto Rico	1928	PR Political
Guarionex Democratic Club	1929	Political
Nueva York Sporting Club	1930	Social Sports
Caribe Democratic Club	1930	PR Political
Casa de Puerto Rico	1930	PR Culture, Economics
Hermandad Puertorriqueno	1930	PR Social, Charity
Club Esperanza	1930	Social
Baldorioty Democratic Club	1932	PR Political
Spanish Grocer's Association	1937	Economic
Camara de Comercio Hispana	1940	Economic
Liga Puertorriquena Hispana Eugenio Maria de Hostos	1940	PR Political, Culture
Circulo Cultural Cervantes	1940	Theater
Pan American Women's Association	1940	Social, Culture
Club Caridad Humanitaria	1940	Charity
Comision Pro Centenario de Hostos	1940	Culture
Mision Episcopal Hispana—Women's Auxiliary Group	1940	
Sociedad de Mujeres Puertorriquenos	1940	PR Civic, Culture
Emergency Unemployment Relief Committee— So. Bronx Headquarters	1940	Welfare, Civic
Asociacion de Empleados Civiles de Correo	1940	Social, Economic
Spanish Association for the Blind	1940	Charity
Club Artes and Letras	1940	Culture

Sources: Vega and Iglesias 1984; Sanchez-Korral 1983

their origin, they "peleaban porque se les reconociera como puertor-riqueno, or, en general, como 'hispanos'" (Vega 1980, 138).[16]

The labor activities of Puerto Rican cigar makers also had as profound an impact within the labor movement as in the Puerto Rican community.[17] Puerto Rican and Hispanic cigar makers, in response to racist exclusion policies by the mainstream union, formed their own union called Trabajadores Amalgamados de la Industria del Tabaco (also known as the Spanish Auxiliary) and were deeply involved in the 1919 strike against cigar manufacturers. That year, the Spanish Auxiliary joined the Cigar Makers' Council and the CMIU to hold a mass meeting where they called "a general strike in New York of all cigar makers, packers, stemmers, and cigar factory workers" (Cooper 1992, 286). That leadership role had repercussions for other Puerto Rican workers. Puerto Rican cigar makers participated for the first time in negotiations with employers and at an equal level with workers from other nationalities. This encouraged Puerto Rican workers in other industries to organize (ibid.). Because of that "se inicio la organizacion de los confiteres, panaderos, empleados de hoteles, restaurantes y trabajadores de la aguja puertorriquenos" (Vega 1980, 158).[18]

Puerto Rican cigar makers not only inspired other Puerto Ricans to organize. They got Puerto Ricans noticed by other unions. Vega reports that it wasn't until the cigar makers battled to organize and fight their employers that "los uniones de otros oficios empezaron a mostrar interes en los trabajadores puertorriquenos" (1980, 156).[19] For example, when the United Garment Workers Union encountered problems organizing Latino button workers in Manhattan who were being paid twelve to fifteen dollars less per week than the $35 per week non-Latinos received, they sought the help of Puerto Rican cigar makers. Harry Dubinsky, of Button Workers' Union Local 132, asked P. Rivera Martinez to "prestar la ayuda" (give assistance) in organizing Latino button workers during 1925 ("Los Trabajadores" 1925).

Puerto Rican cigar makers developed political power for the Puerto Rican community. Their high level of organization, their class consciousness, and their militant leadership represented important values. Cigar makers had proven capable of disrupting production, motivating and catalyzing other workers, as well as inspiring Puerto Ricans in various organizational groupings. Puerto Ricans, as a result, became a concern to employers, unions, and politicians. They became a worry to government officials already frightened into "Red Scare" hysteria by the militant actions of labor, communists, and anarchists during 1919 (Coben 1969, 102). The ultimate impact of getting the attention and interest of other groups in the city was that the Puerto Rican community got to dance, acquiring some political power. The evidence for this consists of deep political bonds and influence with important political leaders, early electoral victories, and congressional attention to the status issue of Puerto Rico.

Only about two thousand Puerto Ricans lived in Congressional District 19 on Manhattan's East Side during 1925. Sol Bloom, who represented that district, made the mistake of calling Puerto Ricans "children" while on a visit to Puerto Rico, and this upset the mostly cigar-making Puerto Ricans in his district. The cigar makers immediately launched a public campaign demanding an apology. They argued that Puerto Ricans had been the deciding vote in Bloom's narrow 1922 reelection victory. They demanded that Bloom apologize for calling Puerto Ricans "*niños*" ("Los Puertorriquenos de Nueva York" 1925, 7). His apology, however, had as much to do with the cigar makers' ability to engage in collective action as with the real impact of the Puerto Rican vote for Bloom. Cigar makers were also an invisible but important force behind the election of such political leaders as Oscar Garcia Rivera, Fiorello La Guardia, and Vito Marcantonio.

The Republican Party showed some early interest in the Puerto Rican community. Republicans supported Victor Fiol Ramos as the first Puerto Rican candidate for City Council from Harlem in 1927. The connection between this support and a 1926 Harlem riot was probably an attempt to thwart future political violence. Ramos was a founding officer of the Liga Puertorriquena e Hispana, formed in 1926 to address the need for community unity and self-defense (Falcon 1984, 27). Republican support also sprang from a wider source. The Republicans had been the party of African Americans since the Civil War and in New York City had often backed progressive and labor policies. Fiorello La Guardia and Vito Marcantonio were both backed by the Republicans.

It was with this behind him and the Republicans that Oscar Garcia Rivera became the first Puerto Rican elected official in 1937 when he won the Assembly seat in the 17th District in East Harlem. He was elected on the Republican ticket as part of that party's strategy to upset the entrenched Democratic Party (Baver 1984, 67). He won his seat, however, because of the votes cast by laborites, Marxists, fusionists, independent Democrats, and Republicans (Delgado 1979, 34). These various political groups had joined together as part of a reform movement opposed to the Tammany political machine (ibid.). Cigar maker leader Pedro Rovira, for instance, was one of the leaders of the fusionist Recovery Party, which, in 1934, strove for nonpartisan political unity to "elect Hispanic leaders for the Spanish-speaking districts" (Thomas 2002, 197). This was the rallying cry and support that got the first Puerto Rican, Oscar Garcia-Rivera, elected to the New York State Assembly in 1937 (ibid.).

Half of the estimated sixty-one thousand Puerto Ricans in New York City during 1940 were registered to vote, and the Puerto Rican vote was mobilized, becoming a critical factor in his election. The Republicans, however, didn't nominate Garcia-Rivera in 1937 simply to attract the Puerto Rican vote, as some researchers have claimed (cf. Sanchez-Korral

1983, 191). Much of the attention and support for the Puerto Rican community from Republican and fusionist parties, like the Recovery, stemmed from an appreciation that the rising New Deal movement spelled an end to the machine-based politics that had dominated Tammany Hall Democrats up till that point. Cigar makers figured in this reform movement as well. A Puerto Rican Vigilance Committee was established in 1934, for that reason, by Puerto Rican labor organizers, mostly cigar makers, and other progressives. This group aimed at exposing and documenting "the numerous complaints collected from East Harlem residents . . . denied work with the Tammany-controlled Sanitation Department" (Thomas 2002, 199).

Just a few years later, in 1945, Patria Gosnell wrote that the Puerto Rican "vote is nonexistent" (Gosnell 1945, 505). The Republicans themselves say that they were drawn to Garcia-Rivera because he had become publicly recognized as "a born fighter" (Delgado 1979, 35). That recognition came to him, in part, because he had impressed others with his willingness to oppose well-established leaders. It was a trait he acquired in his high school days when he opposed Santiago Iglesias, one of Puerto Rico's most esteemed labor leaders. He added to his reputation as a fighter with his career as a trial lawyer.

A more plausible explanation for Garcia-Rivera's candidacy and victory is that fusionists and Marxists "discovered" Garcia-Rivera and then rallied behind him not only because of his fighting spirit but also because he was a radical socialist. The idea of a radical Puerto Rican political leader was planted in the public imagination in New York because of the attention drawn to the Puerto Rican community by the legacy of effective militancy and working-class orientation of the Puerto Rican cigar makers in the 1920s. Almost as a tribute to that fact, Garcia-Rivera spent considerable energy, while in office, trying to defend Puerto Rican seasonal migrant workers in New York and New Jersey (Sanchez-Korral 1983, 191).

Surprisingly, while in office, Garcia-Rivera "was the only laborite lawmaker in the continental U.S.A." (Delgado 1979, 35). He introduced twelve pieces of legislation, of which three became law (ibid., 34). By 1938, Garcia-Rivera was running for reelection with Marcantonio on the American Labor Party ticket (a party the cigar makers helped to found). The cigar makers' militant record had, in fact, drawn the attention of similar reformist and radical politicians like Fiorello La Guardia and Vito Marcantonio to Puerto Ricans (Cooper 1992, 3). Before 1960, La Guardia and Marcantonio had been the two most important defenders of the economic and political rights of the Puerto Rican community in New York and Puerto Rico.

La Guardia became a congressman representing the 20th Congressional

District in 1919 in Manhattan's East Side with the idea that serving the people the right way required that activists use "the liberal cause, supported by conscience, power, and know how" to "remove social evil through proper reforms in government and the economy" (Mann 1959, 73). As Puerto Ricans (cigar makers mostly) began to settle in his district before and after 1920, he became their ardent and vocal champion. His interest in Puerto Ricans was not, as many biographers agree, for the Puerto Rican vote alone. La Guardia was a masterful campaigner who spoke a number of languages and attended, they say, almost every meeting of more than three groups of constituents. But since there were few Puerto Rican voters, La Guardia's interest in Puerto Ricans was mostly ideological.

As a progressive Republican, La Guardia was a champion of the underdog and an opponent of monopolies and "profiteers." In fact, he was a follower of Wisconsin senator Robert La Follette, the nation's leader of the Progressive Movement. He was also a fierce supporter of organized labor. He made speeches to workers supporting unions, fought against court injunctions prohibiting unions, and even served as an unpaid counsel for District Council One in New York City (Mann 1959, 59). La Guardia's connection to the Puerto Rican community started through La Follette and the trade union movement.

Puerto Ricans in New York City supported La Follette, in part because of his relationship both to the Puerto Rican labor leader Santiago Iglesias as well as to AFL president and cigar maker Samuel Gompers (Vega 1980, 182). These labor leaders introduced Puerto Rican labor leaders in New York City to La Follette. The Puerto Rican and Hispanic workers' group Alianza Obrera formed a committee, which had Luis Munoz Marin, Jesus Colon, and Bernardo Vega among others as members to support La Follette's candidacies (Sanchez-Korral 1983, 220). The committee sponsored numerous lectures by La Follette supporters during the early 1920s. La Guardia gave one of those lectures in 1924 (ibid.). Later, Bernardo Vega states that the Hispanic cigar makers' group Alianza Obrera was able to persuade La Guardia in 1927 to denounce the U.S. invasion of Nicaragua (Vega 1980, 193).

When La Guardia announced his candidacy for mayor, the Puerto Rican community was quick to offer its support (ibid., 201). His contact with Puerto Ricans increased. The heart of East Harlem, "El Barrio Latino," was in La Guardia's congressional district. The district was mostly populated, until the late 1920s, by Puerto Rican cigar makers (ibid.). When La Guardia became mayor of New York in 1933, Vito Marcantonio, his protégé and fellow radical, got elected to East Harlem's Seventh Congressional District in 1935. Like La Guardia, Marcantonio became an advocate for Puerto Rico's independence and for the well-being of Puerto Ricans in New York City.

What has been written about the Puerto Rican community's support of Marcantonio ignores the roles played by La Guardia and by cigar makers. Marcantonio represented East Harlem's 7th Congressional District from 1935 to 1937 and from 1939 to 1950. Throughout his tenure in Congress, Marcantonio enjoyed tremendous Puerto Rican support. In general, he won every Puerto Rican district by a 2.5-to-1 ratio (Jackson 1983, 59). It wasn't only votes that attracted Marcantonio to Puerto Ricans, however.

Like La Guardia, Marcantonio was also motivated by ideological concerns about U.S. colonialism and his desire "as a progressive to defend the most exploited victims of a most devastating imperialism" (Schaffer 1966, 45). Radical ideology was as important to Marcantonio as votes. He supported coal miners and farm workers, as he supported Puerto Ricans, even though he had no coal miners and few farm workers among his constituents (Lopez 1979, 20). Marcantonio's interest in Puerto Ricans in New York was, however, most influenced by La Guardia.

From the time they met, La Guardia began training and preparing Marcantonio to make him his "professional heir." La Guardia got Marcantonio appointed assistant U.S. attorney, had him organize the La Guardia Political Club, had him manage La Guardia's congressional campaigns, and, in general, conveyed his own personal and radical style of machine politics. Marcantonio inherited the Puerto Rican community in East Harlem from La Guardia as he inherited almost everything else. Marcantonio's importance to the Puerto Rican community is marked by the fact that his death in 1954 left a leadership void for Puerto Ricans that lasted until the late 1960s (cf. Lopez). But Marcantonio's contribution to the Puerto Rican community was a gift from La Guardia, a gift originally packaged by La Guardia's relationship to the Puerto Rican cigar makers.

The thousand or so Puerto Rican and Hispanic cigar makers who survived into the 1940s remained fiercely militant, independent, and committed to radical political change. They also remained in contact with and were able to influence Marcantonio. In the early years of his stay in Congress, Marcantonio sought advice from Puerto Rican cigar makers, especially with regard to the status of Puerto Rico. On March 6, 1936, Marcantonio wrote to Juan Rovira, secretary of the Cigarmakers' International Union of America—Local 389, to express his regrets that Rovira and local president Ramirez could not meet with him to discuss Puerto Rico. In that letter, Marcantonio agrees with Rovira "that the curse of Puerto Rico is landlord absenteeism."[20] But Marcantonio's relationship to Puerto Rican cigar makers didn't center only on broad, international issues. He also sought the help of Puerto Rican cigar makers on such local issues as housing and immigration.[21]

Marcantonio helped to establish the Harlem Victory Council in April 1942 to build support for World War II. He recommended either "Mr. Ramirez or Santiago of Cigarmakers" for membership on the Executive Committee of this new group to deal with jobs and training.[22] They were the only Puerto Ricans and the only labor activists Marcantonio recommended. A year earlier, Marcantonio had also listed Mr. Andres Santiago as "suggested sponsors for defense council" along with Mayor La Guardia. And in 1945, Puerto Rican cigar makers were still trying to advise Marcantonio on how to vote on particular legislation in Congress. Local 273, the East Harlem section of the United Cigar Workers Union, wanted Marcantonio to reject a bill that would "restrict the right to strike," support another bill that would increase the minimum wage, defeat one bill that would "allow employers to interfere with unions at every step of the way," support the Bretton Woods Bill, and support a number of other bills.[23] In all these cases, Marcantonio expressed agreement with the cigar makers, the only Puerto Rican organization to contact Marcantonio on these issues.

Perhaps the most telling exchange took place between Marcantonio and Juan Rovira of the Cigarmakers International Union of America. Rovira asked for Marcantonio's help in January 1936 to get a gun license "because I have to carry with me cash money in going around the different shops."[24] Marcantonio's response was that Rovira use him as a reference in his application with the police department, a gesture that indicates the high level of trust and respect Marcantonio had for Roviro and Puerto Rican cigar makers.

Marcantonio's role as political leader for the Puerto Rican community before 1950 is undisputed (cf. Jackson 1983). There was no other Puerto Rican or non–Puerto Rican who spoke as well for Puerto Ricans as Marcantonio. The relationship of Puerto Rican cigar makers to Marcantonio was also very close. Marcantonio consulted with them about a variety of issues, and they tried to influence him about what they deemed important. The basis of the cigar makers' influence, however, was largely ideological and local. It was also focused on Marcantonio, one of the more despised and controversial congressmen of his period. The result was that, by supporting Marcantonio, Puerto Ricans experienced even "greater marginalization in the politics of New Deal liberalism" (Thomas 2002, 216).

Their biggest problem was that though they remained tightly organized and militant, there were only about a thousand Puerto Rican cigar makers left in the 1940s. They didn't have numbers or votes. They didn't always have the complete focus of most Puerto Ricans. What they still had was the role of working-class leaders within the Puerto Rican community. This appeared to be good enough. Political leaders like Marcantonio were compelled by them and by their own beliefs to pay them attention. They received that attention, moreover, not just from radicals like Marcantonio.

Harry Dubinsky, leader of the Button Workers Union Local 132, requested the assistance of the Union Internacional de Tabaqueros in 1925 in organizing Latino button workers that were being paid 50 percent below the minimum ("Los Trabajadores" 1925, 1). Even more unusual, Nicholas Butler, the president of Columbia University, met with Puerto Rican intellectuals and political activists in 1926 and spoke to them about "los asuntos politicos de la cuidad y de la nacion" ("El Presidente Butler" 1926, 1).[25] In his talk, he reflected on the advice he gave U.S. president McKinley about what to do with Puerto Rico and the Philippines. He advised that both nations were descendants of a noble race and deserved, some day, to receive full American legal rights and citizenship. Butler is still the only president of a major American university to ever deliver any talk to a gathering of Puerto Rican New Yorkers.

It's hard not to see the smoke of Puerto Rican cigar makers behind Butler's visit. There were many spatial, ideological, racial, and class divisions within the early Puerto Rican community in New York City. *Boliteros* were an important source of leadership and advocacy in Brooklyn. Middle-class and professional Puerto Ricans sought and fought for leadership of the Puerto Rican community in Manhattan. Cigar makers, however, were about the only group able to make Puerto Ricans not simply more visible but also important to other New Yorkers. As one Puerto Rican observed in 1934, for the most part Puerto Rican political leaders found that "politically speaking we are nobody" (Thomas 2002, 200).

The cigar makers' influence, however, drew on old, long-past glories—working-class control of the production process in individual shops and success in a major national strike. Puerto Rican cigar makers had proven able to bring cigar production to a stop. But smoking, unlike wheat or rice, is not a staple. It is a habit that can be shifted to different products. Puerto Rican cigar makers were smart enough to know this. One leader admitted at one point that "La industria nuestra no es una industria basica para ningun pueblo" ("Los anos" 1925, 5).[26] This knowledge made cigar makers both cautious and fearful after the strike since "se puede vivir sin fumar, y por lo tanto la industria puede llegar a un termino."[27] As a result, cigar makers became "mas cuidado de nuestra parte" (ibid.).[28] Caution, however, was not enough protection or good practice on the dance floor.

Good fortune turned bad. The cigar makers had been lucky to find their skills in such demand in the United States. Theirs was a luck founded on the fickle capitalist market, however. As Marx had explained, the need to increase surplus value would sooner or later encourage capitalists to reduce their dependence on skilled labor. Cigar making, thus, provided an inherently unstable and dependent source of political power for the Puerto Rican community.

The African American community, in contrast, did not have such good or bad luck. They had no hold as skilled labor on any industry. Racist discrimination had kept even the most skilled African Americans from occupying anything more than, as one company executive admitted, such positions as "common labor, maid service and the like" (Weatherby and Ottley 1967, 268). Having been denied entry into the economic and political realms of power, the African American community in this period sought power through cultural excellence and autonomy.

Marcus Garvey's great Back to Africa movement of the 1918–1925 period was the first significant example of a continental change in African American political consciousness. James Weldon Johnson warned America in 1933 that the refusal to grant justice to African Americans would produce but one solution: "the making of its isolation into a religion and the cultivation of a hard, keen relentless hatred for everything white" (quoted in Douglas 1995, 322). In actuality, this strategy and movement, which aimed to turn segregation and exclusion into strength, was begun many years earlier in the black churches.

African American religious leaders realized as early as the eighteenth century that if the African American community was excluded from the dance floor, and thus from paths to power, the alternative strategy was to dance with each other, to create their own routes to power. A first step was to create independent black churches. The first such church was created in New York City as early as 1796 (Weatherby and Ottley 1967, 53). That was the African Methodist Episcopal Zion Church, created by free African Americans who could no longer tolerate condescension and discrimination at the white church they had attended. By 1926, there were 140 black churches in Harlem (Katz 1997, 122). One of the most important was the Abyssinian Baptist Church. It was wealthy and secure, having bought land and built its church on West 138th Street by selling its original, downtown lot to the *New York Times* in 1916 (Weatherby and Ottley 1967, 290).

Most black churches, like the Abyssinian, did more than own land, take care of the needy, and provide spiritual guidance. They also helped to nurture and support African American leaders. As early as 1837, African American churchgoers had been urged to oppose discrimination by making their faith a political statement. Rather than accept discrimination in white churches, the *Colored American* suggested that African Americans should "stand in the aisles, and rather worship God upon your feet, than become a party to your own degradation. You must shame your oppressors" (quoted in Katz 1997, 73). That combination of piety and defiance created the black churches and created as well an independent political will and path to power for many years to come.

Over the years, numerous African American political leaders, from Martin Luther King, Jr., to Malcolm X, have found their voice, followers, and economic support in independent black religious institutions. One of the earliest of these leaders was the irrepressible Reverend Adam Clayton Powell, Jr., of the Abyssinian Baptist Church. Before he became a U.S. congressman, Powell preached in a 1936 sermon that "we're not going to the river and lay our burdens down. We're going to look upon our shoulders and dump the burdensome white man off our backs" (quoted in Katz 1997, 159). Because they had the built-in ability to mobilize and organize a large chunk of the African American community, the black churches turned religious and cultural autonomy into a potent electoral and political weapon. They established value in their own readings of the Bible and their own service to God. They moved in step with each other and found or developed skilled dancers whose leadership and potential might have been ignored in the white churches. Puerto Ricans had nothing like this, even with the cigar makers.

The cigar makers were, in contrast, subject to market forces and capitalist retaliation. As early as 1919, more people were smoking cigarettes than smoking cigars (CMIU 1925, 21). The cigar makers' power quickly became a thing of the past. Their skill at rolling cigars and organizing themselves was no longer necessary or respected. In the 1940s, they stood fast to their organizations and militancy, but fewer Puerto Ricans were willing or able to listen. Puerto Ricans were by then located primarily in other industries, earning the lowest wages, unorganized, and with little job stability.

The political and guild-like intellectual sensibility that had sustained cigar makers was irrelevant to a Puerto Rican work force scattered to many different industries and usually organized, if at all, along industrial rather than craft lines. By 1946, Puerto Ricans had been rendered politically passive and economically fangless: relegated by government and private industry to the boundaries of the political and economic dance floor. The class-based and nationalist ideals they espoused were no longer that important to a New Deal reformist political reality based on the new "language of rights" centered on Keynesian economics and social equality.[29] In addition, Puerto Ricans discovered that there was little about their culture (art, music, performance) that drew others to them. Culture, thus, offered little help in counteracting the emergent categorization of Puerto Ricans as nothing more than cheap, disposable labor and as an invisible racial minority. Though culture offered the Puerto Rican community few instruments for influencing the larger society, it did offer them something.

Cultural Power

In the first twenty-five years of the twentieth century, Puerto Ricans had been able to exchange the economic value they had as cigar makers into a modicum of political power that they used to influence politicians and government policies. But in the 1940s, that economic power became increasingly tenuous and shallow. What Puerto Ricans could not overcome, however, was an additional deficit—a lack of cultural power. While Puerto Ricans were drawn by need and interest to dance with American culture, it seemed that there was little about Puerto Rican culture to encourage Americans to dance with Puerto Ricans.

As migrants and a minority, Puerto Ricans could not avoid granting some value to American culture, if only because they had a need to know English and make a living in the United States. For the average American, however, Puerto Rican culture remained something alien, unknown, and undesirable. More so than African Americans, Puerto Ricans remained "immigrants from a foreign country" (Flores 1993, 131). Marcus Garvey had proven that African Americans were capable of publicly imagining, if not living, life outside Eurocentric standards, institutions, and power (Cronon 1969). The Back to Africa movement awakened white and African American alike to the idea that African Americans could dance elsewhere, away from whites. African Americans were, of course, not going anywhere. But by rejecting whites and their culture, African Americans gave themselves value and, eventually, became more attractive as dance partners to those whites seeking the passion and creative expression they thought were missing in their own white culture. Thus, while Puerto Rican cigar makers and culture were being shunted aside, African Americans during the 1920s "quickly became trendsetters on the entertainment scene of Northern cities" (Douglas 1995, 74).

African American music and performance drew a great deal of white attention. Whites were attracted by the perceived novelty, style, and danger of African American culture. No similar passions existed in whites at the time for Puerto Rican culture. What made it even worse for Puerto Ricans was that they had not yet lowered their desire for white culture.

In coming to America, Puerto Ricans were looking for social and political as well as economic rewards. The jobs in New York City did pay more than the jobs in Puerto Rico when they could be had. What is overlooked, however, is that in some respects social life was very different, possibly even better, in America. Puerto Ricans came to America not only for jobs but to loosen the patriarchal and racist chains of life in Puerto Rico. They came to New York for social as well as economic freedom. The evidence for this is substantial though not abundant.

Many if not most Puerto Ricans came to America with the idea of going back to Puerto Rico after making enough money. That dream, however, soon got pushed farther forward in time or got realized only for temporary periods when airline travel became more popular and cheaper in the 1960s. Puerto Ricans actually began to come to terms with the idea of permanent life in America during the 1920s. Even the cigar makers began to make this adjustment. Around 1926, Bernardo Vega and others at the Ateneo Obrero cigar makers' organization committed themselves to life in the United States. They no longer "consideras su estadia en Nueva York como cosa pasejera" (Vega 1980, 190).[30] As a result, the Ateneo Obrero began to offer Puerto Ricans classes in sociology, political geography, and English (ibid., 193). This represented a subtle but profound shift in Puerto Rican interests.

The Puerto Rican drive to learn English, succeed in America, and absorb American cultural values was natural but not assumed without conflict. In fact, the Ateneo's program to teach English during the late 1920s was opposed by many Puerto Ricans during a more nationalist period in the 1930s. Census data shows, thus, that only about 20 percent of Puerto Ricans ten years of age and older could speak English by 1930 (Chenault 1970, 44). Speaking English had also become unpopular in Puerto Rico "on account of the growing anti-American feeling" (ibid.).

Once in New York City, Puerto Rican migrants were reluctant to learn English both because of nationalist feelings and because of a desire to affirm a Puerto Rican identity against rising levels of discrimination in the labor and housing markets. Proficiency in English actually became a more important marker of social status than race. Chenault found that English proficiency was "more important in determining the area of settlement than the degree of color" among Puerto Ricans (1970, 96). English-speaking Puerto Ricans were more likely to live among other English speakers, black and white. Despite that fact, Puerto Ricans were ambivalent about learning English.

Part of their ambivalence stemmed from the fact that what was distinctive about Puerto Rican culture included much that frustrated, riled, or oppressed Puerto Ricans themselves, especially the women. Some scholars suggest that the Puerto Rican sense of social interdependence was among the cultural elements that Puerto Ricans wanted to see diminished. The network of social dependence Puerto Ricans had built over the centuries provided an unsurpassed safety net in times of trouble, a unique fund of cultural virtues and collective life, as well as a source of individual identity. That same social dependence also encroached to some degree on individual freedom and experimentation. Puerto Ricans, for this reason, came to New York, in part, to become less "dependent—on their superiors for favors, on their peers for aid, on their families for support" (Mintz 1975, 45).

Similarly, Puerto Ricans also sought to diminish the unequal relations between men and women, as well as the role of racism and *personalismo* in their lives. Anthropologist Elena Padilla suggested that when Puerto Ricans came to New York, they often sought to replace these cultural traditions with English and with particular American values:

> For recent migrants, the most important and most desirable life goals and adaptations in New York are: working hard and being a "good" worker; valuing formal education and schooling; learning English while not forgetting how to speak Spanish; cultivating the desire to "progress" and get ahead, or "to get the feet off the dish," particularly through the education of one's children; being brave and assertive; not letting anyone take advantage of oneself, or "take you for a ride." (Padilla 1958, 57)

Puerto Ricans, especially in the 1940s, thus, had developed a hopeful and receptive view of American culture, at least initially.

The African American interest in white America was different. While there was much cultural borrowing and exchange between blacks and whites in the 1920s, cultural elites in the African American community projected the hope of a more symmetrical relationship with whites. African Americans, like Puerto Ricans, sought inclusion, "not distance from white America." Unlike Puerto Ricans, however, African Americans saw the possibility of closeness with real "power and recognition" (Douglas 1995, 304).

Puerto Ricans understood the cold of New York, its racist rejection, its ability to make "a man a *spic* instead of a man" (Hamill 1975, 201). Indeed, while Puerto Ricans had come to understand that New York City "could be a mean and nasty and vicious town," they also knew, according to Hamill, that "it was also a great one" (ibid., 206). Great or not, Puerto Ricans had been changed by their survival in New York City, whether they liked it or not. They were certainly changed by a New York City that even in the 1920s had established itself as the irretrievable place for the "sophisticated, witty, wicked, culturally creative and frivolous" (Douglas 1995).

During the 1920s and '30s, Puerto Ricans were increasingly cast as a racial minority by others in the United States. Employers often hired Puerto Ricans cheaply and fired them quickly when economic conditions worsened during the 1930s and made white labor more available. Employers rationalized that this treatment of Puerto Rican labor was merely a response to the fact that they broke too many dishes, didn't speak English, were quick-tempered, and were too inclined to protest against apparent maltreatment (Chenault 1970, 81). The declining demand for Puerto Rican labor thus also depressed the public perception of Puerto Ricans as labor.

Puerto Ricans did not accept the racial recasting of their role as cheap labor. Many union and government officials reported, for example, that Puerto Ricans refused to be used as strike breakers. In what is perhaps a legacy of the lingering authority of cigar makers, observers claimed that Puerto Ricans were usually "found on the side of the workers who are involved in an industrial dispute" (Chenault 1970, 82). At the same time, Puerto Ricans were often discriminated against and locked out by unions. This combination of differentiation, exclusion, devaluation of their value as labor, and their resistance to these forces pulled Puerto Ricans towards a "colored" racial identity during the 1930s (ibid., 79). Puerto Ricans had not yet given up trying to pass themselves off as "white." Nevertheless, the signs of their minority status were as hard to miss in New York as the one that hung outside one Brooklyn factory announcing, "No Negroes or Porto Ricans Wanted" (ibid.).

Puerto Ricans were more bewildered than uncertain about their categorization as "colored." Racial categories in Puerto Rico were complex and consisted of a broad continuum between white and black, often attenuated by social class and personal familiarity. In New York City and the United States, however, people were either white or nonwhite. As a result, dark Puerto Ricans often emphasized speaking Spanish and preferred living with other Puerto Ricans and Latinos to keep a cultural and spatial distance from African Americans. At the same time, Puerto Ricans began to express pride in their own national culture, maintaining an ethnic identity that had little in common with the racial basis of group identity, conflict, and power that was coming into maturity during this time in the United States.

The response of Puerto Ricans to their life in America was, thus, to affirm an ethnic-national identity during the 1930s. This is clear from Puerto Rican organizational history of the time. Most of the organizations created before 1930 emphasized a Puerto Rican identity. After 1930, Puerto Ricans tended to form and join organizations representing Latinos and Hispanics as a whole. Many pan-Hispanic groups actually formed before 1930. These included groups like Trabajadores de la Industria del Tabaco, formed in 1919, as well as the Ateneo Obrero, formed in 1922. Table 2.1 shows, for instance, that the proportion of organizations that were specifically defined as Puerto Rican rose during the 1920s and fell during the 1930s.

The reasons for this are not immediately clear. The rise and fall in the emergence of Puerto Rican organizations may simply reflect the early influence and later decay of Puerto Rican cigar maker leadership, which had been universalistic in its approach to labor issues but nationalist on cultural matters. This was reflected in the Puerto Rican cigar makers' involvement in two separate organizations. Cigar makers were involved in the creation and leadership of the Liga Puertorriquena e Hispana in 1926, an organization with a clear Puerto Rican orientation. They were also involved in the 1927 creation of the weekly newspaper aimed at a general Hispanic audience, called *El Grafico* (Vega 1980, 194).

The year 1926 also brought a clear signal that others in New York City had begun to perceive Puerto Ricans as a racial minority and threat. A series of confrontations occurred in July of that year between Puerto Ricans and Jewish residents of East Harlem. The *New York Times* reported that these "riots" were the result of a rising level of resentment, anger, and fear on the part of Jewish residents towards the influx of "negroes who describe themselves as Porto Ricans" ("Ask Police" 1926, 29). Jewish violence stemmed from a fear about any type of mixing with the "mongrel" population of Puerto Rican migrants. The important consequence was that this violent reaction to their presence provided critical proof that Puerto Ricans could not easily name or identify themselves. Puerto Rican organizational history itself suggests a real ambivalence in Puerto Ricans about their self-identity that was not evident in the larger society.

In short, though Puerto Ricans found aspects of American culture useful if not attractive, the reverse was generally not true. There was little about Puerto Rican culture that other Americans felt drawn to. The sophistication and intellectualism suggested by the Puerto Rican cigar makers' use of lectors meant nothing to wider American culture. In fact, Americans knew little about Puerto Rican culture. This was made very clear by the public response to Puerto Rican music and film in the United States.

In the 1920s and 1930s, when Latin music became a little popular in New York City in the form of "Afro-Cuban" music, the Puerto Rican element was totally ignored. Puerto Ricans had been making music in New

TABLE 2.2

	U.S. Population	# Records
Puerto Rican	20,000	25
West Indian	43,000	355

Source: Glasser 1995, 143

York City for generations. Indeed, as music historian Jorge Javariz has stated, "the bulk of what we today call popular Puerto Rican music was written and recorded in New York. Puerto Rico is the only Latin American country whose popular music was mainly created on foreign soil" (Glasser 1991, 25). Americans, however, knew nothing of Puerto Rican music. If they heard Puerto Rican music or Puerto Rican musicians, they assumed that the music was Cuban or "Latin." Puerto Ricans became "mock-Cubans or simulated Mexicans in a North American entertainment world anxious to see and hear their ideas of what a 'Latin' was like" (ibid., 25). Puerto Ricans got the attention of Americans only by being what they were not. They "found themselves to be a subculture within a subculture, dancing to the Cuban and Argentine sounds that outsiders associated with all 'Latins'" (Glasser 1995, 158). The results were that those Americans charmed by Latin music knew Cuban standards, like "El Manisero," but were oblivious to similar romantic or nostalgic Puerto Rican songs that were extremely popular among Latinos themselves.

What interest there was among Americans for Latin music was limited and shallow. Columbia Records, for example, was the first company to issue Puerto Rican music in 1918 (Glasser 1995, 138). These *danzas* and *aquinaldos*, however, were primarily produced for the "foreign" market in Puerto Rico and Latin America. This initial interest in Puerto Rican music, in any case, quickly waned. Table 2.2 shows, for example, that Victor Records, which also produced Puerto Rican music, did so sparingly in comparison to other groups. As of 1925, the number of Puerto Rican recordings in their catalog paled in comparison to that of West Indian music, although the West Indian population was only about double that of Puerto Ricans at the time. For the recording companies, Puerto Rican music was strictly marginal, a part of what they called the "U.S. Foreign" market.

Though ignored by the U.S. mainstream, Puerto Rican music actually flourished in New York City in the pre–World War II period. Lured by radio, club dates, and recording contracts, Puerto Rican musicians came in droves to New York City, where they did more than keep Puerto Rican music alive. They often reinvented and brought it back to life. One indigenous Puerto Rican music style, the Plena, actually owed a great deal of its popularity and survival to the New York City recording companies and the artistry of Manuel "Canario" Jimenez. According to Ruth Glasser, though Canario was Puerto Rican, he had his first real exposure to Plena in New York City and became its first major interpreter at the behest of the music companies (1995, 178).

For Americans, however, Plena and other Latin music was only "dance music," lacking complexity or real integrity. It was marginal music, enjoyed by a few aficionados only. It did not have the same resonance and penetration into the American musical soul and tastes as jazz did.

Jazz musicians, however, were themselves often enthusiasts and practitioners of Latin music. Dizzy Gillespie and Tommy Dorsey, for instance, collaborated with various Latin musicians, learned Latin music styles, and helped to fuse the two. But it was jazz rather than Latin music that entered the mainstream of American popular musical developments. Unlike Latin music, "Americans of all races and national origins" played jazz (McGinty 1991, 136).

Getting into the American cultural mainstream wasn't that easy for jazz. Indeed, many white Americans rejected it because of its African American origins. Some simply couldn't warm up to jazz's syncopated style, which seemed to violate all of the musical rules with which they were familiar. They quipped that jazz could "never replace the old-fashioned earache" (ibid., 136). But that criticism also suggests that jazz enjoyed a status never enjoyed by Latin music. Americans were engaged with jazz in a way they never were with Latin music.

Collaborators, thieves, lovers, and haters of each other's culture, whites and blacks in the 1920s were, nevertheless, "equals as opponents as often as they [were] friends" (Douglas 1995, 299). The criticism of jazz suggested that at least it was noticed. Puerto Ricans, however, were invisible performers of a marginal and exotic "dance music." Jazz became part of American cultural currency because it was a "ragging" of traditional American melodies and rhythms rather than something completely different and "foreign." Jazz became the language of white musicians like Al Jolson and George Gershwin (Douglas 1995, 356). All of this suggested that the Puerto Rican relationship to the larger U.S. society was not simply unequal but missing. Thus, what was true in the economic and political realms had also become true in music.

Latin music was not invisible to African American musicians. The historical record shows that there was mutual exploration and appreciation of each other's music. John Storm Roberts argues, for example, that "the Latin ingredients in early New Orleans Jazz are more important than has been realized" (1999, 38). That "Latin tinge" in black jazz got stronger in the twentieth century. Black musicians incorporated many Latin rhythms into their music, sometimes taking entire songs and simply translating them into English for American audiences. Cab Calloway and Cole Porter, to name two, made extensive use of Latin rhythms and songs in their shows and recordings for American audiences that could enjoy but not acknowledge the Latin influence. As a result, "Latin rhythms have been absorbed into black American styles far more consistently than into white popular music" (Roberts 1999, 41).

The result was that "while New York's Puerto Rican audiences and musicians were familiar with Porter and Ellington . . . names like Hernandez and Acevedo meant nothing to North Americans" (Glasser 1991, 46).[31] And because Americans were oblivious to the genius of Puerto Rican composer Rafael Hernandez, other important aspects of Puerto Rican community life meant little to them as well.

Puerto Ricans experienced a similar exclusion and rejection in the film industry. Hollywood showed no interest in putting them on the silver screen. Puerto Ricans and Puerto Rico appeared very rarely on film prior to World War II. The few films with Puerto Ricans in significant roles were actually produced by Puerto Ricans. Rafael Colorado's 1915 film, *Un Drama en Puerto Rico*, was the first production done in Puerto Rico. This film was followed by his very *típico* 1916 film, *Por la hembra y por el gallo* (Garcia 1990, 82). After a couple of other films by Puerto Rican filmmakers, Puerto Rico became the setting for a number of Hollywood productions in need of exotic and romantic settings. These films used North American actors and were made for American audiences (Garcia 1990, 83). After the early 1920s, only a few documentaries and films were made that featured Puerto Rico, usually only as an anonymous tropical setting. Between 1936 and 1955, for instance, only fifteen feature films included any mention of Puerto Ricans or Puerto Rico (Richard 1993, 573).

In most of these cases, Puerto Rico merely served as a backdrop for stories about non–Puerto Ricans. But the measure of Puerto Rico's invisibility lies in comparison. Compared to Puerto Rico's fifteen features in that 1936–1955 period, Mexico was a presence in 605 Hollywood productions alone (Richard 1993, 572). In addition, Argentina, that southernmost Latin American nation with no proximate geographic or political connection to the United States, figured in 157 feature films (Richard 1993, 571). Population size was not the main reason behind this oversight. Cuba, Puerto Rico's sister Caribbean isle, with comparable culture and population size, was featured in about eighty-four films and documentaries during the same period (Richard 1993, 572).

Many more films with Latin themes were made in this period. Xavier Cugat, a Spaniard, and Carmen Miranda, a Brazilian, figured prominently in this early Hollywood infatuation with America's Latin "Good Neighbors." The Latin presence in film, however, was essentially marginal, filtered, and watered down for American consumption. Cugat himself admitted that he didn't play authentic Latin music in those films because Americans "have to be given music more for the eyes than the ears" (quoted in Roberts 1999, 87). In addition, the early development of the film industry in New York City made essentially no difference to Puerto Ricans. As Reyes and Rubie state, "Hispanics on the East Coast . . . were virtually shut out from any kind of involvement in the early film industry that was developing there" (1994, 7).

The exclusion of Puerto Rican images from film had important consequences. Puerto Ricans were largely absent from the cultural consciousness of white Americans during this period. That deficit muted Puerto Rican political voices. The Puerto Rican contribution to economic production, meanwhile, already appeared the work of ghosts. This obscurity and exclusion was not a necessary feature of capitalist exploitation, however. Perez mistakes it as such when he claims that "media exclusion, dehumanization, and discrimination are part of the cultural domination inherent in unequal power relations, and a key feature of the historical process by which people of color have been and continue to be subordinated" (Perez 1990, 8). Cultural and economic relations are not this tightly linked together. African Americans, for example, found that cultural power can be enhanced without necessarily reducing economic exploitation. The problem for African Americans during the 1920s was that they "fell prey to the weaknesses inherent in using culture as a substitute for the economic and political arena" (Douglas 1995, 323). Puerto Ricans, on the other hand, found that cultural path to social power essentially closed to them. The dearth of Puerto Rican images on film combined with a lack of recognition of Puerto Rican music to make Puerto Ricans an insignificant, and thus silent, figure on the American cultural dance floor.

Conclusions

The cigar makers' loss of economic power meant that Puerto Ricans had lost an essential source of economic value and power within the U.S. labor market. This loss was particularly distressing since these economic losses came at a time when the United States had begun to emerge as a dominant economic and industrial power in the world. As World War II solidified that movement, Puerto Ricans found themselves increasingly on the edges and falling behind. They had few offers to come out and dance since they could elicit little interest in what they offered as political bodies, as economic producers and consumers, and as creators of music and cultural style. At the same time, Puerto Ricans had become more dependent on non–Puerto Ricans, at least for low-wage, unskilled jobs. This heightened interest and need to hitch their fortunes with others made Puerto Ricans more vulnerable to rejection, failure, exploitation, manipulation, and power.

Puerto Rican political clubs relied on *boliteros* to keep them aloft in the late 1920s because cigar makers no longer could. The clubs had to depend on "the meager dues of their working-class membership," which was no longer composed of well-paid and tightly organized cigar makers (Sanchez-Korral 1983, 175). Whatever power these clubs had to draw political attention and achieve influence disappeared with the demise of the cigar makers and then with the clubs' divorce from the *boliteros* and their money. Puerto Rican groups eventually jettisoned the *boliteros* in an attempt to please Democratic Party officials who enjoyed dominance over the Puerto Rican clubs (Sanchez-Korral 1983, 177). All that the Puerto Rican community got in exchange for this divorce was the "semblance of political representation" (ibid.).

Still, Puerto Ricans danced. They moved, strove, desired, and fought. They were, as Sanchez-Korral observes, "far more politicized than previously assumed" during the interwar years (1983, 184). Their politicization was, however, rooted in institutions and voters that were organized by, inspired by, or benefited from the economic power that Puerto Rican cigar makers had achieved during the first two decades. The cigar makers' decline left a rotten, termite-eaten foundation upon which subsequent Puerto Rican political organizations built houses during the interwar period that were doomed to collapse.

Puerto Ricans were ambitious, original, and independent in their cultural activity. They could not rescue themselves there either. Their musical expressions, no matter how lovely or original, made very little impression outside the Puerto Rican community. Worse still, when *gringos* noticed Puerto Rican music, they called it Cuban or Mexican. A similar fate occurred in film. Puerto Rican images were largely absent from the screen. The few times Puerto Ricans or Puerto Rico appeared on film they appeared as anonymous backdrops for Hollywood productions. As an invisible people, Puerto Ricans had no impact on U.S. cultural consciousness. They were neither devils nor saints. They were invisible and marginal. Lost and inconsequential, firmly relegated to the cultural background, they were neither desired nor feared by others and, thus, had little cultural power.

Culture, thus, played a vital role in the constitution and loss of Puerto Rican power. Its role, however, needs more clarification. A gun, a vote, and a dollar all possess easily recognized power. They are things that superficial observers associate with power. What of an idea, an image, a rhythm, a note, a feeling? We are aware of the dialectical connection, even interpenetration, of the "material" and "cultural" worlds. All social structures require, according to John Fiske, "a system of meanings and values (that is, culture) to hold [them] in place or to help motivate [them] to change" (1993, 73). Culture and material reality are thus tied to each other through such system-maintenance processes as socialization, the development of group identity, the state's need to legitimize itself, as well as the building and erosion of social and nationalist consciousness.

Culture, however, is more than a cloak or a system of meanings covering material reality. It is not something that has a basically ethereal and inconsequential presence. Culture is a form of life in its own right, quite apart from its intersections with the material forces driving economic and state life. Culture can and does make a real contribution to the social order shaped by economic and political relations. Racism is perhaps the most obvious example of a cultural practice that has a profound impact on class relations. It can segment, bifurcate, and shatter the working class, often making it ready for more effective exploitation. It is also true, however, that social agents often have much to gain and lose by creating and inhabiting structures of power that are peculiar to culture.

Culture, like economics and politics, is a system of "power covering different symbolic and material terrains" (Lancaster 1992, 281). Max Weber was, in this sense, correct to insist on the relative independence of culture, or a "style of life," from economics or political life. Culture, or Weber's "status honor," can even decide life or death. Reinhard Bendix once pointed out that in "the Soviet Union . . . where men are sent to labor camps merely for writing a poem, poetry is power" (Coser and Rosenberg 1989, 315). For Puerto Ricans and other minorities in capitalist societies, cultural power often amounts to nothing more than being noticed and taken seriously, even if only within the symbolic terrain created by culture.

Culture is also heterogeneous. Usually, there is more than one cultural structure capable of establishing value and power. They may not all contribute to the fortification of power in the dominant economic structures. However, cultural practices, like language, music, dance, and religion, often provide opportunities for resisting power as well as for creating parallel and alternative systems of power that compete with the dominant structures. Music is an especially effective vehicle for creating a special world of power that runs parallel to or that opposes the dominant economic and political power.

In his study, *Let Us Now Praise Famous Men,* James Agee described the beautiful singing of African American tenant farmers who had been summoned by their white landlords to entertain Agee and his photographer. The African Americans were tenant farmers and it was a Sunday, a day of rest. Yet, the farmers felt compelled, however reluctantly, to meet the landlord's request and sing spiritual hymns for the landlords' guests. In one passage, Agee described the uplifting, deeply moving music he heard:

> The tenor lifted out his voice alone in a long, plorative line that hung like fire on heaven, or whistle's echo, sinking, sunken, along descents of a modality I had not heard before, and sank along the arms and breast of the bass as might a body sunken from a cross. (Agee and Evans 1939, 29)

The singing dug deeply into Agee's heart. The sounds the singers made gave him not only joy but also a good case of Christian guilt. Agee admits to thinking that, compared to the insensitive white landlords, the African American tenant farmers clearly displayed a kind of spiritual nobility that would surely get them "first in the kingdom of heaven."

The tenant farmers were subject to a broad racial oppression in the South that compelled them to obey the white landlords' request to sing. At the same time, their singing created a sphere of beauty, defiance, humanity, and progress missing in other parts of their lives. Their music resonated with similar cultural longings and feelings in Agee. That reach into Agee's deep desires gave the tenant farmers some power. Agee was moved, touched, and lifted. The African American tenant farmers sang to God, then, not only to escape from or to secretly challenge the oppression of their white landlords. They sang also, as Thomas E. Wartenberg said, to elude "the control of their masters" (1992, xviii). The music created a special world where they, the tenant farmers, were on top. Puerto Ricans, in this sense, did the same thing.

Americans were generally indifferent to Puerto Rican music in the pre–World War II period. That indifference made it possible for a few Puerto Rican musicians to record their music with little interference or understanding from the recording companies. The companies usually hired non–Puerto Ricans and non-Latinos to manage the recording process. Because their managers were ignorant of their language and music, the musicians had a great deal of freedom. As a result, they inserted many sexual and political references into the music "that would have been censored in English" (Glasser 1995, 151). The lyrics often incited furious criticism from conservative, Eurocentric elites in Latin America, where the music was mostly sold. The political messages in the music invariably attacked the Yankee "masters." One of the most well-known of these was Rafael Hernandez' "El Lamento Borincano."

Hernandez wrote his "Lamento" while in New York City as a subtle but clear attack on the United States's colonization of Puerto Rico. "Lamento" was actually recorded and became a hit of Manuel "Canario" Jimenez in 1930. The song tells the story of a *Jibaro*, or peasant, who travels to the city to sell his goods, dreaming of the beautiful dress he intends to buy for his wife. But he returns empty handed because "el pueblo esta muerto" (the town is dead). The *Jibaro* then laments in pain and asks of God, "Que sera de Borinquen, mi Dios Querido. Que sera de mis hijos y de mi hogar" (what will become of Borinquen [Puerto Rico], my beloved God. What will become of my children and my home).

Hernandez's words in "Lamento" captured the complex mix of fears, hopes, and regret of many Puerto Ricans as they observed the intrusive capitalist transformation of Puerto Rico as well as the migration of simple, naive, sentimental, family-centered *Jibaros* to cities like New York. For all of its wealth and glory, the city had little to offer Puerto Ricans. The song is, thus, their protest. It is, however, a fairly meek and indirect protest song. It offered colonialism about as much resistance as cold clay, barely maintaining its original shape against the steady pressure and gripping force of capitalism's "potter's hands" (Digeser 1992, 985). The message in "Lamento" is ambivalent and cautious. It lacked the stubborn insistence of Marcus Garvey's call to African Americans ten years earlier to rise "up, you mighty race, accomplish what you will" (Cronon 1969, 70). The ambivalence of the *Jibaro* response later took political form during the 1939–1940 rise to power of the Popular Party. Luis Munoz Marin ran a campaign that made him the first Puerto Rican governor of Puerto Rico and that created the ambivalent legal relationship between the island and the United States, called "Commonwealth," that still exists today. Most people have forgotten that Marin made "El Lamento Borincano" the official campaign song.

"El Lamento" is remembered very differently by Puerto Ricans today. It inspires feelings of pride, nostalgia, patriotism, and spiritual purity. As Ana Celia Zentella says, when she hears "Lamento" today, it makes her feel, as a contemporary *Nuyorican,* that she has somehow "missed out on an essential part of being Puerto Rican" (Zentella 2004, 30). There are good reasons for this. In "Lamento," Puerto Ricans took the essential indifference of people in the United States to their music and culture, to their willingness to work, to their investment in democratic politics, and turned it into an opportunity to condemn injustice, however meekly, as well as capture some self-respect and independence of thought and emotion for themselves.

Puerto Ricans gained strength, unity, and power by the ideas and feelings of opposition that found expression in "EL Lamento Borincano." It is surely all memory and sentimentality today. By recovering and lifting up high the (mythical) values of *Jibaro* peasant life, however, Puerto Ricans gained cultural autonomy and power. Puerto Ricans created a space and music to dance that was theirs. The power they had there to move was limited and small. It was a cramped and uncomfortable space where they could move and dance with each other when nobody else would. Culture was the only space left them by the loss of economic and political power that had rested on the cigar makers.

3

The Rise of Radicalism
World War II to 1965

Abeses me digo yo mismo que me ubiese muerto aste de aber venido
a este paiz es ver que no se ingles y nada Valgo pero para dios
valgo[1]

—Pedro Lopez

Pedro Lopez was a Puerto Rican living in Brooklyn during
1965. His letter to Manuel Cabranes, in the New York City Welfare Department, has a weird combination of self-pity and defiance. Lopez might
be down but at least God supports him, he claims. The Lopez letter is not
unusual. Many Puerto Ricans were denied welfare at that time. Many received it. The Lopez letter, however, symbolizes the complex trajectory of
power for the Puerto Rican community in the post–World War II period.
A time of relative political influence after the war was followed by a quick
decline in power. The entire ride up and down was no accident, however.
It was the result of changing interests. What had been an intensive interest
in the political and economic value of the Puerto Rican community disappeared by the late 1950s. Meanwhile, never having enjoyed any cultural
power in the larger society, Puerto Ricans by the 1960s began to turn in-
wards, to draw strength from their own uniqueness as a culture and to finally see themselves as a "minority group." If the larger society had concluded that Puerto Ricans were worth nothing, Puerto Ricans asserted
that, yes, they were worth something, even if only to God and themselves.

In contrast to the previous period, the Puerto Rican community found
that power could no longer be negotiated or fought for in the economic
realm. The opportunities to connect and develop influence in the city had
become primarily political. Puerto Ricans found more political than economic interest on the part of the larger society. Some of this shift from the
primarily economic source of power Puerto Ricans experienced in the
cigar makers' period originated in the social interest to use Puerto Ricans

as cheap labor after World War II. Puerto Ricans no longer filled an important need for skilled labor in important industries. Puerto Ricans thus became expendable and redundant as labor in the 1950s. The only economic need for Puerto Rican labor was to keep it cheap and plentiful.

This movement of interests in Puerto Ricans towards the larger society ultimately moved each farther from the other. The end result for Puerto Ricans as well as for the larger society was a sudden loss of influence. Puerto Ricans sought greater pleasure and meaning from cultural values that were increasingly independent of the larger U.S. society. The emergence of Salsa, Puerto Rican folk music, and Puerto Rican culture in New York are good examples of this movement. Puerto Ricans could not, of course, remove themselves similarly from the political and economic reality of the United States. But whereas in the past they had tried to fit into this foreign system by accepting low wages or turning to labor unions and other institutions to defend themselves, by the 1960s Puerto Ricans had begun to increasingly assert their rights as independent citizens and increasingly came to recognize and resist the deep inequity of their life here.

This distancing of Puerto Ricans from the larger society meant a loss of power for both. Since Puerto Ricans started out with less power, however, this separation made Puerto Ricans more powerful in their community but more vulnerable outside it. The consequences for Puerto Ricans were economic (low wages and employment, welfare, etc.) and political (the rise of a more passive, manipulated relation to political authorities that James Jennings called "patron-client politics"). The Lopez letter again symbolizes that loss of power. Pedro Lopez was reduced to begging for help in 1965 from Manuel Cabranes, a mere consultant in the Welfare Department. From 1949 to 1955, in contrast, Puerto Ricans had their own institution within the Mayor's Office (the Mayor's Committee on Puerto Rican Affairs) to help them with any problem they might have. Once courted by mayors and congressmen, Puerto Ricans found themselves in the 1960s a community larger in numbers but reduced to making pitiful pleas for the attention of lowly bureaucrats. Puerto Ricans were weakened by a sudden, quick erosion and shift in interests. The political interest that drew others to Puerto Ricans in the late 1940s disappeared a decade later.

There are many signs of this shift in interests. In the larger, non–Puerto Rican society, the level of economic and political interest in Puerto Ricans changed dramatically by the late 1950s. The creation and then termination of the Mayor's Committee on Puerto Rican Affairs (MCPRA) is a prime example. The New York City Housing Authority went from coveting Puerto Ricans as tenants in the early 1950s to instituting a quota system to keep Puerto Ricans out of public housing. Similar changes occurred in the newspaper treatment of Puerto Ricans. What were once glowing reports of hard-working, family-oriented, and law-abiding Puerto Ricans turned into reports of lazy, delinquent, and dysfunctional families. For a time in the late 1950s, many New Yorkers were shocked and appalled at salacious newspaper reports of the barbaric crimes of one Salvador Agron, a young Puerto Rican dubbed the "Capeman." There was also a downward shift in employer interest in hiring Puerto Ricans. On the cultural front, the Puerto Rican presence was represented by *West Side Story*, a Romeo and Juliet tale in which Puerto Ricans alternately sang about how good it was to be in America and turned to gangs and knives to stab Americans.

Puerto Ricans also changed. These changes were much more subtle than the American press would have the public believe. Puerto Ricans didn't turn from hard-working people into gangsters. But they did begin to redefine themselves as a group and to redefine their place in the American system. Essentially, Puerto Ricans increasingly rejected the idea that they were simply national, ethnic migrants to the city. Instead, Puerto Ricans began to see themselves as a minority group, with rights, and possessed not only of a unique cultural and historical inheritance but also of a lowly (and for them unacceptable) place in the U.S. racial and class system.

Again, there are many signs of this. What had been for many years a Hispanic Day Parade was converted in the mid-1950s into a Puerto Rican Day Parade. Puerto Ricans also began to develop their own nonprofit institutions pitched around Puerto Rican needs and to abandon their old hometown clubs.[2] This was a signal of the Puerto Rican desire to become one cohesive, racial-ethnic group rather than a collection of exiles from towns like Ponce and Aguadilla in Puerto Rico. They also took elements of Cuban and traditional Puerto Rican music and developed a musical style that came to be called Salsa. At the same time, Puerto Ricans in New York during the 1960s began to resurrect, sometimes from the dead, those musical styles, instruments, and folk idioms, like Bomba and Plena, that Puerto Ricans in Puerto Rico largely ignored in their search for modernity. In this way, Puerto Ricans in New York forged themselves into a nation, if not a race. By turning inward, away from the larger society, Puerto Ricans learned to move to their own beats, to live and dance without outsider partners, to erect a foundation for power from within their own community. Their success at this led both to the eruption of wondrous, insurrectional political movements in the late 1960s and to greater success at securing elected offices. The failure of this self-defining strategy was that it helped to usher in the economic stagnation that is still being felt today.

Students of power have something important to learn from this particular episode of Puerto Rican community history. The twentieth-century debate about what determines historical change, and thus power, has alternately focused on economics, politics, or culture. Marx, some say, argued for economics, Weber for all three. The Puerto Rican experience shows that it's neither one nor the other. What creates and shapes power is the level and intensity of the interests. Those interests are not inherently economic, political, or cultural. We use theories and methods to separate these social ties into categories like politics and economics in hopes of better understanding a reality that doesn't come so easily divided.

Things happen not because economic, political, or cultural "forces" always assert themselves over the others. These dimensions of life are both too tangled together and too omnipresent for one to always dominate. It is the gravity of the relationship at particular moments that gives any of these dimensions the special ability to pull and push bodies across the social plane and expose its power.[3] Marx understood how gravity comes into play. He knew the unique importance of the economic relationship to long-term survival. It is because capitalism presents an essentially limited set of options to the proletariat that class standing carries so much weight in capitalist reality. That is also why Marx gave class so much theoretical importance.

Marx understood, as Weber would later, however, that politics and culture also have or could develop mass and gravity. He didn't always spell it out. Some say that Marx died as he was about to write about the role of politics in capitalism. He understood that politics and culture also exert great power. They don't just reside in a passive "superstructure" that is pushed around by class processes. They are active and, thus, critical forces in the "reproduction" of capitalist productive relations. Politics and culture are relatively "unshackled" from economics and production but remain important to their perpetuation. The focus on interests and passions is the key that allows us to track the way the various dimensions of social influence shift and unfold over time.

Political scientists and news reporters analyze election results by counting votes as a way to gauge shifting public interest and its impact on power. The thinking in these studies is that each shift in the distribution of votes registers a shift in the voting public's interests. Votes, however, are a narrow representation of citizen preferences or interests. Votes are, in any case, an indicator of individual, not group, interests. A clearer and fuller understanding of why power shifts occur between different groups and individuals actually requires a deeper exploration of interests than voting analysis has provided. Interests point us in the direction of what is good for us and create a framework that gives meaning to what we do (Irvine 2006, 116). We will turn to that now in the Puerto Rican experience.

The Eruption and Erosion of Power

Puerto Ricans found and lost power in the 1950s decade. The loss of power was economic and cultural but mostly political. The Puerto Rican community grew in numbers and lost power in the process. The Puerto Rican experience in the West Side Urban Renewal project is a good place to start understanding this dynamic.

While things began to fall apart for Puerto Ricans in the late 1950s, the exact date of this shift in power is hard to fix. It is clear, however, that in the latter half of the 1950s decade, Puerto Ricans were descending rather than ascending in power. The best sign of this loss was the various projects of urban renewal on the West Side of Manhattan. These projects radically purged that area of Puerto Rican residents. This displacement did not occur, however, without the organized and spontaneous resistance of Puerto Ricans. As soon as the real consequences of this urban renewal became clear, Puerto Rican leaders and organizations emerged and riots erupted in defense of this community's interests. In contrast to the early years of the decade, however, Puerto Ricans found that they could not quite catch the attention of local officials nor get them to marshal the city's resources on their behalf even by asking or demanding it. The change was subtle but significant. Not only did Puerto Ricans find themselves having to knock on and knock down doors to get heard; they also found that the public officials inside those doors no longer gave their needs any priority.

By 1956, there were over half a million Puerto Ricans living in New York City, a large proportion of them on Manhattan's West Side. The exact numbers living on the West Side are hard to establish, primarily because so many of them lived in overcrowded furnished rooms converted by landlords from apartments and brownstones. These landlords made a financial killing by charging excessive rents for undermaintained and dilapidated rooms rented to Puerto Ricans who accepted "less space per person and less building maintenance per unit of space" (Eagle 1960, 149). Some Puerto Rican leaders estimated that the West Side Urban Renewal displaced about ten thousand Puerto Rican households, the majority of those who were forced to relocate.[4] What was clear then as now is that Puerto Ricans were brusquely displaced or "pushed" from prime Manhattan real estate by city agencies. The consequences were devastating to Puerto Ricans. The Puerto Rican community learned that no amount of community organization, leadership, and mobilization could do much to oppose the assault on its well-being if the community is perceived to have very little value.

By the time a small group of Puerto Rican leaders met on July 13,

1961, to review and critique the city's plans for the West Side as they related to Puerto Ricans, it was too late. Thousands of Puerto Ricans had already been evicted to make room for what is now Lincoln Center. And in January of 1961, Mayor Wagner announced the final plans for fifteen renewal projects on the West Side. That small group of Puerto Rican leaders formed themselves into an organization called the Puerto Rican Citizens' Housing Committee, comprised of five members: Roland Cintron, Aramis Gomez, Josephine Nieves, Efrain Rosa, and Petra Rosa (Davies 1966, 133). The committee was right to claim that at that time "the overall housing program seems to envision a New York without Puerto Ricans" (Davies 1966, 133). That official vision was made possible only because, as the committee also realized, the Puerto Rican community had been completely "ignored on the planning and execution of any housing program" (ibid.). The extent to which this was true is important to spell out because it gets at the heart of the Puerto Rican loss of power in this period.

There was little grass roots participation of any kind in the planning for the West Side Renewal. In fact, there was a struggle waged by a group called Strykers Bay that claimed to more legitimately represent the residents of the West Side than the group the city had set up, which was called the Park to Hudson Urban Renewal Citizens' Committee.[5] But Strykers Bay mainly represented white, middle-class residents of the West Side. Of the coalition of forty-three community organizations that comprised Strykers Bay, only two were Puerto Rican (Davies 1966, 126). And those two organizations were actually only two individuals, Aramis Gomez and Efrain Rosa, putatively listed as representing organizations. Puerto Ricans thus came late to and were largely missing from the organized resistance to this renewal process. A similar but more complex situation existed at the city hall and policy level.

The political accommodation between the municipal reform movement and the Democratic Party machine intensified during the 1950s decade. By 1961, even Robert Wagner found it necessary to run as a reform politician despite the fact that the biggest example of political machine corruption, in Title I slum clearance, occurred during his administration. On the West Side alone, Democratic reform clubs captured all assembly districts between 1951 and 1961 (Davies 1966, 114). The rise of reform politics meant the end of the way machine politicians mobilized popular support in order to rule the city.

Machine politicians had always been prepared, as Martin Shefter has said, to "make concessions to important social forces in the city in order to obtain the votes, revenues, credit, and civil harmony that are requisites for gaining and retaining power" (1985, 15). That turned out to be very good for Puerto Ricans, or any working-class and ethnic group, in the immediate postwar period. The increasing grip of reform on city politics, however, hurt Puerto Ricans. The reformers, with some Puerto Ricans among them, wanted to end the system of patronage for votes. This was especially true in the area of social policy. Some of these reformers advocated turning social welfare programs over to grass roots recipients. In general, however, reformers placed great faith in social science and professional expertise as a way to ameliorate poverty.

The reform movement had a noticeable impact on the West Side Renewal project. The West Side was selected, apparently, because an official of the New York City Housing Authority, Samuel Ratensky, thought it would offer a good demonstration site to show what modern rehabilitation and conservation could do to clear slums. Mayor Robert Wagner latched onto this idea as a way to acquire federal funds made available under the National Housing Act of 1954. That law was the federal response to the rising criticism against Robert Moses's "bulldozer" approach to slum clearance. Moses opposed rehabilitation and conservation. As head of the Slum Clearance Committee, Moses believed that only total clearance would work.

The West Side Renewal project proceeded in typical reform fashion, with great attention to studies, hearings, and alternative plans. It followed a rational, professional, and seemingly democratic process. Reform or not, it is also true that these strategies aimed at countering the political weight of Moses in the city. Reform, however, eliminated neither Moses's large and bullying ego nor the corrupt municipal patronage of the old machine. Reform for Puerto Ricans, moreover, amounted to systematic exclusion from the political and policy process.

Puerto Ricans had also been excluded from the public works projects Moses spearheaded during the 1940s and early '50s. In fact, most analysts agree with Joel Schwartz that "Moses was careful to direct his Committee on Slum Clearance onto marginal black and Hispanic neighborhoods, generally isolated, unorganized, and *invisible*" (in Lawson and Naison 1986, 160). While that was largely true, in the early 1950s Puerto Ricans also had an important ally in the Mayor's Commission on Puerto Rican Affairs (MCPRA). This government body provided them with a voice and access to the policy process that was totally missing in Wagner's West Side Renewal project that came later. Puerto Ricans didn't fare any better under Wagner's reform programs than they had under Moses. They were displaced under both programs. It is what happened to them *after displacement,* however, that proved to be very different under the reform-based project.

The Commission on Intergroup Relations replaced the MCPRA in

1955. COIR had a broader mission. It was designed to assist any group in the city, rather than "pinpointing Puerto Ricans," and its staff consisted "mostly of Negroes and Puerto Ricans" (Davies 1966, 62). The 1961 Annual Report of the Commission on Intergroup Relations explained its mission as adapting "social science techniques to *grass roots* problems with a series of interrelated services designed to stabilize *nervous neighborhoods.*"[6] COIR also had "almost no powers except those of investigation" (ibid.).

The most significant element of COIR's work was its social-science and social-work mission. COIR often did radical and unexpected things, like giving public support to Leonard Scarborough, a militant black activist and community leader in Far Rockaway during 1959 (Davies 1966, 61). But its main goal was to *reduce tensions* and to match city services to new problems in minority communities. As a result, though COIR recognized that urban renewal was displacing thousands of Puerto Ricans on the West Side, it insisted that its goal was "to reduce relocation problems, promote integration and keep intergroup tensions to a minimum by working closely with community groups and city departments."[7] COIR even provided a few staff to the Puerto Rican Citizens' Housing Committee on the West Side.[8] However, as Puerto Ricans got pushed from the West Side, COIR was nothing more than a mere bystander. Indeed, one analyst claimed that all COIR did was "to meet minority problems with rhetoric, and with a minimum of commitment of actual resources" (Benjamin 1974, 110). This had not been the case under the MCPRA.

The biggest increase in the number of Puerto Ricans in public housing was the 150 percent increase recorded from 1953 to 1956 (Sanchez 1986, 211). So many Puerto Ricans got admitted during the 1950s decade that by 1960 Puerto Ricans comprised 18 percent of total public housing tenants in the city. Starting from around 0 percent in 1950, this increase in public housing occupancy was the largest in the history of Puerto Ricans in the city. What is most startling is that so many of those Puerto Ricans admitted into public housing came from urban renewal sites, people the Housing Authority generally refused to admit.

The New York City Housing Authority admitted into public projects less than one-third of all families displaced by urban renewal by 1954 (City Planning 1955, 48–49). It was their policy to not admit more than a few of those displaced. The Housing Authority reacted differently towards Puerto Ricans, however. Over 46 percent of all Puerto Ricans displaced by urban renewal between 1954 and 1955, for instance, got admitted into public housing (Housing Authority 1955). In contrast, only 24 percent of whites and 18 percent of blacks admitted into public housing in those years were former urban renewal site residents. Clearly, the Housing

Authority made Puerto Ricans a major exception in an admissions policy that usually gave preference to veterans, whites, and the "deserving poor." But if the Housing Authority had no general interest in housing the poor, neither did Moses.

The powerful master builder Robert Moses had no illusions about urban renewal serving as a means to provide housing for the poor. Slum clearance, he said, "was never designed to produce housing for people of low income . . . [it] aimed solely at the elimination of slums and substandard areas" (Jackson 1976, 246). As a result, between 1950 and 1960, Moses and the city were responsible for the demolition of over twenty-six thousand units renting for less than $10 a room. Those units were replaced by over twenty-eight thousand units that rented at $25 and more (ibid.). What is unusual is that as Moses's slum clearance projects displaced Puerto Ricans from Manhattan sites in the early 1950s, many of them got admitted into public housing. The biggest reason for their admittance appears to be the MCPRA.

As a partner, the MCPRA gave the Puerto Rican community a particular advantage. Where COIR had a professional orientation, the MCPRA was corporatist. New York City mayor John O'Dwyer created the MCPRA on September 12, 1949, with a mandate to facilitate "the integration of United States citizens from Puerto Rico into the life of the city" (MCPRA 1953b, 4). About half of its seventy-seven members were the heads of city departments. About twenty-six of the MCPRA commissioners were representatives from Puerto Rican organizations in the city.[9]

Aside from the many city and private heads of agencies that were members of the MCPRA, there were Puerto Rican doctors, academics, local nonprofit leaders, labor leaders, and newspaper people like the editors of *El Diario de Nueva York* and of *La Prensa*. Each represented an independent base of power, however limited, in the Puerto Rican community. Equally important was the inclusion of two associates of Vito Marcantonio, the radical congressman representing East Harlem. These were Dr. Leonard Covello, a principal at Benjamin Franklin High School, and Eloisa Rivera de Garcia, the wife of assemblyman Oscar Garcia Rivera. Both were good friends of Marcantonio, the biggest thorn in the side of both Luis Munoz Marin, the rising leader of the Puerto Rico commonwealth movement, and local New York City mayors and congressmen. Their presence on the commission was due to the corporatist structure of the MCPRA. Puerto Ricans were brought into government, where they gained some influence in exchange for facilitating city management over the migration of Puerto Ricans into the city.

The inclusion of city department heads and Puerto Rican community leaders on the MCPRA produced many significant, often pioneering, achievements for Puerto Ricans in New York. The Board of Education provided English-instruction classes for Puerto Rican adults and hired Spanish-speaking teachers, many of them from Puerto Rico, for children in the public schools.[10] The MCPRA also set up a Puerto Rican Scholarship Fund that in 1953 awarded seventeen scholarships to Puerto Rican students. It also initiated legislation in the City Council requiring Spanish–speaking caseworkers in the Welfare Department. By 1953, over 480 Spanish–speaking caseworkers had been added to the department. Spanish interpreters were also added to city hospitals. The MCPRA also initiated many cultural and recreational activities and services with church and settlement houses, the New York City Youth Board, the Health Department, the Parks Department, the Police Department, radio broadcasts in Spanish, yearly migration conferences in New York and Puerto Rico, as well as the celebration of an annual Puerto Rico Discovery Day starting on November 19, 1952. As we have seen, one of the most significant achievements came in housing.

Among the members of the MCPRA was Philip J. Cruise, who was the chairman of the New York City Housing Authority, and Robert Moses, whose official title was Commissioner of Parks. Their presence made possible the large increase in Puerto Rican admittance into public housing in the early 1950s. The help came in a variety of ways. In general, the MCPRA made repeated efforts through the Hispanic media and with brochures to "apprise eligible families who met the residence and other requirements of public housing apartments" (MCPRA 1953b, 16). It also held hearings where they heard complaints and where "representatives of the agencies concerned with housing were able to be of some help" (MCPRA 1953b, 17). The MCPRA went so far as to recommend a rent cut for Puerto Ricans admitted into public housing during 1950 ("City Seeks" 1950, 25:1). More generally, the MCPRA helped to change the perception within and without city government that Puerto Ricans were bad tenants and poor economic prospects.

The biggest obstacle to the admittance of Puerto Ricans into public housing was their poverty and status as low-wage workers. The Housing Authority in the early 1950s simply had no use for those who were not "upwardly mobile." It did not see itself as a charity and resisted admitting what Langdon Post, the first Housing Authority commissioner, in 1936 had said were the "permanent unemployables" that would "never be socially redeemable" (Post 1936, 15). The MCPRA helped to change, at least temporarily, the idea that Puerto Ricans were "permanent unemployables."[11] The MCPRA went about this by issuing public statements and reports.

MCPRA public officials went out of their way in the early 1950s to dispel the public impression that Puerto Ricans were nothing more than cheap labor. The MCPRA's 1953 Interim Report, for instance, claimed that the Puerto Rican worker was "indispensable, underpinning, as he does, the essential industries of the city" (MCPRA 1953b, 18). The next year, Mayor Wagner told a conference audience in Puerto Rico that "the mainland needs Puerto Rican migrants to fill jobs" ("Survey Finds New Jobs" 1954). The city's Department of Commerce gave more explicit tribute when it stated that "without the immigration of Puerto Rican labor many of New York City's manufacturing and service industries would face an acute manpower crisis" (NYC Dept. of Commerce 1956). MCPRA member and city welfare commissioner Henry McCarthy addressed directly the need to provide Puerto Ricans with necessary services. In response to public demands to trim the welfare rolls, particularly of Puerto Ricans, McCarthy argued that

> we cannot, on the one hand, attract Puerto Ricans to fill the need for workers in the garment industry, the hotel industry, or as domestic help without extending aid to them when illness or other misfortune strikes. . . . We cannot enjoy the benefits of Puerto Rican labor without assuming some additional welfare costs. On balance, the taxable values created by their labor must far exceed the additional welfare tax burden. (Kihss 1957)

The Housing Authority itself got into this public reclamation of Puerto Ricans. One 1953 Authority report, for instance, expressed delight at finding that "residents of Puerto Rican background make excellent tenants" (MCPRA 1953b, 16). Housing Authority project managers reported that Puerto Rican tenants were above average in paying their rent and had low rates of vandalism, as well as that the "housekeeping habits of the Puerto Rican tenants were above average" (Senior 1965, 104). Even the New York City Planning Commission got into the picture by certifying that the prospect of Puerto Rican social mobility was an "economic fact" since all of the signs pointed to "continued assimilation, with further education and job experience, with consequent gains in rent-paying ability" (1957, 25). The end result of all this public and private pressure initiated through the MCPRA was that, in combination with a drop in the pool of applicants from veteran families, the Housing Authority found it possible to radically increase the admission of Puerto Ricans to public housing in the early 1950s.[12] The significance of this achievement is underscored by what transpired just a few years later.

During the latter half of the 1950s decade, after the MCPRA was replaced by COIR, the Housing Authority reversed itself and began a secret admissions policy to limit the influx of Puerto Rican and black tenants.[13] In 1958, the Authority began to give priority again to white applicants. Apartments were left vacant until white tenants could be found in order to provide what the Authority called "racial balance" ("Bias Laid to City" 1960). These policies had the effect of slowing the admission of Puerto Ricans into public housing. From 1960 to 1970, the Puerto Rican proportion of tenants in public housing increased only from 18 to 23 percent (Sanchez 1990, 558). This 5 point increase was much lower than the black increase of about ten points in the same period (ibid.). This change in the Authority's treatment of Puerto Ricans had a number of causes. The Housing Authority was in some ways responding to the rapid decline in economic demand for Puerto Rican labor. The Authority was not in the poverty business. The more important reason, however, was the replacement of the MCPRA by COIR. The rise of reform and professionalism in COIR deflated the minimal power Puerto Ricans had amassed through MCPRA corporatism.

COIR generalized the government's relation to Puerto Ricans. COIR was mostly a black institution. It could only investigate. It couldn't make policy or take any punitive actions. More importantly, COIR had a social-work approach to reform that was ultimately depoliticizing. The therapeutic approach involved the idea that "social and economic problems would be solved not by political action and empowerment but by the application of scientific clinical techniques administered by properly trained and degreed professionals" (Trolander 1987). Thomas also states that Mayor Wagner ended the MCPRA primarily because, through its work, the "Puerto Rican migration became politicized at the level of social life in New York City" (2002, 296). Its relative success at providing Puerto Ricans with political influence made the MCPRA undesirable and untenable. It was both too political and too Puerto Rican.

What Puerto Ricans lost in the MCPRA was not just convenient access to centers of power in the city. The corporatist structure of the MCPRA had placed Puerto Rican leaders like Perfecto Gonzalez, the business agent of the AFL Local 223 Toy and Novelty Workers of America, on a seemingly equal footing with power brokers like Moses. The MCPRA made it possible for Puerto Rican leaders like Gonzalez to be heard by high government officials and to shape policy agendas. In the MCPRA, Puerto Ricans found themselves in the position to engage and move within the circuits of New York City's ruling elites. The biggest loss, however, was probably conceptual.

As a creature of the political machine, the MCPRA established a quid pro quo practice. The various Puerto Rican organizations represented in MCPRA would do their best to deliver votes to the machine in exchange for government services and benefits delivered to the Puerto Rican community. More generally, MCPRA had become a "key player in debates over how to address the 'problem' of the Puerto Rican migration in New York" (Thomas 2002, 296). In contrast, COIR came into existence with the very different goal of reducing *tensions*. This mission was later amended with vague promises of integration. Mayor Wagner in fact stipulated that COIR appointments *not be* "broadly representative of the religious, racial, and ethnic groups in the community" (Benjamin 1974, 77). The result was that when the Housing Authority changed its admissions policy COIR not only could do nothing to stop it but found itself supporting it.

There were, thus, several reasons why, in the late 1950s, the Housing Authority got little opposition to an admissions policy that hurt Puerto Ricans. First, Puerto Ricans were not well served by COIR. Second, their economic situation in the city had changed. Also, their political response to the city was itself increasingly defined by reform and antipolitical professionalism. These causes point to changes in the political and economic interests that dominated the city in this period. This transformed the lineup of major performers in city politics as well as the rules necessary for dancing in the city. Attention, resources, and action were now centered on those representing political reform. Interests had changed too.

The Housing Authority claimed that it had changed its admissions policy to further integration. What it really sought, however, was to keep Puerto Ricans and other nonmobile workers out of public housing. The chairman of the Housing Authority explained to the public that the quotas were meant simply as a means to "mix up the population" ("Bias Laid to City" 1960). Its real meaning was actually spelled out by friends of the Authority who argued that "middle-class behavior is not something that you can teach a Puerto Rican by imposing fines: fear of eviction does not take the place of socialization" (Miller and Werthman 1961, 285). The Housing Authority decided that the simplest way to keep middle-class tenants was to keep out economically struggling Puerto Ricans and blacks.

The Housing Authority's use of integration goals as a rationale for admissions policies that hurt Puerto Ricans and African Americans was cynical and manipulative. It was also something more. The civil rights movement had a tremendous impact on the language and rules of politics. In the city especially, the demand for civil rights got mixed in with efforts to end political corruption and to modernize the practice of government. In this new political order, discrimination was not eliminated but the terms of its perpetuation, especially in the North, got defined in the language of tolerance and legal rights. As Ronald Takaki found, "racial discrimination was becoming un-American in the post–World War II years" (Takaki 1993, 400). This new political environment made racial issues and integration the main currency of public exchange and debate.

The Housing Authority latched onto integration as the rationale for its discriminatory admissions policies precisely because of the wide public adoption of the language of civil rights. They could also get away with this ruse because the civil rights movement's primary aim was to change the rules for playing the game—the law. The *game* itself was to be left untouched. In fact, both Martin Luther King, Jr., and Malcolm X had come to the realization that the main weakness of the civil rights movement was precisely that it avoided issues that touched on the class and material basis of racism. King once warned that "the eradication of slums housing millions is complex beyond integrating buses and lunch counters" (quoted in Takaki 1993, 410). Nowhere is this more clear than in the New York City Housing Authority's efforts to exclude Puerto Ricans and blacks from public housing in the late 1950s and early 1960s because they were deemed "undeserving poor."

The West Side Urban Renewal project was further demonstration that Puerto Ricans had become inconsequential. Larger in numbers by the 1960s, but weaker, they got pushed around. Herman Badillo's position as head of Relocation didn't help. Full-blown patron-client politics replaced a more specific calculus of interest in machine politics. Is it likely that displacement would have happened anyway under MCPRA? This is, of course, speculation. There is no real way of knowing. The MCPRA probably could not have stopped the displacement of Puerto Ricans from such an increasingly desirable location. But perhaps it would have happened without a callous government's direct sponsorship and with more of a Puerto Rican voice. COIR showed concern about the displacement. They did so, however, as social workers, not as political advocates.[14]

Political Roots of Power

Puerto Ricans, as the MCPRA period demonstrates, began the 1950s decade with some political power. New York City politicians had become concerned about the Puerto Rican community's potential to disrupt their political plans, especially in Puerto Rico. They developed interest in the Puerto Rican community's welfare and adjusted local political agendas to accommodate its needs. Puerto Ricans, meanwhile, believed that they could find the economic prosperity in New York City they could not find in Puerto Rico. While there was substantial economic interest during the early 1950s in using cheap Puerto Rican labor to save the city's rapidly disappearing manufacturing industry, the more important interest in Puerto Ricans was political.

Mayors, businesspeople, and other elected officials courted Puerto Ricans heavily during the early years of this decade. A desire for cheap labor was the major reason. A bigger interest, however, was the attempt to forestall an apparent slide towards the political Left by this new community of voting citizens. The threat was not in the number of votes Puerto Ricans could cast for leftists but in the embarrassment it could bring Munoz-Marin and the Showcase for the Americas the United States was helping him build in Puerto Rico. It was this dual interest that led to the creation of the MCPRA in 1949. This institution was an unparalleled attempt by city officials to harness Puerto Rican labor in the rescue of an ailing local manufacturing industry. It was also used to manage the migration of these thousands of Puerto Ricans by preventing them from casting their lot with more radical and militant political elements.[15] The city's relation to the Puerto Rican community immediately before and after the MCPRA reveals exactly how unique this institution was in Puerto Rican community history.[16]

In the immediate post–World War II period, local government officials debated the real value to the city of incoming Puerto Rican labor. The year 1947 was a pivotal one for all parties. Beginning in that year, Puerto Ricans were blamed not only for the increases in the welfare rolls but also for the post-World War II housing shortage that gripped the city at that time ("Relief Given" 1947, 22:7; "Puerto Rico Acts" 1947, 19:5). Universities were commissioned to study the Puerto Rican problem, while city government departments made feeble efforts to respond to what were basically inaccurate public accusations ("Columbia University" 1947, 31:1). It was in this unsettled climate that the Welfare Department released a report aimed at reassuring the public that the vast majority of Puerto Ricans (96 percent, to be exact) did not, in fact, go on welfare immediately upon their arrival in New York. Even as this report was being issued, the Puerto Rican government was asked by the city to divert and curb the migration of Puerto Ricans to the city because they *drained* the welfare budget ("New York City" 1947, 14:5). The government of Puerto Rico was even forced to take action to calm the fears of white New Yorkers.

In interviews during the summer of 1947, Puerto Rican Governor Pinero tried to reassure the New York City public by making fabricated claims that the migration would decline by the fall ("Pinero Predicts" 1947, 54:5). When fall came and Puerto Ricans kept arriving in New York at an estimated rate of about two thousand per month, the Puerto Rican government announced a new proposal designed by Commissioner

Sierra Berdecia that would have regulated Puerto Rican migrants by requiring that they carry employment credentials.

Another part of the proposal was the creation of a Puerto Rican government agency to advise would-be migrants about conditions in New York and to help divert them to other localities in the United States ("Commissioner" 1947, 17:7; "Resident" 1947, 51:6). Despite these attempts to relieve the fears of white New Yorkers, the Puerto Rican government needed Puerto Rican migration and was working discreetly but purposely for it to happen. In fact, the new development policies taking hold in Puerto Rico at the time demanded migration (Lapp 1990). Demographer Jose L. Vazquez Calzada states that in the 1947 "population projections prepared by the Planning Board (in Puerto Rico), one of the first variables always included was massive migration" (Calzada 1966, 59). The Migration Bureau of the Puerto Rican Department of Labor was created soon after Berdecia made his proposal.

The creation of the MCPRA was very closely tied to the creation of the Migration Division of the Puerto Rican Department of Labor. Both were created in the 1948–1949 period and each played similar yet different roles in the migration of Puerto Ricans to New York. The Migration Division identified places of labor shortages in the United States in cooperation with the U.S. Employment Service and worked out ways for Puerto Rican workers to fill the need. This office also responded to individual businessmen, such as representatives of New York factories who came to Puerto Rico "in search of workers for the garment and needle-trade industries" (Sanchez-Korral 1983, 59). The MCPRA cooperated in this effort by informing the Puerto Rican migrant about conditions in New York City and by marshalling city services to provide necessary assistance, though at very minimal levels, in housing, education, welfare, and recreation. The MCPRA's goals were not, however, to function as a social service provider. Its creation was tied to ideological and political factors centered on

1. the rise of the Populares and Luis Munoz-Marin in Puerto Rico;
2. city hall's reaction to progressive political parties and leaders like the American Labor Party and Marcantonio in New York; and
3. the political mobilization of Puerto Ricans in New York.

Each of these interests contributed to the general political motivation behind the emergence of the MCPRA and led to the temporary increase in Puerto Rican community power. Invited to dance, Puerto Ricans entered the dance floor confident and ready for the pleasures and opportunities for movement aroused by these initiatives.

Puerto Rico's Populares and Operation Bootstrap in New York

In his classic book, *Freedom and Power in the Caribbean,* Gordon K. Lewis notes that the year 1945 represented the turning point in the transformation of Puerto Rico from "a declining agrarian economy into an expanding industrial structure" (1963, 113). An important force in this transformation was the governmental program of technical aids and tax incentives known as Operation Bootstrap, begun in that year. By 1953, Operation Bootstrap was able to attract "over 300 manufacturing plants to the island; more than 25,000 new jobs . . . to the island payroll; and the average annual net income per capita had risen from $122 to $426 some thirteen years later" (Lewis 1963, 116). The emergence of the Commonwealth and Operation Bootstrap was tied in no small way to Congressman Marcantonio and New York City politics.

Since his earliest days in the U.S. Congress, Vito Marcantonio fought for and introduced bills advocating independence for Puerto Rico, attacking the corporate exploitation of Puerto Rican workers, and, in general, resisting what he called "American Imperialism" (Ojeda 1978, 45). His interest in Puerto Rican independence and in the rights of the Nationalist Party had even taken him to Puerto Rico in 1936 as a lawyer to defend Pedro Albizu Campos, the legendary Puerto Rican nationalist who had been arrested on charges of conspiring to overthrow the government. Marcantonio's most vehement criticisms were directed at the various appointed and elected governors of Puerto Rico, whom he saw as acting, along with the whole of Puerto Rico's governing body, as basic servants to American imperialism. The Puerto Rican government, he said, was nothing more than "un producto accesorio del sistema colonial, ya de la explotacion que sufre el pueblo de Puerto Rico" (Ojeda 1978, 151).[17]

Marcantonio's view of the Puerto Rican government as a colonial body did not change with the assumption, by election of Luis Munoz-Marin to the governorship of Puerto Rico in 1948. In fact, Marcantonio capitalized on the popular attention then being given to Puerto Rico's economic experiment called Operation Bootstrap. Marcantonio charged, with satirical delight, that "la administracion de Munoz-Marin, para el pueblo de Puerto Rico es *Operacion Booby Trap*" (Ojeda 1978, 148).[18] Marcantonio made many public and congressional speeches containing well-documented but yet-unproved charges that Munoz-Marin and his government were basically enriching themselves and the American corporations establishing themselves in Puerto Rico. Marcantonio, as a result, introduced numerous measures into Congress that called for Puerto Rico's independence. The last ones were in 1943 and 1950.

All of this certainly did not endear Marcantonio to Munoz-Marin nor to the U.S. government, which was trying to convince the United Nations and Cold War allies that Puerto Rico was not a colony. Their mutual displeasure was eventually vented, in part, in the creation of the MCPRA.

Munoz-Marin's problems with Marcantonio coincided with a rising chorus of opposition to Marcantonio from the leaders of the major parties, organized labor, and the media in the United States and in New York City. The leaders of these institutions had, upon the emergence of the politically more acceptable Liberal Party, begun to label Marcantonio a communist. They painted most of his political opinions and behavior as being too closely tied to the "Communist Line" and as being "anti-God" (Carter 1965, 314).

Confident of the people's support, because of the services he had provided constituents, Marcantonio once answered his critics by claiming that "history and the final judgment of the people will support me in the future as they have so consistently in the past" (Schaffer 1966, 190). Marcantonio was proven correct about his support. Marcantonio was forbidden from gaining the nomination of both the Democratic Party and his own American Labor Party (ALP), something he had done in the past, by the 1947 passage in New York State of the Wilson-Pakula Act, a bill aimed directly at the radical from East Harlem (Carter 1965, 314). This bipartisan legislative repression forced him to run against a Republican and a Democrat in a predominantly Democratic district. Despite this setback, Marcantonio won reelection in 1948 to the U.S. Congress by a margin of close to five thousand votes (ibid., 370). Though he was "opposed by all the organized power of anti-communism," the 1948 election was one that Marcantonio should have lost, but didn't (Ojeda 1978, 190). His victory was ample demonstration of Marcantonio's formidable community support, a support that only caused those seeking to defeat him to redouble their efforts.

Marcantonio and Puerto Ricans in New York

After Marcantonio's big 1948 victory, a number of political leaders and newspapers began to attribute his political success to the rising population of Puerto Ricans living in East Harlem. His power came from dancing with those "hordes," they claimed. With blatantly unabashed racist overtones, the New York *Daily Mirror* observed, for instance, that "Marcantonio's principal strength comes from hordes of Puerto Ricans enticed here from their pitiful poverty, which Marcantonio has done nothing to alleviate—except force thousands on city relief" (Editorial 1950). Marcantonio had, indeed, helped a small "horde" of Puerto Rican workers who needed welfare, but primarily in getting through the maze of paper-work and an English-speaking welfare bureaucracy. The number of Puerto Ricans on welfare had actually never amounted to more than 10 percent of the Puerto Rican population at any time during that period.

But the welfare assistance was only part of the many services Marcantonio's "political machine" provided his constituents. During election time, a more formal organization would take over, as community residents and rank and file members of the ALP climbed stairs and rang doorbells to get the vote out. Marcantonio and his organization turned to the Puerto Rican population in East Harlem for both purposes. Puerto Ricans, unlike other immigrants, were eligible to vote. And Puerto Ricans also had severe needs and problems that weren't being attended to by local authorities. By administering to the social needs of Puerto Ricans, however, Marcantonio did more than simply enlarge this base of electoral support. Working as a kind of agent or catalyst for change, he had also helped to organize the young Puerto Rican community of East Harlem into an impressive electoral and political force. This hadn't been done before, and possibly except for Herman Badillo's mayoral campaign of 1969, hasn't since. It was even more impressive for that time period.

A Columbia University study in 1948 had concluded that the Puerto Rican could not be, and did not want to be, organized politically (Mills et al. 1948). Much later, language barriers and registration laws were offered as reasons for the decline of Puerto Rican electoral politics. Marcantonio's success at getting Puerto Ricans out to vote proved to be a significantly less important issue to academic and political observers, however, than the fact that he had done so, during the late 1940s and early 1950s, as a radical. Congressman Marcantonio himself estimated that Puerto Ricans comprised one-fifth of the total citywide vote for the ALP in the late 1940s (Carter 1965, 399). Because of these factors, Marcantonio's victory caused a few tremors to established powers not only in New York City but also as far away as Puerto Rico.

On July 21, 1949, only eight months after the 1948 reelection of Marcantonio, Governor Munoz-Marin came to New York City to lunch with Mayor O'Dwyer and discuss the problems of Puerto Rico and of Puerto Ricans in New York City. While there is no record of this conversation, subsequent events suggest that the allegiance of Puerto Ricans to Marcantonio must have been the dominant issue at their table. They agreed to a solution that became publicly apparent by September of 1949. This was the creation of institutions, such as the MCPRA, to counter Marcantonio's political movement.

The MCPRA was thus born from these overlapping political and economic forces, most of which were tied to the class dynamics of the city at the time. The MCPRA was created not only to facilitate the migration of cheap Puerto Rican labor to New York City. It was also created to defeat Marcantonio, thereby removing a threat not only to Munoz-Marin and the colonial Puerto Rican government but equally to Mayor O'Dwyer and the New York City political and capitalist establishment. O'Dwyer's opposition to Marcantonio, in fact, had begun almost as soon as he had become mayor in 1945, succeeding Fiorello LaGuardia in the city's highest office. Following upon the split within the ALP and the creation of the Liberal Party, "O'Dwyer began cutting any patronage ties the ALP had with City Hall" (Carter 1965, 187). In 1948, Marcantonio complained publicly that "O'Dwyer and his gang" had reneged on a promise to build a hospital in East Harlem and had instead rescheduled it for a downtown location (ibid.).

O'Dwyer, for the most part, was content to attack Marcantonio in quiet but probably more effective terms by withdrawing patronage and political support. Thus, though he was elected with ALP and Marcantonio support, O'Dwyer spearheaded "an all-out effort by the New York County Democrats to defeat Marcantonio for re-election" (Carter 1965, 357). Marcantonio, however, had neither the power nor the temperament, especially as a fourth-party mayoral candidate in 1949, to act quietly. He fought his battles publicly and vocally. The newspapers of late 1949 are filled with Marcantonio's acrid accusations that O'Dwyer allowed employers and landlords to discriminate against and exploit Puerto Ricans. He also charged that O'Dwyer was a hypocrite, establishing the MCPRA not to solve problems but to capture the Puerto Rican vote.[19]

Marcantonio and Puerto Rico

Towards the end of 1949, Munoz-Marin, the Puerto Rican governor, increasingly answered Marcantonio's many charges against O'Dwyer in the New York media. Never before had political vitriol from more than 1,650 miles away in Puerto Rico been clearer than voices much closer to home. In his replies, Munoz-Marin usually lavished tremendous praise on O'Dwyer for the "splendid" job he was doing for Puerto Ricans in New York City ("Puerto Ricans" 1949, 29:5). But such praise was usually coupled with attempts to discredit Marcantonio. At one point for instance, Munoz-Marin urged Puerto Ricans living in New York City to dissociate themselves from this "follower of the communist line" (ibid.). Later, after Marcantonio's Puerto Rican secretary, Manuel Medina, had narrowly lost an impressive race for state assembly during 1949, O'Dwyer himself spoke to New York City's Puerto Rican population, charging that

Marcantonio was trying to "trick" them into becoming communist in exchange for patronage favors ("Marcantonio Plot" 1949, 5:1; Wakefield 1959, 263). Mayor O'Dwyer went so far as to plead to an audience of Puerto Ricans and other Hispanics at Manhattan's Riverside Plaza Hotel that "they don't have to go to any political clubhouse to get relief" (ibid.). O'Dwyer and Munoz-Marin were apparently doing their best to get Puerto Ricans to turn to the MCPRA rather than to Marcantonio as their source of clubhouse patronage.

This attempt to replace Marcantonio's political machine and its relation to the Puerto Rican community with the MCPRA is also made obvious by the MCPRA's duplication of the services Marcantonio had provided Puerto Ricans. Although the MCPRA was active, and probably more successful, in a number of different areas, none was as important as the reforms the MCPRA helped to institute in the Welfare Department in hopes of luring Puerto Ricans from Marcantonio.[20] O'Dwyer apparently believed that Puerto Ricans had been duped into communism by the assistance Marcantonio's office gave them in securing welfare help. O'Dwyer also seemed to think that Marcantonio was working towards the much broader goal of making the Department of Welfare a "Communist clubhouse for politicians" ("Marcantonio Plot" 1949, 5:1). As a result, O'Dwyer made sure in a speech given to Puerto Ricans in 1949 that they understood that the true objective of the MCPRA was to work "long after election in the fields of education and relief" (ibid.).

The major problems encountered by Puerto Ricans in applying for welfare were, first, knowing about what was available and where to go, and, second, overcoming the barrier of application forms written in English and processed by English-speaking caseworkers. The MCPRA published pamphlets, made radio broadcasts, and even set up a speakers bureau staffed with MCPRA members as part of a general effort to reach out to and inform the Puerto Rican community about welfare and other government services (MCPRA 1954).

The MCPRA's efforts in welfare provision for Puerto Ricans, however, went beyond outreach. Not more than two months after its creation, the MCPRA had maneuvered a bill through the City Council in 1949 to require the Department of Welfare to hire more Spanish-speaking caseworkers and personnel. The intent of these measures was to ensure that Puerto Ricans would not have to resort to the services of "outsiders" or "political party workers" who "often made the applicants feel that they were indebted to them" (MCPRA 1953b, 24). The city was thus required to hire "Spanish-speaking social investigators of Puerto Rican background, thoroughly familiar with conditions and agencies and sources of reference in Puerto Rico" (ibid.).[21] By 1953, 480 Spanish-speaking social investigators and other officials were hired as a result of this law. Ironically, this did not significantly raise the percentage of the Puerto Rican population receiving welfare in the city (it actually declined). It was, however, a sign of unusual local government attentiveness towards Puerto Ricans. The MCPRA's effectiveness, of course, was a function of the mayor's power. But anyone familiar with the more recent struggles of Puerto Ricans for government attention recognizes that, wherever was the true source of the MCPRA's power, the fact that that power was put to use for Puerto Ricans is something this community has rarely experienced.[22]

Cloward and Piven's argument about welfare reform processes provides another plausible explanation for the emergence of the MCPRA. Their argument is that "new welfare programs are typically legislated when political leaders are confronted with mounting concern among their electoral constituencies, often in response to some form of social disruption" (1993, 13). The emergence of the MCPRA can be attributed to the threat posed to local leaders by the radical Marcantonio machine and a militant Puerto Rican community carrying on a tradition handed down from the cigar makers. The MCPRA did not emerge, however, because of any real potential for "social disruption" in the city. Its birth was more closely connected, as we have seen, to economic and political developments in Puerto Rico. The MCPRA, as we've claimed, helped directly to consolidate the Operation Bootstrap program as well as the political power of Munoz-Marin and his Populares movement in Puerto Rico.

In 1979, Social Security payments to individuals in Puerto Rico amounted to over $800 million, or 43 percent of the total transfer payments made by the federal government to individuals in Puerto Rico.[23] The basic role of these payments in the Puerto Rican economy has been to promote a system of "consumption that is geared more to the needs of a producer's market than to consumer needs" (Bonilla and Campos 1986, 148). But these as well as other political effects, such as the institution of the Social Security program in Puerto Rico, might not have arisen early enough to give political legitimacy to Munoz-Marin and his government had it not been for the help of the MCPRA.

Turning Puerto Ricans against Marcantonio

The 1953 Interim Report of the MCPRA states that this committee had become "a channel through which top officers of the Island government can work with government and social welfare leaders in New York City" (MCPRA 1953b, 14). Indeed it had. Eight MCPRA committee members were associated with the island government in 1953. These eight included such prominent Puerto Rican leaders as Jaime Benitez, chancellor of the University of Puerto Rico, and Josefina Rincon, secretary to the city government of San Juan.[24]

The presence of Puerto Rican government representatives helped to secure public and official attention to the political concerns of the Puerto Rican government in Washington, D.C., as well as in New York. During the first year of the MCPRA's existence, in fact, the committee devoted much of its efforts to reversing the growing opposition in Congress during 1950 to the idea of including Puerto Rico in proposals submitted to extend the Social Security Act. The MCPRA acted swiftly. By resolution, it "endorsed extension of Social Security benefits to the Island," and it informed and helped to mobilize most members of the New York State congressional delegation around this issue.[25]

The MCPRA also persuaded Mayor Impelliteri to communicate his official support to Congress. The act passed and the MCPRA went confidently to work on other projects designed to help Puerto Rico and the Bootstrap program. The MCPRA, for instance, also helped to persuade Congress in 1950 to extend the work of the U.S. Employment Service to Puerto Rico, helped Eastern Airlines open up Puerto Rico to the tourist trade, and, through Mayor Impelliteri, officially requested in 1952 that the federal government grant funds for housing projects in Puerto Rico (MCPRA 1953b). The creation of a "commonwealth" government in Puerto Rico during 1952 also stirred the MCPRA into mobilizing, in conjunction with the American Public Welfare Association, to pressure Congress once again into including Puerto Rico in Social Security program increases scheduled for that year (MCPRA 1952).

The relationship between New York City's government, represented at the time by the MCPRA, and Puerto Rico was reciprocal. Puerto Rico provided New York with valuable assistance in recruiting Spanish-speaking teachers and other civil servants from Puerto Rico. It also provided orientation for city government officials unfamiliar with the language, customs, and general background of the Puerto Rican migrant, through a number of conferences held in 1953, 1954, and 1958. The Puerto Rican government, on the other hand, created a street-level bureaucratic and political presence in Puerto Rican communities in New York and other cities through the offices of the Migration Division. This Puerto Rican government agency was created in New York in order to "apply social scientific expertise and bureaucratic know-how to the problems of migration" (Lapp 1990, 4). The Migration Division was, however, also an important weapon in the effort to topple New York Puerto Rican community support for Marcantonio.

Handing Puerto Ricans over to the Professionals

The Migration Division and its director, Joseph Monserrat, helped to organize many of the major private Puerto Rican political and civic organizations in New York. Monserrat and the Migration Division, however, set a general tone of political accommodation and demobilization for this community that lasted for decades. It was a perspective that New York City officials encouraged and supported, especially as official interest in dancing with Puerto Ricans began to disappear. Monserrat's impact was directly felt through his founding and leadership of the Council of Spanish-American Organizations (CSAO), which consisted of numerous civic, social, cultural, religious, and fraternal organizations, many of which were created with the help of the council.

At its founding in 1952, CSAO represented only thirteen affiliated organizations. But by 1956, fifty-seven organizations belonged to the council.[26] The CSAO conducted a number of voter registration campaigns in the 1950s, many of them designed to coincide with the electoral campaigns of Robert Wagner, Jr. Like the many Puerto Rican community organizations to emerge later (the Puerto Rican Forum, the Puerto Rican Development Project, Progress, etc.), the CSAO's perception of the Puerto Rican community and its problems appeared progressive and noble in spirit but was ultimately elitist and therapeutic in form. The CSAO's response to the severe housing crisis faced by Puerto Ricans, for instance, was not to advocate for the community or mobilize it to demand more and better housing from the city. Instead, the CSAO established numerous "housing clinics" during the 1950s where Puerto Ricans were treated as if they were patients inflicted with "housing disorders" (Senior 1965, 103). While being informed of their legal rights as tenants, Puerto Ricans were also warned in these clinics not to maintain "Puerto Rican customs which dictate sharing with others of housing accommodations, no matter how inadequate" (MCPRA 1953b, 7). In 1951, Manuel Cabranes, the executive secretary of the MCPRA, went so far as to attribute the overcrowding and low quality of Puerto Rican housing solely "to the close family ties of the Puerto Ricans, and to their hospitality, where they share their home with anyone who has no home."[27]

Because Puerto Ricans were treated as patients, any real or potential move on their part to secure and control their own "treatment" naturally became a threat to the "healers." The MCPRA became the object of the CSAO's scorn and attack precisely for this reason. The MCPRA was just as ineffective in reducing poverty or promoting Puerto Rican social mobility. Its semicorporatist structure, however, brought together numerous and diverse sectors of the Puerto Rican community into a limited but official city policy-making process. This went against the CSAO philosophy.

The CSAO believed that Puerto Ricans needed "healing" rather than political representation and power. Antonia Pantoja, an activist at that time, recognized this antipolitical perspective in the CSAO even as she advocated it for Puerto Rican institutions. She asked during the 1950s that Puerto Rican New Yorkers withdraw from the CSAO because the "council could have served as our entity to fight for our rights or to conduct activities on our behalf, but it was too dependent on the government agency of Puerto Rico to be an effective representative of our communities" (2002, 111). Along with the Office of Puerto Rico, the CSAO also had "a policy of assimilation and control over the growing influential community of Puerto Ricans on the continent" (ibid., 77).

Eventually, Mayor Wagner and some Puerto Rican leaders in the CSAO complained that by concentrating on the Puerto Rican community, the MCPRA "pinpointed Puerto Ricans as the only group representing a problem."[28] The CSAO also believed that Puerto Ricans were a problem for the city. They were just not the city's *only* problem. The real concern of the CSAO, however, was not the public image of Puerto Ricans in the city but the direction and control over the way city government resources and initiatives were to be utilized by the Puerto Rican community. This is evident in the radically different structures and activities assumed by COIR, the city agency the CSAO promoted as a replacement for the MCPRA.

The MCPRA came into being primarily for political reasons and disappeared as those political purposes got realized. Marcantonio's death in 1954 eliminated the biggest political threat to Munoz-Marin and to local New York politicians. Another important reason was the Puerto Rican nationalist attack in the U.S. Congress in 1950 and 1954. Some Puerto Rican leaders, like Joseph Monserrat, wanted to end it for their own political reasons. Puerto Ricans in New York City began to resent the efforts of the government in Puerto Rico to influence things in the city.

The same year of the MCPRA's demise in 1954, Edward Miller spoke about keeping the MCPRA because of the need for speedy problem solving to help Puerto Ricans. The need was still there in the Puerto Rican community. Puerto Ricans had lost, however, the interest of the larger city and its leaders. As voters, Puerto Ricans were not a real political factor in city and national elections at that time. They were too scattered around the city, and they had low registration and voting rates. In 1952, for example, only about thirty-five thousand Puerto Ricans registered to vote in New York City out of a potential estimated 250,000 registrants (Thomas 2002, 312). One big reason for this was literacy exams that prevented the vast majority of low-educated and non–English-speaking Puerto Ricans from qualifying to vote. Economic changes involving the loss of manufacturing and the defeat of Puerto Rican labor organizing further confirmed the political realization that Puerto Ricans were no longer necessary or wanted in the city. Puerto Ricans were finding themselves increasingly without a dance partner.

Disappearing Interest in Puerto Ricans

> There will come a time when our silence will be more powerful than the voices you are strangling today.
>
> —Vito Marcantonio[29]

The Puerto Rican loss of power in the 1950s was a result of the larger society losing interest in what Puerto Ricans offered politically, economically, and culturally. The decline in political interest, discussed above, was abrupt and painful. The economic losses were just as clear. Puerto Ricans were a desired source of cheap labor in the beginning of the decade and a militant, better-organized sector of labor that employers had begun to avoid by the end. Culturally, Puerto Ricans were seen as a culpable example of ghetto gangsters for movies like *West Side Story* but offered very little that was appealing in music, writing, acting, or dance. This community was weakened further by the way these changes combined with the continued Puerto Rican attachment to the political and economic values of the larger society as well as a nascent but growing Puerto Rican attempt at cultural independence.

Puerto Ricans, as we saw, had power early in this period and lost it. This loss shaped the kinds of relations Puerto Ricans had with the larger society later. In many instances, Puerto Ricans fought back. Economically, they fought against employers and their unions. Politically, they fought against marginalization with activist and militant leaders like Gerena-Valentin and Pantoja as two good examples. Mostly, Puerto Ricans allowed themselves to be handed off to professionals, as available and willing partners. They became patients rather than insurgents, managed rather than disruptive. As a result, they were not independent enough to provide much of a political threat until the Young Lords came upon the scene in 1969.

As the discussion above showed, there is considerable evidence that points to the idea that the wider society, at least as represented by New York City, turned against Puerto Ricans.[30] On the labor front, employers no longer had much interest in hiring Puerto Ricans. The New York City Housing Authority changed their admissions policies to admit fewer

Puerto Ricans. The city replaced the MCPRA with a new organization with less power called the Commission on Intergroup Relations (COIR).

Susan S. Baker once argued that Puerto Ricans have to be credited "with helping New York hold on to the garment industry" in the 1950s (Baker 2002, 159). She was absolutely right. However, the Puerto Rican contribution was temporary and not limited to the garment industry. By the mid-1950s Puerto Rican hard work and skills could not keep light industries from moving south and out of the country. Businesses found cheaper and more compliant labor elsewhere. Similar economic pressures caused Puerto Ricans in Lorain, Ohio, to lose economic status. The small group of Puerto Ricans that worked for U.S. Steel in Lorain in the late 1940s had been among the highest income earners in the U.S. This changed dramatically "in the early 1950s when U.S. Steel stopped housing the Puerto Ricans who then had to look for housing elsewhere" (Baker 2002, 182). Back in New York City, it became clear that the reduced need for Puerto Rican labor required a radical reevaluation of their condition and prospects for upward mobility.

During the MCPRA period, the perception of Puerto Ricans in the media and in the public changed, no doubt as a result of the change in official perception. Puerto Ricans were seen "as social actors rather than as an undifferentiated 'problem' group" (Thomas 2002, 311). During this early 1950s period, "the contextualization and the tone of much of the media attention was now more sympathetic than critical" (Thomas 2002, 300). In a variety of ways, various public authorities began to perceive Puerto Ricans as "undeserving" by the mid-1950s because their economic role had changed. This was also evident in the way newspaper portrayed Puerto Ricans.

Figure 3.1 documents the changes in *New York Times* reporting on the economic condition of Puerto Ricans during the 1950s decade. As is evident, negative reports on the economic condition and value of Puerto Rican labor began to replace positive reports by the middle of the decade. Hard-working Puerto Ricans became unemployable. Responsible workers became "problems" (Barry 1959). There was still some possibility that Puerto Ricans would succeed. Yet amidst the positive was a growing sense that they would not.

Political factors were probably more important in shaping the economic decline of Puerto Ricans in the 1950s as well as the shift in interest that resulted. It was political factors that made Puerto Ricans available to salvage New York City light industries with little future in New York City. Neither of the major architects of this plan, Munoz-Marin and New York City mayors, foresaw that Puerto Ricans would only be a temporary stopgap. What would happen down the line simply didn't matter to them.

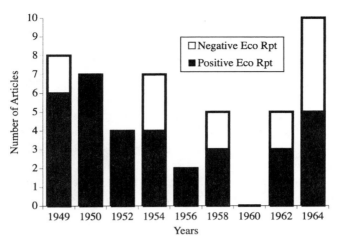

Figure 3.1. Positive + Negative NYT Economic Reports on Puerto Ricans, 1949 to 1964. *Source*: NY Times Index.

They cared more about their own political problems. These were Marcantonio and Operation Bootstrap. In this way, thus, they set Puerto Ricans up for failure.

Unlike the cigar makers of decades earlier, Puerto Ricans were pushed out of Puerto Rico by a combination of economic and political forces over which they had little control. The business cycle thus played a major part in Puerto Rican migration to New York City. As Morales stated, "in times of prosperity the migrants increased, and during depressions they decreased" (Morales 1979, 81). The factors that contributed to the "push" Puerto Ricans felt in Puerto Rico and the "pull" they felt for New York City, however, were driven by politics and policy. The policies in Puerto Rico that led to industrialization wiped out subsistence farming. Changes in U.S. immigration laws created new opportunities for low-wage labor in places like New York City. Then, the emerging commerce between the United States and Puerto Rico created shipping lanes and companies that facilitated Puerto Rican migration. The actions of governments in New York City with programs like the MCPRA greased these rails, producing accelerated movements of decline.

Shifting Puerto Rican Interest

As interest in them declined in the mid 1950s, Puerto Ricans began a hesitant yet steady cultural turn away from the larger society. However, survival meant that Puerto Ricans could not turn much away from what the larger society offered economically. Economic "exits" were few and hard for Puerto Ricans to open.[31] Puerto Ricans were dependent on whatever measly jobs and income they could grab.

Though the obstacles to political independence were lower, Puerto Ricans didn't move that far away politically either. Politicians would not let Puerto Rican citizens lie completely dormant or outside the mainstream. They tapped into the pool of Puerto Rican voters as the need required. This was especially true of Puerto Rican politicians like Herman Badillo.

The period of the late 1950s is marked by a tremendous surge of Puerto Rican political and economic resistance. Puerto Ricans engaged in numerous strikes against employers, sometimes even against their own unions. They fought landlords against evictions and the media when they felt slandered.

Culturally, however, Puerto Ricans found that they had more space in which to develop their own independent forms and, thus, to forge, in culture, their own foundation of power. Puerto Ricans insisted on having their own Puerto Rican Day parade and began to create their own music stores, as well as to recreate and reconnect to traditional Puerto Rican music in Bomba and Plena when Cortijo played at the Palladium in 1955 (Glasser 1995). In essence, Puerto Ricans were dealing with their surfeit of power by awakening to the fact that they were citizens and had rights, realizing that the American Dream would not come easily to them, and finding solace and power in their own ways of dancing in America.

Puerto Ricans began to resist at the workplace. As citizens with rights, Puerto Ricans fought against low wages and poor union representation. They became, in this way, poor partners for the exploitative designs of New York City bosses. They held demonstrations, most of them spontaneous, against media slanders, labor exploitation, housing abuses, political representation, and police brutality (CPUSA 1954). In one example, seven hundred Puerto Ricans demonstrated "against the eviction of Mrs. Marina Gomez on September 3, 1951, in the Bronx" (ibid., 20).

Puerto Ricans also turned towards the general reform movement in politics. This had begun as early as the mid-1950s when Monseratt's CSAO opened housing clinics. In fact, Antonia Pantoja worked in these clinics. Even so, she disagreed with the Office of Puerto Rico because she believed that it "did indeed have a policy of assimilation and control over the growing influential community of Puerto Ricans on the continent" (2002, 78). Radicals like Gilberto Gerena-Valentine, however, were essentially toothless. They were radicals but, unlike cigar makers, essentially alone. Gerena-Valentine worked with Marcantonio organizing Puerto Rican workers. In 1951, he was, however, among thirteen officers of

Local 6 of Hotel and Club Employees who were suspended as a result of congressional investigations into "Communist Activities" ("Puerto Rican Leader" 1964). Actions such as these against Gerena-Valentine and Marcantonio defeated the Puerto Rican Left. The efforts of organizations like MCPRA and, later, the COIR brought Puerto Rican leadership towards the political center.

Deep changes had occurred in the interests Puerto Ricans and non–Puerto Ricans had towards each other. The changes were not monolithic. Complex, sometimes even opposing, interests resided there. One of the most important was the change in culture that unfurled in this period.

Puerto Ricans did not embark on a wholesale abandonment of American culture. They did, however, begin to explore what was uniquely theirs. They dropped their identification with their hometown of origin in Puerto Rico. Gerena-Valentine, the leader of the Puerto Rican Hometown Clubs began to see a steep membership fall. In their place, there emerged a more concrete identification with the idea that they were all Puerto Rican. The first major sign was the creation of a Puerto Rican Day Parade in the mid-1950s to replace the older Hispanic Day Parade. In addition, a distinct Puerto Rican music grown in the city began to emerge.

The first Puerto Rican musical initiative in New York City was actually a return to something old. Rafael Cortijo brought his band to play Bomba and Plena in the Teatro Puerto Rico and the Palladium in 1955. This was the second reappearance of Bomba and Plena in twentieth-century New York. Bomba and Plena was traditional music from Puerto Rico. It was, according to Cortijo's singer, Ismael Rivera, a musical resurrection that "came from the people." Bomba and Plena was music that interpreted the rage and anger of the poor barrios. By 1964, Puerto Ricans in New York focused their anger and particular urban experience to create the musical amalgam called Salsa. Johnny Pacheco, founder of Fania Records (originator of the Salsa movement), created a Cuban-style band rather than the big bands other Latino musicians adopted. In this way, "Pacheco refused to give in to the North American influences" (Ospina and Caistor 1995, 68). The Salsa that Pacheco and others created drew on the hunger and anger of life in "the poor neighborhoods" of New York City (Ospina and Caistor 1995, 46).

A Professional Weakness

A significant achievement for Puerto Ricans in the 1950s was the development of Puerto Rican leaders whose roots were in New York City rather than in the government of Puerto Rico. These leaders were also trained to tackle Puerto Rican problems, for the most part, with social work and bureaucratic solutions rather than politics. As Pantoja said, their goal was to "modernize" Puerto Rican institutional life by developing "administrative, management, and research skills" (Pantoja 2004, 231). "Modernization" provided New York City Puerto Ricans with a mechanism and justification for pulling away from the patronizing shadow of the government of Puerto Rico. This transformation of its leadership into "professionals" would also prove tremendously debilitating for the Puerto Rican community.

Newspaper accounts in the early 1950s were filled with quotes and references to Luis Munoz-Marin, the governor of Puerto Rico, or Joseph Monserrat, the head of the Migration Office set up by the government of Puerto Rico in New York City. During those years, many non–Puerto Ricans also served as spokespeople for the community. Clarence Senior, the well-known author and national director of the Migration Office, is probably the best example of this. By the late 1960s, there were many more New York Puerto Ricans representing the Puerto Rican community. The problem is that these professionally trained Puerto Ricans rose in prominence at the expense of more radical elements in the Puerto Rican community (Sanchez-Korral 2004).

The rise of a professional leadership cadre can be seen in figure 3.2. This chart compares the total number of articles found in the *New York Times* about the Puerto Rican community to the number of articles about Puerto Rican professionals in the years between 1949 and 1964. Figure 3.2 compares the percentage of *New York Times* reporting on Puerto Rican professionals to the total reporting on all issues. Clearly, the reporting changes reflect the rise in the latter half of the 1950s decade of Puerto Rican professional leadership. There were three newspaper reports on professionals in 1954–1956 and fourteen in 1964. A professionally trained (mostly in social work) leadership in the Puerto Rican community emerged during this period as Puerto Ricans began to attend universities and develop fluency in American values. Lost in this achievement was the fact that Puerto Rican radical leadership had been shunted aside.[32]

Anticommunist hysteria affected a broad range of local government offices and occasionally targeted Puerto Ricans. The Housing Authority itself was declared a "security agency" in 1953, giving it the right to investigate employees and residents as well as take action to stop "communist activity."[33] During the 1950s, the Housing Authority took action against a score of employees and tenants. Such repression was not limited to the Housing Authority or only to the early 1950s.

During the late 1950s, the Un-American Activities Committee of the U.S. House of Representatives launched an investigation into the activities

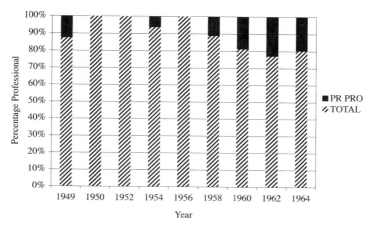

Figure 3.2. NY Times Reporting on PRs + PR Professionals.
Source: NY Times Index.

of Puerto Rican activists in New York City. Hearings were held in November 1959. Ten Puerto Ricans refused to testify about Puerto Rican labor and Communist Party leader Jesus Colon.[34] Accusations of communist affiliation were also made again in 1960 against Gerena Valentin, the radical head of the Congress of Puerto Rican Hometowns.[35] While these investigations essentially went nowhere, they did have a dampening effect on Puerto Rican radicals. Gerena Valentine, for example, found that he had a more difficult time trying to access city government on behalf of the Puerto Rican community. Valentine made repeated and unsuccessful attempts in the early 1960s to speak to Mayor Wagner or to get the mayor to attend Congress activities.[36]

These anticommunist efforts destroyed the independent political leadership of the Puerto Rican community. Some of these, like Jesus Colon, were vestiges of the cigar makers' generation of labor militants. Puerto Ricans no longer had an economic foundation in the workplace as well as in the union from which to incubate new, independent leaders. Puerto Ricans also lacked social and religious institutions that they could control. Without these resources, Puerto Ricans were not able to develop a leadership that was independent enough of the larger society and able to better articulate and represent their interest in that world. What the Puerto Rican community got instead was a professional leadership, trained by universities, skilled at proposal writing, and ready to administer social science solutions to the economic and social crises faced by the Puerto Rican community.

The professional leaders were good enough dancers, skilled at what the rising welfare state demanded of them. They fell short in that they could-n't innovate and were afraid to create a scene. They plodded along when the times required energy. They moved cautiously when the conditions de-manded daring. They introduced and prepared the Puerto Rican commu-nity to and prepared it for the legal and bureaucratic demands of the civil rights movement and the antipoverty programs but for very little else. That movement and those federal programs offered untold promises that mostly came up empty. Eventually, they exhausted the spiritual and emo-tional reserves of the Puerto Rican community.

The professional style of dance was timid, uninspired, and unproduc-tive. Worse yet, the professional style of dancing did nothing to bring Puerto Ricans greater notice or acclaim on the dance floor. In the raucous period of the 1960s, they were easily forgotten. Instead, by pursuing the professional path, the Puerto Rican community became less attractive and less respected as well as cast adrift along the marginal economic, political, and cultural spaces of U.S. society. The power that the Puerto Rican com-munity had attained in the early 1950s had been squandered and lost by the 1960s decade. Amazingly, Puerto Ricans found a way to again create some power by the end of the decade with the emergence of the Young Lords movement.

4

Puerto Rican Marginalization
1965 to the Present

As the garbage burned and the flames grew, people nearby cheered spontaneously. We all felt the spirit of winning, the triumph of good over evil, where justice, in this moment, prevailed.

—Miguel Melendez 2003, 105

Mickey Melendez wrote those words more than thirty years after the Young Lords collected and burned garbage in the barrio of East Harlem as a protest to get the city to clean the streets. Today, he and many others view that theatrical summer of 1969 as the high point of Puerto Rican community influence in New York City (Gandy 2002, 733). By burning the garbage in the streets, the Young Lords got Mayor Lindsay to notice and to negotiate a temporary peace with them. Political scientists like to talk about "authoritative values" in the body politic that shape and inform policymaking. It's clear that the Young Lords pushed against the boundaries of acceptable practice between Puerto Ricans and the rest of society. They lessened the deep official neglect felt by Puerto Ricans in New York City, a neglect that permitted public officials and the public to tolerate dirty streets, poor sanitation, and much else in East Harlem. The Lords made the city heed the needs of Puerto Ricans, even if only temporarily and even if only in East Harlem.

Melendez was right. The garbage protest was a moment of influence and power like no other for the Young Lords, if not for all Puerto Ricans. It wasn't the protest itself, however, that gave Puerto Ricans some power. It was the drama of that high pile of garbage burning in the middle of the street that hot summer evening. It was the feverish image of rage and defiance in the faces of old and young Puerto Rican men and women. It was the presence of the television and print media, drawn by the theater and novelty of Puerto Ricans burning garbage. It was the weight of a media sector possessed of the salient recognition that garbage could bring down a mayor and a city that had barely survived an eight-day sanitation strike the year before.[1] In essence, the garbage protest was effective because it played to the weaknesses and strengths of the city's politics and to the insatiable appetite and impact of the media industry in contemporary U.S. politics.

The rise and fall of the Young Lords organization was the key historic moment in the Puerto Rican community story of power in the period from the 1960s onward. It was key for a number of reasons. The garbage protest was the best effort by Puerto Ricans to make effective use of the symbolic language of the new politics driven by the media. The rise of this radical group also demonstrated, for Puerto Ricans, the extent of this community's alienation from the dominant political and cultural values of the larger society during the late 1960s.[2] This would have a dramatic impact on this community for years to come.

There were various signs of this shift. One sign was the many riots in this period by Puerto Ricans angered by poverty, police brutality, bad housing, and marginalization. Between 1964 and 1971, there were twenty-eight violent riots by Puerto Ricans in different U.S. cities (Carter 1992).[3] It was evident when two thousand Puerto Ricans in the Bronx rioted in October 1966 in response to a boxing official's decision that Puerto Rican lightweight champion Carlos Ortiz had lost a fight ("Mexicans Target" 1966). It was evident to reporters who, digging into the background of the East Harlem riot of 1967, found not assimilation into the wider culture but a "blending of cultures in the teenage generation" between blacks and Puerto Ricans ("The Puerto Ricans: Behind" 1967). It came in the rise of Salsa and the resuscitation in New York of traditional Puerto Rican music like Bomba and Plena.[4] In a variety of different ways, then, Puerto Ricans wrestled some autonomy and separation not only from Puerto Rico but also from what the adopted city of New York wanted and expected from them.

It is tempting to view these activities as a kind of resistance or, at the other extreme, as simply disorganized hedonism. It was neither and both. The alienation of Puerto Ricans from the wider culture was neither planned nor an accidental. It had and didn't have a target. The opposition of Puerto Ricans to the United States was frameless, immature, and conflicted. The alienation of Puerto Ricans from New York City was, however, about power. These movements, like those on the dance floor, happened without long-range strategic plans. Puerto Rican steps were more reactive than deliberate. They did aim at greater power, however.

As the larger society rejected and neglected them, Puerto Ricans simply moved farther away, out of reach. They moved away from the larger society yet closer to new beats and styles that they found more embracing.

They synchronized their moves with those of other Puerto Ricans and of African Americans. At one level Puerto Ricans did seem to understand that their increasing rejection by the larger society required that they take matters into their own hands. They had to demonstrate, as Janeway once put it, their "refusal to accept the definition of oneself that is put forward by the powerful" (Janeway 1980, 167). The Young Lords period is the best example of that. At other levels, however, Puerto Ricans simply pursued dance with more willing partners. What is clear is that in all these different ways, Puerto Ricans pursued interests and reached for power.

The Young Lords were thus pivotal for Puerto Rican community power in the post-1960s period for a variety of reasons. First, the efforts of the Lords stand out as one of the most radical moments in the Puerto Rican community's efforts to wrestle more power for themselves. Second, the Lords were fairly effective in helping Puerto Ricans make better use of the media. Third, the Lords were more successful than most in getting the larger society to pay attention to Puerto Rican community needs and demands. And finally, after the Lords period, both the Puerto Rican community and the larger society turned increasingly away from each other though with more complexity after this period than before.

Puerto Ricans did gain some power in the larger society as a result of the opposition and independence offered by the Lords. Some of it was indirect. Radicalism and extremism made moderates, like Badillo, a lot more attractive to the rest of society. And the rejection of dominant social values represented by the Lords reduced dependence on society and reduced society's power over Puerto Ricans. Still, the withdrawal from the larger society after the Lords didn't immediately increase Puerto Rican power. That withdrawal, however, did initially reduce the impact of the larger society's power over Puerto Ricans.

In the long term, the larger society was able to recover power against Puerto Ricans by incorporating Puerto Rican elites into its economic and political institutions. As a result, Puerto Ricans have experienced a general loss of power since the Lords period. That loss has not been easily checked or reversed by demographic expansion, ethnic solidarity, voter registration drives, voting turnouts, or the election of Puerto Rican and other sympathetic individuals to political office.

Facing rejection and neglect, Puerto Ricans turned from and, in some ways, distanced themselves from the larger society after 1960. Puerto Ricans attempted to displace old needs and wants in order to garner some power. By these various acts of distancing, Puerto Ricans tried to dance to their own music. There was nothing natural or inevitable about this growing alienation from the larger society. Most commentators in the 1950s had predicted, in fact, that Puerto Ricans would assimilate easily into the wider culture. Thus, Oscar Handlin was fairly confident in 1959 that "Puerto Ricans have followed the general outline of the experience of earlier immigrants" (Handlin 1959, 120). Even city administrator Charles F. Preuse claimed in 1955 that he was "convinced that the full integration of Puerto Ricans into the life stream of New York would be swift—perhaps swifter than that of earlier waves of migration" (Preuse 1955).

As late as 1965, Clarence Senior agreed with a social worker that Puerto Ricans were "being assimilated into the life of the city faster than any previous group" (Senior 1965, 53). These predictions were not completely baseless. Puerto Ricans did show some signs of assimilation and incorporation. What most of these commentators missed, however, was that those acts of incorporation had brought more weakness than power for Puerto Ricans.

Puerto Ricans lost power as a result of their wholesale rejection by the larger society from the late 1950s onward. Puerto Ricans no longer seemed to offer the larger society much that had economic and cultural value. As citizens, to be sure, Puerto Ricans still possessed some political value. They could vote and occasionally provided swing votes in close elections. As Puerto Ricans became a racial minority, they found that they were sometimes able to engage the larger society better within the world created by the new public attention given to the fight for civil rights and the plight of minorities. Despite these new possibilities, the specific political interest the city had in Puerto Ricans, during the early 1950s, was gone. In almost every possible way, Puerto Ricans seemed to offer little to interest or entice the larger society. The radical actions of the Lords were, in that sense, a logical, and extreme, flowering of this growing rift between Puerto Ricans and U.S. society.

The Puerto Rican movement away from white society was partial and cautious. Essentially, Puerto Ricans hovered around, not too far away from white America. The reverse wasn't true, however. White America didn't seem to know or care that Puerto Ricans were moving out of sight. The emergence of the Lords was, in many respects, a kind of tonic. They demanded notice and got it. White America seemed surprised to discover a Puerto Rican community "hiding" in plain sight. More importantly and ironically, it was the separatist, militant initiative of the Lords that succeeded in drawing some rudimentary public attention and interest towards Puerto Ricans. The Lords made Puerto Ricans an exciting and exotic novelty as well as a menace whose demands and activities seemed to aspire to the highest humanitarian ideals. In a word, the Lords made Puerto Ricans hard to ignore on political and cultural levels. And that brought some power, temporarily.

The Lords also had some part in changing Puerto Ricans. Though the

Lords' input was not the dominant factor in these changes, they helped to tip them. The changes after 1970 were remarkable. Essentially, the Puerto Rican community became, in a myriad of ways, less interested in the economic, political, and cultural worlds fashioned for them by the wider society. Puerto Ricans dropped out of school and the mainstream economy in greater numbers after 1970. Criminal and drug-abuse activity increased. More Puerto Ricans entered the underground economy.[5] Puerto Ricans also began to turn their cultural concerns towards more specifically Puerto Rican practices. Thus, Puerto Ricans in East Harlem resurrected old musical styles like Bomba and Plena. Also, the first casitas, small-scale replicas of nineteenth-century Puerto Rican dwellings, began to appear in the South Bronx.[6] Many Puerto Ricans also left New York City in a "return migration" to Puerto Rico or dispersed to other U.S. cities and regions.

These were not abrupt developments. In many cases, they were merely an amplification of changes already underway in the Puerto Rican community since the early 1960s. Also, though the post-Lords alienation mentioned above was significant and broad, overall Puerto Ricans remained basically ambivalent about their place in the United States. Were they Puerto Ricans or Americans? Were they white or nonwhite? Was their place in the United States or in Puerto Rico? In most respects, Puerto Ricans then and now continue to struggle with these questions without any clear resolution.[7]

What the Lords accomplished was to make the Puerto Rican option as real and attainable as the other. The consequences, both good and bad, are still being felt today. This was not just an ideological shift. The Lords taught Puerto Ricans new dance steps, new ways to live. They taught Puerto Ricans, essentially, to chart their own course for power in New York by turning towards what is Puerto Rican as well as by more expertly using the media to draw attention to their demands and express their uniqueness. Unlike the nationalists, who called for the preservation of an unconquered past, the Lords were situated in the tumble and conflicts of their own period, in the city, in the media, and in the imagination of a public that aspired to a future virtue even as it remained stuck in racist and inequitable muck. The Lords pointed the Puerto Rican community towards an imagined and more just future.

The Lords could not, however, establish the Puerto Rican community as a permanent and respected dancer in the city. The Lords simply could not change the fundamentally depressed interest of the larger society in what the Puerto Rican community had to offer. Puerto Ricans gained no lasting power from the Lords period because the city and the media acquired no lasting interest in Puerto Ricans beyond the spectacles and theatrics of that period. By the middle to late 1970s, as the city struggled with a fiscal crisis and economic woes, Puerto Ricans were once again forgotten and scorned. When political officials and newspapers sought to understand the impact of these economic problems on minorities, in most cases it was African Americans who got their attention. One typical 1980 *New York Times* article on the problems of youth unemployment in this period, for example, indicated that the bigger problem was a lack of data on *blacks and Chicanos*, no mention was made of Puerto Ricans ("First" 1980).

The Lords and the garbage protest were, nonetheless, a pivotal moment in Puerto Rican community history because it represented the first time that this community took note of the heavy hand played by the media in American politics and power. Puerto Ricans awoke to this new reality and took dramatic and productive action. That the power this produced was not long lasting says more about the limited interests of the larger society than it does about Puerto Ricans. The Lords' actions and contributions were a clear departure from the steady marginalization of the Puerto Rican community in the 1960s period that came before them.

Puerto Rican Marginalization before the Lords

In the October 1969 mayoral debate, each of the three major candidates spoke positively about helping minorities and increasing city services. Surprisingly, even Mario A. Procaccino, a conservative Democrat, spoke about how

> it's very important in the time of crisis that we're in today to see to it that those who are disadvantaged, whether they be Negroes, whether they be Puerto Ricans, whether they be whites, receive what I should call particular and special attention and treatment in order to bring themselves to the level both in education, housing and other areas.[8]

Procaccino's comments are surprising in light of the fact that Puerto Ricans had become increasingly marginalized from the larger society during the decade of the 1960s. This attention from Procaccino may have been one of the first indications of the Lords' impact. During the 1960s, the gulf between Puerto Ricans and the rest of U.S. society had become wider. Puerto Ricans, as a result, had a harder time getting noticed and counted. The exact nature and extent of this marginalization is hard to establish with certitude. Growing poverty and unemployment certainly provide evidence that life had changed for Puerto Ricans in the 1960s. Can we

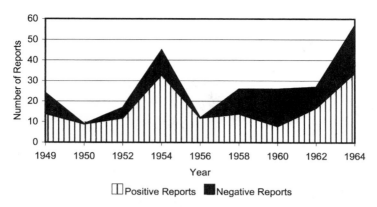

Figure 4.1. Total Positive and Negative *NY Times* Reports on PRs, 1949 to 1964. *Source*: NY Times Index.

attribute this shift to a decreasing interest in the political and economic value of the Puerto Rican community? Yes. One large sign was in the media.

The print and electronic media don't necessarily or always represent the perspective or concerns of elites or social structures. They are certainly "a site of struggle" over the meaningful place of various class and racial groups in our society (Cottle 2003, 6). As a contested place and process, the print and electronic media do often represent the relative short- and long-term strength and success of dominant and subordinate groups in promoting their particular views and political agendas. Newspaper reporting data is thus a useful way to begin to give flesh to the notion of increasing Puerto Rican marginalization in this period.

An analysis of newspaper reporting data shows that, actually, the *New York Times* paid more attention to Puerto Ricans during the 1960s than one would expect. That attention was, however, selective and politicized. Overall, and especially at the national level, Puerto Ricans remained essentially ignored. The analysis of one particular kind of reporting, obituaries, reveals, in fact, that Puerto Ricans and Puerto Rico entered national media consciousness, at least as suggested by obituary reports, only when they posed political problems. This analysis of newspaper reports provides a good way to chart the ebb and flow of the relationship of the larger society towards the Puerto Rican community.

As figure 4.1 reveals, newspaper reports in the *Times* actually increased during the 1960s. There were twice as many reports on Puerto Ricans in 1964 as there were in 1962. A closer look at this data reveals why. Figure 3.2 in chapter 3, which compares *"New York Times* Reporting on Puerto Ricans to Reporting on Puerto Rican Professionals," shows that the *Times* began to pay greater attention to the emerging professional class of leaders in the Puerto Rican community in the 1960s. Thus figure 3.2 shows that the large increases in reporting on Puerto Ricans can be mostly accounted for by the greater attention paid to Puerto Rican professionals. This is in line with the growing role of professionals in negotiating and managing federal antipoverty funds (Padilla 1972, 17). Except for this attention given to Puerto Rican professionals involved in the politics of civil rights and poverty, however, Puerto Ricans basically went unnoticed.

This is clear from the table on subject area reporting. In table 4.1, *New York Times* reporting on Puerto Ricans is broken down by subject area and time period. This table shows that in news reports on Puerto Ricans in the period from 1949 onward, the *New York Times* focused more on economic issues in the early 1950s, on educational issues in the early 1960s, and on political issues in the Puerto Rican community by the late 1960s.

The changes in press attention reflected the changing status of the Puerto Rican community in the city of New York during this period. In the early 1950s, Puerto Ricans were an important factor in helping to meet the city's need for cheap, compliant labor. By the early 1960s, the continued migration of Puerto Ricans, with a preponderance of young children, to New York created considerable strains on a weak and ineffectual public educational system. Public education is also a loaded political issue, often serving as an instrument used by newspapers and the public to evaluate the effectiveness of any mayoral regime. Later, the emergence of the expansion of federal government spending, particularly in the antipoverty programs, created opportunities for funding, political conflict, and greater public attention that were registered in the changes in *New York Times* reporting.

The attention paid to Puerto Rican educational issues are to be expected since Puerto Rican political and professional leaders themselves made a great deal of noise about the problems of education in the Puerto Rican community during the early 1960s. The attention the *New York Times* showed towards these concerns raised by Puerto Rican professionals, however, demonstrates the selective process of incorporation that accepts some Puerto Rican leaders and their demands but not others. Gilberto Gerena-Valentin, for example, was largely ignored despite the fact that he was one of the most prominent, yet radical, nationalists within the Puerto Rican community during the 1950s and 1960s.[9]

Later, Puerto Ricans began to shift their focus to civil rights and the federal government's anti poverty programs. Antonia Pantoja, for example, founded Aspira, the Puerto Rican high school advocacy program, in 1961. The stated goal was to solve some of the problems of Puerto Rican

TABLE 4.1
NY Times *Reporting on PRs by Subject Area, 1949 to 1964*

Year	Hsing	Eco	Educ	Pol	Cult	Pop
1949	0	8	0	12	1	1
1950	1	7	0	0	0	1
1952	7	4	0	1	0	5
1954	5	7	0	23	7	3
1956	0	2	1	8	0	1
1958	3	5	1	9	6	2
1960	11	0	0	15	0	0
1962	9	5	5	3	3	2
1964	8	10	1	30	7	1

Source: New York Times Index.

youth in the schools as well as to "develop educated leaders committed to the resolution of the problems at the policy levels, in the political and economic spheres of the total society" (Pantoja 2002, 98).[10] This was an imitation of the "Jewish Model" for minority community development. It incorporated education, leadership training, and ethnic solidarity. This erstwhile model ignored the fact that jobs, incomes, and racial recalibrations had already landed Jews in the market opportunities and arms of white America before Jews had actually raised their educational levels, organized themselves, and produced what some Jews now derisively label as an ethnic culture of "symbolic Judaism" in America.[11]

Pantoja was not interested in assimilation. She helped to give Aspira a clear mission to advance and retain Puerto Rican culture among the young Puerto Ricans in New York. Pantoja, thus, wasn't interested in a purely professional approach to advancement. However, it is clear that she believed that only the creation of a cadre of Puerto Rican leaders, who could advocate on behalf of Puerto Ricans, could solve the crisis of the Puerto Rican community. This was an approach that coincided with growing concerns in the city about the educational system. Thus, between 1961 and 1963, the *New York Times* published fifty-nine articles about the education of Puerto Ricans in New York City. Almost all of these articles were negative, focusing on low test scores, segregation, and other school problems. It was attention, nonetheless. Most of that press attention was, no doubt, a result of the activities of Pantoja and Aspira. The data so far does not seem to suggest a great deal of estrangement, however.

Clearly, Puerto Ricans were not completely unknown and marginalized. They were certainly not invisible in New York City. Yet the attention Puerto Ricans received was selective, sporadic, very local, and temporary. The key is that, on the national level, Puerto Ricans were and remain invisible. This is substantiated by the analysis of obituary reports.

One way to assess the value of individuals and groups in society is to compare obituaries. In most societies, newspapers devote print space only to those individuals they think have lived noteworthy lives. Since this space is limited, the inclusion of individuals from particular groups and the amount of space devoted to describing their lives are reasonably good indicators of the place and value that a newspaper and, by implication, society gives to that individual and his or her ethnic-racial group. As Ball and Jones explain, "the number of column inches allotted to each soul conveys just how famous or important the *New York Times* thinks that someone is" (Ball and Jones 2000, 6). Unlike other newspapers, the *New York Times* does not charge for obituaries. In fact, the *Times* assigns a special reporter to interview famous people before they die in order to be ready with an obituary when they do pass away. For those reasons, a *Times* obituary is a good indicator of who the newspaper and society thinks has "made a constructive contribution to society" (ibid., 2).

The data in table 4.2 compares obituaries from 1940 to 1978 for Puerto Ricans, Dominicans, Cubans, and African Americans in the *New York Times* and other newspapers. It records the number of obituaries for these groups compiled from different newspapers by *Obituaries on File*. These are listed under four ethnic-racial categories. It also identifies the number of obituaries for people who are not, in fact, members of that ethnic-racial group but who were indexed as an obituary for that group because they had some connection to those groups or places associated with them.

Many obituaries were for individuals who played an important role in the affairs of particular ethnic-racial groups but who were not, in fact, members of those groups. Counted under the Puerto Rican category, for example, were many non–Puerto Rican administrators, military officers, and governors who served in Puerto Rico. As the table shows, furthermore, there were an absolute greater number of obituaries for "Puerto Ricans" in the pre-1961 period than after. These included both Puerto Ricans and non–Puerto Ricans. The 1950s period thus saw more Puerto Ricans noted in the obituaries of U.S. newspapers. This interest in Puerto Ricans reflected the government building efforts then underway in the island of Puerto Rico with Operation Bootstrap. The data on individuals from the other Caribbean islands illustrates, in comparison, the reality that actual Puerto Ricans had relatively low importance in U.S. society.

Despite the close relationship of Puerto Rico to the United States, many more Cubans were revered at death than Puerto Ricans. This was especially true from 1940 to 1960. In fact, Cuban obituary notices in that period were comparable in number to those of African Americans. This period came prior to the emergence of communist Cuba with Fidel Castro.

TABLE 4.2
Obituary Reports in U.S. Newspapers and the New York Times

	Years			
	1940–50	1951–60	1961–70	1971–78
Puerto Rican				
Puerto Ricans	7	15	5	5
Non-PRs	4	6	0	3
In NYT	0	0	0	2
Dominican				
Dominicans	3	9	6	1
Non-DRs	2	4	1	0
In NYT	0	0	0	0
Cuban				
Cubans	29	25	15	8
Non-Cuban	4	6	3	4
In NYT	0	0	0	0
African-American				
AAs	22	42	21	33
Non-AA	2	2	2	0
In NYT	0	4	3	4

Sources: Data from Felice D. Levy (1979), *Obituaries on File, Volumes 1, 2,* New York: Facts on File; *New York Times Obituary Index.*

Cold War fears could thus not be the explanation. Again, like African Americans, very few of these Cuban obituaries were actually for non-Cubans. This fact represents greater U.S. recognition of the particular achievements of Cubans themselves. This kind of attention was simply not there for Puerto Ricans.

The two Puerto Ricans who were included in the *New York Times* obituary page in the 1970s were the Hall of Fame Baseball player Roberto Clemente and the classical musician Pablo Casals.[12] Musicians and athletes have always figured prominently in the *New York Times* obituary section. One research study reports that over 37 percent of all *New York Times* obituaries are for writers, artists, entertainers, and athletes (Ball and Jones 2002, 392). The percentage is a bit higher, at 49.6 percent, for African Americans (ibid.). Though Puerto Ricans have had their share of successful entertainers and athletes, the *New York Times,* did not recognize them.

This analysis of news and obituary reports demonstrates that Puerto Ricans were mostly invisible to the majority of Americans during the 1960s. What's not yet clear is that this invisibility was the product of the declining interest in Puerto Ricans. There is evidence to suggest, in fact, that the larger society had begun to lose interest in the economic value of Puerto Rican labor in the mid-1950s. This loss of interest became stronger in the 1960s and combined with decreasing interest in the political value of Puerto Ricans and the perpetually low interest in the value of Puerto Rican culture to wreck Puerto Rican chances for power.

Depreciating Economic and Social Value

Most of the larger society's interest in the economic value of Puerto Ricans disappeared during the 1960s. The available research on Puerto Rican poverty and depressed power in the U.S. blames either Puerto Ricans themselves or structural conditions and obstacles seen in either market or class terms. The role of interests, both in Puerto Ricans and the larger society, is ignored. Without interests, however, structures loom like monsters ready to block or devour passive human objects. Without interests, there is no possibility of reclaiming the fact that it is people acting, individually or collectively, that make and keep social structures. And it is in their various interests that reason and weight is given to what they do that either upholds or rejects those structures. In a word, these approaches miss the dance of interests that constitutes power.

For the most part, Puerto Ricans were rebuffed and ignored as dance partners in the economic sphere during the late 1950s. They lost jobs, income, and union support during the 1960s, and they reacted with initial bewilderment, anger, sadness, and action to, respectively, the loss of jobs, union betrayal, declining income, and racist reactions from whites. The problem for Puerto Ricans wasn't just this loss of interest but the lack of viable alternatives. The sons and daughters of *bodegueros* and factory workers could not, because of racism, educational deficits, and tastes, take jobs at the next level as accountants, engineers, teachers, etc. These obstacles were structural and institutional. Obstacles alone, however, do not explain the subsequent decline. Puerto Ricans also took action, resisted, and got angry about the lack of options resulting from these crushing developments.

But much of the response from Puerto Ricans consisted not in resistance but in a drifting away from mainstream society. There was purpose to this drifting. It was to recover honor and power. There is evidence to support this position. In fact, there is no other way to adequately account for what Puerto Ricans experienced and the way they acted in this period. For example, as was mentioned earlier, there was the epidemic of suicides for Puerto Rican prisoners during the 1960s. Ten allegedly killed themselves in 1969 alone. There were thirty suicides in the previous five years ("Tenth Prisoner" 1969). These suicides can be explained as the result of sociological or psychological pathologies. In most cases, such arguments would probably be right. However, the sheer number and timing of these suicides suggests that they might also represent something more than individual pathology.

It's clear that many Puerto Rican prisoners felt as though they would rather die than endure prison sentences or the eventual and, for most of these petty offenders, relatively quick delivery back to the world of freedom. We know that prisoners are more likely to commit suicide if they are newcomers to prison, young, drunk, and full of shame and remorse (Hayes 1983). It is possible that the unusually high rate of prison suicide for Puerto Ricans in the 1960s is related to these factors (Tracey 1972). But there is greater likelihood that growing powerlessness and alienation played a major role in encouraging suicides among Puerto Rican prisoners.

Hopelessness and disappointment was general and social rather than individual for Puerto Ricans. Many Puerto Rican leaders at the time complained about repeated instances of police brutality both in the barrios and in prison (Kihss 1965). Police brutality, like suicide, represents a loss of individual power. Both reflect a sharp loss of influence, respect, and status in the larger world. Whether the prisoner does himself in or dies at the hands of a warden or policeman, the causes and results are the same.

Rejection can inspire all kinds of responses: tempestuous rage in one, calm acceptance in another, self-destruction in yet another. This is as true for a community of workers as for individuals who get spurned by others on the dance floor. Obviously, the act of rejection itself may serve simply as the most proximate cause of actions. Behind the suicides is a hopelessness framed by deep economic and political losses. This was documented in the preceding chapter. Suicides were, in that sense, just one more sign of Puerto Rican alienation in this period.

Puerto Rican suicides, thus, were about community history. Suicides represented as much a community as an individual reaction to loss and despair. That the height of Puerto Rican suicides coincided with rise of the Young Lords means something. One aimed at opposing and defeating the monster; the other gave in to it. The fact that they occurred at the same time suggests that though the Puerto Rican community was troubled and distressed by the downward path it experienced, there was no unified, coherent, and strategic response. To a great extent, this is the plight of working-class, poor, and minority communities. There is never enough of a core, enough reinforcements, enough resources, enough leadership, enough institutional capacity to tie such communities together, provide positive and negative incentives to spur action, and offer a vision and goal of what can be possible with the right sacrifices and effort. There wasn't enough present to permit Puerto Ricans to dance or to dance more effectively with a monster that was blind to their existence.

Puerto Ricans in that period thus remained essentially ambivalent—resisting white views of success while adopting white names, resurrecting old Puerto Rican musical traditions while seeking white approval and acceptance of their music, aligning themselves with African Americans and the civil rights movement while keeping some distance from blacks as a racial category. They rioted and destroyed what was around them as well as killed themselves.

Some of that ambivalence may represent generational shifts. The first migrants to the city may have reacted with pain and hurt at the disappointment of being rebuffed by Americans. The second generation may have had lower expectations and moved towards nonwhite and Puerto Rican influences without the complex sense of regret experienced by the first. What is clear is that, in moving away, Puerto Ricans did not move far enough away. They moved out of reach but not so far as to lose sight of the monster. They could have created a clearer oppositional culture like that of African Americans. Doing so would have given them certain advantages, if the larger society noticed and cared about it.

Instead, Puerto Ricans continued to be unsure of their place in the United States. In the 1960s, Puerto Ricans were confused by the fact that in the United States, "they are Puerto Ricans, while in Puerto Rico they are just people" ("Puerto Ricans" 1969). Then as now, Puerto Ricans struggle to get noticed by other Americans (Ferretti 1970). They remain largely unrecognizable as potential dance partners.

That invisibility does not make Puerto Ricans an "underclass." In William Julius Wilson's writings, an "underclass" is defined by chronic, stagnant joblessness and poverty. Wilson claims that "the development of cognitive, linguistic, and other educational and job-related skills necessary for the world of work in the mainstream economy is . . . adversely affected" by high rates of neighborhood joblessness (Wilson 1987, 57). Wilson explains minority poverty as having a cultural dimension that is the product of a lack of opportunities. This is similar to theories that place Puerto Ricans in "segmented labor markets" or in "ethnic queues" (Berger and Piore 1980; Rodriquez 1974). All of these approaches emphasize the "place" where Puerto Ricans are located at the expense of attending to what those places are and how Puerto Ricans got there.

There is more to be gained by examining what groups like Puerto Ricans do in the pursuit of interests and power. The focus should be on the interests and actions rather than on the "obstacles" or "places." Puerto Ricans have, of course, "failed" at times to get more power. What is important here is not the failure or even the obstacle that helped produce that failure. What is important is that Puerto Ricans sought power, even if power could not be found when and where they searched or with the actual partners that were responsive to them there. We must take into account the fact that "desire animates the world" (Irvine 2006, 2). It is in the pursuit of interests and power that communities shape the nature of the relationship they have with others as well as the nature and extent of the power they can achieve.

Sometimes, the pursuit of interests and power results in cultural behavior and values that help perpetuate disadvantage and weakness in the market. It's simplistic, however, to call this a "culture of poverty" or an "underclass culture." That view perpetuates the idea that things happen to Puerto Ricans or other "disadvantaged" groups. It ignores the role of interests and the active pursuit of power that spring from social agents. It focuses, instead, on the temporary "cultural" resting places. It suggests that things are permanent as well as that the group has only itself to blame.

Puerto Ricans do try to get good jobs and often fail. They fail because of racism, "segmented" markets, being last on job queues, cultural defeatism, and more. What's missing is a recognition that Puerto Ricans acted and continue to act. A job is more than a measure of economic power. It is an attempt at power. That goal doesn't disappear with "failure." It simply becomes diverted into other, occasionally unexpected or illegal, activities. These are the activities that Wilson and others label as representative of the "underclass." That designation describes how Puerto Ricans and others appear from a static and objectified perspective. That view can't explain what got them there, what, in some ways, keeps them there, and what may eventually get them out. It's not an "underclass culture" that keeps Puerto Ricans from advancing.

What holds Puerto Ricans back is the lack of opportunities to dance with those who accept them and can provide them with power. Puerto Rican locations in "ethnic queues" and "segmented markets" are, in this sense, a sign that Puerto Ricans had some "success" in achieving power—limited as it may be. What is disheartening is that power gained this way doesn't last and that, in fact, it returns to Puerto Ricans as domination and defeat. That much is true for any group, however. In that sense, it is probably better to refer to this process as a "culture of power." Culture is, in this sense, neither a dependent nor an independent variable (Gould 1999). It is a manifestation of the way power has been pursued. The difference is not just a matter of semantics. The notion of an "underclass culture" suggests that Puerto Ricans and others have become that position or status. The notion of a "culture of power" suggests that the pursuit of power in a racist and uninterested society has delivered Puerto Ricans and other minorities to distressed and painful stations.

It's true that the market does not offer Puerto Ricans many opportunities. In part, this is the case because they can feel the weight of racism in all of society's institutions and social roles. They are devalued and rejected. They have, as a result, developed a "semi-oppositional culture" that often turns them away from traditional pathways of achievement. The argument here is that this turning away, this reaction, is not just negative and pathological. That is the conclusion reached by Wilson and others who adopt static approaches. They deride Puerto Ricans for dancing with each other and those like them, while they ignore that Puerto Ricans are simply seeking their interests and power with those who would dance with them.

Segmented and dual labor market approaches blame "things" like limited opportunities and racism for perpetuating Puerto Rican poverty. They also assert that Puerto Ricans get "tracked" into low-paying, temporary, dead-end jobs in part because they refuse to accept exploitation in "primary" labor markets by insisting on their rights and by becoming more "politicized" (Baker 2002, 172). The problem with these arguments is that they stop there.[13] They do not explore this refusal to accept exploitation in order to discern why and under what conditions it occurs. The "politicization" of Puerto Ricans in the labor market is, in fact, an attempt to gain more power.

Puerto Ricans are not merely short sighted, however, in not pursuing whatever limited opportunities may exist for them in "secondary" or "segmented" labor markets, something other Latinos and immigrants have done. The lower paying and less stable jobs they could receive that way mean that they could engage the monster. Their dance with the monster, however, would be on very weak terms. Instead, they attempt to dance with the monster on their own terms, utilizing the political moves at their disposal rather than economic ones that lack the necessary verve and impact. They organized themselves at workplaces, demanded their rights as citizens, and launched political movements to shame, scare, and negotiate with others to gain more benefits for their beleaguered community. The political arena is perhaps the only stage where they could dance freely and with spirit.[14]

Puerto Ricans do appear to have hurt themselves. Their actions and reactions seem almost "suicidal" in their apparent overreaction to very real limitations. They appear that way, however, only if we use the standards set by the dominant society. Yes, a casual attitude about work, criminal activities, drug addiction, or dropping out of school does have real and, often, deadly consequences for mainstream success. Wilson calls this a self-perpetuating pathological culture that reproduces the "underclass." Nicholas Lemann makes a more specific charge when he attributes the Puerto Rican "underclass" to the "one-two punch of economic factors, such as unemployment and welfare, and cultural ones, such as neighborhood ambience and ethnic history" (Lemann 1991, 97). One big problem with such claims is that they make culture into another deterministic structure. Culture becomes merely another "opportunity structure the underclass confronts" (Gould 1999, 3). Aside from minimizing the causal role of social structure, the underclass arguments can't explain why minority poor are so "foolish" as to perpetuate such self-destructive behavior and culture.

The "negative social dispositions, limited aspirations, and casual work habits" that Wilson claims to be endemic to minority communities were originally, he says, the result of the limited opportunities and isolation confronting minorities in inner-city communities. Thus, again the argument assumes that minorities are passive and focus on the bad things that happen to these minority communities. Neither Puerto Ricans nor the larger society is perceived as an active social agent. There is no doubt that Puerto Rican actions and, perhaps, their culture often serve to entrench their "underclass" status and domination by others. That argument, however, ignores the way Puerto Ricans act as agents, as movers, as dancers. The point is not just that Puerto Ricans had intentions, good or otherwise, that fell short. What's important is that Puerto Ricans took action in an attempt to reject the dominant society's values and to recast Puerto Rican interests towards alternate goals that they believed were more likely, given their context, to deliver power.

Not able to dance with white America, Puerto Ricans sought to dance with each other. Those interests and actions often did make Puerto Ricans more powerful. The "failure" was that this power was often limited, lost in the corridors and streets of their own limited worlds, too local, too flimsy, and too brief. The pursuit of their subjective interest in each other fails them in the long run. In these ways the underclass charges are true. Puerto Ricans could have reacted better, anticipated the challenges with more foresight, and protected themselves. This is probably true of any individual or group. The underclass argument, however, seems stuck on an accusation that Puerto Ricans have somehow been negligent, short sighted, or irrational.

True or not, such claims ignore the role played by other parties, white America, or the United States as a whole. This dialectic of power is easy to see within a community. Some Puerto Rican men in the 1950s, for example, attempted to regain their withering traditional and patriarchal power by abusing their wives and children, by fencing in their families from the outside dangerous world, or by pursuing a religious orthodoxy that insulated their families from the dominant corrupting influences of the larger society. Some Puerto Rican women, especially the young, chafed at these imposed "rescues" by macho fathers and husbands and launched a strategy of resistance and empowerment that often deposited them into single motherhood, welfare dependence, drug addiction, or even the same religious orthodoxy. Individual actions thus need to be seen in context, as part of a dance, a dialectical movement between actors. In the end, what is missing from the underclass argument is a sense of the complicated process of attraction and rejection that determines power for any group.

The problem for Puerto Ricans is not, thus, a lack of market opportunities or Puerto Rican cultural sensibilities. It's not that there is nothing of value to be found in the market (i.e., jobs, education, etc.). Nor is it that Puerto Ricans don't want them. The evidence, in fact, shows over and over that Puerto Ricans, and most working-class people, want the traditional American promise of jobs, education, and good housing. Nor is it that they don't want them badly enough, that they can't postpone immediate gratification to attain them. One of the sad but telling discoveries in studies of high school dropouts, drug dealers, and other criminals is that even they prefer and yearn for the typical America Dream.

The evidence collected here shows that the dominant vector is not Puerto Ricans but the larger society. For the most part, Puerto Ricans find that the larger society has little interest in dancing with them. Puerto Ricans fight an uphill battle trying to get the larger society to see them as possessors of desirable values. This is not simply an economic issue for Puerto Ricans. It is also, as we've seen, a political and cultural one. Opportunity and obstacles thus represent a passive perspective. It lets major social actors, like capital and the state, as well as Puerto Ricans, off the hook and leaves them out of the active process that determines power.[15] Interestingly, that kind of passive, market perspective has been challenged effectively in books like those by Bourgeois and LeBlanc.

Recent research make clear that popular explanations of the Puerto Rican community's plight don't do enough to identify the forces that impact Puerto Ricans. Good explanations must account for the Puerto Rican response to those forces. Baker suggests, for example, that Puerto Ricans have hurt themselves because they are "politicized to recognize and demand their rights" (2002, 171). Similarly, Bourgeois explains how Puerto Rican crack dealers are not simply victims of deindustrialization and racism. Puerto Rican *jibaros*, he says, "are also searching for dignity and fulfillment" (1995, 324). They search for and sometimes find respect, even if what makes respect possible often ends up destroying them as well.

It is the search for respect, for instance, that is the rational framework that explains why they would insist on buying single bottles of beer while hanging out in front of bodegas rather than six-packs that are a lot cheaper. Single bottles take a bigger bite out of their meager budgets. Buying and drinking single beers means, however, that they can avoid sharing their beer and meager budgets with others while they also avoid getting a "reputation for being greedy for refusing your friends" (LeBlanc 2003, 146). In this way, Puerto Ricans end up with a quenched thirst, an intact reputation, and less money in their pockets. Single bottles are thus good for social respect but bad for personal budgets.

Puerto Ricans, like members of any community, seek power and continue to offer much that is of value. The problem is that the larger society doesn't always appreciate the values Puerto Ricans offer. This was, for example, the Puerto Rican experience in the garment industry. Beth Osborne Daponte wrote that Puerto Ricans, especially women, lost jobs in the garment industry during the 1960s primarily because "other Hispanic women would work as operators for lower wages while Puerto Rican women would not" (Daponte 1996, 165). Puerto Rican women didn't lose their skill or desire to work. Employers, moreover, still saw them as skilled. The problem for Puerto Ricans was that there were other Hispanic women with similar skills who were willing to work for less. It was in this context that Puerto Rican women "withdrew from the labor force" (ibid.). Employers no longer valued the skills they still had at the price Puerto Ricans could accept,

Puerto Ricans were also undesired as consumers. They are very poor, and marketing companies avoid them. Even studies on Hispanic consumers have tried to separate Puerto Ricans from the larger Hispanic community and denigrate the opportunities they offered as consumers. One study in 1967, for example, declared that "*ghettos* are mostly Puerto Rican" and thus "not necessarily representative of the standards of the Spanish-speaking population living outside the *ghettos*" (Velilla 1967, 20). That study wanted marketing companies to realize that there were two million Latinos mostly outside the "ghettos," mostly in the suburbs, and "available to be captivated" (ibid., 46). Another study warned that retailers should not expect much from Puerto Ricans since only 47 percent of Puerto Ricans shopped outside their immediate neighborhoods (Andreasen 1982, 9). This compared with the 76 percent of blacks and 60 percent of poor whites who ventured outside their neighborhoods to shop.

This combination of a loss of interest by white employers/businesses and the withdrawal or marginalization of Puerto Ricans was repeated in many different fields, even the music industry. Puerto Ricans, for example, made vital contributions to the origins and development of Hip Hop culture but have been largely ignored and dismissed by the music industry and consumers. Puerto Ricans have been identified as making a contribution to Hip Hop mainly through break dancing. The dance side of Hip Hop, however, has not become as popular as the music, nor has it had much commercial success.[16]

The reasons for this specific marginalization are clear. Rivera writes that African Americans have profited more from Hip Hop because of their "dexterity in the English language, being most easily traceable to a U.S.

Black oral tradition, and primarily employing records of music considered to be Black" (Rivera 2001, 238). The reasons are thus tied to the long wave of social interest and attention to African American culture. In the short run, there is little that Puerto Ricans can do about the comparative advantages of African American culture in American society. What's more important is that this comparison highlights the important role of societal interests in defining a group's capacity to influence others.

Recent history shows that Puerto Ricans are more likely to dance with themselves than with others. This encourages greater marginalization. Certainly, that's what it looks like from the main dance floor. From the perspective of the dominant institutions, Puerto Ricans are located somewhere along the edges. Puerto Ricans have reacted by drawing away from the larger society. Marginalization, however, is not just about Puerto Ricans. It also describes a reality in which the larger society has largely lost interest in Puerto Ricans.

Social Capital

On the surface, this dance argument resembles social capital theory (see Young 1999). Social capital is distinguished from economic and human capital in that it is about the collective bonds and community that define group identity (Goulbourne and Solomos 2003, 332). Social capital is not something possessed purely in individuals. It is more a collective property than human and financial capital. It is treated, however, as a kind of possession that determines individual outcomes. The emphasis in this study, however, is on what the groups value and the actions they take, the dancing, to advance their interests and power.[17]

In one glaring example of the failures of the capital approach, Landale et al. argue that Puerto Ricans drop out and, as a consequence, lose human and social capital (Landale et al. 1999). The more amazing outcome is that of those Puerto Ricans who acquired more social capital in the dominant society by speaking English. Greater social and human capital should, according to the theory, produce greater social mobility in education, work, health care, etc. Landale's study found the opposite happening. It explains the deterioration of Puerto Rican health in the United States as the partial result, among other factors, of what Landale et al. call "negative assimilation." They use this term to account for the fact that the increased ability to speak English for second- and third-generation Puerto Ricans actually correlates with the unexpected and tragic effect of higher infant mortality. The Landale study explains this negative result of "assimilation" as the product of poor education and the fact that Puerto

Ricans "tend to settle in central-city areas of large Northeastern cities, where they experience high rates of joblessness, discrimination, and exposure to negative influences of subcultures of native-born minorities" (Landale et al. 2000, 906). Speaking English is thus a social capital that kills rather than helps for Puerto Ricans living in segregated communities, according to the Landale study.

The problem with social and human capital explanations is the focus on "capital" as a deficit.[18] This deficit model can't explain why Puerto Ricans speak English, drop out, move to the Northeast, or welcome the influence of "native-born minorities" if doing these things makes them weaker and less competitive in the various "capital" markets. Either they don't know they are losing capital, they don't care, or they think they are getting something better. While a lot of recent theory from the Left and the Right assumes the first two positions, this book argues for the last one. The point is to shift the focus away from the "differential possession of resources," of either an individual or collective nature (Goulbourne and Solomos 2003, 332).

Puerto Ricans pursue power, and in the short term often get it, sometimes by valuing the "street" capital of their own people and other native-born minorities. In the process, Puerto Ricans have discovered that, as even the Landale study admitted, "a strong orientation toward Puerto Rican culture does reduce the impact of low socioeconomic status" (Landale et al. 2000, 905). The move towards all things Puerto Rican actually produces immediate benefits.

Dancing often does get better as Puerto Ricans reclaim self-respect, skill, and influence by directing their interests and efforts towards other Puerto Ricans who welcome and enjoy what they have to offer. The problem is that it just doesn't get better for long. Dancing with other Puerto Ricans or African Americans has a long-term liability. It reduces the amount of dancing Puerto Ricans can do with white America, the dominant dancer on the floor. The Puerto Rican ability to get white Americans interested in distinctive Puerto Rican economic, political, and cultural values is seriously eroded by this act of social distancing. This, as a consequence, forms a serious check on Puerto Rican power.[19]

Data hides and reveals. The data shows that in the decade of the 1960s Puerto Ricans dropped into an "underclass," onto the end of the "queue." On one level, this claim is irrefutable. It is the "snapshot" that most people can easily recognize. That snapshot, however, leaves out a lot of information. It leaves out the movements that landed Puerto Ricans at that position in this society. A more comprehensive understanding requires paying attention to the historical interaction of Puerto Ricans to the larger society in this period. It means paying attention to the Puerto

Rican dance of interests and pursuit of power that is so often ignored in current research. Doing so is about more than setting the record straight in some methodological way. It's the only way to adequately account for the changes in power. That historical and relational context helps to reshape the popular explanations for Puerto Rican economic decline in the 1960s.

In 1964, the Puerto Rican Forum reported, "the Puerto Rican rather than the Negro is the bottom man on the ladder here."[20] The report went on to emphasize that "contrary to widespread belief, Puerto Ricans as such are not making their way as did earlier immigrant groups, such as the Irish and Italians" (ibid.). Note the ambivalent racial calibrations presented by the Puerto Rican Forum's remarks, the way the report sought to position Puerto Ricans in some murky space between African Americans and European immigrants. This positioning of Puerto Ricans in a space that overlapped both African Americans and white Americans was representative of the way Puerto Ricans projected themselves to the wider community in the 1960s. The ambivalent nature of Puerto Rican racial identity was a source of both strength and weakness in the Puerto Rican relationship to the larger society.

Economic Decline

Even as Puerto Ricans lost jobs and income in the 1960s period, the Puerto Rican division of labor shifted towards white-collar and professional occupations. Those Puerto Ricans who remained employed, thus, more closely reflected the general contours of the overall New York City economy. Puerto Ricans, however, remained underrepresented in key industries, professions, and the public sector. That correspondence to the larger economy, furthermore, came with real setbacks in wages and employment for Puerto Ricans.

Among the economic setbacks in this period were wages that trailed those of white families by half and of African Americans by $1,200, a drop in white-collar employment from 17 percent of all Puerto Rican white men to 12 percent, and increases in welfare participation from 29 percent of all those on relief in the city to about 40 percent in 1968. The labor-force participation of Puerto Rican women declined from 41.8 percent in 1960 to 27.4 percent in 1970 (Daponte 1996). Puerto Rican school dropout rates also got higher. Only 1.2 percent of all Puerto Rican high school graduates were getting an academic diploma that could lead to college.[21] Given these conditions, it's no wonder that Puerto Rican civil rights leader Gerena-Valentin concluded that Puerto Ricans faced not only a lack of "meaningful jobs" but also a "gap of power" (ibid.). But it wasn't for want of trying.

Structural explanations of the Puerto Rican economic condition are useful but often don't go very far. The decline in Puerto Rican employment and labor force participation is, for example, attributed to the idea that Puerto Ricans migrated to New York City at the wrong time. Puerto Ricans, in this sense, are made to be the victims of bad timing. It's their fate. If only they had come a little earlier. This timing argument suggests that their economic condition would have been radically improved if only Puerto Ricans had come to New York in greater numbers in the early 1900s. The problem for Puerto Ricans, however, wasn't bad timing. Puerto Ricans migrated to New York City when they did precisely because of economic and political forces unleashed by the U.S. occupation of Puerto Rico.

The invasion and colonization of Puerto Rico occurred during a period when industrial and occupational changes in the United States had already begun to produce new professional and white-collar jobs. Educational institutions, like New York's City University, responded by expanding and admitting more students, many from previously despised groups like Jews and Italians. Those industrial changes created professional and middle-class occupations as well as a tremendous demand for cheap labor in the 1940s and '50s. Thus, it was the push of colonial policies in Puerto Rico and the pull of newly available low-paying jobs in the United States that encouraged Puerto Ricans to migrate. The government of Puerto Rico contributed to this process by training Puerto Ricans for low-skilled service and industrial work, like in the garment field. In the late 1940s, the New York State Employment Service collaborated with the government of Puerto Rico to provide Puerto Rican women with training in "modern cleaning methods, home nursing, cooking hygiene and child care" ("Puerto Ricans Here" 1948).

In addition, the governments of the United States and Puerto Rico perpetuated and consolidated the colonial identity of Puerto Ricans as cheap and pliable labor. New York State's Department of Employment very proudly reported in 1950, for example, that they had sent "twice as many Puerto Ricans from New York City on up-state farms between May and November as were placed last year" ("City Seeks" 1950). A noted labor study gleefully predicted in 1954 that the availability of primarily operative jobs would far "exceed the influx of Puerto Ricans" ("Survey Finds" 1954). All of these different measures were a realization of the main colonial goals of Operation Bootstrap in Puerto Rico. The director of Bootstrap, Teodoro Moscoso, explained before the United Nations in 1961 that its goals were to attract industry through "the offer of a

TABLE 4.3
Puerto Rican and Latino Bodegas in New York City, 1970 to 1997

	1957	1970	1985	1997
Number	4,000	7,500	6500*	3,734*
Per 1,000 PRs	7	8.9	7.4	4.6

Sources: Peter Kihss, "Gains Made Here by Puerto Ricans," *NY Times*, 5/31/1957; "City Bodegas Fill Many Roles," *NY Times*, 8/3/1970; "Latin Oasis: To Hispanics in the U.S., a Bodega or Grocery Is a Vital Part of Life," *NY Times*, 3/15/1985; Mireya Navarro, "Puerto Rican Presence Wanes in New York," *NY Times* 2/28/2000.
* Includes Bodega ownership for Puerto Ricans and Latinos

trained, abundant and low-cost labor market, tax benefits, political stability and an attractive climate" ("Puerto Rico Cited" 1961). This was as true for Puerto Ricans in the United States as it was in Puerto Rico

The focus on interests and actions could suggest that Puerto Ricans have acted impulsively, irrationally, and self-destructively. To the extent that this is true, however, Puerto Rican culture is not to blame. Support for this position can be found in Puerto Rican business ownership patterns. Puerto Ricans have owned bodegas and other businesses in the United States since they first started arriving. The rates of ownership for Puerto Ricans are much lower than for other immigrant groups. What's interesting is that Puerto Ricans actually increased their ownership of bodegas as they began to lose their economic footing in the 1960s and then began to drop ownership later on.

As table 4.3 shows, in 1957 Puerto Ricans owned seven bodegas for every one thousand Puerto Ricans living in New York City. By 1970, that ownership rate rose to 8.9 per one thousand. By all empirical and anecdotal accounts, bodega ownership rose but dropped dramatically thereafter.

The decline in Puerto Rican bodega ownership needs a closer look. In 1957 Puerto Ricans owned about four thousand bodegas in New York City (see table 4.3). By 1970, Puerto Ricans owned about seven thousand five hundred bodegas. These changes actually indicate the generally lower level of business ownership for Puerto Ricans as a group. As of 1997, Puerto Ricans still had the lowest rate of business company ownership, with only about twenty-one businesses per one thousand population nationwide (see figure 4.2). In 1997, Puerto Ricans owned only 1,248 bodegas nationwide.[22]

This drop in business ownership has, clearly, negative consequences for the Puerto Rican community. This information also makes clear that Puerto Rican culture or attitudes are not to blame for their low rate of business ownership. Puerto Ricans had significant levels of bodega ownership in the early years of their residence in the United States, a time when Puerto Rican culture was presumably more intact. The declines since then have come in the second and third generation, as Puerto Ricans have adapted to and absorbed elements of U.S. culture. There is no solid research on this issue. The possibility that this decline is due to Wilson's underclass cultural adaptation must be discounted, however. Puerto Ricans have sold off their bodegas but remain interested in owning businesses.

The Puerto Rican politician Ramon Velez charged in the late 1980s that six thousand five hundred "Puerto Rican Judases" had betrayed their people by selling their bodegas to Dominicans (Lemann 1991, 101). Judases or not, Puerto Ricans did start other businesses. Puerto Ricans owned almost thirteen thousand businesses in New York City during 1997.[23] Nationwide, Puerto Rican business ownership has also increased in the last two decades. It does remain low, however, especially in comparison to other Latinos and minorities. Figure 4.2 shows that though Puerto Ricans have increased business ownership, they still lag seriously behind others from 1982 to 1997. The reasons, though complex, may be connected to the reality expressed by one community informant that "the new generation has no regard for the public bullshit. We [Puerto Ricans] wanna make easy money" (Bourgeois 1995, 131).

The second and third generations of Puerto Ricans were schooled with a sense of their rights as citizens, the combative period of the civil rights and Young Lords period, as well as a growing realization of their racialized location at the bottom of U.S. society. The bits and pieces of information that are available suggest that this generation no longer accepts the conditions of work and life of their "old school" parents and grandparents. They project a semi-oppositional, often nationalist stance towards

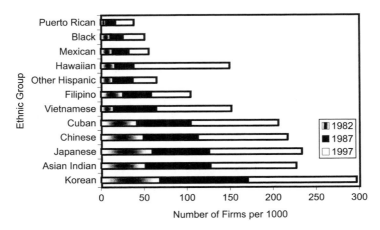

Figure 4.2. Ownership per 1000 by Group. *Sources*: American Demographics, January 1992, p. 34; primary source: U.S. Census Bureau, 1982, 1987, and 1997 Economic Census and Population Estimates

U.S. society and the ideology of achievement. This development in U.S.-born minorities has sometimes been called an "adversarial stance" against the dominant white society (Landale and Oropesa, 2002, 235): "My pop don't know nothin' he still sittin' outside tha' bodega still playin' his dominoes sometimes I drive by 'im jus't look like I GOTTA LOOK like I GOTTA tell myself THAT AIN'T ME, THAT AIN'T NEVER GONNA BE ME."[24]

Puerto Ricans and other minorities develop this opposition to white America in response to poverty and discrimination. As a result, this oppositional stance is also a sign of Puerto Rican agency and the quest for power. Puerto Rican opposition is an attempt to recapture the respect and power Puerto Ricans have lost in the United States as they are pulled to greater poverty, unemployment, and social distress. It is for this reason that Bourgeois argued that Puerto Rican crack dealers "in addition to material subsistence . . . are also searching for dignity and fulfillment" (1995, 324).

Puerto Rican opposition is partial and, probably, inherently limited. Mixed racial identity weakens the level of solidarity as well as their relationship with white America. As Gregory Rodriquez once wrote, "Their diverse origins, plus the absence of a collectively shared history in the U.S., ensure that Latinos will never be as cohesive a group as African Americans" (Rodriquez 2003). The reasons are that Puerto Ricans and other Latinos have an ambivalent and "somewhat fluid status in America's racial order" as well as that Latinos have no history of enslavement in the United States. As a result of these factors, Puerto Ricans and other Latinos inspire neither fear nor guilt in white America.

The primary relation with the rest of America has been one of exclusion and marginalization for Puerto Ricans. Relegation to the margins means there are few opportunities for Puerto Ricans to show off the value of their economic skills, their industrialism, reliability, and dreams for the future. For the most part, white America paid little attention. This made the Puerto Rican quest for power extremely difficult. It also shaped the Puerto Rican search for solutions to their economic, political, and cultural distress. It supplants any resort to more plotting, compliant, and practical approaches in the search for attention and respect with a more militant, oppositional, and, at times, quixotic approach.

Puerto Ricans themselves recognize their own extraordinary stance towards American society. Former Young Lord Wilfredo Rojas is quoted in Whalen as stating that "a lot of folks thought that we were crazy for challenging the system, but it wasn't a question of being crazy. It was a question of gaining respect" (Whalen 2001). Quixotic or not, that Puerto Rican search for respect has a political dimension that has proven just as futile as, though less destructive than, the economic, for the Puerto Rican community.

Political Channels of Interest

The Puerto Rican Forum's 1964 report exemplified all that was right and wrong about Puerto Rican efforts to amass power in the post-1960s period. Puerto Ricans had limited economic capacity to help reverse their economic descent. They were no longer desired as labor nor did they have the support of labor organizations in the garment and other industries to fight on their behalf. As a result, the Puerto Rican community became dependant on Puerto Rican professionals to advocate politically for their economic interests and needs. This professional path was one of the few available to Puerto Ricans at the time. As a path to advancement, however, it was futile so long as the larger society had little interest in the economic, cultural, or political value of Puerto Ricans. Much of the story in the post–Young Lords period consists of recurrent and intense yet futile efforts by Puerto Rican politicians, professionals, and organizations to wrest greater recognition and a little power for Puerto Ricans.

The Puerto Rican Forum worked mightily to confront the challenges of economic decline in the Puerto Rican community. Civil rights strategies eventually gave way to comprehensive approaches involving planning, training, social engineering, and economic development (Falcon 2004, 88). The impact of all of these strategies was minimal, however. Did they not try hard enough? Did they lack good leadership? Did they lack the skills and experience to negotiate the swift currents of American politics? Yes. Sometimes, they did lack these things. However, the main reason for the Puerto Rican Forum's failures has less to do with effort, will, planning, and development strategies and more to do with the reality that Puerto Ricans couldn't get the larger society on the dance floor with them.

The Forum provided Puerto Ricans with fancy dance steps that they didn't get to use enough on a partner. In addition, groups like the Forum believed that Puerto Rican decline was simply a question of deficient human and social capital. Improve Puerto Rican education and training, they thought, and the prospects of Puerto Rican progress would automatically expand. It was an application of what they thought of as the "Jewish Model" of social advancement. This model amounted to economic incorporation with ethnic separation.

The problem with adopting the "Jewish model" was that it ignored the inability of Puerto Ricans to engage the rest of America in serious economic and political ways. It ignored the deep cultural chasm that Puerto Ricans had to span if white and black Americans were ever going give meaning to Puerto Rican needs and group experiences. It ignored the fact that what made the biggest difference in Jewish economic success was that the larger society began to accept Jews as "white" sometime in the post–War World II period.[25] Puerto Rican leaders ignored this deep cultural, racial divide in U.S. society even though it was the association of Puerto Ricans as nonwhites that was at the center of whatever success and failure they had during the civil rights and the antipoverty period.

There are signs that some of the confusion over the racial status of Puerto Ricans has shifted a little. The Puerto Rican community has been increasingly characterized by others, and by themselves, as a nonwhite group. In fact, Landale and Oroposa provide empirical proof that even light-skinned Puerto Ricans are treated as nonwhite by the larger society (2002). There is still some internal and external ambivalence. But, at least on a regional basis, Puerto Ricans have become a kind of black (Sanchez 2005). The larger question is about the foundations of political action and power for the Puerto Rican community. The Puerto Rican Forum's activities in the 1960s were never short of effort, ingenuity, and leadership. What the Forum lacked was an understanding that training, education, votes, and political activity don't automatically produce power. The point is not that they weren't radical enough.

An important part of the Puerto Rican community took the militancy of the Young Lords and tried to channel it into political institutions. Radicals formed other organizations like the Puerto Rican Congress. Reformers tried to utilize that early discontent to continue making demands on the system. This was evident in the creation of the Puerto Rican Legal Defense and Education Fund, Progress, and the various voter-registration drives conducted over the years. Most of these efforts rode on the coattails of the Lords.

The mainstream politicians have utilitarian interest in the Puerto Rican vote. They just want to get elected. Since there are many other Latinos now in cities like New York and Philadelphia, the focus on Puerto Ricans is more diffuse. This is true despite the fact that Puerto Ricans remain the majority of Latino voters in those places. The role of the media is too strong for such facts to matter much. In addition, Latinos are not a homogeneous group that can present itself as one community to the rest of the world. All of this makes it hard to develop a real national identity and presence for Puerto Ricans and Latinos. Neither Puerto Ricans nor whites know what it means to say Latino (see Rivera 2001).[26] Puerto Rican identity is, for that reason, often secured as a kind of black identity. However, even this recognition operates basically on a regional basis (see Sanchez 2005).

What is misleading is that on the surface, Puerto Ricans do appear to be amassing political power. Puerto Ricans have many more elected officials today at local, state, and national levels. As impressive as these achievements are, the complaint by insiders and outsiders alike is that

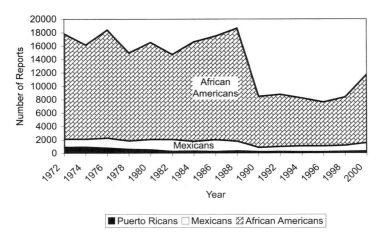

Figure 4.3. Newspaper Reporting on African Americans, Mexicans, and Puerto Ricans, 1972 to 2000. *Sources*: ProQuest Historical Newspaper Database including *New York Times, Washington Post,* and *Times Herald.*

these elected officials don't or can't deliver. Some are locked up within unresponsive political machines. Others push liberal and progressive agendas that make public splashes but get nowhere in local legislatures or the Congress. Some demonstrate great party loyalty and unity in futile hopes of getting grateful colleagues to support bills that address Puerto Rican issues.

Congress members Jose Serrano, Nydia Velazquez, and Luis Gutierrez are good examples of this disconnect. None of them, for instance, has ever dipped below 89 percent in voting along with their party in all their years in the House.[27] They have provided constituents their occasional share of pork barrel grants and some nominal federal grants. For the most part, however, they have accomplished very little. Perhaps too much is expected of them?

What is closer to the truth is the idea that Puerto Rican elected officials have failed because they have not been able to overcome Puerto Rican marginalization. They have not been able to lift the level of national recognition and attention to Puerto Rican issues and needs. As a result, they have not been able to overcome this real limitation. Since the early 1970s period, with the rise of the Young Lords, the coverage of Puerto Ricans in the *New York Times* and other newspapers, for example, has actually declined. Figure 4.3 shows this decline.

The period of highest newspaper attention to Puerto Rican issues and concerns was during the Young Lords period in the early 1970s. The number of articles on Puerto Ricans actually came close to matching the amount of coverage given to Mexicans.[28] Both Puerto Ricans and Mexicans were vastly overshadowed by the coverage given to African Americans.

This history of marginalization can be further demonstrated by an examination of newspaper coverage of the Puerto Rican attempt to stop U.S. military target practice on the Puerto Rican island of Vieques. It was one of the most important and successful protests in Puerto Rican history. The U.S. Navy was forced to end the bombings. Despite that, those Vieques protests in 2000 and 2001 drew more media attention to Al Sharpton than to all of the Puerto Rican leaders that spearheaded those activities.

Vieques Protest

Puerto Ricans have attempted since the early 1970s to stop U.S. military use of Vieques as target practice. Vieques is a partially populated island off Puerto Rico. In 1999, a Puerto Rican/Viequian was killed and several others injured by a stray bomb. The subsequent protests to get the navy out of Vieques rose dramatically after that accident and attracted the attention of various Puerto Rican and non–Puerto Rican mainland political leaders. The use of nonviolent resistance produced arrests that heightened media attention. Most prominent Puerto Rican leaders from Puerto Rico and the United States got involved in this protest movement. The print media, however, hardly noticed them. Instead, as figure 4.4 shows, newspaper coverage was repeatedly drawn to non–Puerto Rican political leaders.

While U.S. newspapers barely noticed Congressman Serrano, New York City mayoral hopeful Freddy Ferrer, or Puerto Rican Legal Defense and Education Fund president Juan Figueroa, they hovered over the words and actions of African American political leader Jessie Jackson and political scion Joseph Kennedy, Jr. The newspapers also absolutely loved Al Sharpton. The coverage he received, as figure 4.4 shows, was greater than that of all Puerto Rican leaders combined. Thus, even on an absolutely Puerto Rican political issue, the national media and the American public hardly noticed Puerto Ricans.

Puerto Rican Protest

Puerto Ricans have a long and distinguished history of protest against discrimination, expensive and poor housing, workplace exploitation, and

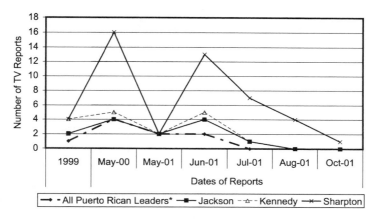

Figure 4.4. TV Reports on Vieques Issue by Political Leader, 1999 to 2001. *Source*: Vanderbilt University Television News Archive (http://tvnews.vanderbilt.edu).

political repression, as well as for political freedom. The record of organizing and institution building has also been impressive. The work of Aspira and the Forum are just two examples. The comparison with African Americans yields some important differences. Puerto Rican membership in the Catholic Church has been a real liability since the church has not proven to be a reliable ally or resource in support of Puerto Rican interests. On the other hand, Puerto Ricans have streamed into Pentecostal churches that have been reluctant to enter the political realm or to incubate an independent Puerto Rican leadership.

Like African Americans, however, Puerto Ricans electoral participation has been historically very low in the United States. Voting data shows that few Puerto Ricans register and few vote. When they do register and vote, Puerto Ricans find that not much happens. Rosa Estades writes that in 1972, two hundred thousand more Puerto Ricans became registered to vote (1978). Badillo led that campaign. Sanchez explained that successful political mobilization and a series of demonstrations had little impact on the public housing policies that kept them from getting admitted (1996, 263). The conclusion seems inescapable. The reason for these failures is that there is little political connection between Puerto Ricans and the larger society.

The gulf between Puerto Ricans and the larger society has been mostly economic and cultural. Politicians needing votes have often turned to Puerto Ricans. Except for those moments discussed in earlier chapters, Puerto Ricans got very little out of these wanton moments of political attention. Now, there are signs that many Puerto Ricans in the United States are beginning to draw away politically from established political leaders and institutions. Some of this increasing political gulf is expressed by Puerto Rican ethnic nationalism.

Flags and Nationalism

Information on the nationalist orientation of the Puerto Rican community is hard to find. The degree of Puerto Rican nationalism is, however, an important element in the movement of Puerto Ricans away from white America. The few studies that are available do suggest that Puerto Ricans have a slightly higher degree of nationalism than other groups. The survey data presented in the *Latino Voices* book, for instance, suggests that they have more nationalism. The authors of this study reported that "only among some of the Puerto Rican respondents was this attachment [to the U.S. government] tempered, with 23 percent expressing 'somewhat' strong love and 8 percent expressing 'not very strong' love" (de la Garza and DiSipio 1992, 79). This data, however, came from a survey of individuals. It lacked insight into whether such nationalist sentiments were more than an individual thought or attitude.

Ethnographic studies have also found some evidence for the salient presence of nationalism in U.S. Puerto Rican communities. Ana Y. Ramos-Zaya's study of the Humboldt Park Puerto Rican barrio, for example, demonstrated that "the performance of Puerto Rican nationalism in Chicago's barrio was premised on separatist rhetoric, community-building strategies, and historical narratives that discredited the very ideological foundation of the American nation and of the American Dream and its postulates of meritocracy, individualism, and equality" (Ramos-Zaya 2003, 236). Ramos-Zayas' study is very insightful. It could not establish, however, the exact extent of nationalism in this Chicago community, or the larger Puerto Rican community in the United States for that matter. To begin to address this issue, I conducted observations of Puerto Rican flag displays during the day on which the Puerto Rican Day Parade is held in Manhattan.

I chose the Bushwick community of Brooklyn in which to study Puerto Rican flag displays because it is a moderately old Puerto Rican community that has experienced tremendous arson, crime, poverty, and political neglect, as well as the recent influx of Latinos from Mexico, the Dominican Republic, and other parts of Central and South America. The block chosen for study was centrally located within a census tract (427) that still has a strong presence of Puerto Ricans.[29] Observations were made in

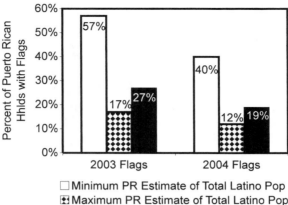

Figure 4.5. Percent of PR Households Displaying PR Flags as an Estimate of Latino Population in CT 427 Bushwick, PR Day Parade 2003–2004. *Source*: Bureau of the Census, U.S. Department of Commerce Block Data Polygonal Mapping from Claritas website.

2003 and 2004 during the Saturday when the Puerto Rican Day Parade is held. The data is presented in figure 4.5.

Ramos-Zaya has argued that the increases in Puerto Rican nationalism in U.S. barrios has been partially "sustained by a constant emphasis on its proponents' binding legal identity as citizens of the colonial power" and on the undocumented status of other Latinos (2003, 37). Puerto Rican nationalist strategies are thus compelled by complex acts of distancing from other minorities as well as from white America. This complex process of separation and attraction thus probably motivates displays of Puerto Rican flags by Puerto Rican households in Bushwick. They display flags to remind other minority, Latino, and other Americans that they are there. The observations of flag displays made in 2003 and 2004 do suggest that this one block of Puerto Ricans exhibited a similar complex of Puerto Rican nationalist "performance."

Calculations establish that the proportion of Puerto Rican households exhibiting Puerto Rican flags range from 17 to 57 percent in 2003 and from 12 to 40 percent in 2004.[30] There is no way to extrapolate these block findings to the larger Puerto Rican population. These numbers do suggest that there is a fairly high degree of nationalist sentiment in this small sample of the Puerto Rican community, even if only the lowest estimates of Puerto Rican concentration (at 12 percent) are considered.

Displaying a flag takes much less effort than joining an organization or participating in a demonstration. One survey study documented, for instance, that only 4.5 percent of Puerto Ricans had ever volunteered for a Puerto Rican organization, compared with 5.5 percent of Mexican Americans and 2.5 percent of Cuban Americans (de la Garza and DiSipio 1992, 137). What's interesting is that Puerto Rican flag displays are also not traditional acts of participation. Since there is no independent Puerto Rican state, flag displays do not constitute simple acts of Puerto Rican patriotic or nationalist loyalty (Skitka 2005). Flag displays, in this context, must then reflect Puerto Rican efforts to negotiate their presence in the United States. They may very well represent what Wilkinson has called nation-building efforts. As Wilkinson has written, "The planting of the flag signals Puerto Rican rootedness and belonging within mainland communities, even as it evokes emotional connections to an island past" (Wilkinson 2004, 62).

Flag displays are thus examples of the separation-and-attraction complex that Ramos-Zaya described. This particular study of flag displays provided no access to the meanings Puerto Ricans give to their displays. The study does point, however, to one significant finding. Whether this or any Puerto Rican community does anything more than display a flag, the persistence of this "nationalist " gesture is astonishing for a community that is deep into its second and third generation and that has experienced significant social erosion and impoverishment.

This Bushwick flag study and the Ramos-Zaya Chicago study shows that nationalism remains a strong current among Puerto Ricans in the United States. Even Aspira is part of that militant and nationalist tradition. At its creation, Puerto Rican youth were urged by founder Antonia Pantoja and others to fight for their rights and proclaimed Puerto Rican identity "a revolutionary factor" in Puerto Rican history.[31]

Puerto Ricans in Congress

These separatist, nationalist currents pull on Puerto Rican political loyalties both at the community and the leadership levels. The radical and militant political position taken by Puerto Rican elected officials in Congress is one consequence. In fact, Jose Serrano was identified in 2001 as the leader of four New York City congressmen from a list representing the top ten "most liberal in the country" (Malanga 2002). Their generally radical position is demonstrated by the high ratings that congresspersons Serrano, Gutierrez, and Velazquez have received from groups on the Left. In the period 1990 to 2002, Congressman Serrano did not receive a congres-

TABLE 4.4
Interest Group Ratings for Congressman Serrano, José E.

Year	ACLU	ACU	ADA	ASC	CCUS	CFA	COPE	LCV	NEA	NTU
2002	93	0	90		37		100	100	100	24
2001	93	0	85		35		92	71	100	10
2000	88	0	90		42	86	90	86	100	16
1999	88	4	95		12	83	89	100	80	17
1998	93	0	90		25	100	100	72	90	13
1997	93	8	95		30	100	100	75	90	20
1996	94	0	95		19	85	91	92	100	31
1995	94	4	100		13	88	100	92	100	25
1994	86	0	95	0	42	90	78	92	100	17
1993	86	4	100	0	0	100	100	75	100	18
1992	100	0	95	10	13	93	91	88	100	27
1991	100	0	100	10	10	89	100	85	100	20
1990	100	0	88	0	14	94	100	75	100	14

Source: CQ Press, a Division of Congressional Quarterly Inc., 2005.
American Civil Liberties Union (ACLU); American Conservative Union (ACU); Americans for Democratic Action (ADA); American Security Council (ASC); Chamber of Commerce of the United States (CCUS); Consumer Federation of America (CFA); Committee on Political Education (COPE); League of Conservative Voters (LCV); National Education Association (NEA); National Taxpapers' Union (NTU)

sional rating below 78 percent from liberal interest groups like the American Civil Liberties Union or the Committee on Political Action of the AFL-CIO (see table 4.4). In fact, during that thirteen-year time period, Serrano received a rating of 100 percent at least seven times. Also in that thirteen-year period, there were ten times when he received a rating of 100 percent from the liberal organization the National Education Association. Congressmen Gutierrez and Velazquez also have very liberal voting records, at least as measured by interest groups. In his first ten years in Congress, Gutierrez had a 100 percent rating from COPE each of those ten years. Similarly, Congresswoman Velazquez recorded a COPE 100 percent rating for eight out of the ten years she has been in office, from 1993 to 2002. She has also received a 100 percent rating from the NEA seven out of those ten years.[32]

This raises several hard-to-answer questions. Are Puerto Rican politicians simply out of touch with their fellow members of Congress, with their constituents? Are they unable to steer successful legislation through Congress because they refuse to or can't make practical alliances? Has their militant posturing hurt their credibility in Congress? Have the public employee unions captured them? The answers are hard to get. The data is simply not readily available. More importantly, these are the wrong questions.

Perhaps the problems faced by Puerto Ricans in Congress are not personal or institutional. Perhaps what pushes them leftward and limits Puerto Rican influence and effectiveness, whether in Congress or in their communities, is the status of their overall relation to the larger society.

This can be demonstrated by a review of Puerto Rican congressional legislative patterns.

The relative success of individual legislators can be attributed to a number of factors. Constituent interests, financial support, personal ambition, and attractiveness obviously all play parts. The individual skill of an elected official plays a strong role as well. Some politicians make adroit maneuvers, establish effective coalitions, and exude enough charm to produce successes. These differences aside, however, there are specific factors that make such individual attributes and strategies more or less effective. The media, for example, can be a tremendous boon to politicians both in running for office and in gaining support for their initiatives from fellow legislators after election.

The media pays attention to elected officials for reasons beyond the charms of individual personality or skill. The national importance of an elected official as well as the salience of particular issues plays a major role in why the media pays attention. This is especially true for officials who serve as representatives of minority groups and women. The ability of elected representatives to enlist the help of fellow lawmakers is, for similar reasons, also affected by national and public considerations.

Elected officials seek cosponsors for their legislative initiatives in order to give weight and legitimacy to their bills (Cook 2000). Cosponsorship is, no doubt, also affected by extra-individual concerns, especially for legislation related to ethnic-racial issues. Among, and near the top of, these considerations is the perceived status of the group the legislation targets. Herman Badillo, for example, the first Puerto Rican elected to Congress, was hampered considerably by the invisibility of Puerto Ricans at the national level during his tenure in Congress.

An examination of Badillo's and Charles Rangel's legislative histories shows that both accomplished very little during 1970s. From 1973 to 1978, no legislation that Badillo sponsored was passed in the House. Rangel, the long-term congressman from Harlem, only had three. Rangel's relative success compared to Badillo's may be due to the national television exposure he received during the 1974 Watergate controversy.

As figure 4.6 shows, Rangel appeared on national television stations twenty-four times during 1974. Rangel's major success in getting his legislation passed came during the 1974–1979 period. Badillo had almost no exposure on national television. Admittedly, television exposure is no guarantee of political influence. However, as Richard E. Neustadt once showed, even presidential power depends on the "image of the office" portrayed by the media (Neustadt 1976, 163). Though true, both congressional success and national television exposure are best seen as signs of ef-

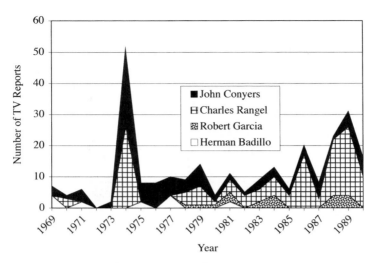

Figure 4.6. National TV Coverage of Minority Congressmen, 1969–1990. *Source*: Vanderbilt University Television News Archive (http://tvnews.vanderbilt.edu)

fective networking and the confluence of mutual interests. One does not have to be the product of the other.

In contrast to Badillo, higher levels of networking seemed to be at work in Jose Serrano's legislative history. He both has been a more effective legislator and has received more national television exposure than Badillo, though far less than Rangel. Congressional networking is also important. Both Serrano and Rangel had more success in Congress when their bills had cosponsorship. All of their rejected legislation had no sponsors in the period between 1989 and 2000. Similarly, the majority of their successful legislation had sponsors in the same time period (see figure 4.7). While no direct relationship exists between media exposure and the record of legislative success, there was some impact.

Media exposure may encourage members to forgo sponsorship, especially if the costs of those ties are too high. The member may believe that media exposure provides a level of public attention and support that allows him or her to escape the need to bargain and compromise to get cosponsorship. Thus, table 4.5 shows that a lower percentage of Charles Rangel bills were cosponsored as compared to Jose Serrano's. Rangel was also, in general, more successful in getting his bills passed even with less sponsorship.

Media attention is thus a resource that provides members of Congress

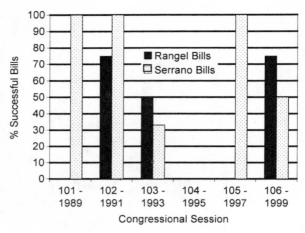

Figure 4.7. Cosponsored Bills Passed in the House by Congressman, 1989 to 1999. *Source*: THOMAS Legislative Database of the Library of Congress at http://thomas.loc.gov/.

with greater opportunities for developing successful congressional strategies to get their legislation passed. That ability to attract media attention is, furthermore, subject to the capacities and limitations not just of a particular congressperson but also of the ethnic-racial group her or she represents. Puerto Ricans, in that sense, are usually not considered "newsworthy" by the news media (Wolfsfeld 2003, 85). It is thus the inability of Serrano or Puerto Ricans in general to get media or public attention that debilitates and weakens Puerto Rican influence in Congress.

This claim that Puerto Rican political leaders lack not just media but also public attention can be supported by an examination of the data on "junkets," or free trips given to congressional officials, sometimes in violation of their own ethics rules.[33] Corporations, lobbyists, interest-group organizations, foreign governments, and universities fund congressional travel in exchange for speeches, networking, and influence. It is a measure of the importance that these public groups give individual members of Congress, deserved or not. Are those who fail to take these free trips morally superior to those who do? Are they less partisan or less captured by special interests? We can't know much about these things from the raw data. What the data does show, however, is that Democrats are more likely than Republicans to take advantage of these free trips.

Democrats in Congress took 2,729 trips, valued at $7,805,362.87, from 2000 to 2004 (see table 4.6). In contrast, Republicans took 2,095 trips in the same time period, valued at $6,512,990.35. Even in New York

TABLE 4.5

*Bill Success and Sponsorship in the House by
Congressman, 1989–99*

Congress	# Bills	Sponsored	Not Sponsored
Jose Serrano			
101-1989	21	2	0
102-1991	10	7	3
103-1993	9	7	2
104-1995	23	18	5
105-1997	19	15	4
106-1999	17	7	10
Charles Rangel			
101-1989	57	42	15
102-1991	51	27	24
103-1993	25	12	13
104-1995	17	11	6
105-1997	27	14	13
106-1999	47	30	17

Source: THOMAS Legislative Database of the Library of Congress at: http://thomas.loc.gov/.

TABLE 4.6

*Sponsored Congressional Trips by Political Party,
2000–2004*

Democratic Party	
Number of trips for party members	2,729
Total spent on party members	$7,805,362.87
Percentage of total spent on party	54.30%
Independent Party	
Number of trips for party members	22
Total spent on party members	$53,830.93
Percentage of total spent on party	0.40%
Republican Party	
Number of trips for party members	2,095
Total spent on party members	$6,512,990.35
Percentage of total spent on party	45.30%

Source: http://americanradioworks.publicradio.org/features/cong travel/index.html (accessed 4/22/05)

State, where most Puerto Rican members of Congress are situated, Democrats were eighteen out of the top thirty-one trip recipients from 2000 to 2004, not including Democratic senators Clinton and Shuman.

In such a context of bipartisan congressional use of sponsored junkets, not participating is an anomaly that can only reflect a lack of interest on the part of the different public groups to fund such trips. Unlike lobbying and campaign contributions, these sponsored trips are usually a direct attempt to influence a member of Congress. This makes offering and accepting such trips an even more revealing measure of the way public groups

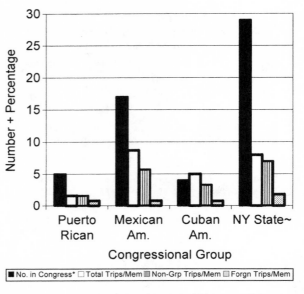

Figure 4.8. Sponsored Congressional Trips per Member, 2000–2004. *Notes*: * Number of members actually taking trips may be less than this total; ~ Does not inclues Senators. *Source*: http://americanradioworks .publicradio.org/features/congtravel/index.htm.

rank the member and how much importance the member assigns to his or her relationship with those groups.

Puerto Ricans do not get many free lunches or trips. As figure 4.8 shows, by almost any measure Puerto Rican members of Congress are not very often tapped by outside groups to take these missions. The Puerto Rican members of Congress took, on average, 1.6 trips per member during the four-year period ending in 2004. This compares to 8.7 for Mexican American members, 5 trips for Cuban Americans, and 8 trips on average for the New York State delegation to Congress as a whole.

More interesting is the data on nongroup trips by group representatives. This data reveals how often members of Congress were asked to take trips by organizations that were not connected to their ethnic-racial or state (for New York State delegation) affiliation. It is a measure of the connection of Congress members to organizations outside their closest networks. As such, it reflects how much attention and importance outside groups give members of Congress and the people they represent. Puerto Ricans, again, fall far short.

Puerto Rican members of Congress had only 1.6 per member compared to 5.7 for Mexican Americans, 3.3 for Cubans, and 7 trips for the

New York State delegation. The senior Puerto Rican member of Congress, Serrano, had no trips whatsoever in that four-year period. The Puerto Ricans with the most trips, at 7 between them, were Anibal Acevedo-Vila and Carlos Romero-Barcelo, both of whom represented Puerto Rico in Congress. The latter had been governor of Puerto Rico and the former became governor in 2004. Delete those trips and that leaves only one trip for the three Puerto Rican members of Congress representing New York City and Chicago. This paucity of trips reflects how scarce Puerto Ricans really are in the public and corporate imagination.

Puerto Rican Congress members are ineffective even on symbolic issues. Over the years, they have proven unable to get honorific awards for their community. This is shown by figure 4.9, which indicates how many Congressional Medal of Honor awards have been given to different groups. The only two ever awarded to Puerto Ricans were given during the early 1970s, the period of Young Lords activity.

During that same early 1970s period, a poll administered by Harris showed that Puerto Ricans enjoyed higher levels of public attention and approval than they have since. Table 4.7 shows the results of this poll. Female and male survey respondents thought that a Puerto Rican had a greater probability of becoming president in 1971 than did a woman (of any race) or an African American. Only Jews and Native Americans were thought to have a better probability of becoming president than Puerto Ricans. Strangely, those same respondents didn't think that Puerto Ricans

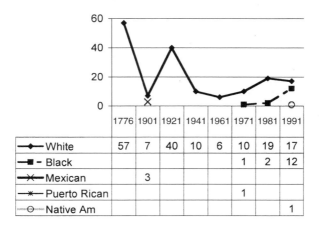

	1776	1901	1921	1941	1961	1971	1981	1991
◆ White	57	7	40	10	6	10	19	17
■ Black						1	2	12
✕ Mexican		3						
✳ Puerto Rican						1		
◉ Native Am								1

Figure 4.9. Congressional Gold Medals Awarded by Racial Group, 1776–2002. *Source*: CRS Report for Congress, Congressional Gold Medals 1776–2003, July 23, 2003. Stephen W. Stathis, Specialist in American National History.

TABLE 4.7
1971 Harris Poll on Electing Minority President by Group

When?	Puerto Rican or Mexican	Woman	Black	Jew	American Indian
Women					
Now	10	6	7	26	14
5 Years	7	10	13	12	8
10 Years	13	21	21	13	13
20 Years	16	20	19	11	14
50 Years	11	8	10	5	9
Never	25	26	18	15	24
Not Sure	18	9	12	18	18
Men					
Now	9	7	7	32	19
5 Years	5	9	8	10	
10 Years	11	23	17	12	11
20 Years	16	19	20	9	12
50 Years	12	9	15	6	11
Never	31	22	23	18	27
Not Sure	16	11	10	13	14

Source: Survey by Virginia Slims.
Methodology: Conducted by Louis Harris & Associates during October, 1971, and based on personal interviews with a national adult sample of 4,000. Sample consists of 3000 women and 1000 men [USHARRIS.71VASL.R21E].
Question: 7c. When do you think the country will be ready to elect a (READ FIRST ITEM ON LIST) as President—now, in the next 5 years, in 10 years, 50 years, or never?

had much of a chance of becoming president five or ten years later. Perhaps they foresaw how limited and short was the window of public attention the Puerto Rican community actually had at the time.

Conclusion

The discussion in this chapter on the economics and politics of Puerto Rican moves has made clear that Americans had a hard time noticing and appreciating Puerto Ricans in this most recent period. American society made few moves toward Puerto Ricans. They were oblivious to Puerto Rican economic skills and productivity. Puerto Rican ability to work has been largely discounted and wasted. They were ignorant of Puerto Rican political goals and needs. Puerto Ricans have been industrious and effective in building organizations and producing leaders. The larger society has ignored and discounted them, even when it paid attention to issues Puerto Ricans themselves have brought to the table. The consequences of this political and economic blindness and inertia have been huge for Puerto Ricans. The cultural dimension has been equally as toxic. The discussion of media impact has already suggested the important role of culture. These movements are worth exploring in more detail.

5

The Young Lords, the Media, and Cultural Estrangement

He smothered her hurt feelings with hugs, making it into a game, drowning out her crying with laughter and kisses and silly smooching sounds. In the tyranny of that moment beat the pulse of Cesar's neighborhood—the bid for attention, the undercurrent of hostility for so many small needs ignored and unmet, the pleasure of holding power, camouflaged in teasing, the rush of love. Then the moment passed, and Cesar's three-year-old daughter walked back out into the world and left him behind.[1]

A great deal of the problem Puerto Ricans have in making real economic and political connections with this society is due to the reality that Americans place such little value on Puerto Rican culture. In this, Puerto Ricans and Latinos differ markedly from African Americans. Another major reason why Puerto Rican culture is often not appreciated is that it does not fit the "interpretative frames" within which the news media make sense of and give importance to different events, issues, and groups (Wolfsfeld 2003, 88). The intermediate or fuzzy nature of Puerto Rican racial identity contributes to this interpretative dissonance.[2] The problem is not just, however, that Puerto Ricans are not "clear." It is that Americans *can't see* them clearly.

It is in the cultural realm, then, that Puerto Ricans find their most ambivalent and paradoxical relationship to the rest of America. From music to movies to racial identity, Puerto Ricans find themselves partially attracted to the rest of society yet mostly rejected by it. In a variety of different ways, white America has either largely ignored or rejected Puerto Rican cultural expression and values. The result of this curious mix of cultural repulsion and attraction is a further weakening of the Puerto Rican community. Puerto Ricans, on the other hand, are unable to make a clear rejection of a white America that has up to now basically ignored and rejected them. This leaves them vulnerable, dependent, and, thus, less powerful.

The fuzzy nature of Puerto Rican racial identity has not prevented Puerto Ricans and Latinos from moving increasingly towards a nonwhite identity. The reasons are not just that they feel they don't belong in this society. The reality is that they've adopted a nonwhite identity, in part, because whites make them feel as if they don't belong. The difference is important.

There are few studies of what white Americans have done to make groups like Puerto Ricans and Latinos marginal. What studies there are usually examine individual attitudes rather than the more important actions and expressions of white institutions and group leaders.[3] There are signs, however, that what white America has done, thought, and felt as a community, and through its institutions, has made a large contribution to the construction of Puerto Rican and Latino racial identity. Some clues can be found in those white decisions and actions that produce and establish what is important in music, postage stamps, and film. These cultural artifacts are more revealing than polls and surveys precisely because they are natural indicators of where Puerto Ricans reside in the public imagination as institutions and organizations go about their normal activities.

The evidence suggests that Puerto Ricans have not resided often or long in America's public consciousness. And yet the Harris poll of American political and social attitudes reveals that in 1971 white America was more ready to accept the idea of a Puerto Rican president than a woman of any race or a black (see table 4.7). They were also more likely to imagine Native Americans or Jews becoming president. These relatively positive attitudes towards Puerto Ricans are puzzling. It's possible that the Young Lords' activities during this same period contributed to this positive public perception of Puerto Ricans. We will get back to this issue later.

One has to wonder how Native Americans, who have been one of the most neglected and repressed minority groups, could achieve a similar positive public reception. Perhaps the very act of asking the question influenced the responses the poll got? The liberal orientation of that time period could have also persuaded Americans to give the idea of a minority as president some plausibility. The problem is that while the idea of a minority as president became more plausible, the respondents avoided choosing African Americans or women in general. One speculation is that, at that time, these groups represented more threat and trouble than whites could entertain and accept.

These kinds of problems highlight the difficulty in relying on survey and poll research to examine popular consciousness. This is where the study of naturalistic phenomena like postage stamps and music offers real advantages. It allows insight into white thoughts and feelings without the distorting lens of survey methods. Before examining that data, it is important to get a sense of the thrust of Puerto Rican culture during this period.

Puerto Rican Mixed Cultural Moves

So much of Puerto Rican cultural effort is deeply ambivalent. Puerto Ricans seek to establish their own autonomous cultural expression while they continue to pursue closer connection and acceptance by white America. The movement towards a more autonomous Puerto Rican culture is evident in the increasing adoption of nonwhite racial identities. It is also evident in the rise of Salsa in the 1960s and '70s as well as in the resurrection of more traditional Puerto Rican music in Bomba and Plena.

The movement towards a closer identification with white America is also evident in the findings that more educated and financially successful Puerto Ricans appear more often to claim a white identity (see Landale and Oropesa 2002). The movement towards closer connection to white America is also suggested by the repeated Puerto Rican "crossover" dream or hope that white American audiences would adopt Puerto Rican cultural expression, in music and film for example.

There is some evidence that the intermediate racial identity of Puerto Ricans and Latinos is more than an inheritance from their past. Puerto Ricans have, over the last two decades, begun to drop their identification with European and white conceptions of race. Some of that rejection of U.S. racial categories can be seen in the fact that Puerto Ricans and other Latinos insist on keeping their national identity (Landale and Oropesa 2002, 237). On top of that, more and more Puerto Ricans and Latinos refuse to place themselves in the existing racial categories common to official records and popular thinking in the United States.

In the 2000 Census, more than 42 percent of all Hispanics called themselves "Other" and refused to label themselves as "White," "Black," or "Native American" on the census racial question (Tafoya 2004). A similar proportion of Puerto Ricans, at 38 percent, identified themselves as "Other." The Puerto Rican percentage of "Others" is a little lower than that of Latinos but is increasing. Puerto Ricans also have larger cohorts of third- and fourth-generation households living in the United States than other Latinos. These tend to be more incorporated into American society. In any case, Puerto Ricans, even of these generations, tend to prefer Puerto Rican as well as Other as their identity.

In one recent survey, Puerto Rican mothers in the United States chose Puerto Rican as their preferred identity (at 67 percent) over all other racial and panethnic options, including Other (at 4 percent) as their preferred identity (Landale and Oropesa 2002, 241). In one other national survey conducted in 2002, over 52 percent of Puerto Ricans chose a panethnic identity like Hispanic or Latino when given this choice among racial categories (PEW 2002, Chart 8). These results for Puerto Ricans in this national survey were lower than those for Mexican Americans but higher than those of Columbians, Cubans, and other Latin Americans living in the United States.

Some of the research shows that the Puerto Rican selection of "Other" was strong as far back as 1980. More education and higher class standing, furthermore, do not diminish the use of "Other" in Puerto Ricans by very much (Rodriguez 2000). The use of "Other" thus appears to be a good indicator of Puerto Rican efforts to racially separate and distinguish themselves. The key question is, from whom? The data so far suggests that it is both from white and black America. When Latinos in one sample were asked their race in a question that closed the options, the percentage of respondents answering white and black increased (Rodriguez 2000, 147–49).

The use of "Other," therefore, "raises the question of whether they had an aversion to classifying themselves as black or whether they really believed that they were simply not identified as black" (ibid., 148). The answer is probably somewhere in between. Puerto Ricans draw closer either to a black identity or to some more amorphous Other depending on their experience and their evaluation of the possibilities for power.[4] It is for that reason that researchers have found that Puerto Ricans tend to adopt "Other" when they reside in communities with high Latino densities while they gravitate towards a white or black identity when they reside in communities with more African Americans (ibid., 219 fn 26).

The issue of density in Latino identity is ignored by some researchers who argue that Puerto Ricans are moving towards and incorporating African American culture (Flores 2000). In music, language, dress, and many other cultural ways Puerto Ricans have "an identification and solidarity with American blacks perhaps unmatched by any other group in the history of the *nation of immigrants*" (Flores 2002, 50). This cultural move towards black culture is significant. It signals solidarity with the black diaspora as well as an attempt to join blacks in opposition to white culture. It suggests the possibility of racial and political alliances that could prove a formidable challenge for white America. It also suggests something else.

The Puerto Rican move towards black culture could actually be an attempt to impress white society. Flores inadvertently puts his finger on this critical issue when he argues that Puerto Rican moves toward black culture are a threat because "on the streets and in the dominant social institutions 'brown' is close enough to black to be suspect" (Flores 2002, 50). Puerto Ricans become a threat, Flores correctly points out, when they are seen as another kind of black. Puerto Ricans move towards black culture because it scares white America. The use of "Other" and the reluctance to fully adopt a black identity springs from the realization that to pose a real and independent threat in most places, Puerto Ricans must stand on their own.

These mixed and opposed racial moves are, nevertheless, significant and recent (Tafoya 2004). Puerto Ricans are abandoning a white for a racialized, minority identity as registered by their increasing use of Other, Puerto Rican, and pan-Hispanic identities. Can this trend, however, be attributed merely to the working out of structural forces like racism, segregation, unemployment, and poverty that encourage the redefinition Puerto Ricans as Other? Or, how much of this trend represents the work of Puerto Ricans themselves insisting on a nonwhite identity for reasons having to do with pride, nostalgia, resistance, or as an irrational and self-destructive gesture aimed at declaring their commitment to a separate or an "underclass" culture? The answer is beside the point.

We know that the movement towards a nonwhite identity is growing among Puerto Ricans, even in U.S.-born generations. Much of this movement springs from the treatment Puerto Ricans have received in the United States. Tafoya confirms this in a study that found that "Latinos are categorized as a minority group that is significantly different from the white majority due to factors including a history of discrimination and persistently lower educational outcomes and incomes" (2004, 4). The 38 percent of Puerto Ricans who identified themselves as Other in the 2000 Census were, like other Hispanics, more likely to "have lower socio-economic status, and were less politically engaged and more often feel discriminated against" (21). The data reveals also that low education and employment levels lead Latinos to adopt a nonwhite identity. More importantly, it was those Latinos "born during the post-war baby boom" that were more likely to acquire "a lower level of white racial identity" (16). Tafoya's research suggests further that those Latinos who identify as nonwhite are also more likely to have had experiences with discrimination and disrespect in the United States (23).

There is evidence that Puerto Ricans had made earlier moves away from white America. As was discussed before, Puerto Ricans rioted about twenty-eight times between 1964 and 1971, exposing their deep alienation from and rejection of white America. The Young Lords and FALN (Fuerzas Armada Para la Liberacion Nacional) periods of the early 1970s established a heightened level of Puerto Rican opposition (Susler 1998,

145). In the area of culture, however, except for the refusal to accept a white identity, Puerto Ricans have exhibited ambivalence and equivocation about how much connection and acceptance they desired with white America. This is not unique to Puerto Ricans. African Americans also experience this kind of "dialectical interplay between accommodation and resistance" (Lipsitz 1998, 149). The problem for Puerto Rican, however, is that the culture that emerges from this ambivalence doesn't attract or endear Puerto Rican bodies, images, music, and art to the rest of America.

Structural forces are, of course, at work here. The racism and rejection that litter their experience on the U.S. dance floor demands reaction and moves from Puerto Ricans. Yet the structural push to dance is also something Puerto Ricans internalize and attempt to turn into something theirs. More than this process of internalization, Puerto Ricans turn the rejections that racism and poverty represent into opportunities for pride, respect, and power. They claim and see themselves as different kinds of dancers—as Others, as nonwhite. What they accomplish is not just another identity, although that is important. They also change the equation that, for them, delivers value and power to "whiteness" in this society. They rob "whiteness" of its ability to control, shame, diminish, and destroy. They reject it even as whiteness itself rejects them. And yet, it is in those acts of rejection that the Puerto Rican and Latino pursuit of power fails. It doesn't go far enough.

Locked in an ambivalent and fuzzy conception of race, the Puerto Rican and Latino adoption of a nonwhite identity is internally unstable. The rejection by whites inspires a rejection of their own in the adoption of a nonwhite identity. The impression Latinos give, however, is that they are likely to easily drop the pursuit of a nonwhite identity if "whiteness" gives any small hint of embracing them. This is particularly true for those individual Puerto Ricans and Latinos living in less segregated communities and whose "in-between" physical appearance makes it easier to "pass."[5] Latinos also have few public complaints with the whiter Latino faces that populate and represent them in both the gringo and Latino media.

A nonwhite identity is unstable for another reason. Whites do not value what is "nonwhite" about Puerto Ricans and Latinos in any way similar to the way they value African American otherness. The power that Puerto Ricans generate by rejecting "whiteness" is fine as long as Puerto Ricans limit their interactions to other Puerto Ricans and, sometimes, other minorities. It disappears in the larger society if being Puerto Rican itself remains without special value or attraction to white America. Interaction in that larger world brings Puerto Ricans no real influence, in that case, and ultimately weakens the reasons Puerto Ricans have for keeping that identity.[6]

Puerto Ricans have found repeatedly that their hesitant moves towards rapprochement with white America is rejected and defeated. Puerto Ricans don't have the spiritual and psychic connection to white Americans that blacks do. Some have argued that both white racism and white attraction to African Americans spring from a deep investment in projecting African Americans as representatives of a primitive, mysterious, and soulful culture (Lipsitz 1998). White Americans are both repulsed by and attracted to this myth. In both cases, however, white Americans find personal redemption and meaning in the myth of the African American primitive. Puerto Rican culture has never come close to having that kind of psychic and spiritual connection to white America.

When Puerto Ricans have offered whites their cultural products with hopes of simple commercial gain or recognition, they have found that they get little attention. What's more, their rejection of and opposition to white culture acquires relevance and meaning mostly when it comes connected to black culture. A large part of the reason for the failures of Puerto Rican cultural moves has to be that, unlike African Americans, Puerto Ricans are not "a locus of both contempt and envy onto which whites projected their own repressed desires for pleasure and unrestrained free expression" (Lipsitz 1998, 150). To paraphrase Mailer, Puerto Ricans have found that there are no "white Spics."

White America's Cultural Moves

Puerto Ricans, as we've seen, have made some moves to separate and become autonomous from white America. Mostly, however, Puerto Ricans have largely been pushed away. It wasn't that Puerto Ricans just had a hard time getting others to notice their musical and other forms of cultural production. Puerto Ricans were just plain devalued and rejected. They were overlooked in most of the ways in which society takes note and signifies the contributions of people in the culture. The absence of Puerto Ricans in popular music taste, postage stamps, obituaries, and other signs of public recognition and attention demonstrates the degree of rejection Puerto Ricans experienced.

Though not completely invisible, Puerto Ricans are generally not found in popular television or film. It's ironic that one of the high points for the Puerto Rican presence in film was the 1961 movie *West Side Story*. Puerto Ricans were main protagonists in the film, acting primarily as the evil, primitive thugs who battled the undisciplined and unruly, yet misunderstood ethnic American white gang. *West Side Story* underlines all of the worst stereotypes invented to racialize Puerto Ricans. They were overemotional, lazy, dark, and violent.[7] What's more fascinating is that even in a film where the Puerto Rican presumably had star billing, non–Puerto Ricans played the two main characters (Bernardo was played by George Chakiris and Maria by Natalie Wood) and the producers did not actually conceive the film with Puerto Ricans as the original dramatic foils.

West Side Story was first conceived as a play about a Jewish girl and an Italian Catholic boy. When producers first decided to turn the play into a movie, they considered inserting Chicano gang members. They finally settled on utilizing Puerto Ricans because "in New York we had the Puerto Ricans, and at the time the papers were full of stories about juvenile delinquents and gangs."[8] So at the height of Puerto Rican "visibility" on film, their presence was actually an afterthought. They were marginal, colorful "extras."

More recently, some Puerto Ricans, like Jennifer Lopez, the late Raul Julia, and Jimmy Smits, have become stars. These are the few, however, that prove the rule. There is also some evidence that Puerto Ricans are often utilized more than Mexicans when Hollywood wants to depict a Latino. Thus, Jennifer Lopez played the Chicana Selena, while Jimmy Smits and Freddie Prinz have also played Chicanos. This is interesting and reflective of some small cultural advantages Puerto Ricans possess over Mexican Americans in the acting field.

Puerto Ricans have been able to present a pan-Latino identity mostly when it is harnessed to the added value of African cultural idioms just below the surface.[9] Zimmerman thus argues that "Lopez's Mexican crossover abilities stem not only from her great performance skills, but also from the fact that she could translate her hip hop and also her Salsa cultural capital into Chicano capital" (Zimmerman 2003, 120). These successes, however, don't reverse the bigger reality that both Puerto Ricans and Mexican Americans are generally missing from television and film. Latino projections on film, moreover, lack interest without a recognizable subliminal connection to Hip Hop and African American culture.

For the most part, research supports the idea that Latinos are generally scarce on the small and large screens. As Joseba Gabilondo writes,

> Hispanic realities sprinkle any contemporary Hollywood film but they do not occupy central subject positions. Selma Hayek, Antonio Banderas, or Jennifer Lopez reappear in films where their Hispanic exoticism stands for many forms of otherness. But to this day, they have never starred in a blockbuster film in which a Hispanic character is the central focus of representation. *Selena* or *The Mask of Zorro* were the closest phenomena. (Gabilondo 2001, 5)

Numbers are hard to come by on the presence of Puerto Ricans in Hollywood. Judging from Oscar nominations and awards, however, there have been very few. In over seventy-five years, there have been only four Latinos who have been awarded the Oscar. These were Jose Ferrer in 1951, Anthony Quinn in 1957, Rita Moreno in 1962 for *West Side Story*, and Benicio Del Toro in 2001. Two of them were Puerto Rican. More striking is that non-Latinos have played Latinos in over five hundred films, from Paul Muny in *Juarez* to Marlon Brando in *Viva Zapata*.[10]

More important than the underrepresentation is that, unlike African Americans, Latinos have not projected a distinct cultural style worth widespread coveting or theft by others, at least not since the Carmen Miranda fruit basket head dress and Desi Arnaz "babalu" days. What made the Will Smith character in *Independence Day* so appealing, for example, was precisely the fact that he was a "black man" rather than of "any race." The role could have been played by anyone, but the fact that it was played by an African American introduced distinctive dramatic and comedic possibilities of speech and style that were flagrantly displayed in the movie and understood and enjoyed by American viewers of all races. One example is the way the audience ate up the bravado and "cool" with which Will Smith dispatched the alien by punching him in the face.

Sadly, the same could not have been said had a Latino, like Jimmy Smits or John Leguizama, been put in that role. Latino actors often state that they wish to play roles that could be about anyone. They don't want to be limited to Latino character roles. The problem is that a Latino playing such a role would not bring much more to the acting than a white actor. That may be one reason why Latino actors have such little appeal in Hollywood.

Part of the problem for Latinos is that non-Latinos can slip into Latino roles rather easily. Latinos can be of "any race," according to government, Latino, and the prevailing U.S. social standards about race. This has given whites a freedom to represent Latinos that whites no longer have with African Americans. But the difference is social and historical rather than biological. It's not that Latinos are "whiter" than African Americans. It wasn't long ago that whites routinely portrayed African Americans in blackface. White imitation of African Americans continues today though it now primarily takes the form of borrowing or stealing, and profiting, from black cultural styles in music and dance (see Douglas 1995). Somehow the "multiracial" nature of Latino identities and origins as well as the continuing Latino preference for whiteness has made it a lot easier for a non-Latino, like Madonna, to slip into Latino "brown face."

Puerto Ricans and Latinos have been mostly overlooked in television as well. They are absent on prime time programs as well as commercials while overrepresented in televised news reports of criminal activity. Latino characters on prime time situation comedies and dramas have been no higher than 4 percent of all characters (Hoffman and Noriega 2004, 2). Another study shows that Latinos are also not found in the commercials that pay for this programming. In a study of 2,889 commercials, only 1 percent of the characters were Latino compared to 12.4 percent black, 2.3 percent Asian, and 83.3 percent white (Mastro and Stern 2003, 5).

While Latinos are absent in prime time programming and commercials they are overrepresented in news reports on crime. One recent study found, for example, that "Latinos were more likely than Whites to be portrayed as perpetrators. When only felons were included in the analysis, Latinos were almost twice as likely as Whites to be portrayed as felony perpetrators" (Dixon and Linz 2000, 12). There was no specific data on Puerto Ricans. This data on Latinos suggests, though, that the Puerto Rican situation on television was probably a bit worse.

Though white America does not seem to know it, Latinos do, of course, have a distinct cultural repertoire. The "pieces" can be seen in the brooding work of Edward James Olmos as well as the pointed frivolity of Cheech and Chong or the late Freddie Prinze. Many students of Latino culture point to a traditional dialectic between respect and frivolity ("*respeto y relajo*") as its central defining feature (Lauria 1964). What Latinos lack is an interest by non-Latinos in putting these pieces together except in the most superficial and negatively founded stereotypes as lazy and dirty.

Even the multiracial character of Latino origins goes unrecognized in the United States. Tiger Woods has become the symbol of a growing community of "mixed-race" individuals in the United States who are making new demands on the political and racial expectations of white and black America. The media and political attention paid to this growing miscegenation seems, however, to have forgotten or never known that Latinos have long practiced this "new" art of racial mixing.

White America cannot enjoy Puerto Rican and Latino music without wrapping its otherness in African American culture. Thus, Salsa becomes "Afro-Cuban" and Samba becomes "Afro-Brazilian" music. Without the Afro wrapping, white America doesn't know what to do with Latin music. As figure 5.1 shows, white Americans have not had much taste for Latino music in almost every decade since the 1950s. Latinos did not have top twenty musical artists in the U.S. market until the 1990s. In every decade, Latinos have, moreover, trailed African Americans by large margins.

Even the music critics and experts find nothing of excellence in Latin music. More recently, *Rolling Stone* magazine published its list of the top five hundred music albums of all time. As table 5.1 shows, the Latino representation on that list was miniuscule at less than 1 percent. There was

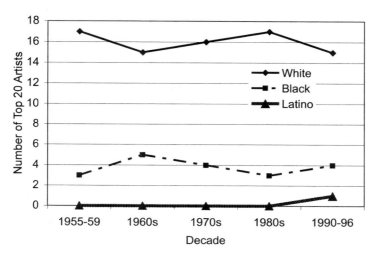

Figure 5.1. Top 20 Musical Artists by Decade and Race. *Source*:
Joel Whitbum (1996), *Top Pop Albums, 1955–1996*, Menomonee
Falls, WI: Record Research Inc.

TABLE 5.1
Rolling Stone *Magazine Top 500 Music Albums*

Black	Latino	White
98 Total	4 Total	398
5 (1%) Jamaican	3 Mexican / 1 Cuban	
20% Black	0.8% Latino	80% White

Source: *Rolling Stone* magazine, December 11, 2003.

no Puerto Rican musical album on that list and only one Cuban. The
problem for Latinos has been, in part, language. That hasn't been the
whole of it, however.

Many Latino artists tried repeatedly to "cross over" to the English
market without success. Joe Cuba was one of the most successful with
his "Bang, Bang" hit in 1966.[11] The song had some success in the white
American market, particularly because it had almost no lyrics except the
ubiquitous "Bang, Bang." What's more important is that language has not
been a barrier for African Americans. Latin music has a long history of
appreciation by African Americans according to most musicologists. African American musicians borrowed from Latin music and often invited
Latino musicians to play in their bands. Some researchers trace the earliest collaborations between African Americans and Latino musicians to
the 1880s (Roberts 1999). Some surveys suggest, moreover, that average

Americans have some appreciation for Latin music. Table 5.2 shows that Latin music has more fans than opera or even rap and yet it goes largely unnoticed. Unlike African Americans, Puerto Ricans and Latinos have simply not had the impact "that blacks have had from slavery onwards on the musical tastes and expressions of all Americans and through them on the whole world" (Redner 1991, 319).

What is important in all of this is not that Puerto Ricans are not being incorporated into American culture. The scarcity of Puerto Rican representation in film and television is important because it reveals white America's very low interest in Puerto Rican cultural products. A lot of other information documents the idea that Latinos do not exist in the public consciousness of the United States. One example is an important 1992 study by the American Jewish Committee that probed Americans about the relative social standing of various ethnic, racial, and religious groups. The results were ironic and tragic for Puerto Ricans and Mexican Americans. As table 5.3 shows, these two groups were rated below "Wisians," a fictitious group placed in the questionnaire as a control measure. Moreover, Puerto Ricans and Mexican Americans scored below "Wisians" both in 1989 and in 1964. Apparently, Americans know more about the fictitious "Wisians" than they do about Puerto Ricans and Mexican Americans. The American public believed that the "Wisians" had a higher social standing.

The reasons are not due simply to the relatively small size of the Puerto Rican and Mexican populations. There are fewer Greek Americans in the United States than Puerto Ricans and Mexicans, and yet Greeks scored significantly higher than these two Latino groups in social standing. These findings suggest something more than simply that the average American has very little knowledge of Puerto Ricans and Mexican Americans. It also suggests that Americans have a "null" rather than simply a negative image of them. After all, Negroes also scored below "Wisians" in 1964 and were barely above this fictitious group in social standing in 1989. The change for African Americans has probably been the result of an increase in visibility combined with a dialectic of attraction and repulsion they have in the minds of the average white American. Other information about public consciousness also points to this conclusion.

The idea that Puerto Ricans and Mexican Americans have little visibility in American culture compared to African Americans is further demonstrated by information on who has been represented on U.S. postage stamps since 1900. Postage stamps are a good indicator of public visibility since people are selected to appear on U.S. postage stamps by an official committee of private citizens who are supposed to be representative of the population. The selections made by this committee are thus a good

TABLE 5.2
Musical Taste Survey, 2002

Classical	27.2%
Musicals	16.6%
Reggae	14.7%
Dance	16.5%
Latin	18.2%
Opera	10.0%
Jazz	26.2%
Rap	15.0%
Blues	28.8%
Big Band	23.8%
Parade	11.9%
Country	42.6%
Bluegrass	21.1%
Rock	48.3%
Ethnic/Nat	16.3%

Source: Survey of Public Participation in the Arts, 2002 (UC Berkeley), www.cpanda.org/sda-cgi-bin/hsda3.

TABLE 5.3
Social Standing of Selected Groups, 1964 and 1989*

Group	1964	1989
Native White American	7.25	7.03
Catholics	6.36	6.33
British	6.37	6.46
Germans	5.63	5.78
Italians	5.03	5.69
Japanese	3.95	5.56
Jews	4.71	5.55
Greeks	4.31	5.09
Latin Americans	4.27	4.42
American Indians	4.04	4.27
Negroes	2.75	4.17
"Wisians"**.	—	4.12
Mexicans	3.00	3.32
Puerto Ricans	2.91	3.32
Gypsies	2.29	2.65

Source: "What Do Americans Think about Jews?" American Jewish Committee, Literature Dept., 165 E. 56th Street, New York, NY 10022, 1992.
   * 1989 mean "social standing" is based on a 9-point scale, with 9 as the highest ranking.
   ** "Wisians" are a fictitious people invented as a control for the study.

indicator of both a group's visibility as well as how positively or negatively a group is viewed by the American public. Figure 5.2 shows, in that context, that Puerto Ricans and other Latinos would appear to be almost nonexistent in the public consciousness of the American people. Puerto Ricans, for example, have only had two of their own appearing on U.S. postage stamps. These two were Roberto Clemente, a major

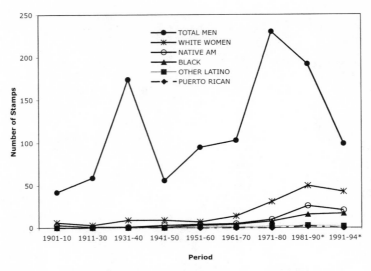

Figure 5.2. Persons on U.S. Postage Stamps by Sex and Racial Group, 1901–1994. *Sources*: Donald J. Lehnus (1982), *Angels to Zeppelins: A Guide to the Persons, Objects, Topics, and Themes on United States Postage Stamps, 1847–1980*, Westport, CT: Greenwood Press; United States Postal Service (1995), Hispanic People and Events on United States Postage Stamps; website: www.philately.com/usa_19.

league baseball player who suffered a tragic and heroic death, and Luis Munoz Marin, the first Puerto Rican elected governor of Puerto Rico. Their appearance on U.S. stamps highlights the general absence of Puerto Ricans and other Latinos.

In another example, high school and college students, asked in a series of yearly polls to select their cultural heroes, chose white and black actors and athletes, but not a single Latino. Thus Eddie Murphy, Michael Jordan, and Oprah Winfrey have been selected, along with Burt Reynolds and Alan Alda. In that nine-year period, as table 5.4 shows, five white Americans and four African Americans received the highest votes as "heroes" by American youth. In a similar survey of American adults in 2001, 33 percent of the respondents selected an African American as their "hero." As table 5.5 shows, Jesus was the number one choice, followed by, among others, Martin Luther King, Jr., and Michael Jordon. The lack of Latinos can be attributed to their absence from television and movie screens as well as from the public imagination, as discussed earlier.

But Latinos are well represented in sports like baseball and boxing, which have produced African American cultural heroes. Perhaps the

TABLE 5.4
Heroes Selected by U.S. High School and College Students, 1980–89

Year	Person
1980	Burt Reynolds
1981	Burt Reynolds
1982	Alan Alda
1983	Sylvester Stallone
1984	Michael Jackson
1985	Eddie Murphy
1986	Bill Cosby
1987	Tom Cruise
1988	Oprah Winfrey
1989	Michael Jordan

Source: 1990 World Almanac.

TABLE 5.5
Heroes Selected by Adults in the U.S., 2001

Rank	Selected Hero
1	Jesus Christ
2	Martin Luther King—AA
3	Colin Powell—AA
4	John F. Kennedy
5	Mother Teresa—Indian
6	Ronald Reagan
7	Abraham Lincoln
8	John Wayne
9	Michael Jordan—AA
10	Bill Clinton
11	John Glenn
12	Norman Schwartzkopf
13	George Washington
14	Oprah Winfrey—AA
15	Franklin Delano Roosevelt
16	Princess Diana
17	Dwight Eisenhower
18	Pope John Paul
19	George W. Bush (current president)
20	Jimmy Carter
21	Nelson Mandela—African
22	Jesse Jackson—AA
23	Tiger Woods—AA
24	Malcolm X—AA
25	Thomas Jefferson
26	Eleanor Roosevelt
27	Muhammad Ali—AA
28	Venus Williams—AA
29	Hillary Clinton
30	Neil Armstrong

Subtotal = 10 African Americans or 33% of Heroes

Note: These results are based on spontaneous, unprompted replies. All persons listed were mentioned by 1 percent or more of the individuals polled.
Source: These results are from *The Harris Poll*, a Harris Interactive survey based on a nationwide telephone sample of 1,022 adults surveyed July 20–25, 2001.

difference is that Latinos in sports have not been marketed as extensively as have African Americans like Michael Jordan. This has no doubt had an impact, since such marketing invariably takes place on the small television screen where young Americans are likely to view them. However, what is striking is that marketing of this sort has either not been seriously entertained by promoters and advertisers or has been less successful with Latino sports stars.

Advertisers may be weary of using Latino personalities precisely because they elicit little recognition by the American public. In one report on the "most liked celebrities" conducted by a marketing company in 1994, not a single Latino was selected. There was, however, one African American man (Bill Cosby) and three African American women (Whoopi Goldberg, Whitney Houston, and Oprah Winfrey) among the top ten men and women (Berkowitz 1994).

There is other information that points to the idea that Latinos have a weak psychic connection to white America. Despite years of attempts by Latinos to "cross over" and attract the attention and interest of Anglos, the results have been largely unsuccessful. For example, in 1996, *Entertainment* magazine published its list of the 101 most powerful people in entertainment. This list included executives, like Rupert Murdoch, and actors, like Tom Hanks. On that list were twelve white women, seven African Americans, one Asian, and *no Latinos* ("Power 101" 1996). While Latinos could not get on that list, Madonna's baby, all of a few months old, did. Latino talent, skill, and experience are, apparently, as fruitless and hopeless as Sisyphus's rock.

The media appreciates the connection between public recognition and power. This is suggested by their various attempts to identify the influential and powerful. These efforts, themselves a cultural artifact, have repeatedly resulted in the exclusion of Latinos. *Time* magazine's 1996 list of the 25 "most influential people in America," for example, included five African Americans but no Latinos (1996). Even Luis Farrakhan, the leader of the Nation of Islam and someone usually despised by large chunks of white America, made the list.

In 1997, *Time* also selected no Latinos in its list of twenty-five influential people. What is interesting is that *Time* seemed totally unaware of this omission. In explaining how the magazine selected its twenty-five influential people, *Time* editors proclaimed their pride in "the fact that we have a good number of women and minorities—we didn't go out looking for it—it was there" ("Time's 25" 1997). The fact that there were no Latinos was completely overlooked by the editors. They claimed the list to be representative because, apparently, it included three African Americans and one "Asian" (Tiger Woods).

More recently, *People* magazine published its list of the "Fifty Most Beautiful People." That list, in table 5.6 below, includes African Americans and Latinos at apparently similar proportions. There were 16 percent people of African origin and 12 percent of people of Hispanic origin. Many of the Hispanics, however, were from Spain and other countries in Latin America. Of the six Hispanics included as most beautiful, only three were Latino, with one Puerto Rican and two Mexican Americans. Jennifer Lopez was the only Puerto Rican. In contrast, only one of the most beautiful blacks (Sophie Okonedo) was not African American.[12] This pattern of indifference or exclusion of Puerto Ricans and Mexican Americans is not limited to the mainstream press, however.

Utne, a popular progressive journal, publishes a list of influential people. *Unte* calls them "visionaries." *Utne*'s 1995 list of one hundred people in the United States with vision included eleven African Americans, two Africans, and four Asians, but no Latinos. In 1996, *Utne* published a list of an additional twenty visionaries. This addendum included three African Americans as well as two Latinos. Thus, out of the 120 visionaries in the United States identified between 1995 and 1996, *Utne* could only find two Latinos! More recently, *Utne* published a list of young leaders it called "Movers and Shakers" in 2002. That list, table 5.7 below, had greater representation of people of color. This was accomplished, however, by including many more young leaders from Third World countries

TABLE 5.6
People *Magazine 50 Most Beautiful People in 2005*

Group	Number
African American	8 (16%)
Asian	1 (2%)
Hispanic	6 (12%)
PR and Mexican Am	3 (6%)
White American	34 (68%)

Source: *People* magazine, May 21, 2005.

TABLE 5.7
Utne *Magazine Visonaries and Leaders*

Group	1995–96 Number	2002 Number
African American	14 (12%)	5 (17%)
Asian	2 (2%)	0
Mexican Am	2 (2%)	1 (3%)
PR	0	0
Other Third World	0	4 (13%)
White American	102 (85%)	18 (60%)
Totals	120	30

Source: *Utne* magazine, 1995, 1996, Sept.–Oct. 2002.

like India. Only one Mexican American was chosen and no Puerto Ricans.

Puerto Ricans and Latinos fared no better in New York City, where they have historically received a bit more public recognition. A recent issue of *Time Out New York*, the popular guide to New York City activities, listed twenty-five artists, activists, "and other players" that they believed would "be making some noise this year" (TONY 2005).[13] This list of twenty-five young leaders consisted of twenty whites, three Asians, one African American, and 1 Latino. Somehow, in a city where African Americans and Latinos make up a majority of the population, this magazine believed that 80 percent of its future leaders would be white.

African Americans also perceive Latinos as making few cultural contributions or possessing little influence. One example was the September 1995 issue of *Vibe*, an African American music and culture magazine, which was devoted to identifying of who or what has "juice" or power in American society. The only Latina identified as having any power by the magazine was Rosie Perez. Actually, it wasn't Rosie that *Vibe* chose. *Vibe* actually selected her bra because, as they stated, "you didn't think it was just that loud Nuyorican accent that made her a star, did you?" (*Vibe*, 1995, 113).

Puerto Rican Cultural Moves

The invisibility of Puerto Rican culture makes Puerto Ricans move away from white culture. They have also moved closer. One example of this ambivalent relation to white culture can be found in the names that Puerto Rican parents give their children. As Lee explains, "Latino immigrants who decide to 'Anglicize' their names upon immigration or naturalization make a choice that is rife with consequences for how they view themselves, how they wish others to view them, and how they view their relationship to their new homeland" (Lee and Ramakrishman 2002, 8). First names are a good window into group tastes and interests since, "compared with fashions in clothing, cars, and sodas, the naming process can be studied without worrying about the effect of organizations dedicated to influencing these tastes" (Lieberson 2000, 23). While the names that parents give their children are normally not the product of marketing forces or laws, they may, of course, be influenced less directly by other groups, popular trends, and forces of assimilation and separation that are internal to the group to which the parents belong. Parents may also have their own particular reasons and hopes for assigning a particular name to their child. Overall, thus, the naming process offers a unique opportunity

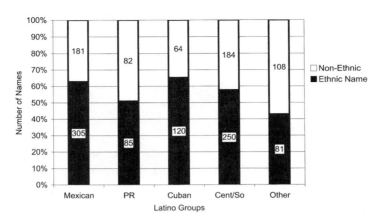

Figure 5.3. Latino First Names. *Source*: Data from Taeku Lee,
"What's in a Name?" 2002 APSA Annual Conference paper.

TABLE 5.8
Boy and Girl Baby Names by Ethnic Group, New York City, 2002

Group	White	Black	Hispanic	Asians
Boys				
% Ethnic	100	20	30	0
Ranked Ethnic Ratio	1	0.19	0.39	
Girls				
% Ethnic	100	35	30	0
Ranked Ethnic Ratio	1	0.58	0.28	

Source: New York City Department of Health, 2003.

to expose the shift in tastes as well as the influence of "external forces, internal mechanisms, and historic factors" (ibid.). [14]

Figure 5.3 describes the name patterns among different Latino groups culled from a national survey. Compared to other Latino groups, Puerto Ricans are more likely to give their children ethnic names (ibid., 16). Almost 54 percent of Puerto Ricans in this sample had ethnic names compared to 37 percent of Mexican Americans and 35 percent of Cuban Americans. This is supported by a study of baby names reported to the New York City Department of Health.

Table 5.8 shows that Hispanics in New York City give their baby boys ethnic names at a rate that is greater than that of African Americans or Asians. Thus, Hispanics give ethnic names to 30 percent of their boys, while African Americans give ethnic names to only 20 percent, and Asians give none of their boys an ethnic name. The differences are greater when name ranking is taken into account. The "ranking" measure factors in how often the name was used within the top twenty ranking. This measure shows that while about 19 percent (.19) of all African American baby boy names in the top twenty were ethnic, 39 percent (.39) of all Hispanic names were ethnic. The results are very different for baby girl names.

Fryer and Levitt found in their study of California baby names that "blacks, much more than other minorities, choose distinctive names for their children" (Fryer and Levitt 2004, 787). African American girls receive distinctive names much more often than African American boys. Fryer and Levitt found evidence, for instance, that "more than 40 percent of the Black girls born in California in recent years received a name that not one of the roughly 100,000 White girls born in California in that year was given" (787). Lieberson and Mikelson's study showed that about 60 percent of black girls in Illinois received unique names in 1980 (Lieberson and Mikelson 1995). The New York City results in table 5.8 are consistent with this and other studies.

The slightly lower rate of ethnic names for African Americans in table 5.8 may be due to the higher presence in New York City of people of African descent who originate in the West Indies. The slightly higher rate of ethnic names for Hispanics may be due to the increasing immigration of Latinos from Mexico and other parts of Latin America. Recent Latino immigrants are more likely to give their children ethnic names.

Ethnic names are an important measure of the interest in assimilation and acculturation of different groups. Lee found "strong evidence that individuals with ethnic first names are significantly more likely to value the retention of cultural distinctiveness, more likely to perceive discrimination against Latinos as a pervasive problem, and more likely to believe that Latinos share a linked fate in the United States" (Lee and Ramakrishman 2002, 22). Ethnic names, thus, move Puerto Ricans and Latinos away from other Americans. It's not clear, however, that such moves hurt them in the economic arena.

The unique names that African Americans give their children seem to be a product of the influence of the Black Power period of the late 1960s and early 1970s. Fryer explains that the sharp rise in the use of black names in the early 1970s was due, in large part, to "the rise of the Black Power movement" (Fryer and Levitt 2004, 801). Unique black names are thus "a signal of community loyalty" (ibid., 789). They inform others of a commitment to and solidarity with the black community. What's more interesting is that there appears to be "no relationship between how Black one's name is and life outcomes after controlling for other factors" (ibid., 801). Black names, thus, don't result in negative job market chances. Black names do appear to be a reaction to poverty and segregation, how-

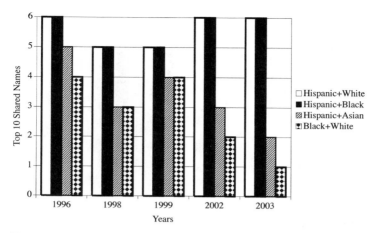

Figure 5.4. Boys' Shared Top 10 Names between Ethnic/Racial
Groups, 1996–2003. *Source*: New York Dept. of Health,
http://www.NewYorkCity.gov/html/doh.

ever. This conclusion is important in helping us to understand the reasons
why Puerto Ricans adopt more ethnic names as well.

Sociologists examine the names that parents of different ethnic groups
give their children not as a measure of "assimilation" but as an indication
of the desire of those parents to "reinvent" themselves as "American."
Puerto Ricans and Latinos have, in this vein, substituted the Catholic
saint names popular in their own homelands for more "American"-
sounding names. The data also shows that Puerto Ricans have maintained
and reverted back to ethnic names, possibly in an attempt to separate
them from what it is to be American.

There is no detailed data on Puerto Rican naming in New York City,
aside from the survey discussed above. There is data, as we saw, on Hispanic naming. An examination of recent naming practices in New York
City shows some interesting trends. Figures 5.4 and 5.5 show how many
names are held in common between Hispanics and other groups as well as
blacks and whites. Shared names are important because they reveal more
than simply the interest in separation versus assimilation. The number of
shared names reveals the extent to which the groups share the same uni-
verse of experiences and influences. The data in these two charts demonstrates that Hispanics and blacks live in a world of influences that is
largely separate from that of whites.

Figure 5.4 shows that white and black boys had few names in common
among the top ten given in 1996 (at four) and even fewer more recently.

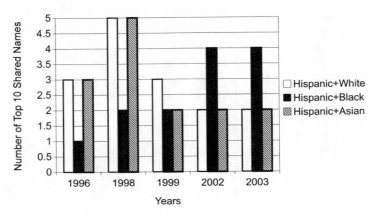

Figure 5.5. Girls' Shared Top 10 Names between Ethnic/Racial Groups, 1996–2003. *Source*: New York City Dept. of Health, http://www.NewYorkCity.gov/html/doh.

Hispanic boy-naming patterns are more complex. Hispanics are as likely to give their boys a name that is also given by either blacks or whites. The number of shared names between Hispanics and either whites or blacks has been equal and has stayed fairly consistent at around five or six names out of the top ten. This would suggest that Hispanics occupy a position somewhere between whites and blacks. That is, of course, consistent with a lot of other research and anecdotal evidence about Latino racial perspectives. The data on girl naming complicates that conclusion.

Figure 5.5 shows that although Hispanic girls have recently been given names that were often also given to white girls, that pattern has changed more recently. In both 2002 and 2003, Hispanic girls shared names with black girls at twice the rate of the names they shared with white girls. It is possible that Hispanic girls would share even more names with black girls if the latter didn't often have such a high frequency of names designed to be uniquely theirs.

In almost every group, girls are more likely to be given ethnic or unique names. Some attribute this to the idea that sons are the "bearers of tradition" (Lieberson 2000, 205). It is also true, however, that boys are expected to enter the larger public world in a way that girls still are not. Those sexist expectations give parents more liberty in naming girls. The naming patterns for Hispanic, Asian, and black girls in New York City show, however, that each group perceives that liberty differently.

Black girls have not shared with white girls any name in the top ten in any of the years from 1996 to 2003 in the chart. Black girls have shared names with Hispanic girls. This has increased from only one shared name in the top ten in 1996 to four in 2003. Many of the names that black girls received in 2003, like Jada, Aaliyah, Imani, and Nia, were connected to black singers and performers who were important to the black community. Hispanics were reluctant to use these names. The ones they did adopt in common with blacks were Kayla, Brianna, Ashley, and Destiny. These names held no particular connection or significance for the black community, except that they liked them. As a result, Hispanics used those names too. Without trying to wrench too much meaning from these patterns, Hispanic naming data suggests that though Hispanics share a common experience with black Americans, they don't share a similar oppositional perspective or set of cultural preferences.

Survey data also appears to show that the level of Latino attachment to American culture is quite low. One study showed, for example, that few Latinos indicate a preference to identify as "American." Only about 8 percent of Puerto Ricans, 9 percent of Mexicans, and almost 17 percent of Cubans indicate that they prefer to be called "American" (de la Garza and DiSipio 1992, 63).

Despite this response, Latinos also demonstrate a love for the United States. About 39 percent of Mexicans, 32 percent of Puerto Ricans, and 57 percent of Cubans expressed an extremely strong love for the United States (de la Garza and DiSipio 1992, 80). In contrast, about 50 percent of Anglos expressed a similar love. This suggests either an essential ambivalence or an appreciation by Latinos of the practical benefits they have achieved by residing in the United States.

Puerto Ricans in the United States thus seem to be struggling with their relationship to the dominant culture. It is clear that Puerto Ricans no longer want simple entry into an American "melting pot." Some Puerto Ricans, for example, seem to be drawn to African American culture much more intensely than to white culture (Flores 1996, 183). At the same time, Puerto Ricans and Latinos seem to recognize that they cannot continue to see themselves the way they have traditionally—according to their national origins. Latinos born in the United States, for this reason, are more likely to express identification with a "panethnic" label, such as "Latino" (de la Garza and DiSipio 1992, 40).

The sum of the cultural moves that Puerto Ricans and white America have made with each other results in cultural weakness for the Puerto Rican community. Puerto Rican culture is either overlooked or recognized in connection to black culture. Puerto Ricans, meanwhile, have not resolved the nature and extent of their separation from white culture.

The data on film, music, stamps, and magazine lists all points to the general absence of Puerto Ricans from public consciousness. At the same time, the data on racial identity and first names points to a Puerto Rican move away from and rejection of white culture that falls short and remains ambivalent. They proclaim a difference that falls short of making a clear racial separation. Puerto Rican and Latino identity has what Torres-Saillant has called a "radical porosity" (Torres-Saillant 2003, 140). That combination makes the Puerto Rican community both marginal and too responsive to white culture, often entering "the territory of whiteness in phenotype and in shared prejudices" (ibid., 142). All of this is put in sharp contrast by the Young Lords period that brought clearer cultural movements and relatively high power for the Puerto Rican community.

This analysis of cultural moves is also about the importance of the media as a player/dancer in the relations of power. From the standpoint of the dance theory of power, the ambivalent interests such moves represent don't bode well on the dance floor. They suggest too much hesitancy and indecision. The projection of such images, whether in direct public interaction or through the media, informs wider audiences of the unattractiveness of Latino dancers. The image a group projects is thus an important element in that group's power. It is the equivalent of bad marketing. It's interesting in that context that Pablo Guzman once explained that the Young Lords decided on the garbage protest in 1969 because "garbage is visible" (Gandy 2002, 736). The Puerto Rican ability to dance with the rest of society was at an all-time low in the late 1960s. The perception that Puerto Ricans had little to offer was stamped into public consciousness as an economic, political, cultural fact. Into this reality and appearance of public loss and decline sprang the Young Lords.

The Garbage Protest

Scientific studies of Puerto Rican community power usually concentrate on voting rates, the election of Puerto Ricans to office, and patterns of political participation (de la Garza and DiSipio 1992; Miyares 1980; Jennings 1977). They assume, in contrast to this study, that those measurements of formal participation are always more accurate indicators of the extent of Puerto Rican community power.[15] A major reason they focus on such measurements is that doing so seems like an easy way to satisfy the scientific goal of finding patterns in social behavior. Their goals are noble. Voting patterns, however, don't usually provide a good indicator of power. The almost 100 percent voting rate in the old Soviet Union did not provide its citizens with power anywhere near that level of voting. In the case of Puerto Ricans, voting patterns reveal more about the degree of Puerto Rican integration into the formal channels of political power in the United States than they do about power itself.

Low voting patterns also don't necessarily mean there is little power. Puerto Ricans have one of the lowest voting rates among any group in the United States. That is often taken as an explanation for Puerto Rican powerlessness and poverty. Cruz, for example, blames the Puerto Rican community's "relative absence from the polls" for the "failure of poor Puerto Ricans to influence and shape the power structure" (2004, 45). Such arguments ignore, however, the fact that Puerto Ricans in Puerto Rico have an extremely high voting record and that their voting has yet to produce real economic and political benefits for Puerto Ricans there (Falcon 1984). In addition, there have been historical periods in the United States when Puerto Rican voting and political participation rose without resulting in any substantial increase in power. Voting and other examples of formal political participation do little to explain the extent of Puerto Rican community power and the way such power gets generated and lost in contemporary American society.

The continuing problems of poverty and low education remind us that incorporation is not the same as power.[16] Political influence is not an easily observed or a clearly linked product of formal participation. The number of votes cast by Puerto Ricans does not usually lead to desired policy outcomes. Electing more Puerto Ricans to political office does little to directly alleviate total levels of poverty or housing distress. Voting rates and elected officials offer, in this sense, merely the promise of influence, not its guarantee. And it's a promise realized, for the most part, on minor, symbolic issues and, perhaps, only for individual voters. The socioeconomic data provides, in any case, ample proof that, potential or not, formal incorporation has not had any real impact on Puerto Rican community life. This leaves the much weaker counterargument that voting and the election of in-group members to political office is in and of itself a political good and a harbinger of, at least, a potential influence down the line (see Dahl 1991, 21).

Let's examine the issue of political power in a different way. The relationship between particular events and influence has, arguably, a commonsensical component. On the surface, it is much easier to make the case that the Young Lords' garbage protest led to particular results. The Lords burn garbage in the streets and the mayor sends sanitation trucks. The study of political events such as this, thus, has obvious merit for the study of power. The focus on particular events is not, admittedly, without its problems. Though particular events can more easily be linked to situations of influence, it's harder to establish whether such "correlations" are actually causal.

There are innumerable processes at work in any event that may have contributed the necessary or sufficient push to make something happen.

More narrowly, it's hard to establish the real impact of events on the conditions of power for the Puerto Rican community. The reason is that power itself is not so easily measured. Events can help us to understand the extent of Puerto Rican power only if they are analyzed in the context of existing social structures, which requires theoretical and empirical analysis of how the garbage protest fits into the larger historical plane for Puerto Ricans and the city of New York. Given that requirement, what exactly did garbage do?

Even as an event, some may question whether that 1969 protest was, in fact, the high point of Puerto Rican community influence in the last thirty years or so. Perhaps Herman Badillo's 1970 election to Congress was more significant? Were Badillo's many failed candidacies for mayor of New York City more important? There is, also, the Aspira Consent Decree that established bilingual education in 1974. What about the 1977 takeover of the Statue of Liberty by Puerto Rican Independentistas? Then there is the 1973 Puerto Rican Legal Defense and Education Fund victory in court that established the right to bilingual voting instructions and election ballots. There can be no debate with the idea that each of these events was significant for the development of the Puerto Rican community in New York and in the United States. It is also clear that each of these very significant events succeeded in large part through the ability of the primary actors to project their demands on and to make effective use of the media. Each profited, furthermore, from an image of Puerto Ricans as tough and inventive defenders of their rights as citizens, an image that owed a huge debt to the earlier militant efforts of the Lords. More about this later.

If the garbage protest was, indeed, a turning point, it was also not the only time when Puerto Ricans achieved notable power in this period. What is true is that the garbage protest was not just another protest or riot by Puerto Ricans during this period. In the garbage protest, the Lords actually capitalized and amplified on a number of earlier protests by the Puerto Rican community against the lack of sanitation in the East Harlem community.[17] The garbage protest, therefore, was pivotal not just for the trivial reason that particular results can be traced back to this action. It was pivotal because it marked a turning point in Puerto Rican orientation towards the media and because it incited public attention and political influence even if that influence was not unmediated or lasting.

The garbage protest was the best example of the explicit recognition by Puerto Ricans of the new opportunities for power presented by the growing role of the media in American politics. The pre-Lords protests by Puerto Ricans over garbage, in contrast, were routine, almost timid efforts. They received media coverage but the reports merely showed Puerto Ricans doing their civic duty to clean up the streets with their own volunteer labor and materials. The pre-Lords garbage protests served instead to remind political leaders and the public of their respective political and civic responsibilities. There were also moments prior to the Lords when Puerto Rican protests achieved a high level of inventiveness and demonstrated ability to draw media attention.

One significant protest occurred in the mid-1960s when the Aspira Club Federation (ACF) protested a new policy to raise City University of New York's (CUNY) admissions standards.[18] The new standards would have hurt the admissions chances of many college-bound Puerto Rican high school graduates. Scores of ACF students picketed in front of Governor Nelson Rockefeller's home dressed as symbolic "mothers," "fathers," and "children." Parents led the demonstration holding a casket and signs proclaiming that Rockefeller had "killed the future of high school Puerto Rican youth" (Pantoja 2002, 105). The results were swift and prophetic. Rockefeller met with Aspira, the ACF, and parents. The results were that "all students affected entered college the next autumn" (106). The success of this media-conscious protest was a harbinger of what would come later with the Lords.

Aspira used media-friendly symbols to get a message across to politicians. The mechanism that made the casket protest work was, however, a psychological and moral one. Rockefeller and other public officials got shamed. The Lords protest, on the other hand, *scared* political leaders and the public. By scaring them, the Lords, as Machiavelli once argued, gained a measure of respect and power that had been missing for the Puerto Rican community. In the early 1970s, as Elena Padilla explained, Puerto Ricans became "a potent political force in the city, involved in struggles for self-determination through community control" (Padilla 1972, 18).

Protesting Garbage and Authority

Everything the Lords did about the garbage in their streets in 1969 was done a year earlier by the Puerto Rican residents of El Barrio—except burn it. Infuriated by the piles of garbage festering in the streets after the Sanitation Department strike, residents of El Barrio and the Lower East Side took to the streets on February 1968 to clean it up any way they could. Scores of residents and community organizations volunteered their labor, while local merchants contributed food and cleaning tools to the effort. Some volunteers even suggested that theirs was an act of militancy, calling themselves the "East Harlem Liberation Front."[19] They did every-thing the Lords did about the garbage except burn it, disrupt the peace, and confront the police and other city institutions.

The Lords burned the garbage in 1969 as a spontaneous solution to the problem of what to do about the garbage they had collected in huge piles. Though unplanned, the burning was significant. In the 1968 effort, the volunteers simply hauled away the garbage themselves, in rental trucks they had paid for. Disposing of the garbage was not very important for the Lords. Confronting institutions and challenging their legitimacy, espe-cially by the use of the media, were more important.

The Lords asked the Sanitation Department for brooms. When they were denied, they took them. They could have bought their own. They went on to burn the piles of garbage, fully expecting "a confrontation with the police" (Melendez 2003, 103). They chose to burn garbage be-cause they knew that in order to "stun the community," they had to do "something with a sense of drama, and a flair" (Young Lords Party 1975, 246). The Lords recognized that they had launched a new chapter in Puerto Rican politics in the United States with their collective act of defi-ance. They believed and hoped that the "garbage offensive" had over-turned the Puerto Rican "colonial pathology of docility" (Melendez 2003, 106). They probably did help to change attitudes towards political au-thority, even if only temporarily. Their most important contribution, how-ever, was to help change the Puerto Rican relation to the media. One can say that in this area, the Lords even changed themselves.

Power and the Media

The garbage protest is representative of a more general pattern of political power for Puerto Ricans from the late 1960s to the present. Over that pe-riod, Puerto Ricans rode a fluctuating wave where political power came tantalizingly close only to fall farther away. Repeatedly, Puerto Ricans ap-peared to make considerable political strides only to see any burgeoning power vanish quickly. The reality is that much of what Puerto Ricans achieved politically in this period, from electing Puerto Ricans to public office to victories in the courts, however, amounted to nothing more than political incorporation without real power. Some would attribute that in-corporation to the organizing and mobilizing efforts of Puerto Rican lead-ers (Cruz 2004, 15). That incorporation, however, seemed to gain mo-mentum only with the heightened public attention Puerto Ricans began to receive in the 1970s. Each moment of attention came only after a radical shift in public and media perceptions about Puerto Ricans. This was especially true about their eventual inclusion within the socially proscribed categories of protected minority as well as "social menace."

Until the Lords, Puerto Ricans had been a different sort of menace to New York City. In 1967, one New York City policeman summarized the dominant view that Puerto Ricans "all feel the world owes them something, but they are inherently lazy" ("East 96th Street" 1967). Puerto Ricans were thus seen as lazy low-lifes and as a defiant, perhaps criminal, element. The Lords played an extremely important role in altering this perception of Puerto Ricans. Violent protest, like those Puerto Ricans resorted to with riots during the 1960s and the more strategic activities of the Young Lords, created opportunities for third parties to enter the fray on behalf of the protestors (Fording 2001). Social workers, teachers, and, above all, politicians profited from the newfound attention given to Puerto Ricans. This was made possible, furthermore, by the use of the mass media. Such a process was clearly at work in the Lords' occupation of the Methodist Church. It is not only the aggrieved group that receives the benefits that can accrue from violent protest, however. Third parties to the dispute can also benefit. This is especially true if members of these third parties are also members of the aggrieved group.

The election of Herman Badillo to Congress in 1970 has been largely attributed to a redrawn congressional district (Cruz and Santiago 2001, 26). Given Badillo's previous electoral failures, a large portion of this congressional victory has to also be attributed to his association with the Young Lords during 1970. Badillo jumped into the fray during the Lords' occupation of the Methodist Church as a mediator to the dispute ("Badillo Confers" 1970). Melendez argued that Badillo was instrumental in getting the legal charges against the Lords dropped and was able to get the National Council of Churches to provide the Lords with other space (2003, 129). For all of his help to the Lords, Badillo helped himself more. When he won the election to Congress, he was essentially unopposed since "there was no Republican candidate, and Mr. Badillo had only a Conservative opponent, 30-year old George B. Smaragdas" ("Lowenstein" 1970). It seemed as though local political leaders in the city had cleared the path for Badillo's election.

Throughout the year 1970, it seemed as though most of the political establishment was eager to promote Badillo as a leader for Puerto Ricans, perhaps hoping he could prevent further problems with the Puerto Ricans. In January of 1970, a new "Puerto Rican" district was created out of pieces of Manhattan, the Bronx and Queens.[20] Many politicians at the time believed that this new district was "tailored-made for the expected Congressional candidacy of former Bronx Borough President Herman Badillo, a Democrat who was born in Puerto Rico" (ibid.). That view was more than mere speculation since the incumbent congressman, a Democrat, decided not to try for reelection in the new district and instead opted to "challenge one of two incumbent Democrats in contiguous districts" (ibid.). There were other behind-the-scenes political maneuvers designed to make Badillo a congressman.

In March, Mayor Lindsay appointed Badillo to the board of a new quasi independent corporation to run the city's eighteen public hospitals.[21] It didn't help. The Lords and community organizations took over Lincoln Hospital in the South Bronx in July. Then, later in July, Puerto Ricans in the East Village section of Manhattan rioted, looted and attacked police cars. Puerto Ricans in other parts of the city attacked and burned police cars, telephone trucks, and other official vehicles.[22] City authorities had clearly lost the respect and trust of significant portions of the Puerto Rican community. It was becoming increasingly clear that what city officials and reporters saw as they surveyed Puerto Rican communities in the various barrios of New York was "a threatening crowd of Puerto Ricans" (ibid.).

These events suggest that it was this emerging perception of Puerto Ricans as a growing social menace that helped to get Badillo elected to Congress and led to the greater political incorporation of the Puerto Rican community.[23] It is hard, as a result, to imagine anything that Puerto Ricans have attained since then or that others have said or written about them that does not spring from the perception and reality that Puerto Ricans were now both a protected minority and a social menace. The first category was as important as the second.

The path towards becoming a legally protected minority began seriously for Puerto Ricans on June 13, 1966. On that date, the U.S. Supreme Court heard two cases involving the voter registration of Puerto Ricans.[24] In these two cases, the Court drew on the growing concern with civil rights. It essentially upheld the right of non-English speakers to register to vote without having English literacy. It also did more. It established the legally protected status of Puerto Ricans in the United States. In Justice Brennan's deliberation over the Equal Protection Clause of the Constitution and section §4(e) of the Voting Rights Act of 1965, he stated that "§4(e) may be viewed as a measure to secure for the Puerto Rican community residing in New York nondiscriminatory treatment by government—both in the imposition of voting qualifications and the provision or administration of governmental services, such as public schools, public housing and law enforcement."[25] This decision established the necessary legal precedence for the civil rights battles and victories Puerto Ricans waged later. It also established Puerto Ricans as a group the Court had determined had experienced legal harm that required legal/political remedy.

This placed Puerto Ricans potentially at the same level as African Americans whose history of slavery and movement for civil rights were much more central to U.S. history and its social conscience. This potential remained unrealized until the Young Lords propelled Puerto Ricans into national political life.

Ultimately, perceptions are ephemeral. Public opinion may be something managed effectively by politicians, consultants, and media organizations. Its structures, however, are unstable and hard to control. It didn't take long for the New York City Sanitation Department and Mayor Lindsay, for example, to get over their initial caution and compromise to the Lords of 1969. The Young Lords and Puerto Ricans had made a bold and outrageous statement.[26] They had taken control of their small part of the city. The Lords' protest brought media and public attention. It also made them better known to law enforcement. As a result, they became the subject of counterintelligence, some got arrested, and one died suspiciously in prison. This coercive response by law enforcement, by the state, is a strong sign of the threat the Lords posed, of the real power they wielded.

The Lords themselves saw it that way. Their power was real enough. They got quick results. It was also essentially generated by and rested on the use of the media. It was a power that was grown and transmitted primarily by the TV screens and newspapers that reported their story to the world (Bennett and Entman 2000). That made their power suspect and vulnerable. The Lords lacked "the access to money, power and friendly media that sustains the established institutions of society."[27] The problem is not that media, as a cultural institution, doesn't have the causal heft of material means of production. The problem is that Puerto Ricans and most working-class groups have no leverage, no easy mechanism for striking, influencing, and punishing the media. To paraphrase Marx, since Puerto Ricans and other workers are not the primary creators of value for mediated means of cultural production, they lack lasting cultural and media power.

All power, however, contains an unavoidable element of public opinion. Political power relationships especially, must be established, maintained, defended, and promoted publicly. Very often, the very core of power depends on a public recognition, perception, and approval of who has and who doesn't have it. It is for that reason that when powerful people get treated, mistakenly, like weak minions, they are quick to assert and remind onlookers of their power by asking rhetorically, "Do you know who I am?" Knowing who occupies various positions within the galaxy of power players is as important for those with power as it as for those with little power. It is also a job of power that is focused on managing perception and public opinion. That was the contribution of the Young Lords.

They told the rest of the world what Puerto Ricans themselves already knew: that Puerto Ricans were to be reckoned with.

Yet despite this truth about power, the problem for Puerto Ricans was that their power in this period consisted largely of mediated public perception. The influence Puerto Ricans achieved in this period was mostly gained through the use of the TV media. It was real and effective. Yet it rested on blown-up images, on their ability to offer spectacles in what Jean Baudrillard called the contemporary political economy of symbolic exchange (1993). It rested on their ability to scare, shame, and surprise. More importantly, the Lords delivered a string of events "easily pictured by the TV cameras and narrated with melodramatic logic" (Nimmo and Combs 1990, 29). They could not, however, keep this up. Perhaps, no one could.

The Lords raised some power for Puerto Ricans by virtue of their mediated events. There is nothing very unusual about what made this possible. Ever since television became a dominant force in American politics in the early 1960s, researchers have argued that television has had the unique capacity to set the public agenda of what is important for people to think about and do (Oliver and Myers 1999). There is even evidence that television not only shapes what we think about but how we do so. As Kerbel stated, "television structures how we think about things through the context in which information is presented" (1999, 6).

Before television can influence the public in any way, however, it must identify the content, the subjects of its broadcasts. Typically, television has a preference for dramatic "episodes of celebration, crisis, conquest, crime, and contest" (Nimmo and Combs 1990, 29). More specifically, some research shows that "conflictual events are generally more likely to receive media coverage than other events of similar size and form" (Oliver and Myers 1999, 39). The Lords presented episodes of conflict by the bushels. More interestingly, the Lords engaged in a kind of conflict that appears to have particular appeal to American publics. In late 1969, after the garbage protest, the Lords began to specialize in taking buildings hostage.

Nimmo and Combs argue that Americans have had a long fascination with stories of captivity, real or imagined. Thus, Americans have a long historical attraction, going back to the early nineteenth century, to stories where individuals are held "hostage for some ransom, booty, or consideration" (Nimmo and Combs 1990, 46). In December of 1969, the Young Lords seized the First Spanish Methodist Church in East Harlem ("Puerto Rican Group Seizes" 1969). This inspired a level of media attention Puerto Ricans had never encountered or enjoyed in the past.

As figure 5.6 shows, reports on the Young Lords surged to 40 percent of all news reports on Puerto Ricans appearing in the *New York Times*

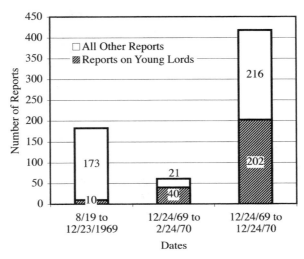

Figure 5.6. *New York Times* Reporting on PRs and Young Lords. *Source*: New York Times Index.

during the first two months of 1970. The church takeover actually received more attention from the press than did the garbage protest. The Young Lords also became a major television story. Table 5.9 below also shows that national television paid more attention to the Young Lords than to leading Puerto Rican politician Herman Badillo.

The seizure of the church made a compelling television story for a number of reasons. It was a hostage story with a twist. The Lords captured a building rather than people. It was the same thing with their later capture of Lincoln Hospital. They appeared dangerous yet used the church space for a free breakfast program and free medical care. The mixed messages in the Lords' actions made their story more appealing. Their actions had the drama and spectacle of traditional hostage taking without the actual violence. They were like a "made for TV" movie. Though the ending was unknown to observers at the time, they understood that the hostage moment was essentially benign.

The results were not just media attention but significant public approval. Not long after the church seizure, eighty-four elected executives of the Protestant National Council of Churches requested in a petition that charges be dropped against the Lords for occupying the East Harlem church ("84 Church Aides" 1970). These executives, including high-ranking officials in Methodist and other Protestant church institutions, declared the need to identify "with the weak and the poor and their needs" (ibid.). Clearly, the Lords had captured not just a church but the public's imagination and interest.[28] The power they garnered from this action stood, however, in stark contrast to the kind of power Puerto Ricans had achieved and strived for in the past.[29]

It was the city's need for Puerto Rican labor that was at the center of earlier Puerto Rican community power. Cigar makers represented the apex of power for Puerto Ricans in the pre–World War II period. Later, the larger society and New York City sought Puerto Ricans to satisfy both their need for cheap labor as well as their need for pawns to present as glorious exhibits in the great American experiment to lift Puerto Rico by its "Bootstraps."[30] Chapter 2 presented this nexus of economic and political needs that established a "political machine"–like core of influence for Puerto Ricans in the 1950s.[31] Since then, several processes have altered the interests of New York and the United States in Puerto Ricans. With those changes, the prospects for power for Puerto Ricans were transformed.

The deindustrialization of northern cities as well as the successful casting of Puerto Ricans as disposable, cheap labor severely weakened this formula for power after 1960. The successful launching of Puerto Rico's Associate Free State and the forging of a legitimate government in Puerto Rico weakened national and local political interest in the welfare and political behavior of Puerto Ricans in the United States. In addition, the rise of the civil rights movement and the rapidly increasing role of the media in American politics during the 1960s appeared to end old opportunities for power while it created new ones Puerto Ricans were not very prepared to exploit.

The rise of mediated politics more than anything changed the landscape for power. In the past, it was a sufficient and effective mechanism of influence to go on strike and take other actions to affect individual employers. The ability to influence was once built on the capacity of Puerto Ricans to satisfy needs for cheap labor, or on the fact that they stood in the way of "progress" in Puerto Rico, or even on the need to offer Puerto Ricans favors, housing, and jobs to entice them away from local radical politicians like Marcantonio. Now, to have a significant impact, Puerto Ricans have to reach political leaders, economic bosses, and the general public not directly in factories, stores, or street corners. Increasingly today, influence has to be generated through the media. Increasingly, it appears that "reality is created, or constructed, through communication— not expressed by it" (Nimmo and Combs 1990, 3). Through groups like the Young Lords, Puerto Ricans took major but flawed steps towards taking advantage of these changes in the political and economic terrain of power in the post-1950s period.

Today, as a result, Puerto Ricans have more Puerto Rican elected officials, several talking media heads, and celebrities even as the Puerto Rican community as a whole continues to lose its economic footing and social compass. These examples of Puerto Rican power and formal political incorporation have some origin in what the Young Lords initiated. It's hard to say exactly how much. In some ways, the garbage spectacle represented the height of what was possible for a working-class community cast as a racial minority and as cheap labor in this new realm where so much of power and politics came "mediated" (Gandy 2002).

The Lords were able to capture the public's attention and imagination to a degree that no Puerto Rican politician or leader has been able to do since then. Puerto Ricans had become alienated from traditional economic sources of power in workplaces and unions by the loss of jobs and union manipulation. Politically, Puerto Ricans were marginal factors both as clients of the Democratic machine and as participants in the political reform period of the 1960s. Commentators, at the time, shared a "widely held view in the early 1960s, reinforced by both media stereotypes and academic treatises . . . that the Puerto Rican community was docile and politically inactive" (Gandy 2000, 732).

The Young Lords, however, freed Puerto Ricans from the fruitless pursuit of traditional avenues of political incorporation by the adoption of a political style centered on dramatic confrontation played before the cameras. Puerto Rican political power, or its potential, soared as a result. Many Puerto Rican political leaders and institutions have taken this lesson to heart. It is true that, in the end, the Lords' impact could not reverse the deep, corrosive impact of poverty and social instability during this recent period. Despite all their efforts and their significant achievements, Puerto Ricans have lost most of the power they acquired during the Lords period. That, however, is a reflection of the fact that perhaps Puerto Ricans don't have enough or a lasting value in the minds and eyes of the rest of America.

Post-1960s Dance of Power

The impact of the Lords' garbage protest can be gauged by the period that followed it. What specifically was achieved as a result of the protests? One particular achievement was to reverse the increasing lack of interest by the rest of New York City in whatever political, economic, or cultural values Puerto Ricans offered. The evidence for this comes from a number of natural indicators of public preferences.[32] Most public entities, as we have seen, paid Puerto Ricans almost no attention during this period. Puerto Ricans went unnoticed and unvalued. The Young Lords period was a heroic and extraordinary exception to all that. That they succeeded even for a limited period was a tribute to their ingenuity and will.

In very real but limited ways, the Puerto Rican situation in the United States has improved. Economically, there are fewer Puerto Ricans living in poverty today than ten years ago. Educational levels have improved. More Puerto Ricans have been elected to political office. Many Puerto Ricans now also work in corporate America. And Puerto Ricans have increasingly left New York City, wandering off to other eastern cities and towns in search of a better life. The Puerto Rican community has also been very resourceful in orienting itself towards the new reality of mediated politics. This hasn't generally been a conscious and deliberate process. Nevertheless, the Puerto Rican community in this period discovered the critical importance of media in contemporary American politics.

Media's role in power and politics had been growing for decades. Even as early as 1948, Paul F. Lazarsfeld and Robert K. Merton had concluded that "increasingly, the chief power groups, among which organized business occupies the most spectacular place, have come to adopt techniques for manipulating mass publics through propaganda in place of more direct means of control."[33] The Young Lords, in important ways, took advantage of that emerging reality and advanced the Puerto Rican community's efforts to harness media to its needs. It's true that, despite these achievements, Puerto Ricans, as a group, remain far behind most other groups. They also remain, as a whole, largely marginalized from the main avenues of economic and political action. While Puerto Ricans, thus, were able to grab a share of mediated power in this period, in all the other areas that count, they remain relatively powerless.

The Young Lords became a focal point for the post-1960s period in a number of specific ways. They, of course, took outrageous public actions and received abundant media attention. They also represented the moderate levels of Puerto Rican alienation and distance from existing political and economic structures. Their rise as militant opponents to American values and practices had the effect of bringing more attention and some influence to Puerto Ricans. Some have attributed very specific achievements to the Lords, from the creation of the Lead Poisoning Project at Montifiore Medical Center to the funding of the free breakfast program in city public schools (Gandy 2002, 249). The Lords organization didn't last very long. Their impact, however, extends beyond these very specific achievements.

The Lords taught Puerto Ricans that the media had become not just a channel but also a major object of power in this most recent period. They introduced the Puerto Rican community to the heights of what was possible. They placed the Puerto Rican community at center stage and pushed

TABLE 5.9
National Television Reporting

Years 1969–1971	Herman Badillo	The Young Lords
Featured in Report	0	2
Mentioned in Report	6	0

Source: Vanderbilt University Television News Archive.

TABLE 5.10
Percentage New York Times Reporting

Dates	All Other Puerto Ricans	The Young Lords
8/19/1969 to 12/23/1969	95%	5%
12/24/1969 to 2/24/1970	60%	40%
12/24/1969 to 12/24/1970	67%	33%

Source: New York Times Index.

it to dance to the larger society's media-driven style. In some ways, everything else that has happened since then has benefited from their actions. The creation of the Puerto Rican Legal Defense Fund in 1971, its court victories, Badillo's electoral success, the creation of the Institute for Puerto Rican Policy in 1979 and all of its pioneering policy work, and much more owes a great debt to the Lords.[34] This is a big claim.[35] It is also not without some evidence to support it. The Lords during the three year period from 1969 to 1971, for instance, made it to the national media stage almost as much as Herman Badillo. As table 5.9 shows, the Lords actually had more featured stories on national television than Badillo, who found himself merely mentioned in stories about the New York City mayoral race and as a congressman.

There is additional empirical information available to support the position that the Lords made the media pay more attention to Puerto Ricans. The Lords received a lot of local television coverage. The records that could verify this idea are, however, not available. Newspaper reporting on the Young Lords, however, did increase dramatically in 1970. Table 5.10 shows the large impact of the Lords on local media. In particular, it shows that the *New York Times* reports on the Young Lords became 40 percent of all stories written about Puerto Ricans in early 1970 and 33 percent for the entire year.

It's clear that the Young Lords movement created tremendous media attention for Puerto Ricans. They may also have helped Puerto Ricans achieve some of the political victories described above. It wasn't mere coincidence. Some of this success can be attributed to the new political climate created by the civil rights movement and the federal War on Poverty programs. Those movements and programs, however, existed before the

Lords period, and they did little for Puerto Ricans. The Puerto Rican community had, also, plenty of organizations and leaders before and after the Lords. These organizations and leaders worked, however, within the norms of convention and probity more compatible, unfortunately, with an earlier period. The difference maker, what stands out, was the four- or five-year period of the Young Lord's political movement and spectacle.[36]

Puerto Rican politics prior to the Lords was locked into a movement by professional, middle-class Puerto Ricans to establish their independence from the government of Puerto Rico and to secure their place within the formal political institutions of the city. The Puerto Rican Forum, in particular, tried mightily to wrest money for Puerto Ricans from antipoverty funds (Pantoja 2004). Others battled African Americans to get Puerto Ricans a fairer share of public funds (Cruz 2004). The overly ambitious Herman Badillo became Bronx borough president in the 1960s. Still, Badillo was not that respected within the Puerto Rican community. Badillo was identified by fellow Puerto Ricans as having less political influence than Gilberto Gerena-Valentin, a long-time political activist and the president of the small and new National Association for Puerto Rican Civil Rights ("Mexicans Target of Riot" 1966).

Puerto Rican activists, responding to this university study in 1966, identified Gerena-Valentin as having the most influence. Badillo came in fourth. In any case, Puerto Rican leaders of this period churned out studies and proposals, made policy recommendations, and occasionally held protests. They did all of this with a careful eye not to ruffle too many feathers or to appear uncivilized.

One telling moment came in 1968 when leaders of the Puerto Rican Community Development Project (PRCDP) attempted to make their own organization more accountable by removing board members and a director who they thought were working at odds to the mission of the organization. These efforts resulted in some humiliation, however, when the city ordered them to reinstate their board and director ("Puerto Ricans" 1968). Twenty-seven dissident members of the PRCDP Board reacted to the city's actions by resigning (Pantoja 2002, 118). In her memoirs, Pantoja lamented that the primary mistake of the mostly professional leaders within the PRCDP was that they did not fully understand "the extent to which some of our leaders would go to obtain money and power" (116). A more important lapse was that they did not understand that it was the city and local officials and not the PRCDP leaders who called the shots.

The point isn't that these groups were still trying to work the reformist game of incremental reforms, that they had not yet become as militant as the Young Lords. Militancy and radicalism were not unknown to the Puerto Rican community. Puerto Rican nationalists, after all, displayed considerable militancy by shooting at President Truman in 1950.[37] The point is that these pre-Lords organizations and leaders were simply too naïve about the nature of city politics, the dance of politics, as well as unable to recognize that the politics of that period made the media a dominant force. Any substantial amount of influence would require the generation of colorful, perhaps menacing, images and sound bites.[38]

The Lords also influenced other Puerto Rican organizations, leaders, and events. Some researchers like to connect the dots to make this argument about the Lord's impact as a question of networking and personal contacts. It's true that many of the institutions and leaders that emerged after the Lords, like the Puerto Rican Legal Defense and Education Fund and El Museo, had ex-Lords or associates as leaders and founders. The connection, as I have said, is actually even more intimate and telling. What these institutions and organizations shared with the Lords was the recognition that political success required channeling their demands and requests through the media. That they didn't achieve as much as the Lords says more about the limitations of media-generated power than about the special gifts found in the leadership of the Lords.

The downfall of the Lords and the continued socioeconomic decline of the Puerto Rican community is also a reminder of how limited this kind of mediated power proves ultimately to be. It's true that "much of the Puerto Rican future . . . will depend on this community's ability to shape its own image" (Falcon 2004, 156). It's even truer that the way others perceive Puerto Ricans isn't completely in Puerto Rican hands.

Established powers eventually lost much of their interest in continuing to engage with a Puerto Rican community that, since the Lords, had lost its sharp and menacing media edge. The Lords proved that power could be generated through the skillful use of the media, by making one's group story spectacular, menacing, and novel. This kind of power also tends to easily drift away. Spinning such images is the kind of work that, in the long run, is simply not easily sustained.

It may be that this modern period requires herculean efforts of will and enterprise to generate a constant stream of sensational, media-friendly activity, especially with media institutions owned and tied to dominant social structures. This was something the Lords and the Puerto Rican community didn't have. The Lords proved that images are part of the process of group interests and interaction that create and limit power. They also proved that the Puerto Rican community was not up to the task of satisfying this appetite for images and color. This study has proven that this failure is due as much to puny interests in Puerto Ricans found in the larger society as it is to Puerto Rican failure to make the right moves.

Conclusion

It consisted of irregularity, change, sliding forward, not keeping in step, collisions of things and affairs, and fathomless points of silence in between, of paved ways and wilderness, of one great rhythmic throb and the perpetual discord and dislocation of all opposing rhythms.

—Musil, 1935

Musil was writing about cities.[1] He could have been writing about dancing. He could have been writing about the dancing of the Puerto Rican community in the city of New York. He could have been writing about the moves they made, the moves they didn't make, and the way others responded. He could have been writing about the power they won and the power they lost. Musil tried to capture the feverish action of city life. His words came very close to capturing the devilish energy of the city. In some ways, they didn't. It's not that Musil didn't have the language skills. It's just hard to accurately describe anything while trying, at the same time, to capture the speed and direction of its movement. Even cameras have a hard time with this. We have, as a result, cameras that are better for taking still pictures and others that are better for taking moving pictures.

Words don't easily capture the movements, rhythms, invitations, rejections, compliance, conflict, notice, communion, and anonymity of what takes place on the social dance floor. They don't always reveal the internal mechanisms and external social pressures that produce the cacophony and complexity of activity on the dance floor. Words don't always reveal the usually invisible moments of influence that result from all that activity and what inspires it. Words wrapped up in observations, insight, explanations, and theory are, however, all we have.

Dancing was the key to Puerto Rican power. It was the Puerto Rican entrance onto U.S. dance floors, in New York City and elsewhere, and the reaction of those they encountered there that created the opportunity for and shattering of power for this community. It was about what they wanted and desired. It was about what others wanted from them. Power, as we learned early on, is fluid and alive. Shifts in interests, a desire to dance or a need for companionship, create moments of influence and vulnerability. Any movement is toward and away from something and someone, connecting and disconnecting. Movements establish what is desired and what can be left behind. By doing so, they create and destroy possibilities to influence. They create a dance where interests reveal a "pure tension, cyclic struggle in its steps."[2]

Those dance steps, the engagement and interaction with others, and the moments of influence that result are, of course, infinite in number and varied in their complexity. There is no easy way to capture all of these moments in their entirety. Power doesn't stay still long enough. Our tools and skills as researchers are limited and inadequate. I think, nonetheless, that we captured the critical and important moments in Puerto Rican community history in this study. There are bound to be objections. I certainly hope I inspired some debate. I am confident that I did the best I could to capture both the movement and origins of power for Puerto Ricans with the data and archival materials available.

Puerto Rican community history validates this dance model of power. The previous chapters showed that the Puerto Rican community has been systemically weakened through a two-way process. They became dependent on values controlled by the larger society while society became less dependent on values controlled by Puerto Ricans. The Puerto Rican story with power is tragic but, to a large extent, not unique. Power comes and goes for everyone in similar ways. It comes to the extent that one controls values that others cannot do without. It goes to the extent that one pursues and cannot do without values that others control.

Each of the previous chapters is an attempt to document and explore this dance of interests and power. There was the cigar makers' period in chapter 2, the rising tide of new Puerto Rican migrants in the 1950s in chapter 3, the loss of political and economic interest in chapter 4, and the media-focused gains inspired by the Young Lords in the 1970s in chapter 5. Each period witnessed efforts by Puerto Ricans to engage America and wrest moments of influence from the engagement.

Sometimes Puerto Ricans moved with dance steps that accentuated their economic value and at other times they emphasized their political value. Their ability to beautifully wrap cigars or to work hard for very little pay attracted notice and got them on the main dance floor in the United States. As naturally born citizens since 1917, on the other hand, Puerto Ricans have always stirred some sporadic interest, especially from politicians who believed that their votes could make a difference in their election.

Dance steps sprung from Puerto Rican cultural values, on the other hand, never got them much attention. Their musical, artistic, culinary, and performance styles never seemed to charm Americans or catch on. Puerto Ricans stepped onto that dance floor, moved, and exhibited what they had with exquisite skills, confidence, determination, and flare. When they had partners, Puerto Ricans moved well, often in their own ways and at their own pace. Most of the time, however, they found that they had to dance, when they could, the way others wanted.

There were moments when Puerto Ricans rejected dancing with non–Puerto Ricans. Mostly, these moments came after Puerto Ricans had been repeatedly rebuffed on the dance floor. In response, they patrolled the sidelines and gave ominous message to those others lucky enough to still be engaged on the dance floor. As in *West Side Story*, they drew lines, rejecting and menacing those others that hovered near them. Sometimes, they opted for a cool distancing and indifference that proved to be more impotence than lure. Puerto Ricans could not entice those who could not see or want to see them.

When Puerto Ricans have been able to attract interest and move well, they achieved some influence. This always occurred because others, especially "important" others, had some need or concern for Puerto Rican industrial skills, their capacity to work for low wages, their ability to distract from or disrupt official plans, their entrance into the category of social menace or protected minority, or because the media found them to be an enticing bundle of images for popular consumption. Have I proven this argument?

As I've said, the moments when power accumulates or drifts away are real but hard to document. Mostly, they pass unnoticed and unrecorded. Power is a "circularity of impositions, negotiations, and upheavals" that originates from and transforms the internal emotional and intellectual states of the dancers. As such, it "permanently reproduces subjection and rebellion" (Savigliano 1995, 70). The interests and passions that lie behind them are not written down, easily observed, or apparent.

What can be seen, documented, and measured easily is the dancing, the guiding influence of one partner's hands on another. What drew them together or apart, the inner and outer dynamic bundle of interests and emotions behind the dancing, is not so easily observed. In addition, the small resistance of the follower or the imposition of a different pace on the leader goes largely unnoticed to outside observation. The data presented in this study, thus, does not provide conclusive proof. It can't. The data consists of snapshots or tracings of moving subjects. Taken together, these tracings are more than suggestive of the interests that lie behind the movement, however.

The patterns of interest and dance suggested by stamps, obituaries, newspaper coverage, first names, music consumption, and lists, as well as by historical records, provide good indicators of those changing interests. These indicators do not lend themselves easily to regression or correlation coefficients. They are too nominal, complex, and fragmented. Statistical measurements, in any case, do not provide a sure way of getting at the truth. The margin for error is always present, even if those margins of error are accounted for in the statistic. More importantly, it is extremely difficult to subject dynamic phenomena, like power, to statistical manipulation. As W. Phillips Shively once said, "concepts that can be measured directly are usually trivial in and of themselves."[3]

The more important problem is that most social science methods are geared towards accounting for the behavior of individuals rather than groups. Statistical methods are thus largely useless for understanding the behavior of a community and group like that of Puerto Ricans. Though this study is about group interactions, some people will insist that no groups are monolithic. Puerto Ricans are poor and rich. Puerto Ricans turn against American life as well as embrace it. I've tried to account for this complexity while trying to identify collective identity and movement. The answer, in some ways, is that the complexity of the Puerto Rican condition doesn't matter.

What's important for groups is the way others perceive and interact with them. What's important for this study is what that perception and interaction reveals about their interests and power as a group. The complex and differentiated economic, political, and cultural reality of Puerto Rican life in America is, in that sense, irrelevant. Jennifer Lopez's stardom and wealth isn't enough to counter the reality and the treatment of Puerto Ricans by others as mostly poor, marginalized, and invisible. The election of three Puerto Ricans to Congress doesn't change the essential powerlessness of the Puerto Rican community. In fact, this study showed the connection between these individual politicians' effectiveness as legislators and the community's powerlessness. Treating Puerto Ricans as one group is, thus, legitimate and worthwhile. In fact, this particular study of group interests and interaction provided some valuable lessons about the nature of power as well as about why Puerto Ricans and other minorities find themselves, as groups, so poor and with so little power.

Lessons

What have we learned about power from this study of the Puerto Rican community? First, there is the discovery that the Puerto Rican community has not been completely powerless nor has it lost power consistently over the years. Much of the research on Puerto Ricans has simply misunderstood this. The Puerto Rican story with power has in fact been quite complex and remarkable. Puerto Ricans had tremendous success along with dramatic failures.

Power is always relative. There is less or more of it but only in relation to others. Power fluctuates as the relationships that give it life evolve. That makes power fluid and hard to measure. The origins of power in interests and its effects on dancing are, however, open to observation. It is clear, in this context, that Puerto Ricans had moments with more power during each of the three periods studied in this book.

The cigar makers had an impact both within and outside the Puerto Rican community. Their power "went up in smoke," however, as employers made their moves and the larger society began to pay more attention to "minorities" who could demand and use the language of "rights."[4] The rapidly growing Puerto Rican community of the early 1950s was able to leverage unusual influence in New York City government that lasted as long as there was sufficient economic interest and political fear of the Puerto Rican community. The Young Lords period brought media attention, some political influence, and greater Puerto Rican independence from the larger society. Media attention produced influence for the Puerto Rican community in New York City politics and in Congress, produced increased group confidence and independence, and increased public recognition.

The key to Puerto Rican power in each of those periods was the dance with the larger U.S. society. Puerto Ricans gained power to the extent that they found themselves needed or desired or feared. Puerto Ricans took advantage of the economic need for their talent at rolling cigars in the second and third decades of the twentieth century. The United States wish to propagandize Operation Bootstrap in Puerto Rico made Puerto Ricans in New York City important, dangerous, and worth placating in the early 1950s. Puerto Ricans got more from the New York City government than they have in any other period since. Then, because the electronic and print media found the Young Lords an intoxicating brew of bravado, color, and controlled menace in the early 1970s, Puerto Ricans gained some power again.

Puerto Ricans also lost power because of dancing, or rather the lack of it. They lost power when others in the larger society lost interest in Puerto Ricans and whatever values they possessed. In the process of losing power, Puerto Ricans demonstrated the fallacy of so many popular assumptions about power.

First, it is clear from the Puerto Rican experience that numbers alone do not equal power. The Puerto Rican community has enjoyed power when its numbers as a population were small and lost it when its numbers were much larger. This may not seem like an important revelation, except that demographic growth continues to seduce many political researchers into the flaccid argument that power inevitably follows larger numbers.

Second, poverty does not have to mean little power. Power can be generated from all kinds of values, as long as those values draw interest. The Puerto Rican community has gained power, as in the early 1950s, when it was poor and inexperienced. It has lost power despite being relatively affluent, as happened to the cigar makers.[5]

Third, the Puerto Rican community has shown that voting does not always equate with power. Despite the periodic emphasis on voter registration and turnout, voting does not provide many opportunities to dance and influence political leaders. In the absence of other mechanisms for interacting with political leaders, voting becomes an activity that can be easily manipulated and marginalized by others.

Fourth, Puerto Ricans showed that a strategy of professional development, pursued in earnest during the 1960s, has limited payoffs. A professional strategy avoids politics in hopes of fashioning success through a cunning and strategic infiltration of dominant institutions. Success dooms the strategy, however. The few new Puerto Rican professionals got jobs tending to the needs of the poor or simply forgot the community that helped to get them into their profession. Puerto Rican infiltration turned into cooptation by those dominant institutions. More importantly, this strategy does nothing to increase the value of the Puerto Rican community to others in society.

A fifth lesson is that the achievement of minority group status did permit Puerto Ricans to move more freely in the new political vernacular and medium launched by the civil rights movement. It didn't, however, make Puerto Ricans more powerful in the long run. Puerto Ricans became a legally recognized " protected minority" with the passage of the 1965 Voting Rights Act, but they never attained the level of menace nor did they enjoy the psychic engagement that African Americans had with white America. Short of that, Puerto Ricans found that they could become part of the conversation and debate about the rights and plight of minorities in America but not part of the negotiations. Only in places like New York City did Puerto Ricans come close to the level of respect accorded African Americans in negotiating over federal antipoverty dollars. But not close enough.

Finally, the Puerto Rican experience with power reveals the critical new role of media in politics and power. Puerto Ricans were, of course, not the first to discover this, nor did they make extraordinary use of the media compared to other groups.[6] What is clear is that so much of the power of contemporary minority groups depends on the media. Indeed, it has become truer than ever, and as Nimmo and Combs have argued, "reality is created, or constructed, through communication" (1990, 3).

Why have so many theorists not learned these lessons about power? Part of the answer is perspective and the other is expediency. Like most social scientists, researchers of the Puerto Rican experience view power as a necessary evil and as an object to be possessed.[7] It is also true that something that is always in motion, like power, is cumbersome if not impossible to study. The tendency is to go with the quick, easy, and officially sanctioned methods despite their obvious limitations. Research on power thus concentrates on voting rates and population figures. Each additional vote or body becomes an additional level of power. One result of the superficial attempts to measure power is that they never seem to get right the role and influence of media.

Media has, in fact, become a vital part of politics for all Americans. The ability to influence the larger society depends on the ability of minority groups to use the media to raise public awareness of themselves as a group, to increase the legitimacy of their claims on the larger society, to shame and embarrass the larger society into action, as well as to sometimes frighten society with the possibility of minority violence. As a result, minority groups find themselves fighting to appear in the mass media, to reduce negative stereotypes, and even to place themselves in a position to present news and images about themselves to the public. Is it any wonder that the civil rights movement gained national momentum during the 1950s when average white Americans first became able to watch video on their new black and white televisions of the battles to end black segregation in the South and of the white violence against African Americans engaged in peaceful protest?

Media Power

The media has become a key dimension of modern U.S. politics and power. It is, for that reason, vital to Puerto Rican and minority politics. The media is, however, not just a tool of political influence. It also creates and constructs identities and bodies. Minority groups are, in many ways, "made" through the media. The media helps individuals discover their membership in particular groups, the kinds of behavior and symbols associated with that group, as well as its place within the hierarchy of groups in America. This is but one facet of the role the media plays in the general process of socialization of the American people.[8]

Even as adults, the American people have a hard time becoming independent of the messages provided by the media. In fact, the average American has actually become more dependent on the media for basic information and survival. When it comes to an identification of the facts and how to interpret them, Americans rely to a large extent on the media since they "rarely have enough information and understanding to form" independent views "about the many complex national and international issues that succeed one another with bewildering rapidity" (Graber 1984, 142).

The media's role in socialization can be seen in capitalist terms. The media, thus, not only "trains" the way people think; it does so in order to advance capitalist economic and political objectives. Indeed, as Arlene Davila has argued, minority group identities are often the product of capitalist marketing. She argues that the marketing industry has successfully reconstituted individuals of different Latino groups into "Hispanic" consumers and markets (Davila 2001, 2).[9]

Puerto Rican Choices

As important as the media has become to Puerto Ricans and minorities in general, many of the questions about Puerto Ricans have to do less with how much power they have and more with how they've used it. In particular, many critics believe that Puerto Ricans have not made wise decisions with whatever power they do have. This study disagrees with this assessment. Puerto Ricans have made incredible moves to gain power, have sometimes succeeded, and have made generally good decisions with the power they've attained. The quality of the choices they've made is, in any case, beside the point. The problems they've had have come about because of a lack of interest in dancing with them and because of the way they've used the power they've gained. Their problems have mostly come from not having enough power.

As this study has shown, constructed or not, Puerto Ricans have tremendous reserves of energy and pluck. They've repeatedly gotten off the mat and achieved, at various moments, considerable power. The key to their success is that they've not stopped *moving*. Poverty and defeat never stopped them from moving—from Puerto Rico, from Manhattan into the Bronx, away from New York City, from low-paying factory jobs, from a lack of respect, from useless voting, from white notions of racial identity, from American cultural values and to long-forgotten Puerto Rican cultural values, and from their own political and professional leaders. Their restless energy has often resulted in power. They've also lost power because it does "take two to tango."

Some could assume that Puerto Rican powerlessness has come about because Puerto Ricans have waited too long to dance, found bad suitors, acted mostly as followers on the dance floor, been easily colonized and conquered, or retreated into the background. The truth is that though they have often been the marginalized and wounded material of greater forces, Puerto Ricans were, at least, also "passionate objects, not passive ones. Objects that had, if not a say, at least a *move* to make in the power game" (Savigliano 1995, 70). Cigar makers, populist leaders like Gerena Valentin and Pantoja, the MCPRA, *Jíbaros,* professionals, and the Young Lords were the great *movers* in Puerto Rican community history.

This book has argued that if their power didn't last it was usually because their relations with others changed or hadn't really changed enough or in terms of fundamental interests. In many ways, Puerto Ricans were simply no longer being asked to dance. Were Puerto Ricans responsible for their rejection? Could they have dressed better, learned newer dance steps, or chosen better dance partners? Perhaps. Liberals are ever optimistic about the effectiveness of such strategies. They believe that anything is possible. They assume that individual and group progress is assured if only they can "stockpile all of the information drawn from every successful program in public education, employment, and community development so that an actual model for the future can be imagined."[10] The liberal perspective ignores the role of social structures.

These kinds of questions have also been a particular preoccupation of conservative critics in recent times. The essence of their complaint, however, is that blacks and Latinos do not take personal responsibility for the female-headed households, criminal violence, and drug addiction that plague and often perpetuate their own underclass status (Steele 1990). The dance model offers a way to explain this riddle of contemporary minority life in a way that accepts the small truths in both the conservative and liberal complaints. It all comes down to what happens on the dance floor. The conservative complaint that minorities perpetuate their own subjugation is equivalent to claiming that dancers are responsible for how they move and who they encounter when they do.

The conservative complaint is really about the kinds of dancing that minorities tend to do and with whom they do it. Conservatives think that minority moves are usually pointless and self-destructive. They also believe that minorities have a choice that they don't take to move and dance differently, to dance better, and to dance with better people.

The response to this charge is that there is both choice and experience. Dancing always has a history of hidden and open desires and the particular dance form that expresses them. Dance moves and forms evolve over time. The evolutionary development of dance styles is, moreover, something that is not controlled by any particular individual. It is a group experience. Each individual act of dancing comes with a trail of experiences for its practitioners. What happens before has a bearing on whether and how particular individuals move. Dancing leaves its mark.

There is, for example, the issue of rejection. Practically everyone has felt some self-doubt after experiencing rejection on the dance floor. Active and assertive agents are more likely to experience rejection. High expectations make rejection more painful. Conservative critics, however, don't believe that rejection leaves a mark or a mark that can't be overcome. Shelby Steele insists, for instance, on the idea that "a margin of choice is always open to blacks (even slaves had some choice)" (Steele 1990, 27). In a similar way, Linda Chavez once argued that Hispanic poverty and powerlessness were due to Hispanic failures, to their "emphasis . . . on rights, never on obligations" (Chavez 1991, 166). They are absolutely right. Individuals are always responsible for how they move, for not trying hard enough. They are not responsible, however, for what they move like, what dances they are trying to imitate, for how they channel their choices and desires. And though they are accountable for their actions, it doesn't mean that the moves they make will be successful.

The action on the dance floor is mostly an individual responsibility. Each dancer must take care to advance and move on the dance floor without disturbing and endangering his or her partner or other dancers. This is the margin of choice available in any dance. Mambo can be danced in an infinite number of different ways. The variation in style introduced by individual dancers makes dancing colorful and exciting to watch and do. Most people would agree, however, that the margin of individual decision is not unlimited. The reason is that what happens on the dance floor is a collective product of many individual actions. That product is greater than the sum of individual inputs. What people dance is not in the hands of specific dancers. The group rather than the individual, in that case, has ultimate control.

The "underclass" behavioral patterns that Steele and Chavez condemn are the unintended and unexpected consequence of multiple and uncoordinated, even opposed, individual actions that define and move the collective whole. It is, thus, the group as a whole rather than the individual that possesses and perpetuates "underclass" behavior. And that community behavior is simply the accretion over time of different individual dances that are rational and irrational responses to rejection, marginalization, opportunity, success, influence, dashed hope, lost ambition, raised desires, and racism. The individual, in most cases, simply dances along with everyone else. It's silly to complain about the moves of particular individuals if they are simply trying to follow the beat and to move in imitation of particular dance styles.

The conservative complaint is thus actually with the dance forms that dominate at a particular place and time rather than with the individual dancers. Though conservatives would not agree, individuals really don't have much opportunity to oppose what has become common sense around them. Not many individuals are able to dance against all others. Most people conform to the dancing that is current and that dominates the social group, on the particular dance floor, the society within which they move. In that sense, "we can choose what we desire, but we are 'programmed' to think some things are more desirable than others" (Irvine 2006, 171).

Groups and societies tend to exist at what economists call near equilibrium. Most people follow "the behavioral pattern that is expected of them and almost everybody wants to follow this behavior given the behavior they expect of others."[11] Minority and poor people cannot be held to a higher standard of responsibility than the rest of society. Everyone chooses within the set of values his or her society has presented him or her. A Bantu goat herder is not likely, thus, to *choose* the life of a New Jersey suburbanite. The conservative critique, therefore, ignores the role played by society and social groups in shaping individual behavior.

Pantoja's professional strategy, conservatives would argue, could have worked if Puerto Rican individuals had simply been more responsible, cooperated, and stayed in school to become professionals. Some Puerto Rican individuals did just that in the late 1960s and early 1970s. But not Puerto Ricans as a whole. Why most didn't can be traced to racism, insufficient social and cultural capital, and limited opportunities. These are not excuses, but facts about the slim and frail opportunities to take alternate paths. Yes, there was, even under those circumstances, a sliver of opportunity to move against the grain and ahead. Puerto Ricans didn't take it. They didn't take it in sufficient numbers to make a difference for the community as a whole. They didn't take it for good reasons. Puerto Ricans concluded that the costs of staying in school and getting a good job were just too high. They assumed that there was just too much to lose. They calculated that as a group rather than as individuals. In this sense, they were unlike the mythical Asian immigrants in their assessment of risk and personal investment.

But why did Puerto Ricans and Asian Americans, conservatives claim, react so differently? How did Puerto Ricans come to such different conclusions and assessments of their chances for success in the U.S.? It is easy to assume that the difference was simply one of individual failure or of cultural temperament, that Puerto Ricans are simply less *patient* than Asians, for instance. Or there are those, like Steele, who claim that Puerto Ricans, like African Americans, mistakenly hold too tightly onto their race, their identity, their culture, and their victimization. As a consequence, they fail school and work simply because "they are afraid of all-out competition" with whites (Steele 1990, 28).

That argument by Steele and others is psychological. It assumes that the removal of legal forms of segregation and inequality in America means that the races have achieved a basic structural equality.[12] With these corrupt and immoral legal impediments gone, minorities, presumably, have little standing in the way of their success. This makes the defeatist, undisciplined, and anti-educational outlook assumed by many (working- and middle-class) minorities nothing more than a psychological ploy or crutch used by these individuals because they are "intimidated by that eternal tussle between the freedom to act and the responsibility we must take for our actions" (Steele 1990, 28).

This study showed, however, the importance of historical experience to the movement of a people through society. The Puerto Rican condition cannot be understood without taking into account their history of contact with American society in Puerto Rico and the United States. As a result of those experiences, young and old Puerto Ricans have larley made assessments that the costs of staying in school were worse than the costs of dropping out. The larger society also developed a negative sense of Puerto Ricans, their value, and where they were going as a people. These assessments changed over time, sometimes significantly, as we saw with the cigar makers. They didn't change enough or for long, however, to make a lasting difference.

The idea that minorities value and choose what's in their community against what the larger society offers riles conservatives like Steele. They can't imagine that there is anything worth choosing in poor, minority communities. Puerto Ricans and other minorities, however, do not come to that assessment lightly. It requires that they take into account their immediate and past economic and social situation. It requires that they take into account recent and past experiences with rejection, racist degradation, isolation, marginalization, and pain. It requires that they rediscover wonder in their own people and ways, that they aspire to comfort and recognition within their own community, and that they value what others in their group think of them.

Minorities do not attempt suicide. They think they are coming alive by not pursuing mainstream routes to success and power. Death is what they believe the larger society offers them. When they have taken the "hard" path, competing with white Americans, and striving to reach mainstream success in school, they have suffered. Mostly, they have suffered silently and invisibly, dying more from the work, stress, and illness they got from the larger society. It was more pain than they got from the violence, drugs, poverty, and limitations they occasionally visited on each other within their own communities. In fact, the interplay between minority and larger communities has become more complex. As some researchers have discovered for African Americans, young black boys drop out of school because the "cool-pose" culture of sharp clothes, petty crime, sexual conquests, and partying is both too gratifying to them as well as rewarded by the larger society.[13] Puerto Rican boys are also drawn to "cool-pose" culture though they get few rewards for it from outside their own community. In Pedro Pietri's immortal words, many Puerto Ricans in America simply "died broke, they died owing, they died never knowing what the front entrance of the first national bank looks like."[14]

Colonialism and exploitation, thus, leave a very deep, deadly mark. They make most Puerto Ricans sad, angry, destructive, and restless. They make Puerto Ricans and African Americans look inward to their own communities for sustenance and power. It is for that reason that a similar "underclass" process has been observed in some Asian immigrants. This includes Cambodians and Vietnamese in the United States and Pakistanis in England, and others who have had comparable colonial experiences.[15]

Agency and Power

These issues raise some interesting questions about agency, determination, and power for individuals and groups. The dance model of power, of course, suggests an abundance of agency and force on the dance floor. It also provides a useful way to understand the relationship of agency to social structures. People choose to dance with those who are willing or they wait for more desirable and productive dancing opportunities with others who are not (yet) interested or present. Those choices are not, however, entirely free and each one has an impact on subsequent choices. Each decision to dance or not results in more or less power. Each of these decisions also has a cumulative impact. Who one dances with and how well one can dance will affect future opportunities to dance. Earlier decisions provide the context for future dancing.

This is what makes history, or what happened before, so important. Puerto Ricans tried repeatedly to get power, and at times succeeded, only to lose it. These experiences taught them important lessons, even if those lessons were not completely understood or understood well. The point is that each dance, each aspiration, effort, and move, creates the conditions for both power and weakness later.

The focus of the dance model is not only on history but also on group consciousness and action. Some analysts have, in fact, in contrast to conservatives, blamed the economic degradation of the Puerto Rican community on a lack of group unity, poor leadership, and the circular migration with Puerto Rico. These arguments all question the very possibility of a Puerto Rican community identity. Like conservatives, these arguments suggest that Puerto Ricans lack the necessary coherence, in a variety of ways, to fight effectively for themselves. If a Puerto Rican identity exists, some say it is as a negative response to colonialism and marginality. Puerto Ricans are wrecked by the shame of what it means to be Puerto Rican in America.[16]

Although shame could be one feature of Puerto Rican identity, it is not the only element that draws Puerto Ricans together. This study found that the Puerto Rican community has been united enough to remember, as a community, both the pride and shame of being Puerto Rican. It has also remembered the successes and failures of its previous efforts to attain power. It is precisely the coherent unity of Puerto Rican community life that carries an additional burden. Puerto Ricans remember and, thus, must assess and respond to the past injustices and losses of power.

The rise of the Young Lords and the support they received from the Puerto Rican community depended on that community's memory of injustices and disrespect in the past. The Puerto Rican community hangs together enough that younger generations seek to avoid the hardships and mistakes of previous generations. This was the story with Puerto Rican bodegas.[17] The Puerto Rican community has maintained enough unity that it displays that unity in abundance each year in New York City's largest parade and in scores of Puerto Rican Day parades all around the country.[18] If the issue is truly about the impossibility of group coherence and identity, rather than about individuals, who's in charge? This notion of group identity gets back, then, to the timeless debate about agency and structure. The dance model offers particular benefits in this area.

Contingency and Determination

Power, as we established, is not locked up in a bank or in someone's pocket. It is not a constant that never changes. It is not a thing. It is not a permanent state of inequality. Power is also not the product of accidents, contingent processes, or a random and chaotic world. Power comes to life in relationships and in the yearnings that bind people together. For that reason, power is both real and always in flux.

Many studies about power assume one of two opposing yet wrong positions. One is that everything is determined. The other is that nothing is determined (contingency). These, however, are two sides of same coin. Both suggest that power is not in anyone's hands. In one, power arrives by chance. There are no structures or processes that determine, in this sense, who or what has more power. In the other, power is possessed only by abstract, remote, and individual *structures* that are out of anyone's hands.

Each position, by itself, is absurd. There are structures of power. These structures are, however, not completely independent of social agents. At the same time, though social agents can change things, they can't do it always or by themselves. It is never completely one or the other. Structures and agency happen together. As in dancing, neither partner can do just as he or she pleases. The music, the dominant dance styles, and the dancers themselves on the floor all affect what happens. Individual dancers control how they move but cannot invent new ways of dancing independently of other dancers. As Leiberson has argued about the taste in first names, "an individual's distinctive preferences are obviously important, but they are really the last factor to consider in analyzing tastes, for individual responses are molded by the standards of a specific time and place, as well as by an individual's activities and membership in a variety of subgroups and organizations" (Lieberson 2000, 5).

Individuals have some control over when and with whom they dance but not the need to move or what to dance. The consequences of making those decisions and taking those actions are also not usually clear when they make them. Each dance or rejection also has an impact on what a dancer does later on the dance floor. After ten dances, the legs and the spirit don't move as easily as they did in the first. Each step, moreover, contains both the personal agency of the individual dancers (their personal style, energy, passion) and structural determination of the dance form that dominates at that moment and that serves as the model that the dancer tries to replicate.[19] Even oppositions or violations of dominant dance styles require that rebellious dancers be aware of what is dominant in order to be able to reject or avoid it (Lieberson 2000, 7).

Dancers may introduce slight variations in pacing, positioning, and style that reflect their status as agents. Some innovate because they're creative. Others are defiant, deviant, or simply nonconformists. Some dancers insert variations, by accident or design, into their dancing all the time. They are not, in that sense, faithful imitators of current dance styles.

Some innovations catch on with other dancers. New dance styles are invented in this way. Most innovations, however, are lost, ignored and forgotten in the whirl of activity on the dance floor. These variations can only be submitted, in any case, within certain limits. Too many and an agent is either dancing out of sync with everybody else or has introduced a new dance that others may or may not imitate.

Variations and innovations usually alter a dance style at the margins and over time. As J. D. Applen writes,

> for a riot, trend, fad, or social movement to gain a critical momentum, there needs to be a "vulnerable cluster" of people who are not known as innovators (as they lack perfect knowledge of the initial elements of a potential event) but who will join in when they see just one of their neighbors do so.[20]

New dances come into existence this way. Thus, in the 1950s some dancers introduced variations into Mambo and created Cha-cha-cha. In most cases, the pressure to conform is too great both from other dancers and from the music. Not every dancer is privileged or talented or bold enough to go against the flow.

The dancer also possesses an inner sense of what's appropriate and acceptable. Dancers know something about what it means to "do it right" even when they know they can't. An assertive woman, a *milonguita*, dancing tango, for instance, cannot bring too much of herself to the tango, cannot resist her partner completely, cannot defy her partner by refusing "to read his *marks* or to perform the expected figures" or she would risk being left "out of the tango-dancing game" (Savigliano 1995, 60). Being left out means losing the opportunity to have power.

Taken together, these individual and collective processes help to reproduce existing, traditional dances and social structures even as they allow agents to exert their own will into and by dancing. This is not just simple determinism. Agency does not disappear in "determining structures." An agent's moves in the past actually get carried forward into the future as "structures" in the form of customs, traditions, and styles of dancing that guide the actions of subsequent agents.

Very often, the product of those processes appears as if it came from nowhere, struck by chance. It surprises and awes. Luck could, some would say, very well play a part in making Puerto Ricans more powerful. Some innovation in their dancing, some cultural asset, or some economic value of theirs could catch public attention. One example is the current popularity of the Puerto Rican music called "Reggaeton."[21]

Puerto Ricans could find at some future date that they have unexpectedly become highly attractive to other people, to other dancers. Puerto Ricans might even be able to strategically plan and develop the specific values they think can have high public interest. Such a tactic could resemble the efforts of Native Americans to get the right to build casinos or of the Saudis to capitalize on the discovery of oil beneath their desert tents.[22] That stroke of good luck (and planning) may be all a group needs to "take off" and advance economically and politically. Puerto Ricans could gain considerable power in this way. Luck, however, would not really be what created power in these cases.

The opportunity for power can occur by chance, as it has for oil-producing states. Power itself, however, is still created the same old dancing way. Power got created for Native American tribes and for Saudi Arabians because of society's large need to gamble or to consume oil. Moreover, the values controlled by Native tribes and the Saudis were locked in easily protected real property and land. Gamblers and drivers don't have many other options for satisfying their needs. Luck only explains the fact that tribes and the Saudis came into sudden possession of highly desirable, not easily found values. It doesn't reveal how interaction and dependence by the public on particular values creates power. Power is created in relationships and not out of thin air.

This suggests that the conservative complaint about the Puerto Rican and African American rejection of mainstream paths to achievement and power amounts to nothing more than a call for blind faith. It is a complaint that minorities have refused to maintain faith in the possibility, no matter how remote, that their continued exertion and sacrifice along mainstream paths will eventually pay off. Conservatives cannot explain, however, what change in value or interest will actually bring about an increase in power. They simply demand that the poor and the weak plod on and not lose faith.

Determination and Change

One of the more important lessons we learned from this study of the Puerto Rican community is, thus, about the nature of determinism. What causes change? Decades ago the raging debate was about whether economic or political factors are the "determining" factors in the "last instance." Within the context of that earlier debate, this study found that economic power did have more weight. It did so, however, not for the reasons given in the past by the likes of Marx or Weber. The reasons have little to do with the traditional argument that it is basically economic or class factors that shape and dominate human history. Marxists explain that workers are made weak because they must sell their labor to capitalists in order to survive. Capitalists are powerful because they own the "means of production." This suggests that power springs from an abstract, macro process, like class exploitation or the "economic base."

Yes, Puerto Ricans seemed to have a firmer grip on social power when they had control of their economic fate. The cigar makers were the best example and yet even their power disappeared. As good as it may be, there is nothing permanent about economic and class power, at least for particular social groups. However, economic and class power does seem to carry more weight, or offer a more lasting power than other forms. What gives economic factors such weight is not history as an abstract entity. It is not the fact that this is a "capitalist stage" of class society. We know, in any case, that even economic or social structures are nothing more than "secondary formations or products of the activity of people acting according to rules, customs and conventions" (Harré 2002,115). It does not come from the idea that capitalism is a class system, a form of class society based on economic exploitation that imposes itself as the "essence" of capitalist society. The power of economics and class is generated, instead, from the role played by the everyday activities and interactions of individual and collective social agents like workers and bosses.

The power to move society is greater and more easily available (for both workers and capitalists) within the economic base. Workers lose but also gain power as a result of what they do in the workplace. They can't overturn class exploitation, the expropriation of the surplus by capitalists, but they can damage, lessen, and even stop that expropriation process. They can do that by individual and collective acts of sabotage, slow downs, collective organizing, work stoppages, and strikes. They can do those things because the capitalist needs the worker to perform in the workplace in order to extract a surplus. It is precisely their repeated contact and the necessity of their contribution to surplus value, a contact that is both fraught with conflict and imbued with cooperation, that creates power for labor and capital.[23]

Class and race, like power, get created by moves and contact. They require opportunities to exchange, establish value, and establish levels of need and desire. Those opportunities happen more frequently and intensely in the workplace. Who is a capitalist and who is labor, and their short- and long-term power, are things that are continuously produced and negotiated on the shop floor. That this negotiation seems to generally favor the capitalist class reflects the fact that labor is more dependent on capital. Labor needs a job and money more than capitalists need individual workers to work.[24] That dependence normally gives capitalists the upper hand in their negotiations with labor. It also creates repeated opportunities for interaction between working and capitalist classes. That dependence and repeated interaction means that power is both created and challenged every day. Sometimes, labor organizes and gains some power. Most of the time, labor's needs make capitalists more powerful. Aside from the cigar makers' period, Puerto Ricans have had few opportunities to engage capital and extrude power from that contact.

If conservatives are right about something it is that Puerto Ricans and other "underclass" minorities cannot gain power if they are not engaged in mainstream venues. They must be on mainstream dance floors to gain power there. They are wrong to assume that Puerto Ricans and others are not on that dance floor simply and purely out of misguided individual choices. Simply getting on that main dance floor is no guarantee, however. The incorporation of African American "cool-pose" culture into mainstream culture, with Hip Hop for instance, has provided glory and wealth for some, but mostly despair and failure for most black men.

Puerto Ricans, as a group, can't make it to the main dance floor. Racism, class segmentation, and dual market sectors create a limited field of movement for Puerto Rican labor. The problem with both conservative and liberal explanations of Puerto Rican and minority experience is that they place too much emphasis on individual actions. Group and collective experiences are generally discounted and ignored.

In this context, Austen-Smith and Fryer have provided an excellent analysis of the way cultural elements block minority achievement. They view this process, however, as involving individuals subject to group peer pressure. Their argument centers on the rational calculus of individuals who "prefer to be accepted by their peers" (Austen-Smith and Fryer 2003, 4). This is where their model goes wrong. The pressure individuals face to be accepted is more than an individual preference, for instance. As Robinson points out, "in reality individuals act not purely in isolation, but also as part of larger social groupings and networks."[25]

What's missing is the realization that those individuals become Puerto Rican or African American before they act to make that rational calculation as *individuals*. This makes an individual's membership in a group an important element that is often hard to fit within the process required by individual rationality. Indeed, individual Puerto Ricans will aspire to "be depended upon to support the group in difficult times" before they strive to act rationally (Austen-Smith and Fryer 2003, 4). A Puerto Rican, in that sense, seeks group approval simply by becoming and accepting membership within the group that calls itself Puerto Rican. This identity shapes Puerto Ricans before they attempt to rationally choose, as individuals, between the costs and benefits of allocating "his or her endowment of effort" (7). The decision to dance comes with the territory defined by membership in an ethnic-racial group identity rather than as a consequence of individual rational analysis. It comes because of what they like and how they identify rather than because of what they think.

Even so, whether the decision was a product of affective or cognitive processes, there were, no doubt, "crossroads" moments when the Puerto Rican community could have taken a number of different paths within the limited set available to them. The assumption is that since some minority groups prosper, those paths of success are available to all minority groups equally. What is difficult is describing a particular path as wrong or irrational or mistaken, especially given that this was a group process and that most Puerto Ricans must sell their labor to survive. Such conclusions are as illogical as condemning individuals for dancing like everyone else. They also can't be blamed for dancing with the "wrong" people if those are the ones most interested in dancing with them. The problem with the conservative insistence that minorities are agents responsible for their own condition is the assumption that they have an *unfettered* ability to "make society."

A 1935 Riot

In 1935, a Puerto Rican "de color" unwittingly sparked a riot by African Americans who were seeking revenge for a beating supposedly administered to him by a white department storeowner. Both the riot that spread to other stores on 125th Street in Harlem and the official investigation that followed ignored completely the fact that the young man who sparked the riot was Puerto Rican. His Puerto Rican identity was ignored as everyone focused on his black color. Most Puerto Ricans were also happy to keep the fact that the boy was Puerto Rican out of sight. Most sectors of the Puerto Rican community in New York City in 1935 desired "not to align themselves with African Americans, and not to complain about the same injustices that African Americans objected to" (Thomas 2002, 165). Puerto Ricans sought distance rather than alliance or identity with African Americans. They hoped to slip into the category of whiteness in a society where whiteness counted for so much.

This 1935 event provides an interesting illustration of the problems with the conservative critique of minority impoverishment. It provides an opportunity to examine more closely exactly how we can argue both that Puerto Ricans move and that their actions and decisions are also *fettered*. Puerto Ricans at that particular moment in the 1930s had three options: align with African Americans, align with whites, or seek some intermediate middle ground. Mostly, Puerto Ricans did the second and eventually moved to the third option. The moves they made were group ones and they reflected their own experiences and the prospects for power they faced as a group.

That path of moving towards white America, towards "assimilation," is presumably what conservatives want. They assume that wealth and power can be gained that way. It's clear that since the 1930s Puerto Ricans have, for the most part, rejected the assimilation path because they didn't think it could succeed for them. What if, however, they had taken the first option and aligned themselves closer to African Americans? Would their prospects for power in America have been any better? In general, the answer is no.

There existed considerable public perception at the time encouraging a "black" identity for Puerto Ricans. In those early years in New York City, many New Yorkers already saw Puerto Ricans as a "lighter-skinned nigger." Many New Yorkers and public officials tended to view Puerto Ricans as "colored" in the 1930s, to the chagrin of most Puerto Rican leaders (Chenault 1970, 79). Puerto Rican leader Carlos Tapia was also deeply conscious of the fact that Puerto Ricans were a nonwhite racial community. Tapia was very critical of the "*blanquito*," or white elite within the Puerto Rican community, who, he claimed, had no interest in Puerto Rican "civic dignity or progress."[26]

What if Puerto Ricans had taken these signs and perceptions and accepted a clear nonwhite, oppositional, and black identity in the 1930s? What if they had listened to the Puerto Rican writer Pales Matos and asserted, at least, an *Afro-Antillan* identity?[27] They could have admitted their blackness, as a culture if not as a race. They could have accepted a black self-identification with a clear "pervasive oppositional stance."[28] Doing so could have also helped them reinvent the notion of blackness for whites and blacks.

Blackness could have been reformulated into the kind of international concept that many people suggest by the notion of an African diaspora. Blackness could have meant Salsa and Spanish as well as R & B and Hip Hop. Puerto Rican could have meant blackness to whites "with all the social danger, marginality, and inferiority that such status implied" (Thomas 2002, 178). Political, economic, and cultural exchange with whites would have radically changed, placing Puerto Ricans within the bipolar racial orbit of American consciousness or at least stretching it to include them. The possibilities for power for Puerto Ricans could have been radically different. They may not have been better, however. The reasons have little to do with the rational calculation of individual Puerto Ricans. They are tied to the existence of Puerto Ricans as a group and the dance of power in America at that time.

Successful inclusion within the black racial category would not have made Puerto Ricans more powerful. The major reason is that Puerto Ricans would not have had more opportunities to dance with white America. They would have been absorbed within the larger category of black and lost opportunities for independent contact and power as a group. This is evident in the experience of other "black" groups in the United States. The blackness of Haiti or Angola has not produced a level of influence for immigrants from those countries living in the United States that is comparable to or apart from that of original African Americans, despite their general inclusion within the African American racial orbit.[29] These groups continue to be perceived as different from and less important than African Americans, probably because of the low status of their country of origin in the American imagination.

Puerto Rican Mixed Race

Puerto Ricans were unlikely to achieve full inclusion within the black racial category because of the mulatto and mestizo element of Puerto Rican racial experience. That racial mixture serves to complicate any effort to easily lump Puerto Ricans into one or another racial category as they are defined in the United States. That racial complexity dampens Puerto Rican prospects in this hypothetical "blacks" scenario. It prevents Puerto Ricans from achieving opportunities for power similar to that of African Americans in the United States. The first reason is that this complexity prevents African Americans from fully accepting Puerto Ricans as black. Second, white Americans also reject the racial mixture they find so confusing in Puerto Ricans.[30]

Those problems are magnified by the existing relationship between African Americans and white Americans. Their close, historic dance makes it very difficult for anyone else to step in and dance with either of them. Dancing with Puerto Ricans, as was explained above, can mean dancing with someone who identifies and can be identified as "white," "black," or "other." Their *in-between* racial identity means little in a bipolar racial world. It offers none of the advantages of being white and none of the threat/excitement of being black. White Americans could not be sure that they were dancing with a true "opposite." The continued difficulty of fully accounting for Puerto Rican and Latino racial identity within the American racial system thus creates obstacles for their relations with white and black America.

There is little that Puerto Ricans can do to simplify their mixed racial identity since each racial component represents not discrete racial groups but individual *phenotypes* that often occur within the same family unit. Puerto Ricans and other Latinos, as a result, find it hard to unambiguously oppose white America. An aunt or brother may be perceived or identify as "*blanco*." In the same way, "black" Puerto Ricans are different and feel inferior not just to other Puerto Rican groups, but to members of their own families. "Black" and "white" are often found within the same family. This makes it hard for Puerto Ricans to figure out who is the "enemy" both in Puerto Rico and in the United States. Black Puerto Ricans and other Latinos have, for that reason, never organized very effectively in defense of their civil rights within their own communities.

Racial mixture and ambiguity thus get in the way of Puerto Rican relations with both black and white America, making it difficult to develop a sufficiently distinct and opposed "racial" culture that can compete with and replace white American culture. A *Latino* identity would offer no sure remedy.

Some have argued that a distinct Latino racial identity that celebrates and emphasizes mulatto/mestizo origins, as in the notion of "La Raza," could become an accepted third category for racial identification within the United States.[31] That possibility has yet to happen in any real way, though there are some interesting trends. Recent census data shows, for instance, an increasing number of people who identify themselves as "mixed" or "other" race, especially among Latinos. Also, the fastest-growing racial category in the United States is Native American, a group that is more mixed-race than people acknowledge.

The population of people who identify themselves as Native American has more than doubled since the 1960s.[32] Many of them are people, however, whom others would easily identify as white or black but who, through a process of "ethnic shifting," now identify themselves as Native American. What is interesting is that these people became Natives rather than identify as mixed. The reason appears to be that they realized that there were great benefits in becoming a "pure" Native American, "a member of the one people who have been here all along" (Hitt 2003b). Puerto Ricans face a radically different dilemma.

Puerto Rican racial problems come not from claiming a race that doesn't match their appearance. The problem comes from claiming a "racial" identity, based on nationality, that others in the United States do not easily understand.[33] The fact that there are Puerto Ricans and Latinos who could identify, or "pass," as white or black or Indian further weakens the chances of widespread success for a *Latino race* option within the United States: Latinos have an extraordinarily difficult task trying to cast themselves as "the other" to white America. African Americans don't have the same problem as this character in Zadie Smith's novel *On Beauty* makes clear: "*This* is what it's all about, being *this* different; this is what white people fear and adore and want and dread. He was as purely black as— on the other side of things—those weird Swedish guys with translucent eyelashes are purely white."[34]

The impenetrability of American racial categories points to some of the existing limits to power for Latinos. White America already has a main dance partner in African Americans. In many ways, white Americans actually define themselves against African Americans. Whites establish who they are in the context of a long historical struggle, or dance, with African Americans. It amounts to, as Norman Mailer once said in exaggeration, a "wedding of the white and the black," the Square and the Hip, the Civilized and the Primitive, and the cold and the hot.[35] This dialectic of mutual being can be observed in the way that many men dance tango.

Men require, some say, not simply a submissive but a challenging woman with whom to dance tango. The reason is that men dance to conquer/control the woman and thus assert their maleness through dance for all other machos to see. A submissive woman prevents the exposition of his macho-ness. Whites see and create themselves in opposition to as well as through African Americans. They receive their "cultural dowry" from African Americans. This makes it very difficult for Puerto Ricans and other Latinos to step in and dance on a steady and consistent basis with white America.

Puerto Ricans and Latinos are weakened in American society, then, because they do not offer the same psychic and social rewards to white America. They cannot easily "cut in." They are barely recognized or recognizable as a minority, let alone as African American. Their racial complexity makes it difficult, then, for Puerto Ricans either to fit neatly within a black identity or to benefit from an attempted inclusion. It explains why, despite the fact that Puerto Ricans have been included in the category of protected minority along with African Americans, Puerto Ricans have not received nearly as many benefits.[36]

This claim is not an idle speculation. As James P. Smith states, "the average economic status of Latinos appears to be deteriorating at an even more alarming rate than that of African-Americans" (1999, 2). These theoretical and empirical arguments, thus, support the Puerto Rican community's choices. They stayed apart from African Americans for a variety of good reasons.

Puerto Ricans didn't quite understand African Americans or share the same experiences. More importantly, Puerto Ricans saw African Americans as their main competitors at the bottom of the racial social order. Puerto Ricans understood that joining blacks so completely was a strategic mistake. They received some economic benefits from their attempted inclusion within the white category. Had they instead admitted to blackness, they would have probably been absorbed and disappeared completely as Puerto Ricans or become, at best, weak younger siblings within the black orbit.[37] They already knew in the 1930s that they were "*personae non gratae* in the black-and-white political relations in Harlem and in the city at large" (Thomas 2002, 206). They sensed their essential marginality to the already existing and intimate dance of black and white. They accepted their compromised and ambiguous position in the American racial system much as the Indians of South Africa did theirs during the apartheid period (Ben-Rafael 2001).

Thought Experiment

This analysis is really more thought experiment than speculation.[38] We may never have all the information we need to explain the Puerto Rican decision not to side with African Americans. Was it caused by Puerto Rican pride, invisibility, racism, political realism, or mixed (confused) racial identity? Was it due to African American economic and political competition, lack of understanding, or ignorance? Was it due to white racism, domination, or their preference for dancing with African Americans? The best answer actually has to do with power.

Power is a natural human goal, pursued by all living individuals and groups. Puerto Ricans sought power. They wanted to dance because only by dancing could they get power. One way to view the decision not to join blackness is to see it as a move conducted on a crowded, hectic, and foreign dance floor on the fly by Puerto Ricans. They moved with the repertoire of moves they knew and had brought with them to America. Some of those moves can be characterized as racist, myopic, cowardly, and selfish as well as idealistic, brave, and passionate. Puerto Ricans came to America, for instance, with ideas about race that were different from the bipolar model prevalent in the United States. Those notions, nevertheless, still placed blacks at the bottom. They were also more complicated.

What can be said is that Puerto Ricans tried to survive and gain some power on that crowded and incoherent dance floor in the United States. They were hesitant to dance with African Americans because they saw them as undesirable dance partners within this society. They chose not to dance with African Americans because they could not gain much power that way. Puerto Ricans found later, however, that the path towards whiteness eventually closed to them even as they themselves had begun to turn away from it.

As Puerto Ricans began to acquire the role of minority, it was equally true that Puerto Ricans themselves actively pursued that status. The signs of this shift, as explained above, can be found as early as the 1930s, and it solidified considerably in the 1950s. They recognized that opportunities for political battle and advance could be found increasingly within the terms defined by civil rights and minority status. Puerto Ricans recognized the increasing possibilities for power within the struggle for minority rights. Antonia Pantoja saw in the 1950s, for instance, that the civil rights movement had created an opportunity for Puerto Ricans to fight for their rights not only in "each locality, but also in the courts of the nation through the legal process" (Pantoja 2002, 86). They made many right moves. They just didn't make enough of them.

Not Just Culture

So far this discussion appears to be limited to identity and culture. Wasn't that moment in the 1930s also an economic and political crossroads? Were there not political and economic decisions that Puerto Ricans failed to make that could have taken them along different and better paths? Could Puerto Ricans have presented a new and improved set of human and social capital to radically change the course of their journey through the thicket of American politics and market economy? Could Puerto Ricans have sacrificed more, dedicated themselves more, been more patient about their schooling, been more aggressive in pursuit of better jobs, and been more diligent about monitoring their kids' education and social networks? In the abstract, they could have done many of these things. While individuals could and did do these things, the group couldn't. Puerto Ricans made moves, both as individuals and as a group. Their moves were filtered through and weighed down by their relations as a group to the larger society.

The research on the intersection of culture with political economy assumes that the level of motivation and effort between groups is similar. Those groups that fail in the marketplace do so because they lacked some necessary social or human capital. Political critics, on the other hand, blame either outside institutions or Puerto Ricans themselves for their lack of success. Liberals, for instance, charge non–Puerto Rican institutions with failure, while conservatives charge Puerto Ricans themselves.

The reality is that Puerto Ricans have tried to advance both individually and as a group. Overall, much of the time, they've failed to advance. It wasn't because others failed them, as liberals might argue. It wasn't because they failed themselves, as conservatives may argue. They've failed because their dancing wasn't good enough or done with the right partner.

Wrapped up in all of this is an assumption that part of the problem for Puerto Ricans is that they have not stopped being Puerto Rican. If only they would accept their place and identity as Americans. Liberals work to make this happen and conservatives think it is Puerto Ricans that keep it from happening. The persistence of Puerto Rican ethnic identity is not the problem, however. From the academic side, there is, for instance, some evidence to show that ethnic identity in some places has actually helped social mobility. Researchers have identified ethnic social capital, particularly in the community, as a mechanism that can be used to overcome social barriers to advancement. As Giorgas explains, "ethnic community formation has served as a positive strategy for immigrants in overcoming social isolation and economic difficulties by providing employment opportunities and a sense of familial surroundings within their own ethnic group."[39] The social resources and networks of an ethnic community can "provide the second generation with the appropriate economic and moral support necessary for social mobility" (Giorgas 2000, 11). That positive contribution of family and community social capital is not something that individual members of the community control, however.

In particular, the degree of ethnic community cohesiveness in combination with the perception and acceptance of the dominant culture is what determines whether the contribution of social capital will be positive or negative for individual ethnic members.[40] Is it fair to argue that whatever is the contribution from social capital, individuals still have opportunities to decide? Do individuals have a choice about what to do with the social capital they inherit from their community and family? This is what Theodore Dalrymple argues. He claims that, in England, "the children of successful Indian parents . . . choose the underclass way of life" despite their middle-class advantages and social capital.[41] Dalrymple is not realistic.

Agency is in many ways about imagination and creativity. In order to break the weight of institutions, structures, "economic bases," and rules, individuals and groups must imagine that things can be different. They must refuse to accept the meaning of what is dominant and act to create new meanings and moves that could result in new rules. This is the way on the dance floor. That conceptual transformation is really about culture, about ideas and imagination. Culture is, for that reason, at the center of material social life. People use culture

> as a guide to accomplishing their purposes; make things, alter their physical environment, create social groups, and establish rules by which to conduct their affairs with one another. . . . The artifacts of ideational culture give structure to the phenomenal world in which people live, a structure that itself keeps changing over time (Goodenough 1996, 295).[42]

Taking an independent economic and political path thus requires some cultural creativity. It requires a rejection of the symbolic meanings and actions that prop up the existing political and economic world.[43] This is not naïve idealism talking. The cultural rejection or break that occurs can just as easily take the form of action and motion (dancing) as well as of an idea.

Many Puerto Ricans were, in fact, exceptional in their dedication and talent. Many Puerto Rican individuals became middle-class and professional.[44] Most didn't. Many tried. These results are to be expected. In any population, the natural distribution of talent, intelligence, perseverance, etc., is a curve, with most people squarely in the middle. Exceptional individuals are, by definition, fewer in number. Moreover, it is clear from their history that Puerto Ricans did try very hard and against steep odds to ascend the ladder of success.

That unflinching striving for upward mobility in the mainstream world was largely the Puerto Rican story up until about 1970. By that date, it appears that many, but not all, stopped believing that dancing with other Americans was still a real possibility. It seems as though after that date, they relaxed a little and put their energies into community-focused activities rather than into conventional avenues of success.

What was the point? Like any other group with so few resources, interest, and support, they found it really difficult and unproductive to stretch a penny, to work more than twenty-four hours a day, and to grow an extra pair of hands.[45] Moreover, like many other minority groups around the world, Puerto Ricans rejected the sacrifices and grateful subjugation of the previous, largely unsuccessful generation, especially since they found themselves becoming increasingly marginalized in America.

Puerto Ricans are, in this sense, similar to the Pakistani youth today in Great Britain. Both groups lost the "ballast" of work that gave the previous generation a purpose and foundation. In America's alien and unforgiving culture, Puerto Ricans like them found that "they sometimes seem to be living in rooms without walls."[46] The major difference is that though Puerto Ricans are treated as an ethnic-racial group, they don't hold together very well as a group. Unlike the Pakistanis, Puerto Ricans lack an established religion that is completely theirs and that could be reshaped into a weapon of indignation and opposition.[47] They cannot bank on a historic legacy of victories against colonial oppressors. And even though they are comfortable with being Puerto Rican, they lack a transparent and coherent sense of who they are as a race in American terms. As Negron-Muntaner writes, "were it not for the 'shame' of being Puerto Rican, there would be no *boricua* identity, at least not as we know it" (2004, xiii).

It is in this way that the material conditions of class and race act as a very effective brake on individual and group ambition. They get internalized. They get digested in, sometimes, unique ways. Most conservatives would like us to believe otherwise. Occasionally, some conservatives do get close to the idea that group perception and ideology can be a *brake* on social mobility. As Shelby Steele once said, "The greatest problem in coming from an oppressed group is the power the oppressor has over your group. The second greatest problem is the power your group has over you."[48] Steele clearly flirts with the idea that groups can exert their collective power and will on individuals. He then promptly ignores it. He is more interested in attacking individual failure.

Steele reduces the collective power of minority-group identity to a self-serving "mask." He calls minority group ideology, their identity as "victims," a kind of "mask" because each individual member must wear it in order to serve "his group's ambitions in these politics" (Steele 2002, 37). The mask, he says, advances and capitalizes on white guilt. Steele thus places a great deal of blame for black poverty and underachievement on a black emotional and intellectual attachment, as a group, to the notion of "racial victimization." The mask is worn both as an affirmation of that victimization and as the "only release from racial shame" (2002, 36). Steele sees affirmative action and African American studies programs as evidence of the way African Americans gain politically from advancing this Faustian mechanism of white guilt and black militant "masks."

Steele is right about the notion that African American and Latino impoverishment is no longer the result of simple material forces (if it ever was). *Masks* and other symbolic expressions are often more immediately effective than material forces in perpetuating exploitation and oppression. He is wrong about everything else.

The postmodernists agree with him. Language, politics, identity, and symbols in general have become as important as "social structures" in the perpetuation of class and racial exploitation. Legal segregation in housing, jobs, and transportation is, for example, insignificant today. What perpetuates poverty and powerlessness for African Americans and Latinos is not simply an obvious oppression by "others" (Steele 2002, 36). What's at work operates at the level of symbols and consciousness. This "symbolic oppression" doesn't mean, as Steele believes, however, that social mobility is now easier to overcome because the "obstacle" is nothing more than an *idea* that minorities carry in their heads.

Social structures of inequality are also symbolic. They take the form of "rules and conventions" about the notion of labor, how to work, and what is necessary for survival in capitalist society (Harre 2002, 119). Since most people follow those "rules," it is not easy for individuals to cast them out. They limit, channel, and push. Symbolic or not, the continuing oppression of minority groups still means that an individual can't just dance whatever he or she wants to.

Steele and other conservatives see individual agents remaking society everywhere because they only see other professionals, political leaders, and capitalists like themselves. These are the people whose actions are normally enabled by the existing social structures. Minorities don't have that experience. For them, social structures limit more than enable. As a result, they accept themselves as limited. Their inability to decipher the "cultural capital" of mainstream success gets internalized as personal stupidity and laziness. As a result, many seek success and meaning elsewhere. Individual agents, in that sense, carry the social structure, with its powers and limits, within.

Minorities are "held back" in the larger society, thus, because of what they believe and perpetuate about themselves. Some could, and have, overcome the obstacles, self-imposed and otherwise. Many, instead, embroil "themselves in the underground economy and proudly" embrace "street culture" as an alternative vehicle for social mobility (Bourgeois 1995, 143). Minorities, thus, do appear to hold themselves back. They withdraw, collectively, from competing on the same dance floor with whites but only because they know they can't dance there.

Where Puerto Ricans and other minorities go to dance and acquire power points to an additional problem with Steele's argument, however. He argues that the ideas and practices that minorities perpetuate and that hold them back from the main dance floor are simply irrational, and a complete mistake for minorities. He also asserts, incorrectly, that the only real and lasting social benefit that minorities can extract from those masking ideas results from the fact that, in the larger society, minorities "collect the fruits of white guilt" through programs like affirmative action (2002, 41).

It is true that Puerto Ricans and other minorities do collect benefits from the ideas they perpetuate about themselves. The benefits they get, however, are mostly on the street and outside the mainstream. The benefits they get in the street are mostly slim and temporary yet important. It may be that like Muslim youth in England, Puerto Ricans have found that the "underclass life offers them the prospect of freedom without responsibility, whereas their parents offer them only responsibility without freedom" (Dalrymple 2000).

Puerto Rican individuals often choose "street" or "ethnic" culture because those communities, bodies, and groups offer more benefits than the mainstream. Puerto Ricans gain some power from each other by withdrawing from the larger society, as well as by desiring and needing each other more, and by championing and becoming more dependent on the values found within their community. They dance with those fellow group members who accept and desire them.[49] They ignore and become more remote from whites and their many slights and refutations. The power they gain comes against rather than with whites, however. They gain power within their own community but it is limited.

Limits of Cultural Strategies

Culture is, thus, an important mechanism for power. The irony is that culture is actually not a good place to acquire power. The reason is that, in general, the realm of meaning, art, and music does not provide enough opportunities for contact and dancing between groups. The opportunities for realizing interests, for engaging and moving others (in a word, for dancing), and, thus, for power are limited in culture because few cultural relations can normalize frequent interaction between classes and groups. Ethnic group and dominant culture are each very highly segregated places for the creation, circulation, and exchange of cultural value. Each usually exists to the exclusion of the other. The most democratic locations, where contact and interaction are likely to occur, are the public schools and the market, places where, in fact, deep, hidden inequalities perpetuate the expression of the dominant culture. The problems with the use of culture as a direct vehicle for social advancement thus get to the bottom of the nature of power.

Some of the research on minority economic mobility recognizes the complex and, in some ways, limited role of social capital. Borjas, for instance, states that ethnic concentration "may effectively hinder the move to better-paying jobs by reducing the immigrants' incentives to learn the culture and language of the American labour market."[50] The real problem, however, is not with the social capital but with the kinds of interactions the minority group and the dominant society have with each other and the interests that lie behind that interaction. Conceptualizing these limits as a function of minority group "social closure" and "social distance" to the dominant society does not fully explain the limited role of social capital (Giorgas 2000).

The problem with the concept of social capital is that it is often used to explain change and power. Social capital refers to social networks, but its use in most theories makes it nothing more than an object that can be accumulated and exchanged. It refers less to the interaction that takes place in those networks and more to its product. As a result, power gets defined by the quantity of social capital rather than by the nature of the interaction in those networks. The dance model, however, provides a more realistic explanation of the dialectic way power gets created with either material or social capital.

Power gets created for both capitalists and labor in the same way. It gets created in the relationship they have with each other. Since power springs from relationships, workers are well positioned to extract benefits and influence the capitalist in the workplace. Workers are well positioned because they are there most days and in repeated contact with their capitalist bosses. It is, as Marx once wrote, their "social being." Other opportunities for proletariat power, through the use of state power or public opinion, are not as readily available, intrinsic to the work they do, or very effective.

Dancing is, thus, an unavoidable fact for workers and bosses. Their very existence as classes depends on their interaction. Surplus value, capital, and class are the products of that repeated interaction in the workplace. Power, in fact, is the more important product of that interaction for both classes. A similar process does not happen in the cultural and political realms. There are few political and cultural arrangements that compel and place the weak and the strong in each other's arms for repeated contact. The creation of political and cultural products (votes, legitimacy, music, art, etc.) can take place with very limited, genuine input from labor or the weaker groups in society.

Contacts between the strong and the weak in politics and culture are, thus, mostly sparse, limited, and diffused. A worker's, or anyone's for that matter, contact with political leaders is basically limited to Election Day when voters can exercise a very small influence on the political process by choosing from a largely elite-derived list of candidates. There are, course, other forms of political activity that can be conducted more regularly. But those activities, like lobbying or protest, are too difficult, logistically or financially, to mount on a consistent basis by the poor and the weak.

The cultural arena is an even more complicated and diffused place. Subordinate groups often produce cultural innovations. Capitalism, in fact, needs those contributions from below to satisfy its relentless hunger for cultural products to produce and sell. Rock and Roll and Hip Hop are some good examples. But a subordinate class or group origin does not prevent cultural products from being captured, managed, and produced independently by the strong. It happens in music all the time. African Americans have experienced this repeatedly. Critics of this process in Hip Hop are left to bemoan the fact that "hiphop is money at this point, a valued form of currency where brothers are offered stock options in exchange for letting some corporate entity stand next to their fire."[51]

The cultural dimension is, for that reason, not a secure or lasting path to power. Cultural value is just too easy to capture and manage by more powerful agents. The weak can only look on as their cultural inventions benefit others or complain about the authenticity of this now-captured product. All they have left is a claim that they, unlike corporate managers and their "money-shakers," have kept it "real."

The notion of *cultural capital* further illustrates the difficulty of a cultural strategy to power. Proponents of this approach suggest, for example, that accumulating cultural capital eventually generates cultural influence. The real question is really, Whose cultural capital? The reality is that there is no real way to know this since cultural or "social capital is not actually a commodity exchangeable through other forms of free commodities; it has little meaning or use outside the group" (Goulbourne and Solomos 2003, 333). Unlike in the capitalist market, there is no easily identified standard or currency of exchange, except money itself, in the cultural realm to facilitate exchange and accumulation between groups and communities.

Workers often amass cultural capital in hopes of ratcheting their power upwards. Most of the cultural capital they can amass, however, is likely to actually enhance their influence within their own working-class world and not outside it. Because of segregation, the social interaction and transfer of social and human capital tends to result in the accumulation of capital that ensures solidarity within the group rather than competitive advantages in the larger society. Thus, because of segregation and racism, even middle-class African Americans "with college educations have more than a 20 percent chance of coming in contact in their neighborhood with someone receiving welfare, whereas college-educated whites have an 8 percent chance. This pattern was repeated for interaction with blue-collar workers, high school drop-outs, and the unemployed."[52] "Black English" among African Americans and *Jibaro* traditions of reciprocity among Puerto Ricans are but two examples of the way segregation produces in-group cultural capital accumulation that creates little influence outside minority communities (Bourgeois 1995, 136). The continuing segregation of African Americans and Latinos means that much of their cultural contact, cultural capital, and power will be with members of their own community.[53]

Accumulating the cultural capital of dominant groups in society can, on the other hand, make working-class and minority groups weaker. Speaking English is a necessary tool for individual advancement for any Latino. But it comes with a price. When English is spoken with an accent, shame and discrimination usually follow.[54] English also represents a triumph for individualism, elite control, and colonial ideology.[55] Latinos have an intuitive understanding that losing Spanish for English can make them weaker as a group. Elders arch their eyebrows and deliver other re-criminations to young Latinos who have lost the ability to speak Spanish. They have the implicit recognition that what is lost is more than a lan-guage. Speaking English means losing mechanisms for group conscious-ness, solidarity, power, and culture.

Alternatively, a strategy of empowerment based on developing aspects of their own worker or group culture, like Spanish, may provide opportu-nities for inclusive group power but limit opportunities for power within the wider society. This has been the case for those in the Puerto Rican and Chicano communities who have resurrected their respective musical styles like Bomba and Mariachi.

It doesn't matter whether group culture is oppositional to the larger so-ciety, compliant, or both at the same time. The point is that the cultural realm provides no consistent position or opportunity from which to con-tact, interact with, and influence the larger society. Subordinate group members can acquire the cultural capital of dominant groups, but that does not bring the group any power. In fact, the group loses members, and power, to the larger society as talented members acquire dominant cul-tural capital and defect. The group recognizes this and responds nega-tively. That is why, very often, promising Latino or "black students are ridiculed for speaking standard English, showing an interest in ballet or theater, having white friends, or joining activities other than sports."[56]

What they object to is, of course, the classic assimilation process where individuals acquire the language, manners, goals, and habits of the domi-nant culture. That acquisition allows those individuals to engage more easily in social transactions with the larger society. It may even allow for an ascent in social rank. This is a process that happens to some extent for individuals in all minority groups. It is also a process that just as often devastates individuals because it forces them to "choose between who we were as students and our ethnicity or race" (Anselmo and Rubal-Lopez 2005, 146).

Given these realities, most members of the ethnic or racial group won't acquire most of the dominant cultural capital even though many try. They will be forced to ask themselves, "Where am I most socially accepted?" and "How can I show that I, too, am worthy of respect and admira-tion?"[57] As racial and class minorities, they will hold themselves back and hold each other back because they find that they can't get much respect outside their own group. The wider cultural values are either unattainable or damaging.

The cultural contact between the wider culture and minority cultures is thus fraught with conflict, pain, alienation, and paradox. Minority cul-tures find this contact, at bottom, unmanageable. Absorption of dominant cultural values becomes a form of treachery within a minority community or is absorbed in a distorted and fragmented manner that often parrots elements of the dominant culture (like individualism, violence, misogyny, criminality) that hurts the individual and community. Culture is, for those reasons and ironically, not an easy place to engage others, to dance, and to get power.

Media Struggle?

Culture, in general, is thus not an efficient place for the struggle for power. What about the media, the primary instrument of cultural and symbolic power in this society? It seemed to work for the Young Lords and other Puerto Ricans in the 1970s.[58] Though the media is a vital component of power, it is not, as some argue, a primary site for "domination and contestation."[59] That notion is actually absurd.

Aside from the creation of music, and music only at the creative stage, opposing class and racial groups do not come into consistent contact to struggle over their representation and the meaning of their existence in media institutions. It may be true that cultural forms, like television, sometimes reflect the "impulses, tones, and consciousness of contemporary black life in the United States" as they are actually "lived, practiced, and understood by blacks" (Gray 1995, 11). But it does so not because predominant and subordinate groups confront each other within the television industry over what images and meanings to produce.

Television offers a complex, often contested, set of images and meanings because of its contradictory need to appeal to viewing audiences. If the images appear in conflict, it is because television marketing extrudes conflicting impulses and sentiments from its study and knowledge of the viewers. The media then presents those images back to the public it seeks to attract.

The struggle over meaning in television is thus quite "mediated," removed from the everyday consciousness and activity of subordinate groups. Blacks, for example, developed a presence in television programming because "black-oriented programs were cost-efficient and advertisers could be attracted" (Gray 1995, 68). The "struggle" that takes place in television is in the imagination and plans of its managers. It is precisely this mediated form of "struggle" that makes culture a vital, yet less effective site for class or racial struggle and power than the work site. Its remote connection to struggle does not spring from its location in the capitalist "superstructure." Its remoteness springs, again, from the limited opportunities it offers for contact, dancing and conflict between the strong and the weak. As effective as the Young Lords were in their use of the media, they could not keep themselves in front of the cameras.

How to Dance with the Monster

There is one more lesson to be derived from this study. The monster is not such a monster after all. It is not omnipotent or always prepared for the dance of power. Puerto Ricans have had their moments with it. The cigar makers and Young Lords showed that it was possible to dance and influence the monster. Their experience provided clues for how a poor, minority community can influence the economic and political life of the larger society.

Though the lessons are real, no specific instructions about how to dance come out of this study. What we have is, instead, a sense of the rhythms, parameters, and conditions that define good possibilities of dance and power for minority communities. At bottom, this amounts to the conclusion that minority communities can advance in society only to the extent that they can carry over the dancing they do so well with each other to dancing with the monster. This is simplistic and crude. It is also the closest we are going to get to a general rule.

Over the last thirty years, the route to power for minority communities has been defined by politics. Puerto Rican and Latino leaders have made politics, rather than the media, culture, or economics, the main arena for the Latino struggle for power. Conservatives, as we discussed, have criticized this minority political orientation for creating a dependence on liberal policies, the welfare state, and affirmative action. They argue, instead, for a complete submission to the economic market where minorities would be forced to compete and, they assume, succeed in climbing out of the bottom rungs of American society.[60] Social mobility for Puerto Ricans will not occur, however, by pursuing either conservative or liberal strategies. It can happen, though, with better dancing, by a better understanding of the role of interests and group actions.

Neither liberals nor conservatives have much to offer Puerto Ricans, Latinos, and African Americans because they see the world in individual rather than collective terms. Liberals are right—affirmative action programs do work, *for individuals*. Conservatives are also right—welfare does perpetuate *individual dependence*. Welfare's main purpose wasn't, however, to help individuals but to serve as a component of broader fiscal policies aimed at correcting the unruly and dangerous fluctuations of the market economy on behalf of Americans as a whole. Individual assistance or dependence was irrelevant in the effort to fix economic depression and inflation.

The market economy offers Puerto Ricans no easy or automatic remedy for their problems. Admittedly, if enough individual Puerto Ricans acquire sufficient education and get good jobs, they will create a critical mass that could change the collective fortunes of Puerto Ricans as a whole, becoming numerous enough "to tip society from one near-equilibrium to another" (Young 1998, 19). Pantoja would have been proven correct. That scenario is unlikely, however. Individual Puerto Ricans do succeed every day and they should keep trying. They succeed, however, against tremendous odds.

Those "odds" are not an abstract statistic, a wall of bad risks. They instead consist of the dancers, their interests and passions, as well as the kind of dancing that individual Puerto Rican agents encounter as they make their way through U.S. society. Individual Puerto Ricans find that mainstream success requires them to learn very different ways of dancing (in language, social relations, style, etc.).

They must face other dancers (at school, at work, and in politics) who ignore them, don't quite understand them, reject them, or expect more from them. They must also face fellow Puerto Ricans, other Latinos, and African Americans who equate academic and mainstream success with a betrayal of their ethnicity, race, and class (see Anselmo and Rubal-Lopez 2005; Steele 2002; MacLeod 1987). They must "work twice as hard to get half the credit."[61] Admitting to these "odds" doesn't mean that Puerto Ricans and other minorities are victims and that society is the only "agent of change" (Steele 1990, 14). These odds do point, however, to both the difficulty and the infinite complexity of change. They point to the interactive, combustible, and intimate nature of power. They point to the importance of group interests to any dancing its members try to do.

Institutions, social structures, and dances can exist largely unchanged for generations or change overnight. Whether they change or not depends on what happens to group and class interests. The complaint of conservatives like Steele is really with the interests and motivations of minorities. They can't understand how minorities can reject education or why minorities, except for a few individuals, see education as worthless. The reality is that even individual social mobility is possible and gets a terrific boost when the dominant groups become more receptive to and interested in minority-group culture and other values. Individual social mobility is, thus, also dependant on the interest the larger society has in that individual's minority group.

Austen-Smith and Fryer have taken this one step further. They've argued the counterintuitive position that "as the probability of leaving the community increases, those who opt for cooperation invest less in human capital" (2003, 16). The increased opportunity to succeed in the larger society causes minority individuals, according to this model, to more often reject mainstream success. This is ultimately caused by segregated housing, which increases the probability that group members will interact mostly with other group members in the future. The high probability of in-group interaction creates incentives and mechanisms that encourage maintaining group culture and values instead of acquiring those of the mainstream society.

The Austen-Smith and Fryer model explains the puzzling behavior of individuals from second-generation immigrant groups and middle-class minority communities who appear to resist assimilation and accommodation to mainstream social values. It doesn't account, however, for those recent developments wherein a group's cultural products, like Hip Hop or basketball skill, become valuable commodities and avenues for success in the larger society. These counterexamples ultimately weaken the value of their model.

The success of Hip Hop suggests that maintaining group culture can make success in the larger society possible. An investment in group cultural capital can become an advantage and provide for future mobility for members both within and outside the group provided the larger society has interest. Latino failures, in this sense, may have come about because they have not had similar opportunities to transform in-group success into mainstream success. Nobody cares when Puerto Ricans present "cool poses."

Strategies for group success vary but are likely to have several things in common. One, they don't require extraordinary efforts from agents. Extraordinary efforts, intelligence, or anything is, by definition, not normally available for any group. Two, the strategy must make it possible for individual agents to succeed in the dominant culture by pursuing success and solidarity within their own group. They should create a seamless boundary between group and societal success. And three, they make the penalty for failure in the dominant society the same as the penalty for failure in the group. There are many historical examples to support this pattern.

African Americans have had countless experiences where musical forms that they've invented became popular not only within their communities but also in the larger society. This has happened to African American blues, jazz, R & B, Rock and Roll, and, more recently, Hip Hop. What made African American performers important and successful inside their culture brought some success in the wider culture.

It is true that many African American performers got cheated or even lost their lives prematurely when their music got discovered, commodified, and captured by white businesses. Those African Americans who succeeded did so, however, not by fundamentally changing the music they had long performed within their own communities. They succeeded by "crossing over," by being "discovered," by becoming more widely popular, and by becoming more commercial. R & B succeeded because people like Berry Gordy were coolly observant and strategically prepared enough to pay "attention to economics."[62] At bottom, they succeeded by taking African American culture to white America.

Something similar occurred for the Irish in America. An Irish American identity was reinforced by several processes that were internal to that community. This was mostly accomplished by the Catholic Church, which "promoted an Irish Catholic identity in order to insure their loyalty to the church."[63] In addition, their collectivist orientation made the Irish work together in the building of canals, railroads, sewers, water systems, and garbage pickup. The Irish were, in this way, able to make economic advances in early-twentieth-century America. The critical element was that America industrialized and introduced new technologies, occupations, and ways of life that included improving public health conditions. The Irish were in a good position to benefit from these economic and political changes. The Irish found that they had little to change about themselves in order to benefit from the fact that "America had an expanding economy with almost unlimited jobs."[64]

When the U.S. economy changed and required new hands and minds to tend to newly emerging technologies, policies, and occupations, the Irish were in a good position to dance. As Richard Jensen has observed, "the Catholic school system generated high school and college graduates well-equipped to make their way in the white collar world entirely as individuals."[65] It wasn't luck that placed the Irish in the right position to accept the offer to dance with the larger society. There is even plenty of historical evidence that the Irish protected with violence and determination the economic niches they had carved for themselves as well as their rapid incorporation within the white racial category. Here again, Irish economic and political advances did not require them to do anything extraordinary to get them.

Similar processes have been observed in studies of ethnic groups in Australia (Giorgas 2000). Italian and Greek immigrants to Australia achieved considerable social mobility because they maintained a cohesive and tight ethnic identity and community that provided "alternative social and economic resources not available elsewhere in society" (Giorgas

2000, 8). Dutch immigrants to Australia, in contrast, had a more individualistic culture and were equally as mobile.

The Dutch didn't have to depend on the social capital of their ethnic community, since they were more integrated into Australian culture and institutions. This suggests the dancelike quality of the interaction between the group and the society that can make social capital both a necessary and effective tool for social mobility. Giorgas concludes that

> although the cultural heritage of ethnic communities needs to be maintained, it also needs to be progressively integrated into the dominant Anglo-Celtic heritage. In other words, the core values of a given ethnic community need to be drawn upon in Australian society more generally and drawn into the institutions of Australia specifically (2000, 10).

As this passage explains, the key to success was not really the group's social capital. The key was how much interest the larger society had in what a group had to offer as a community. When society has no preexisting, built-in or new interest in a group's racial identity, financial assets, technical skills, and other values, the ethnic group's social capital will often serve as an alternative, critical tool and resource for individual social mobility. A group without the insider status of the Dutch, thus, needs the group social capital of the Greeks.

Similar interactions have been noted by research into ethnic mobility in Great Britain and Canada. Platt and Thompson report, for instance, that social mobility for immigrant groups has occurred largely as a result of economic and occupational changes that have opened "room at the top" with more and new professional and managerial jobs.[66] Thus, Caribbean and Indian immigrants in Canada have benefited most from economic changes that have opened opportunities for advancement. Education and social capital have also played a part. Their impact would have been greatly diminished, however, had there not been changes in occupational structure. As one researcher has noted, social mobility for minority immigrant groups depends on "the degree of fluidity within society as a whole."[67]

In all of these cases, groups advanced and succeeded by pursuing their interests, by moving and taking what they knew and did best from their own group to the larger society. This is often characterized as social and human capital. These concepts, however, don't do justice to the dynamic nature of the actual process involved. For one, they don't account for how and why these different kinds of capital first begin to have an impact within the dominant society. Social and human capital often get wasted when the larger society doesn't value it. Second, these accounts forget the role of social interests by focusing on social and human capital. Social interests foreshadow the moves the capital make possible. Social interest foreshadows the dancing. It is these interests that create newly felt demands and pressures that pull and draw the minority group into the bosom of the larger society.

In many ways, this is a story about groups that is really more familiar as a story about individuals. Throughout modern history, personal accounts of individual social mobility have explained the key mechanism to success as a mutual seduction between the individual and the larger society. This can take place in several ways. Subordinate-group individuals are either insulated from their own group values and rituals by distance and psychology, or they turn against it. The other mechanism is to get attention from dominant-group individuals who seek to rescue subordinate individuals from the "savagery" that is their group culture. In both cases, the subordinate individual seduces and is seduced into accepting, desiring, and relocating within the values and behavior of the dominant society.

Norman Podhoretz writes about his own assimilation into the "superior" class. Podhoretz explained that when he was thirteen a teacher in his Brownsville school took a special interest in him because he had "so beautiful a mind."[68] He admits that "she flirted with me and flattered me, she scolded me and insulted me." Her fierce efforts were aimed at turning a "filthy little slum child" into the recipient of a Harvard scholarship. The seduction went both ways, however.

Podhoretz realized that even though he had not consciously known it, he had already begun to change his speech, to drop his slum and Yiddish accent, before he met the teacher. He had begun to take fundamental action on his own that "would eventually make it possible for me to move into some other world." It was a move for entry and power in the "Superior class" that he had already prepared for before he met his meddling and patronizing teacher.

Puerto Rican activists and leaders tell many similar stories of mutual seduction. El Comite leader Esperanza Martell attributes her development to the experiences she had with settlement houses, citywide leadership training, and non–Puerto Rican counselors.[69] For Iris Morales of the Young Lords, the first transformational moment was her exposure to African American history and the writings of Malcolm X while in college.[70] Felipe Luciano, another Young Lord, has written that even at a young age, he "knew that to the extent that we became white—we would advance in school."[71] His teachers criticized him for not trying to reach his "potential." He also had a teacher who introduced him to Shakespeare and got him to love it. Again, like Podhoretz, Luciano had already committed himself to the larger world before meeting this teacher. He claims that he used to "rape" books, devouring dozens of them at a time locked up in his room. It was, he says, his "way of escape" from the ghetto.

In all of these experiences, the process of seduction worked for individual and society because each had a preexisting interest in the other. Individual strategies don't work very well for groups, however. Groups, for instance, can distance themselves from their own culture only with great difficulty. In fact, the more cohesive the group is, the harder this will be. Research shows that it is immigrant groups with low levels of cohesiveness that have found it easier to assimilate and advance. That was the experience of the Dutch immigrants who settled in Brooklyn (originally from the Dutch town "Breuckelen") and Australia (Giorgas 2000). Group cohesiveness, on the other hand, can also be an asset to mobility, as we discussed above with Greek immigrants.

What is hard for groups is easier for individuals. Whether it is with or against the restraints of their group of origin, individuals often have some opportunity to move upwards and out of their group. Persistence does often pay off for them. An opportunity to dance with the right partner does often become available. While mutual seduction is necessary for a group to assimilate and become absorbed within the larger society, it does not work as cleanly as it does for individuals. Persistence does not pay off for a minority group because the dynamics of the seduction process are complicated by far fewer opportunities for contact with the larger society.

One Last Move

Puerto Ricans have lost power because of the particular historical mix of values and interests found in them as well as in other parts of the larger society. Many Puerto Ricans have rejected the larger society because they think, perhaps correctly, that the costs of moving towards it are too great. This is especially true since opportunities to dance and gather power are more readily available, as a result of segregation and poverty, with other Puerto Ricans and other minorities. Puerto Rican desire for the larger society is, however, less important than the lack of desire the larger society has for them. That lack of interest keeps Puerto Ricans at bay, at the margins, and out of most real opportunities for power. "They flee from me that sometime did me seek."[72] Puerto Ricans have, as a result, exchanged the remote possibility of future success dancing on the main dance floor with "the monster" (that rejects them) for more limited and real opportunities for dancing with partners just like them, on their own dance floors.

Puerto Ricans have exchanged the possibility of power in the distant future for power today. They've rejected what appears like a big gamble in mainstream striving. The risks in pursuing that gamble might be exciting and worth taking if life itself in the barrio was not already in jeopardy and short. Moves to "opt out" of local, community life and strive for mainstream success might also be worth taking if that dance floor were easier to get to and remain on. It's the choice that any dancer or group makes all the time—dance and gain power with those who are present and willing. Dance, move with the monster even, when you can. Some power may be had that way. Move anyway, with anyone when you can't. Power can be had this way too.

> O air-born voice! long since, severely clear,
> A cry like thine in mine own heart I hear:
> "Resolve to be thyself; and know that he,
> Who finds himself, loses his misery!"[73]

Notes

1. Amos H. Hawley, "Power as an Attribute of Social Systems," *The American Journal of Sociology* 68 (January 1963): 422.

2. Pierre Bourdieu et al., *Academic Discourse: Linguistic Misunderstanding and Professorial Power*. Richard Teese, trans. (Stanford, CA: Stanford U. Press, 1996).

3. The most prominent alternative metaphor for power found in social theory literature is that of a game (Clegg 1989, 209). Bowles and Gintis argue, for instance, for the use of chess as an analytical metaphor because it offers "both an activity (playing chess) and a structure (the rules of chess)" (1986, 118). Power, like chess, is a game with roles and rules. But, real-life power is very different from chess. Chess is deliberative and calculating. The creation, destruction, and use of power very often are not. In addition, those with great power are often in a position to change the rules. The ability to ad-lib and modify the rules, even to change them, makes dancing a much better metaphor for power. Historians of social dancing argue, in fact, that the role of leader and follower evolved as a mutual agreement between dance partners needing a system for deciding when to turn, in what direction, and how to avoid bumping into other couples. It is for that reason that "the leading partner was responsible for steering a safe course around the ballroom, and the other partner had

to follow the leader" (Gerald Jonas, *Dancing: The Pleasure, Power, and Art of Movement* [New York: Abrams, 1992], 124).

4. Karl Marx, *Grundrisse* (London: Penguin Books, 1973), 92.

5. Data in this paragraph from March 1994 *Current Population Survey (CPS)*, Bureau of the Census, U.S. Department of Commerce.

6. Boricua First press release, May 16, 1995. See also on this issue Angelo Falcon, "De'tras Pa'lante: Explorations on the Future of Puerto Ricans," in Haslip-Viera et al., 2004, 156.

7. "Puerto Rican Obituary" in Santiago and Galster 1995, 182.

1. Bourdieu also pictured power as a game complete with players, rules, and the tokens of value that the players compete over and capture (see Pierre Bourdieu and L. J. D. Wacquant, *An Invitation to Reflexive Sociology* [Chicago: U. of Chicago Press, 1992]). He also recognized the limitations of the game metaphor—power is not a deliberate creation and has mostly implicit rules. The more important difference is that most agents in the social relations that create power aren't involved in and don't perceive what they do as a competition. This is what makes dance a more appropriate model.

2. Many theories of power identify its existence as a function of conscious and unconscious resistance. Thus, Dahl claims that A has power over B to the extent

that A can make B do something B would otherwise not do. I avoid this overly narrow definition, which ignores the role of social structures that make things happen and often at such a distance that B is not even aware. I define power as the ability to shape the way others think, act, and feel.

3. Something similar is also at work in the relationship between attorneys and clients as well as doctors and patients. See Marcia A. Hillary and Joel T. Johnson, "Social Power and Interactional Style in the Divorce Attorney/Client Dyad," *Journal of Divorce* 12 (4) (1989) 89–102.

4. See Martin Tolchin, "Congress's Influential Aides Discover Power but Little Glory on Capital Hill," *New York Times,* Nov. 12, 1991, A22. Also see Harrison W. Fox and Susan W. Hammond, *Congressional Staffs: The Invisible Force in American Lawmaking* (New York: Free Press, 1977)..

5. See Michael W. Malbin, *Unelected Representatives* (New York: Basic Books, 1980), 29.

6. This is one of the critical lessons in any dance class. In an early dance instruction manual, Lawrence A. Hostetler states that even "an excellent dancer, is nevertheless handicapped to the extent of her partner's ability—or inability" (*The Art of Social Dancing: A Text Book for Teachers and Students* [New York: A. S. Barnes, 1934], 41).

7. Geoffrey Canada relates an episode in his childhood when he and his friends stared down a man with a gun. They gave the man the look of cold hardness, a

look that said that they were "willing to die, to sacrifice themselves" and forced the man with the gun to run off (*Fist, Stick, Gun: A Personal History of Violence in America* [Boston, MA: Beacon Press, 1995], 62).

8. Jose E. Limon writes about the popular Mexican American and Latino folk tale concerning disobedient young people who attend a dance and then find themself dancing with the devil. Interestingly, some of his respondents blamed the female dancers for the appearance of the devil because they were "never satisfied," always wanting this and that. The devil that appears and tempts them is rich and white. These characteristics, the respondents believe, will help the women "learn that they can't have everything." What is clear is that the devil overpowers the women because their unquenchable desires lead them to dance with him. (*Dancing with the Devil: Society and Cultural Poetics in Mexican-American South Texas* [Madison: U. of Wisconsin Press, 1994], 175).

9. This is what Haugaard means when he states that "social structure does not exist materially outside its moment of reproduction" (Haugaard 2000, 65).

10. Adam Smith, *The Wealth of Nations* (New York: Penguin Classics, 1982), books 1 and 2.

11. Some of the most recent intellectual descendants of social power theory include the literature on the powers of the weak. See, for instance, Elizabeth Janeway, *Powers of the Weak* (New York: Knopff, 1980) and James C. Scott, *Domination and the Arts of Resistance: Hidden Transcripts* (New Haven, CT: Yale U. Press, 1990).

12. Afsaneh Nahavandi, *The Art and Science of Leadership* (Upper Saddle River, NJ: Prentice-Hall, 1997). Leadership training makes use of social power theory because it assumes agency and an agent in leaders.

13. *New York Newsday* reporter Craig Gordon explained Cheney's enduring presence and influence in the White House as a result of the fact that "Cheney is too important to Bush." See "Cheney Plays by His Own Rules," Feb. 18, 2006.

14. Wartenberg agrees with Hannah Arendt in defining power as resulting "from a mutual decision made by a group of people to create a social hierarchy in order to run their common life efficiently" (1990, 41).

15. Isaac Balbus argues that, in contrast to Marxism, classical liberalism and pluralist theories ignore objective interest and define interest "in purely subjective terms" ("The Concept of Interest in Pluralist and Marxian Analysis," in Ira Katznelson, G. Adams, P. Brenner, and A. Wolfe, eds., *The Politics and Society Reader* [New York: McKay, 1974], 282).

16. Peter de Jonge, "Television's Final Frontier," *New York Times Sunday Magazine,* August 22, 1999.

17. Anthony Giddens makes clear that "human societies, or social systems, would plainly not exist without human agency. But it is not the case that actors create social systems: they reproduce or transform them" (*The Constitution of Society* [Berkeley: U. of California Press, 1984], 171). Social actors are, in this sense, not entirely free to make society. But they do make it. That much is also asserted in the dance model.

18. As Mark Hugaard has said, "Structural constraint works through the agency of others because of the need for collaborative others in order to reproduce social structure" (in Goverde et al. 2000, 62).

19. This is similar to what Murray Edelman argued in *The Symbolic Uses of Politics* (Edelman 1964). For Edelman, the basic unit of analysis in political science is not the individual, organizations, or structures. It is the social transaction that he claimed was the "mechanisms through which politics influences what they want, what they fear, what they regard as possible, and even who they are" (1964, 19).

20. Objective interests suggest the element of need. Preferences are more like desire. Thus, while "I may have my own subjective reasons for desiring something, I cannot have my own reasons for needing something" (Dowding 1996, 22).

21. Bernard Berk, "Face-Saving at the Singles Dance," *Social Problems* 24 (5) (1977): 19, 543.

22. See Anne Schneider and Helen Ingram, "Social Constructions and Target Populations: Implications for Public Policy," *American Political Science Review* 87 (1993): 334–47, as well as their "Response to Robert C. Lieberman," *American Political Science Review* 89 (1995): 443–46.

23. Here I agree with Arts. Power can be *assessed,* not *measured.* What data and historical records make possible is, at best, "well-educated guesses" (Arts 2000, 137). See also John Ramsay, "Power Measurement," *European Journal of Purchasing and Supply* 2 (2/3) (June/September 1996): 129–43.

24. Edward J. Lawler, S. R. Thye, and J. Yoon, "Emotion and Group Cohesion in Productive Exchange," *Journal of Sociology* 106 (3) (November 2000): 616–57.

25. For an excellent analysis of the use of historical interpretation in political science, see Ian S. Lustick, "History, Historiography, and Political Science: Multiple Historical Records and the Problem of Selection Bias," *American Political Science Review* 90 (3) (September 1996): 605–18.

26. The Turner model has four essential elements. The first is the moment when the "regular, norm-governed social relations" between social agents is violated. The second is a period of "mounting crisis" during which regular, norm-governed social actions are under question. The third phase involves "redressive action," where leading social agents of the disturbed social system attempt to limit the spread of crisis by bringing to bear formal and informal mechanisms. The final moment results in either "the reintegration of the disturbed social group or. . . . [t]he social recognition and legitimization of irreparable schism be-

tween the contesting parties"
(Turner 1974, 37–41).

27. This, of course, assumes
that prominent and excellent life
achievements are not the exclu-
sive property of mainstream,
white America.

28. See Robert E. Stake, *The
Art of Case Study Research*
(Thousand Oaks, CA: Sage Publi-
cations, 1995).

29. It is usually the case that
"concepts that can be measured
directly are usually trivial in and
of themselves" (Shively 1998,
40).

30. Although the recent problems with establishing that Sad-
dam Hussein had weapons of
mass destruction show that even
this kind of measurement can
pose formidable obstacles.

31. Baltasar Gracian, *The Art
of Worldly Wisdom*, edited by
Willis Barnstone, translated by
Joseph Jacobs (Boston, MA:
Shambhala Library, 1993).

NOTES TO CHAPTER 2

1. A similar government effort
existed at the time for African
Americans. A Division of Negro
Economics was created in 1917
to seek employment and "mobilize the black work force in the
U.S." (Guzda 1982, 40).

2. See Marcantonio Papers,
New York Public Library
Archives, Box 52, "Puerto Rican
Construction Workers'" file.

3. Such a perception eventually
compromised the Puerto Rican
labor movement as well. During
the Depression, the Puerto Rican
labor movement collaborated
with the New Deal program in
Puerto Rico to keep wages in
Puerto Rico lower than in the
mainland so as to prevent factories from closing and throwing
people out of work (Carrion
1983, 230).

4. See Marcantonio Papers,
New York Public Library
Archives, Box 53, "United Cigar
Workers Union" file. Also between 1930 and 1936, cigar
making represented the eleventh
most sought after position by
Puerto Rican men seeking employment from the Puerto Rican
government's employment agency

in New York City (Chenault
1970, 74).

5. Over four million workers
in different industries went on
strike in late 1919, reflecting a
crest in national union membership and power that declined
soon after (cf. Irving Bernstein,
*The Lean Years: Workers in an
Unbalanced Society* [New York:
Houghton-Mifflin, 1960]).

6. The condensed fruit of the
worker's own labor.

7. The workers in New York
will have in their struggles the
help and solidarity of the feder-
ated worker's movement in New
York, which has about seven
hundred thousand organized
members.

8. We cigar makers who pre-
tend to be the leaders and
spokesmen in social workers'
struggles have proven the contrary in our ability to create a secure and efficient base to defend
our own occupations.

9. Work below the contracted
wage.

10. In most cases, Puerto Ricans found that politicians
quickly forgot them after the
election. Some Puerto Ricans recognized the dancelike quality to
their relationship with politicians. Invariably, politicians
come around "with banquets,
drinks, and false promises," according to one Puerto Rican.
They then respond after the election with, "I do not know you"
(Thomas 2002, 200).

11. This argument contrasts
with that of Virginia Sanchez-Korral, who explains the proliferation of Puerto Rican organizations in New York during the
1920s as a mere response to demographic expansion as well as
to experiences with racism. Thus,
she states that one 1920s organization, the Puerto Rican Brother-
hood, was among the first to realize that "the *colonia* needed
groups to represent them before
the host society, to handle particular problems such as discrimination" (1983, 153). More importantly, if in fact the existing
Puerto Rican organizations, like
the cigar makers' unions, proved
limited in dealing with racism,
the question should be why

Puerto Ricans would abandon
organizations with power, like
the cigar union, for new organizations possessed of only a potential power? Sanchez-Korral, in
fact, admits that Puerto Rican
labor was concerned with racism
in the United States. She states
that *Grafica*, a Puerto Rican
working-class newspaper, often
editorialized and "broached the
subject of discrimination against
Puerto Ricans in New York"
(1983, 72). It would have made
more sense for Puerto Ricans to
turn to the experience and organizational skills of the cigar makers. To some extent, this is, in
fact, what they did.

12. The first serious effort to
create an organization that
would unify the community.

13. No political party, neither
the Democrat nor the Republican, was seriously interested in
Puerto Rican support.

14. Potential voter to an inqui-
sition to stop him (from voting).

15. Jesus Colon himself admits
that "the workers and the cigar
makers taught me—they gave me
pamphlets and papers to read—
they told me that we were a
colony—a sort of storage house
for cheap labor and a market for
'seconds' (cheap industrial
goods)" (Colon 1982, 199).

16. Would fight to be recognized as Puerto Rican or, in general, as Hispanics.

17. Cigar makers and their
union, the Cigar Makers' International Union, enjoyed considerable prestige and political
power in part because cigar
maker and long-time CMIU vice
president was none other than
Samuel Gompers, a founder and
long-time president of the American Federation of Labor. Gompers's major accomplishment as
AFL president was to enshrine
his business-unionism philosophy
in the American labor movement.

18. The *confiteres,* bread makers, hotel, restaurant, and garment workers got organized.

19. Other industrial unions
began to show interest in the
Puerto Rican worker.

20. Marcantonio Papers, NY
Public Library, Box #6, 18th

Congressional District Cases, 1935–36.

21. See the exchange of letters between Marcantonio and Juan Rovira, secretary of the CIAU-Local 389, regarding the naturalization problems of a Mrs. Klumpp (Marcantonio Papers, ibid.).

22. See Marcantonio Papers, NY Public Library, Box # 3, General Correspondence Legislative Conference.

23. Marcantonio Papers, NY Public Library, Box 53, United Cigar Workers Union file, letters of December 7, 13, September 12, and April 23, 1945.

24. Marcantonio Papers, NY Public Library, Box # 6, 18th Congressional District Cases, 1935–1936, January 28th letter.

25. The political issues of the city and the nation.

26. Our industry is not a necessary industry for any people.

27. You can live without smoking, and for that reason the cigar industry can come to an end.

28. More cautious on our part.

29. See Alan Brinkley, *The End of Reform: New Deal Liberalism in Recession and War* (New York: Vantage Press, 1995), 164–70.

30. Consider their place in New York as a passing thing.

31. Rafael Hernandez composed and created thousands of songs. He was a leading musical creator in Latin America and a national hero in Puerto Rico. According to one source, the *New York Times* wanted to interview him in 1965, the year he died, but never did. The *Times* had "thirty or forty years to do so" but hadn't "discovered" him till he died (Bloch 1973, 51).

NOTES TO CHAPTER 3

1. Translation: "Sometimes I tell myself that I should have died before coming to this country, seeing as how I don't know English and I am worth nothing—except I am worth something to God." February 2, 1965, letter from Pedro Lopez, of Brooklyn postal zone 32, to Manuel Cabranes, consultant to the

Commissioner of Welfare, New York City. Cabranes was earlier the executive director of the MCPRA. (Cabranes Papers—Case Records 1965, January–March, New York Public Library.)

2. Antonia Pantoja described how the creation of the Puerto Rican Forum included dropping the word "Hispanic" from its name at its creation in 1957 as she and other Puerto Rican leaders realized that they no longer "needed to include other Spanish-speaking groups in our activities in order to obtain strength." Antonia Pantoja, *Memoir of a Visionary: Antonia Pantoja* (Houston, TX: Arte Publico Press, 2002), 91.

3. See Amelie Oksenberg Rorty, "Power and Powers: A Dialogue between Buff and Rebuff," in Thomas E. Wartenberg, ed., *Rethinking Power* (Albany: SUNY Press), 9.

4. Letter from Ruperto Ruiz of the Puerto Rican West Side Urban Renewal to Urban Renewal Board, March 30, 1961 (Municipal Archives Box 3503).

5. See Davies 1966, 116–42.

6. Municipal Archives of New York City, Box 6633.

7. COIR Annual Report, 1961 (Municipal Archives of New York City, box 6633).

8. COIR was also involved in the creation of Aspira, the Puerto Rican educational organization, and of the Puerto Rican Forum, an institution-building organization. See Antonia Pantoja, *Antonia Pantoja: Memoir of a Visionary* (Houston, TX: Arte Publico Press, 2002).

9. Fifteen of those were actually Puerto Rican (Thomas 2002, 290).

10. Unless otherwise stated, all of this information is from MCPRA 1953a and 1953b.

11. Here is a typical example from Jack Lait and Lee Mortimer's famous book, *U.S.A. Confidential* (New York: Crown Publishing, 1952): "In the last twenty years some 600,000 of the Little Brown Brothers have been funneled into our town, mostly in East Harlem."

12. In 1950, veterans, almost

all white, represented 84 percent of all families admitted into public housing (NYC Housing Authority Annual Report, 1950, La Guardia Archives, Box 18, 590.25).

13. In 1958, 49 percent of public housing tenants in New York City were white.

14. Puerto Rican activist Gerena Valentine did continue to battle authorities on behalf of the Puerto Rican community during the 1950s and '60s.

15. Something very similar to the MCPRA was also created at the national level for African Americans during the early part of the twentieth century. During World War I, the Labor Department created the Division of Negro Economics to assist black workers newly migrant to the labor-short, industrialized North (Guzda 1982).

16. Puerto Rican Affairs Committee reported that the Communist Party in New York City showed a "catastrophic drop of 90 % from the 1948 Puerto Rican membership" to their membership in 1953 (CPUSA 1959, 65). No actual numbers were mentioned.

17. "An accessory of the colonial system of the exploitation suffered by the Puerto Rican people."

18. For the people of Puerto Rico, the administration of Munoz-Marin has been Operation Booby Trap. *Boriquen*, or garden of flowers, he told his House audience, was the Puerto Rican Indian's name for the island. But, he continued, the colonial economic and political situation on the island had destroyed Puerto Rico's natural beauty and tranquility. As a consequence Marcantonio felt that it had become increasingly true that for the average Puerto Rican "Puerto Rico no tiene nade de jardin" (Puerto Rico is no garden) (Ojeda 1978, 126).

19. See the *New York Times* Sept. 14, 1949, 36; Sept. 22, 1949, 37; Oct. 8, 1949, 30; Oct. 17, 1949, 10; and Thomas 2002, 297.

20. The public assistance program in New York during the

1940s was unlike the one in Puerto Rico where a very small amount (nine dollars a month) was granted only to the most destitute person, and none was given to poor but employed persons.

21. The MCPRA also provided Spanish-speaking teachers for the public schools.

22. The percentage of New York Puerto Ricans on welfare in 1950 was 12.7 percent but only 4.5 percent in 1953.

23. Calculated from Bonilla and Campos 1986.

24. There were twelve members in total from private and public institutions in Puerto Rico. Another twenty-six Puerto Ricans or Spanish were associated with organizations in New York City. The thirty-nine non–Puerto Rican or Spanish members of the MCPRA included heads of city government departments.

25. Extension of Social Security to Puerto Rico and the Virgin Islands, 81 H.R. 6000, was passed in the House on February 6, 1950.

26. Based on comments by Robert Wagner at Annual Meeting of CSAO, April 14, 1956, Box 1967, New York Municipal Archives.

27. Cited in CPUSA 1954, 63.

28. Letter from H. L. Present, Counsel for the Spanish-American Youth Bureau, Inc. (a part of CSAO) to Munoz-Marin, April 26, 1954. Municipal Archives Box #1967.

29. Quoted at http://www.bookrags.com/ebooks/11009/3.html.

30. Baker recognized this dimension in explaining Puerto Rican poverty when she stated that she studied the extent to which the city of Chicago "embraced or did not embrace" Puerto Ricans (2002, xv).

31. This is where I disagree with Albert O. Hirschman, who argued that exit was a neat and "uniquely powerful" option in most situations. Hirschman assumed competitive environments and consumptive rather than productive activities. See his *Exit, Voice, and Loyalty* (Cambridge, MA: Harvard University Press, 1970).

32. Ironically, Antonia Pantoja led this rise in professional leadership, though she claimed to be a radical.

33. La Guardia Archives, Box 39 B4–06, documents on NYHA Security Investigations, Feb. 22, 1957.

34. *New York Times,* November 17, 18, 19, and 20, 1959.

35. Municipal Archives, Box 2136, letters and report of Police Commissioner investigation on behalf of Mayor Wagner.

36. Municipal Archives, Boxes 117, 4991, 2136.

NOTES TO CHAPTER 4

1. The 1968 garbage strike pummeled Lindsay. Like the snow-cleaning issue, the garbage strike became the signature negative moment in his tenure as mayor. At one point in 1968, Lindsay walked those same East Harlem streets, at East 127th Street, during the strike, heckled by a citizen demanding to know when he was "going to get this garbage mess fixed up, chief" ("A Weary Lindsay Views the Pile-up and Finds It Bad," *New York Times,* Feb. 10, 1968).

2. See José E. Cruz, and C. E. Santiago, 2001.

3. This number of riots is puny in comparison to those of African Americans who in the same time period engaged in 752 riots throughout the United States. (See Gregg Lee Carter, "The 1960s Black Riots Revisited: City Level Explanations of Their Severity," *Sociological Inquiry* 56 [1986]: 210–228.) For Puerto Ricans who were mostly concentrated in New York City and in the Northeast, the number was small yet significant

4. The first Bomba and Plena festival was held in December of 1975 at the Beacon Theater in Manhattan ("Arts and Leisure Guide," *New York Times*, Dec. 21, 1975). Willie Colon, Mon Rivera, and others performed.

5. See Jose E. Figueroa, *Survival on the Margin: A Documentary Study of the Underground Economy in a Puerto Rican Ghetto* (New York: Vantage Press, 1989).

6. See Mitchell Pacelle, "An Oasis of Island Culture under Siege in the Bronx," *Wall Street Journal* (Eastern Edition), Feb 24, 1994, A16.

7. As Rogler, Cooney, and Ortiz have argued, in a study of Puerto Rican families in this 1970s period, the majority of Puerto Rican children saw themselves as either exclusively Puerto Rican or as Puerto Rican American. They found that "not even one of the Puerto Rican children considers himself or herself to be exclusively American" (Rogler et al. 1980, 212).

8. "Transcript of Debate by the Three Major Candidates in the Mayoral Election," *New York Times*, Oct. 11, 1969.

9. Gerena Valentin appeared in only 158 *New York Times* news reports from 1963 to 1982. In most of these, he was merely mentioned as a participant in a protest or meeting. In contrast, Badillo had 3,876 reports in his career of political "firsts."

10. Pantoja's father was a cigar maker in Puerto Rico. She attributes much of her militant politics to the example set by her cigar maker father.

11. See Tim Wise Commentary in Zmag at www.zmag.org/weluser.htm, 8/29/2000.

12. Clemente was also one of the only Puerto Ricans to receive a Congressional Gold Medal.

13. Baker does attempt to examine "the interactions between the barrios and the institutions of those cities" where Puerto Ricans live to explain their poverty. This dynamic perspective falls short, however. Baker ends by placing most of the blame on "double exploitation" in Puerto Rico and the United States, which prevented Puerto Ricans from establishing an economic niche (2002, 203).

14. The problem with "political dancing" is that it is mainly an Election Day event. "Economic dancing" at workplaces gives workers opportunities to affect employers every day they work.

15. See Richard Delgado's critique of affirmative action:

"Affirmative Action as a Majoritarian Device." *Michigan Law Review*. Vol. 89, 1991.

16. Raquel Z. Rivera, "Hip-Hop, Puerto Ricans, and Ethnoracial Identities in New York," in Agustin Lao-Montes and Arlene Davila, eds., *Mambo Montage: The Latinization of New York* (New York: Columbia U Press, 2001), 235–61.

17. Even Gould's critique of the way Wilson conflated cognitive and normative values assumed that values are the product of socialization both successful and unsuccessful. His vantage point remains that of the structures (1999).

18. I'm not arguing that Puerto Ricans don't lack capital. Puerto Ricans, for example, do lack education. As Rivera-Batiz found, during the 1990s "the educational gap between Puerto Ricans and the white population has grown" (Rivera-Batiz 2004, 122).

19. In contrast, African Americans don't quite have that problem. Moving closer to what people perceive as more authentic African American culture and styles, like in music, dance, sports, and language, has the ironic impact of making African Americans more rather than less attractive and interesting to some segments of white America. Rap music, for that reason, sells more to the white community than to African Americans (Katz 2004).

20. "Group Organizes Puerto Rican Aid," *New York Times*, Nov. 7, 1964.

21. "Woes of Puerto Ricans in City Found Increasing," *New York Times*, July 25, 1968.

22. Data on "Food Stores" is from the *1997 Economic Census—Minority and Women-Owned Businesses in the U.S.,* U.S. Bureau of the Census, 1997.

23. *1997 Economic Census,* table 7.

24. Abraham Rodriquez, Jr., *Spidertown* (New York: Hyperion, 1993), 69.

25. Puerto Ricans had direct experience with the recalibration of Jewish racial identity. During the clashes with Jews in Harlem during 1926, Puerto Ricans found that while they remained "Porto Ricans," the Jews involved in the incident were transformed by the *New York Times* into the avuncular and generic "old residents of Harlem" ("Ask Police Protection: Porto Ricans Complain of Being Attacked," *New York Times*, July 30, 1926).

26. Landale and Oropesa show that being a light Puerto Rican is not the same as being white (2002).

27. The party unity rate for Serrano is 89.2 percent, 91 percent for Guiteirrez, and 93 percent for Velazquez.

28. The data in this chart is raw. Articles about Puerto Ricans in Puerto Rico or Mexicans in Mexico have not been removed. This was done for practical and methodological reasons. It is more efficient not to remove them and it's important to include them because they contribute to the entire public image and response to these groups.

29. The exact boundaries were Starr and Troutman as well as Knickerbocker and Wilson.

30. Each estimate reflects a different assumption about the proportion of Puerto Rican households on the block. The minimum estimate assumes that Puerto Ricans are 23 percent of the households on the Starr-Troutman block. (This is the percentage of residents born in Puerto Rico.) The maximum estimate assumes that the percent of Puerto Ricans on the block is 77, representing the proportion of the total number of Census Tract 427 residents born in Puerto Rico together with the number of Hispanics born in the United States (most of these tend to be Puerto Rican). The 40 percent assumption is based on population figures for CT 427, which report this as the proportion of Puerto Ricans. Another major assumption was that Puerto Rican households were all visible from the street. That is, of course, not true. It was a necessary assumption, however, that underestimated the actual proportion of Puerto Rican households on the block.

31. "Puerto Ricans Here Drive to Train Youths for a Future," *New York Times*, March 5, 1962, 25.

32. Congressional database at CQ Press, a Division of Congressional Quarterly Inc., 2005.

33. Under rules enacted in 1995, members of Congress are effectively banned from accepting any gift worth more than fifty dollars. They may accept sponsored trips so long as these trips are not sponsored by a lobbyist or foreign agent.

NOTES TO CHAPTER 5

1. Adrian Nicole LeBlanc, *Love, Drugs, Trouble, and Coming of Age in the Bronx* (New York: Scribner, 2003), 162.

2. Occasionally, some Puerto Ricans have recognized this difference. As early as 1962, one member of the Latin Artists Union lamented that Latinos "are either not white enough or not black enough" to appear in theaters or on TV (Anderson 1962, 13).

3. An exception is Ira Katznelson's 2006 book, *When Affirmative Action Was White: An Untold History of Racial Inequality in Twentieth-Century America* (New York: Norton, 2006).

4. In one recent study, 65 percent of Puerto Rican activists believed that the Puerto Rican community was "besieged by outside forces." They believed that the undercount of the Puerto Rican population in the 2000 Census was the result of a deliberate "policy in Washington" (Falcon 2004, 152).

5. Juan Flores argues that the commercial projection of Latinos has selected whiter Latino faces both to facilitate the transaction with nonwhites as well as to mollify white fears of a Brown invasion (2002).

6. There is an implicit recognition of this fact in recent reports by some civil rights organizations that promote "interdependence" between minority groups and white society. (See Maggie Potapchuk, *Cultivating Interdependence: A Guide for Race Relations and Racial Justice Orga-*

nizations [Washington, DC: Joint Center for Political and Economic Studies, 2004]. Also, see Gary Delgado's *Multiracial Formations: New Instruments for Social Change* [Oakland, CA: Applied Research Center, 2002].)

7. American high school textbooks perpetuate a similar stereotype about Puerto Ricans and Latinos. Barbara C. Cruz's study of textbooks found that "most popular history textbooks currently in use at the secondary level reinforce the stereotypes of Latin Americans as lazy, passive, irresponsible, and somewhat paradoxically, lustful, animalistic and violent" ("Stereotypes of Latin Americans Perpetuated in Secondary School History Textbooks," *Latino Studies Journal* 1 [1] [January 1994]: 55).

8. Screenplay writer Arthur Laurents quoted in Alberto Sandoval Sanchez, "West Side Story: A Puerto Rican Reading of *America*" in Clara E. Rodriguez, ed, *Latin Looks: Images of Latinas and Latinos in the U.S. Media* (Boulder, Co: Westview, 1997), 168.

9. Some Puerto Rican advantages in Hollywood may have originated in the use of Puerto Rico to produce Mexican movies in the 1950s and 1960s. As Beer writes, "beginning in 1963, both Columbia and independent Mexican producers began to make a substantial number of feature films on location in Puerto Rico" (Beer 2001, 148).

10. Roberto Rodrigues and Patrisia Gonzales, "Latino Spectrum" E-mail.

11. Joe Cuba "Bang! Bang! Push, Push, Push" CD (Tico 1146), released 1966.

12. *People*'s list of 50: Jessica Alba • Jennifer Aniston • Drew Barrymore • Mischa Barton • David Beckham, international soccer star • Halle Berry • Orlando Bloom • Penelope Cruz • Patrick Dempsey, *Grey's Anatomy* • Johnny Depp • Hilary Duff • Sara Evans, Country singer • Colin Farrell • Jamie Foxx • Tim Green, former NFL star and best-selling author • Mariska Hargitay, *Law & Order: SVU* • Tyler Hilton, *One Tree Hill* • Josh Holloway, *Lost* • Scarlett Johansson • Angelina Jolie • Juanes, Colombian musician • Alicia Keys • Heidi Klum • Jude Law • Lindsay Lohan • Eva Longoria • Jennifer Lopez • Ann-Margret • Matthew McConaughey • Eva Mendes, *Hitch* • Jesse Metcalfe, *Desperate Housewives* • Sienna Miller, *Alfie* • Catalina Sandino Moreno, *Maria Full of Grace* • Sandra Oh, *Sideways, Grey's Anatomy* • Sophie Okonedo, *Hotel Rwanda* • Clive Owen, *Sin City, Closer* • Tyler Perry, *Diary of a Mad Black Woman* author • Brad Pitt • Julia Roberts • Seal • Maria Sharapova, Russian tennis player • Jessica Simpson • Elizabeth Smart, Utah teen • Martha Stewart • Hilary Swank • Usher • Dwayne Wade, Miami Heat basketball player • Oprah Winfrey • Kate Winslet • Ziyi Zhang, *House of Flying Daggers*.

13. TONY had a circulation rate of over 1.3 million in 2002, according to *MediaWeek* magazine.

14. Some of the issues involved in the use of naming data can be found in Philippe Benard, "The Study of Social Taste through First Names: Comment on Lieberson and Bell," *American Journal of Sociology* 100 (5) (March 1995): 1313–1317.

15. In contrast, Charles Tilly and other scholars, like Nhu-Ngoc T. Ong and David S. Meyer, have conceptualized protest as an extension of conventional politics (Ong and Meyer 2004, "Protest and Political Incorporation: Vietnamese American Protests, 1975–2001," posted at the eScholarship Repository, University of California. http://repositories.cdlib.org/csd/04–08; Tilly 1984).

16. Some researchers suggest that incorporation means political influence (see Browning, Marshall, and Tabb 2003). I don't. The reason is simple. I don't think we should equate the absorption of a group into existing political institutions with the ability to influence the way those institutions behave.

17. See "Hundreds of Volunteers Pitch In and Haul Refuse to Incinerators," *New York Times*, Feb. 10, 1968.

18. See "City University Plans Cut in Admissions Standard," *New York Times*, March 20, 1965, 28.

19. "Hundreds of Volunteers Pitch In and Haul Refuse to Incinerators," *New York Times*, Feb. 10, 1968.

20. "State Remapping of Congress Lines Helpful to GOP," *New York Times*, Jan. 10, 1970.

21. "Mayor and Council Name 15 to New Board," *New York Times*, March 13, 1970.

22. "Violence Recurs in East Village," *New York Times*, July 27, 1970.

23. That same year, Puerto Rican representation in state government quadrupled. Three Puerto Ricans were elected to the State Assembly and one to the Senate ("4 Puerto Ricans Will Take Seats," *New York Times*, Dec. 6, 1970). It was the first time since 1966 that that many Puerto Ricans served in the state legislature.

24. The two cases were *Martha Cardona v. James M. Power, et al.* (No. 673, 86 S.Ct. 1728, 1731) and *Nicholas de B. Katzenbach, etc., et al. v. John P. Morgan, et al.* (Nos. 847, 877, 86 S.Ct. 1717).

25. *Race Relations Law Register* 11 (3) (Fall 1966): 1092.

26. The mediated nature of this action was made clear by the Lord's Melendez, who explained that "on a typical news-dead summer Sunday, we became the lead story" (2003, 106).

27. Frank Browning, "From Rumble to Revolution: The Young Lords," in F. Cordasco and E. Bucchioni, *The Puerto Rican Experience* (Totowa, NJ: Littlefield Adams and Co., 1975), 245.

28. In almost exactly parallel fashion, many of the doctors and nurses at the Lords' Lincoln Hospital takeover in 1970 also joined and supported the Lords ("Lincoln Hospital: Case History of Dissension that Split Staff," *New York Times*, Dec. 21, 1970).

29. It was mediated power because their capacity to influence

was transmitted through the media. Lindsay and others complied with the Lords because they were afraid. They didn't fear losing an election to Puerto Ricans nor that Puerto Ricans could take work actions to cripple any city industry. They feared that the public perception of them would be tarnished by a potential Puerto Rican riot or by the suggestion that they coddled poor and minority lawbreakers.

30. By 1961, the United States was so confident about what it helped to produce in Puerto Rico that it began to promote Puerto Rico at the United Nations as a model of development for the Third World (see "Puerto Rico Promoted in U.N. as a Model," *New York Times*, March 30, 1961).

31. That period was, no doubt, the last gasp of the traditional political machine. Later, in the 1960s War on Poverty, a different kind of political machine developed. This machine, in agreement with Charles Hamilton, took the form of "patron-recipient" relationships that were more about charity than power ("The Patron-Recipient Relationship and Minority Politics in New York City," *Political Science Quarterly* 94 [2] [Summer 1979]: 211–27).

32. Collective preferences are impossible to establish by using the usual survey and interview methods that are so popular among social scientists. All that can be learned from such efforts are individual preferences. Thus, in order to get at the actual degree of public interest in Puerto Ricans, this study identified and measured public interest by probing such things as postage stamps, obituaries, and newspaper articles.

33. Quoted in Bernard Rosenberg and D. M. White, eds., *Mass Culture: The Popular Arts in America* (New York: Free Press, 1957), 457.

34. The Institute for Puerto Rican Policy, Inc., has, for example, clear connections to the Lords' heritage. The popular media description of their work was that they were "Young Lords

with computers." In addition, founders Angelo Falcon and Jose R. Sanchez were associates and collaborators with the Lords. They helped the Lords to acquire the space at Columbia University for the Lords' famous September 1970 conference. Gerson Borrero, an early associate of the Institute, had also worked with the Lords, particularly helping them to put together a musical concert to fundraise money in order to pay the bail debts of ex-Lords arrested for the Statue of Liberty protest in 1977 (Melendez 2003, 210).

35. I'm not suggesting that what happened in New York City is the only experience of Puerto Ricans worth discussing. The Puerto Rican community has become more dispersed around the country and has made many pioneering and significant achievement in those places, including the election of the first Puerto Rican mayor in Hartford, Connecticut, in 2003. Just as for the rest of the country and the mass media, however, New York City and the Puerto Ricans who live there are vital centers and leaders of change for the rest of the country.

36. A Google search on July 19, 2004, for pages about the Young Lords (excluding references to Battlestar Galactica or to a musical group with the same name) resulted in 1.940 entries. In comparison, a search for pages about Puerto Rican politician Herman Badillo resulted in 2,370 entries. That the Lords almost matched Badillo in the number of entries is telling since Badillo has been in the public eye for generations. He was Housing Relocation Commissioner in the 1960s, served as a multiterm congressman, was a repeated New York City mayoral hopeful, served as deputy mayor, and more recently has served as chair of the CUNY Board of Regents. Many of the entries are not about Badillo since there are many schools and community centers named after him.

37. Puerto Ricans also attacked the Congress in 1954. See also "Five Congressmen Shot in

House," *New York Times*, March 2, 1954.

38. Interestingly, Antonia Pantoja explains that she founded the educational agency Aspira and the school-based Aspira Clubs in an attempt to capture and repackage the socially beneficial and menacing elements of Puerto Rican youth gangs. Gangs, she said, provided "such symbols as jackets and names that meant power and elicited fear" (2002, 97). By creating school clubs, she had hoped to give Puerto Rican youth an alternative, similar mechanism for building identity, power, and prestige.

NOTES TO THE CONCLUSION

1. From Robert Musil's *The Man without Qualities* (1935), quoted in Ben Highmore, *Cityscapes: Cultural Readings in the Material and Symbolic City* (New York: Palgrave MacMillan, 2005), 10.

2. Marta E. Savigliano, *Tango and the Political Economy of Passion* (Boulder, Co.: Westview Press, 1995), 214.

3. W. Phillips Shively, *The Craft of Political Research*. 3rd ed. (Englewood Cliffs, NJ: Prentice Hall, 1990).

4. Alan Brinkley, *The End of Reform: New Deal Liberalism in Recession and War* (New York: Vintage Press, 1995).

5. In 1940, Puerto Rican males had median incomes that were almost twice as close to those of white Americans as African Americans (at 82.9 percent to 43.3 percent). See James P. Smith, "Race and Ethnicity in the Labor Market: Trends over the Short and Long Run," paper prepared for a National Research Council Conference on Racial Trends, June 1999.

6. As early as 1949, some Puerto Rican leaders complained that the Puerto Rican community had not learned from the way African Americans used the media, attributing "much of the progress of the colored Continental people today" to the "constant *hammering* of their press . . . [to] demand

respect for them" (quoted in Thomas 2002, 267).

7. See Sanchez 1986.

8. Doris A. Graber, *Mass Media and American Politics*. 2nd ed. (Washington, DC: CQ Press, 1984).

9. Arlene Davila, *Latinos Inc.: The Marketing and Making of a People* (Berkeley: University of California Press, 2001).

10. Stanley Crouch, "On Watts: The Birth of the Hustle," *Daily News*, August 15, 2005, 29.

11. H. Peyton Young, *Individual Strategy and Social Structure: An Evolutionary Theory of Institutions* (Princeton, NJ: Princeton University Press, 1998), 19.

12. For an excellent analysis of the way structural processes can create unequal results, even in the absence of outright racism, see Christopher Prendergast, "Why Do African Americans Pay More for New Cars? A Structural Explanation," in Peter Kivisto, ed., *Illuminating Social Life: Classical and Contemporary Theory Revisited*. 3rd ed. (Thousand Oaks, CA: Pine Forge Press, 2004), 197–225.

13. Orlando Patterson, "A Poverty of the Mind," *New York Times*, March 26, 2006, op-ed. section.

14. Pedro Pietri, "Puerto Rican Obituary," in M. Abramson and Young Lords Party, *Palante!* (New York, McGraw-Hill, 1971).

15. Some researchers have argued that the plight of minority groups in the United States has fluctuated very closely with the colonial fortunes of their country of origin (see Peter Kwong, *Forbidden Workers: Illegal Chinese Immigrants and American Labor* [New York: New Press, 1997]).

16. Frances Negron-Muntaner, *Boricua Pop: Puerto Ricans and the Latinization of American Culture* (New York: New York University Press, 2004), xiii.

17. A similar process of generational memory has been documented with contemporary American farmers. Jared Diamond writes that young people in Montana leave for the city because "they don't want a life

forcing them to do literally back-breaking physical work into their 80s" (*Collapse: How Societies Choose to Fail or Succeed* [New York: Penguin Group, 2005]). No one blames these white young people for making these individual and collective choices since, in most cases, for them, the move to the city is more than likely to result in a white-collar job paying more than they would get in Montana.

18. There are at least forty-nine established Puerto Rican Day Parade organizations in cities around the United States, according to one website: http://elconcilio.net/News/2005_Puerto_Rican_Festivals_(schedules).htm (accessed 8/7/05).

19. This is one solution to the theoretical question about social structure: "Is it dynamic or is it static?" (Rom Harré, "Social Reality and the Myth of Social Structure," *European Journal of Social Theory* 5 [1] [2002]: 111–23).

20. J. D. Applen, "The Effects and Dynamics of Networks, Texting, and Power Relationships on the Construction of Identity," *Post Identity* 4 (1) (Spring 2004).

21. Reggaeton combines Reggae, Hip Hop, and Latin rhythms. It has become popular among different Latino groups as well as with African Americans and white Americans. See Mireya Navarro, "Mad Hot Reggaeton," *New York Times,* July 17, 2005.

22. As William N. Evans and Julie H. Topoleski write, "Four years after tribes open casinos, employment increases by 26 percent, and tribal population increases by about 12 percent, resulting in an increase in employment to population ratios of five percentage points or about 12 percent. The fraction of adults who work but are poor declines by 14 percent" (4), "The Social and Economic Impact of Native American Casinos," August 7, 2002 (accessed on Aug. 7, 2005, at http://www.src.uchicago.edu/prc/pdfs/evans02.pdf).

23. P. Edwards, J. Bélanger, and M. Wright come close to this argument in "The Micro-foundations of Class Compromise,"

paper to International Sociological Association World Congress, Research Committee 10, Brisbane, Australia, July 2002 (accessed on Aug. 7, 2005, at http://users.wbs.warwick.ac.uk/irru/publications/conference_papers/teams.pdf).

24. Anselmo and Rubal-Lopez describe the personal negotiation involved in creating racial-ethnic identity. One of the authors remembered her tortured reaction at requests to help fellow Puerto Ricans who needed translation assistance in dealing with Americans at school, work, or businesses. She explained that "one part of me wanted to be helpful and kind, but the other did not want, in the process of translating, to be identified as a *Spic*" (2005, 99). Each act of translation was a moment of negotiation about her identity as a Puerto Rican. Clearly, her worries also point to one of the racial differences between most Puerto Ricans and most African Americans. Most African Americans can be easily identified as such by the color of their skin. There is, admittedly, still some negotiation of race for African Americans. Black skin is not always *black*. If it were, black Puerto Ricans and other Latinos would not be able to differentiate themselves from African Americans by insisting on speaking Spanish in public.

25. James A. Robinson "Social Identity, Inequality, and Conflict," *Economics of Governance* 2 (2001): 89.

26. Lorrin R. Thomas, "Citizens on the Margins: Puerto Rican Migrants in New York City, 1917–1960," Ph.D. Dissertation at University of Pennsylvania, 2002, 98.

27. Felicia Fahey, "Beyond the Island: Puerto Rican Diaspora in 'America' and 'América,'" *Post Identity* (Summer 2001): 25–26.

28. Silvio Torres-Saillant, "Inventing the Race: Latinos and the Ethnoracial Pentagon," *Latino Studies* 1 (2003): 139.

29. See D. D. Caulkins and C. Peters, "Grid-Group Analysis, Social Capital, and Entrepreneurship among North American Ethnic Groups," *Cross-Cultural Re-*

search, 36 (1) (February 2002): 48–72.

30. Clara E. Rodriquez has written the best analysis of Puerto Rican racial consciousness in her "Puerto Ricans: Between Black and White," in Roberto Santiago, ed., *Boricuas: Influential Puerto Rican Writings—An Anthology* (New York: Ballantine Books, 1995).

31. José Vasconcelos, *La raza cósmica : misión de la raza Iberoamericana, Argentina y Brasil* (México: Espasa Calpe/El Colegio Nacional, 1994).

32. Jack Hitt, "The Newest Indians," *New York Times,* August 21, 2005.

33. This is illustrated by a recent controversy in major league baseball. A debate broke out about the list of players included in a "Latin Legends" team ballot. In particular, Reggie Martinez Jackson and Ted Williams were left out despite having some Latino in their background. An official explained that one of the reasons was that these names *"would distort the ballot* and *cause havoc* because [their] ethnicity is not widely known" (Richard Sandomir, "Williams and Jackson Omitted from Latino Ballots," *New York Times,* August 26, 2005, D1).

34. Zadie Smith, *On Beauty: A Novel* (New York: Penguin Press, 2005), 242.

35. Norman Mailer, "The White Negro: Superficial Reflections on the Hipster," *Dissent* 17 (2) (1957). Spring.

36. See, for example, Daniel Sabbagh and Ann Morning, "Comparative Study on the Collection of Data to Measure the Extent and Impact of Discrimination in a Selection of Countries, Final Report on the United States," May 2004, at www .economie-humanisme.org (accessed Aug. 30, 2005); James P. Smith, "Race and Ethnicity in the Labor Market: Trends over the Short and Long Run," published at website, revised June 1999, Rand Corporation; and Thomas Sowell, *Civil Rights: Rhetoric or Reality?* (New York: William Morrow, 1984).

37. This does not have to be the outcome. There are some examples of collaborative alliances between minorities. See Amy Foerster, "Race, Identity, and Belonging: 'Blackness' and the Struggle for Solidarity in a Multiethnic Labor Union," *Social Problems* 51 (3) (August 2004): 386–409.

38. See "Thought Experiments" in *Stanford Encyclopedia of Philosophy,* at http://plato .stanford.edu/entries/thought-experiment/ (accessed July 26, 2005).

39. Dimitria Giorgas, "Community Formation and Social Capital in Australia," 7th Australian Institute of Family Studies Conference, Sydney, 24–26 July, 2000, http://www.aifs.gov.au/ (accessed Aug. 28, 2005).

40. Lucinda Platt and Paul Thompson, "Researching the Role of Family Capital in the Social Mobility of Migrant Ethnic Minorities," paper contributed to the "Whither Social Capital? Past, Present, and Future" conference, London South Bank University, 6–7 April, 2005.

41. Theodore Dalrymple, "Choosing to Fail," *City Journal* (Winter 2000). http://www .city-journal.org/html/10_1_ oh_to_be.html.

42. Ward Goodenough, "Culture," in David Levinson and Melvin Ember, eds., *Encyclopedia of Cultural Anthropology.* Vol. 1. (New York: Holt, 1996), 291–99.

43. See Murray Edelman, *Constructing the Political Spectacle* (Chicago: University of Chicago Press, 1988).

44. This is a truism that even Shelby Steele admits. He quotes and agrees with Martin Luther King, Jr., that the only way for African Americans to get ahead is to work harder, "to run faster than the [white] man in front of you" (1990, 138).

45. Ira Katznelson argues that whites have received considerable "affirmative action" from supposedly neutral federal government policies that boosted their postwar rise up the ladder of success. See his *When Affirmative Action Was White: An Untold History of Racial Inequality in Twentieth-Century America* (New York: Norton, 2005).

46. Amy Waldman, "Seething Unease Shaped British Bombers' Newfound Zeal," *New York Times,* July 31, 2005.

47. As Eliezer Ben-Rafael has written, "a religious faith is particularly able to inspire dedication to believers, and sustain the cohesion of communities, throughout centuries" ("Sociology of Ethnicity," *International Encyclopedia of the Social and Behavioral Sciences* [New York: Elsevier, 2001]).

48. Shelby Steele, "The Age of White Guilt," *Harper's Magazine,* Nov. 2002, 37.

49. Assimilation and rejection of American culture probably occur simultaneously for Puerto Ricans. They also occur in complex, unpredictable ways. Juan Flores writes, for example, that Puerto Ricans have "assimilated" towards African American rather than white culture in *From Bomba to Hip-Hop: Puerto Rican Culture and Latino Identity* (New York: Columbia University Press, 2000).

50. G.I. Borjas, *Heaven's Door: Immigration Policy and the American Economy* (Princeton, NJ: Princeton University Press, 1999), 55.

51. Greg Tate, "Hiphop Turns 30: Whatcha celebratin' for?" *Village Voice,* January 4, 2005.

52. Roland G. Fryer, Jr., "An Economic Approach to Cultural Capital," Harvard Society of Fellows and NBER, June 2003, accessed on Aug. 20, 2005, from http://post.economics.harvard .edu/faculty/fryer/papers.html.

53. See Federico Echenique and Roland G. Fryer, Jr., "On the Measurement of Segregation," March 2005, accessed on Aug. 20, 2005, from http://post .economics.harvard.edu/faculty/ fryer/papers.html.

54. Salvador Vidal-Ortiz, "Puerto Ricans and the Politics of Speaking Spanish," *Latino Studies* 2 (2004): 254–58.

55. See Lea Ramsdell, "Language and Identity Politics: The Linguistic Autobiographies of La-

tinos in the United States," *Journal of Modern Literature* (Fall 2004): 28.

56. David Austen-Smith and Roland G. Fryer, Jr., "The Economics of Acting White," Working Paper 9904, http://www.nber.org/papers/w9904, August 2003, accessed on Aug. 20, 2005.

57. George T. Rowan, E. Pernell, Jr., and T. A. Akers, "Gender Role Socialization in African American Men: A Conceptual Framework," *Journal of African American Men* 1 (4) (Spring 1997): 12.

58. Television personality Geraldo Rivera, for example, created a career out of his representation of the Young Lords in this period.

59. Herman Gray, *Watching Race: Television and the Struggle for Blackness* (Minneapolis: University of Minnesota Press, 1995), 4.

60. More recently, these ideological positions have infected each other. The welfare state has been shrunken by neoliberals while conservatives have learned to advance their political agendas with a more "compassionate"

tinge that accepts some kind of government "safety net."

61. Kerry L. Riley, "Bourgeois Blues: Intergenerational Relationships and Manhood as Post–Civil Rights Discourse," *Journal of African American Men* 1 (4) (Spring 1996): 55.

62. Craig Werner, *A Change Is Gonna Come: Music, Race, and the Soul of America* (New York: Penguin Books, 1999), 18.

63. Cumann Na Saoirse Naisiunta, "The American Irish: From Oppression to Freedom, An Introduction," available at http://irishfreedom.net/Cultural/THE%20AMERICAN%20IRISH.doc, accessed Aug. 31, 2005.

64. Ibid.

65. Richard Jensen, "No Irish Need Apply": A Myth of Victimization," *Journal of Social History* 36 (2) (2002): 405–29.

66. Lucinda Platt and Paul Thompson, "Researching the Role of Family Capital in the Social Mobility of Migrant Ethnic Minorities," paper contributed to the *Whither Social Capital? Past, Present and Future* conference, London South Bank University, 6–7 April, 2005.

67. Lucinda Platt, "The Intergenerational Social Mobility of Minority Ethnic Groups," *Sociology* 39 (3) (July 2005): 459.

68. Norman Podhoretz, "The Brutal Bargain," *Making It* (New York: Random House, 1967).

69. Esperanza Martell, "*In the Belly of the Beast*: Beyond Survival," in Andres Torres and Jose E. Velazquez, eds., *The Puerto Rican Movement: Voices from the Diaspora* (Philadelphia, PA: Temple University Press, 1998).

70. Iris Morales, "Palante, Siempre Palante! The Young Lords," Torres and Velazquez 1998, 211.

71. Felipe Luciano, "Palante: Young Lords," in Roberto Santiago, ed., *Boricuas: Influential Puerto Rican Writings—An Anthology* (New York: Ballantine Books, 1995), 246.

72. "They Flee from Me" by Sir Thomas Wyatt, Poetry Archives, accessed at http://www.emule.com/poetry/?page=poem&poem=2568, on March 30, 2006.

73. Matthew Arnold, *Empedocles on Etna, and Other Poems* (London: B. Fellowes, 1852).

Bibliography

"Age of Hand-made Cigars Gives Way to Machine Era" (1926). *New York Times*, Aug. 22, A18.

Agee, J., and W. Evans (1939). *Let Us Now Praise Famous Men*. Boston: Houghton Mifflin.

Alvarez, J. (1994). *In the Time of the Butterflies*. Chapel Hill, NC: Algonquin Books.

Anderson, D. (1962). "Hearing Shunned by Puerto Ricans." *New York Times*, Nov. 1.

Andreasen, A. R. (1982). "Disadvantaged Hispanic Consumers: A Research Perspective and Agenda." *The Journal of Consumer Affairs* 16, 1.

Anselmo, A., and A. Rubal-Lopez (2005). *On Becoming Nuyoricans*. New York: Peter Lang.

Ashley, David (1997). *History without a Subject: The Postmodern Condition*. Oxford: Westview Press.

Aponte-Pares, L. (1994). "What's Yellow and White and Has Land All Around It: Appropriating Place in Puerto Rican Barrios." *Centro Journal*, 7, 1.

Arts, B. (2000). "Political Influence of NGOs on International Environmental Issues." In H. Goverde, P. G. Cerny, M. Haugaard, and H. H. Lentner, *Power in Contemporary Politics: Theories, Practices, Globalizations*, pp. 132–47. Thousand Oaks, CA: Sage.

Austen-Smith, D., and R. G. Fryer (2003). "The Economics of Acting White." *National Bureau of Economic Research Working Papers*, 9904, August.

"Ask Police Protection: New York Porto Ricans Complain of Being Attacked" (1926). *New York Times*, July 30, 29.

Bachrach, P., and M. S. Baratz (1962). "Two Faces of Power." *American Political Science Review*, 947–52.

"Badillo Confers with Young Lords" (1970). *New York Times*, Feb. 1.

Baker, Susan S. (2002). *Understanding Mainland Puerto Rican Poverty*. Philadelphia, PA: Temple University Press.

Ball, John C., and Jill Jones (2000). *Fame at Last: Who Was Who According to the New York Times Obituaries*. (Kansas City, MO: Andrews McMeel Publishing).

Ball, T. (1992). "New Faces of Power." In T. E. Wartenberg, (Ed.) *Rethinking Power* (pp. 19–31). Albany: State University of New York.

Balzer, M. (2005). "Essays on Leading and Following." (Accessed at http://www.eijkhout .net/lead_follow/).

Barry, D. W. (1959). "The Puerto Rican Adapts Remarkably Well." *Washington Post*, March 8, E3.

Baudrillard, J. (1993). *Symbolic Exchange and Death*. London, UK: Sage.

Bauman, Z. (1990). *Thinking Sociologically*. Cambridge, MA: Blackwell.

Baver, S. (1984). "Puerto Rican Politics in New York City: The Post–World War II Period." In J. Jennings and Rivera.

Beer, A. B. (2001). "From the Bronx to Brooklyn: Spanish-Language Movie Theaters and Their Audiences in New York City, 1930–1999." Northwestern University Ph.D. dissertation.

Bendix, Reinhard (1989). "Inequality and Social Structure: A Comparison of Marx and Weber." In Coser and Rosenberg.

Benjamin, G. (1974). *Race Relations and the New York City Commission on Human Rights*. Ithaca, NY: Cornell University Press.

Bennett, W. L., and R. M. Entman (2000). *Mediated Politics: Communication in the Future of Democracy*. Cambridge, England: Cambridge University Press.

Ben-Rafael, E. (2001). "Sociology of Ethnicity." *International Encyclopedia of the Social and Behavioral Sciences*. New York: Elserier. (Accessed on Aug. 22, 2006 at: http://spirit .tau.ac.il/socAnt/benRafael/ ethnicity.doc.

Berger, Bennett M. (1995). *An Essay on Culture: Symbolic Structure and Social Structure*. Berkeley: University of California Press.

Berger, S., and M. Piore (Ed.) (1980). *Dualism and Discontinuity in Industrial Society*. Cambridge, England: Cambridge University Press.

Berkowitz, H. (1994). "Williams Tops 'Q' List." *New York Newsday*, October 6, A.57.

Bernstein, B., and A. J. Matusow (Ed.) (1969). *20th-Century America: Recent Interpretations*. New York: Harcourt, Brace and World.

Bernstein, Irving (1960). *The Lean Years: Workers in an Unbalanced Society*. New York: Houghton-Mifflin.

Best, Steven, and D. Kellner (1991). *The Postmodern Turn.* New York: Guilford Press.

"Bias Laid to City in Tenant Choice" (1960). *New York Times,* July 4.

Blau, Peter M. (1996). *Exchange and Power in Social Life.* New Brunswick, NJ: Transaction Books.

Bloch, P. (1973). *La-Le-Lo-Lai: Puerto Rican music and its performers.* New York: Plus Ultra.

Bonilla, F., and R. Campos (1986). *Industry and Idleness.* New York: Centro.

Boulding, K. (1990). *Three Faces of Power.* London, England: Sage.

Bourdieu, P. (1992). *The Logic of Practice.* Stanford, CA: Stanford University Press.

Bourdieu, P., and L. J. D. Wacquant (1992). *An Invitation to Reflexive Sociology.* Chicago, IL: University of Chicago Press.

Bourgeois, P. (1995). *In Search of Respect: Selling Crack in El Barrio.* Cambridge, UK: Cambridge University Press.

Bowles, S., and H. Gintis. (1986). *Democracy and Capitalism.* New York: Basic Books.

Bowman, K. L. (2001). "The New Face of School Desegregation (Latino Segregation in Public Schools)." *Duke Law Journal* 50, 16, 1751–93.

Brettell, C. (2002). "The Individual/Agent and Culture/Structure in the History of the Social Sciences." *Social Science History* 26, 3, 429–45.

Brisset, D., and E. C. (Ed.) (1990). *Life as Theatre: A Dramaturgical Sourcebook.* New York: Aldine de Gruyter.

Brown-Graham, A. R. (1999). "Housing Discrimination against Hispanics in Private Rental Markets." *Popular Government* 65, 1, 45–51.

Browning, R. P., D. R. Marshall, and D. Tabb. (2003). *Racial Politics in American Cities.* New York: Longman.

Calzada Vazquez, Jose (1966). *El Desbalance entre Recursos y Poblacion en Puerto Rico.* San Juan, PR: Centro de Estudios Demograficos.

Cardona, L. A. (1987). *A History of Puerto Ricans in the United States.* Volume 2, *Sojourner from Puerto Rico.* Silver Springs, MD: Carreta Press.

Carrion, A. M. (1983). *Puerto Rico: A Political and Cultural History.* New York: W. W. Norton.

Carter, G. L. (1992). "Hispanic Rioting during the Civil Rights Era." *Sociological Forum* 7, 2, 301–22.

Carter, R. F. (1965). "Pressure from the Left: The American Labor Party, 1936–1954." Syracuse University Ph.D. dissertation.

Case, C. V., and R. Campbell (2002). "A Study of Minorities in Selected Non-Metropolitan Communities in Missouri." Missouri Department of Social Services.

Centro de Estudios Puertorriqueños (1979). *Labor Migration under Capitalism.* New York: Monthly Review Press.

Chavez, L. (1986). "Striving but Still Lagging: Puerto Ricans Wonder Why." *New York Times,* June 5, B1–2.

Chavez, L. (1991). *Out of the Barrio: Towards a New Politics of Hispanic Assimilation.* New York: Basic Books.

Chenault, L. (1938, 1970). *The Puerto Rican Migrant in New York City.* New York: Russell and Russell.

City Planning (1955). *Tenant Relocation Report.* New York: Department of City Planning.

"City Seeks U.S. Aid for Puerto Ricans" (1950). *New York Times,* April 21, 25.

Clegg, S. R. (1989). *Frameworks of Power.* London, England: Sage.

CMIU (1919). *Cigar Makers Official Journal.* Volume 15.

——— (1920). *Cigar Makers Official Journal.* Volume 16.

——— (1925), *Cigar Makers Official Journal.* September, Volume 21.

Coben, S. (1969). "A Study in Nativism: the American Red Scare of 1919–1920." In B. Bernstein, et al.

Colon, J. (1982). *A Puerto Rican in New York and Other Sketches.* New York: International Publishers.

"Columbia University Submits Plan for Study of Puerto Rican Migration" (1947). *New York Times,* Oct. 14.

"Commissioner Sierra Berdecia Suggests That Puerto Rican Migrants Bear Credentials" (1947). *New York Times,* Oct. 28.

Cook, J. M. (2000). "The Social Structure of Political Behavior: Action, Interaction and Congressional Cosponsorship." University of Arizona Ph.D. dissertation.

Cooper, P. (1992). *Once a Cigar Maker: Men, Women, and Culture in American Cigar Factories, 1900–1919.* Urbana: University of Illinois.

"Corsi Offers Plan for Puerto Ricans" (1950). *New York Times,* April 20.

Coser, L., and B. Rosenberg (Ed.) (1989). *Sociological Theory: A Book of Readings.* Prospect Heights, IL: Waveland Press.

Cottle, S. (Ed.). (2003). *News, Public Relations, and Power.* Thousand Oaks, CA: Sage.

CPUSA (1954). *Handbook on Puerto Rican Work.* New York: Puerto Rican Affairs Committee of the Communist Party USA.

Cronon, E. D. (1969). *Black Moses: The Story of Marcus Garvey and the Universal Negro Improvement Association.* Madison: University of Wisconsin Press.

Cruz, J. (2004). "The Changing Socioeconomic and Political Fortunes of Puerto Ricans in New York City, 1960–1990." In G. Haslip-Viera, et al.

Cruz, J., and C. E. Santiago (2001). "The Changing Socioeconomic and Political Fortunes of Puerto Ricans in New York City, 1965–1990." Paper presented at the American Political Science Meetings, San Francisco, California, in September.

Dahl, R. (1991). *Democracy and Its Critics.* New Haven, CT: Yale University Press.

——— (1957). "The Concept of Power." *Behavioral Science* 2 (July), 201–15.

Dalrymple, T. (2000). "Choosing to Fail." *City Journal,* Winter. accessed October 20, 2005 at: www.city-journal.org/html/10_Loh_to_be.html.

Daponte, B. O. (1996). "Race

and Ethnicity during an Economic Transition: The Withdrawal of Puerto Rican Women from New York City's Labour Force, 1960–1980." *Regional Studies* 30, 2, 151–67.

Davies, J. C., III (1966). *Neighborhood Groups and Urban Renewal*. New York: Columbia University Press.

Davila, A. (2001). *Latinos Inc.: The Marketing and Making of a People*. Berkeley: University of California Press.

de la Garza, and R., and L. DiSipio (1992). *From Rhetoric to Reality: Latino Politics in the 1988 Election*. Boulder, CO: Westview Press.

Delgado, R. T. (1979). *El Primer Legislador Puertorriqueno*. San Juan, Puerto Rico: Coleccion Hipatia.

Digeser, P. (1992). "The Fourth Face of Power." *Journal of Politics* 54, 4, 977–1007.

Dixon, T. L., and D. Linz (2000). "Overrepresentation and Underrepresentation of African Americans and Latinos as Lawbreakers on Television News." *Journal of Communication* 50, 2, 131–54.

Douglas, A. (1995). *Terrible Honesty: Mongrel Manhattan in the 1920s*. New York: Farrar, Straus and Giroux.

Dowding, K. (1996). *Power*. Minneapolis: University of Minnesota Press.

Edelman, M. (1964). *The Symbolic Uses of Politics*. Chicago: University of Illinois Press.

Eagle, M. (1960). "The Puerto Ricans in New York City." In N. Glazer and D. McEntire. *Studies in Housing and Minority Groups* (pp. 144–77). Berkeley: University of California Press.

"East 96th Street: Wall between Worlds" (1967). *New York Times*, July 27.

Editorial on Vito Marcantionio (1950). New York *Daily Mirror*, Oct. 23.

"84 Church Aides Plead for Lords" (1970). *New York Times*, Jan. 24, 40.

"El Presidente Butler de Columbia University hablo a los puertorriquenos" (1926). *La Prensa*, Oct. 30, 2.

"El Senador Iglesias exhorta a los

Obreros Hispanos a Organizarse" (1925). *La Prensa*, Aug. 16, 6.

Emerson, Richard M. (1993). "Power-Dependence Relations." In M. E. Olsen and M. N. Marger, *Power in Modern Society* (pp. 48–58). Boulder, CO: Westview Press.

Engels, F. (Ed.) (1909). *Capital: A Critique of Political Economy*. Volume 3, *The Process of Capitalist Production as a Whole*. By Karl Marx. Chicago, IL: Charles H. Kerr & Company.

Estades, R. (1978). *Patterns of Political Participation of Puerto Ricans in New York City*. Puerto Rico: Ramallo Bros. Printing.

Etzioni, A. (1993). "Power as a Societal Force." In M. Olsen and M. N. Marger, *Power in Modern Society* (pp. 18–28). Boulder, CO: Westview.

Angelo, F. (1983). "Puerto Rican Political Participation: New York City and Puerto Rico." In J. Heine, *Puerto Rican Political Participation: New York City and Puerto Rico*. Lanham, MD: The North-South Publishing Company.

——— (1984). "Early Puerto Rican Politics in New York City, 1860–1945: Prolegomenon to a History." In J. Jennings and Rivera, M.

——— (2004). "De'tras Pa'lante: Explorations on the Future History of Puerto Ricans in New York City." In G. Haslip-Viera, et al.

Ferretti, F. (1970). "Survey Sees Bias in Broadcasting." *New York Times*, Jan. 21, 75.

"15 Puerto Rican Leaders Are Rated in Study Here" (1966). *New York Times*, June 5, 118.

"First, Get Good Data on Youth Joblessness" (1980). *New York Times*, July 6.

Fiske, J. (1993). *Power Plays, Power Works*. New York: Verso.

Flores, J. (1993). *Divided Borders: Essays on Puerto Rican Identity*. Houston, TX: Arte Publico Press.

——— (1996). "Pan-Latino/Trans-Latino: Puerto Ricans in the *New Nueva York*." *Centro*, 8 (1,2) 170–86.

——— (2000). *From Bomba to Hip-Hop: Puerto Rican Culture and Latino Identity: Popular Cultures, Everyday Lives*. New York: Columbia University Press.

——— (2002). "Nueva York—Diaspora City: U.S. Latinos Between and Beyond." *NACLA Report on the Americas* 35, 6, 46–51.

Force, H. T. (1982). *Sources for the Study of Puerto Rican Migration: 1879–1930*. New York: Centro de Estudios Puerto rriquenos.

Fording, R. C. (2001). "The Political Response to Black Insurgency: A Critical Test of Competing Theories." *American Political Science Review*, 95, 1, 115–130.

Foucault, M., and C. Gordon (Ed.) (1980). *Power/Knowledge: Selected Interviews and Other Writings, 1972–1977*. New York: Pantheon.

French, J. R., and B. Raven (1959). "The Bases of Social Power." In D. Cartwright, *Studies in Social Power* (pp. 150–67). Ann Arbor: University of Michigan Press.

"From Latin League in Harlem Centre" (1926). *New York Times*, Sept. 9, 5.

Fryer, R. G., and S. D. Levitt (2004). "The Causes and Consequences of Distinctively Black Names." *Quarterly Journal of Economics* 119, 3 (August).

Gabilondo, J. (2001). "The Global Phallus: On the Digital and Allegorical Economy of the Hispanic Subaltern in Hollywood Film." *Discourse*, 23, 1 (Winter), 4–24.

Gandy, M. (2002). "Between Borinquen and the Barrio: Environmental Justice and New York City's Puerto Rican Community, 1969–1972". *Antipode*, 34, 4, 730–61.

Garcia, K. (1990). "Puerto Rico: Hacia un cine nacional." *Centro Journal* 2, 8 (Spring).

Giddens, A. (1984). *The Constitution of Society*. Los Angeles: University of California Press.

——— (1995). *Politics, Sociology, and Social Theory: Encounters with Classical and Contemporary Social Thought*.

Palo Alto, CA: Stanford University Press.

Gilderbloom, J. I., and J. P. Markham (1993). "Hispanic Rental Housing Needs in the United States: Problems and Prospects." *Housing and Society* 20.

Giorgas, D. (2000). "Community Formation and Social Capital in Australia". *Family Futures: Issues in Research and Policy,* Paper presented at the 7th Australian Institute of Family Studies Conference in Sydney, July 24–26.

Giroux, Henry, and P. McLaren (Eds.) (1994). *Between Borders: Pedagogy and the Politics of Cultural Studies.* New York: Routledge.

Glaeser, E. L., and J. L. Vigdor (2001). *Racial Segregation in the 2000 Census: Promising News.* Washington, DC: Brookings Institution.

Glasser, Ruth (1995). *My Music Is My Flag: Puerto Rican Musicians and Their New Communities, 1917–1940.* Berkeley: University of California Press.

Goodenough, W. (1996). "Culture." In Levinson, D., and M. Ember. New York: Henry Holt, 291–99.

Goodsell, Charles T. (1988). "The Architecture of Parliaments: Legislative Houses and Political Culture." *British Journal of Political Science,* 18, 3, (July).

Gosnell, P. A. (1945). "The Puerto Ricans in New York City, 1945." New York University Ph.D. dissertation.

Goulbourne, H., and J. Solomos (2003). "Families, Ethnicity, and Social Capital." *Social Policy and Society* 2, 4, 329–38.

Gould, M. (1999). "Race and Theory: Culture, Poverty, and Adaptation to Discrimination in Wilson and Ogbu." *Sociological Theory* 17, 2, 171–200.

Goverde, H., P.G. Cerny, M. Haugaard, and H.H. Lentner (Ed.). (2000). *Power in Contemporary Politics: Theories, Practices, Globalizations.* Thousand Oaks, CA: Sage Press.

Graber, D. A. (1984). *Media Power in Politics.* Washington, DC: CQ Press.

Gray, H. (1995). *Watching Race: Television and the Struggle for Blackness.* Minneapolis: University of Minnesota Press.

Green, D. P., and I. Shapiro (1994). *Pathologies of Rational Choice: A Critique of Applications in Political Science.* New Haven, CT: Yale University Press.

"Group Organizes Puerto Rican Aid" (1964). *New York Times,* Nov. 7.

Guzda, H. P. (1982). "Labor Department's First Program to Assist Black Workers." *Monthly Labor Review,* 107, 5, June, 39–44.

Halperin, E. C. (2001). "The Jewish Problems in U.S. Medical Education, 1920–1955." *Journal of the History of Medicine* 56, 140–67.

Hamill, P. (1975). "Coming of Age in Nueva York." In F. Cordasco and E. Bucchioni, *The Puerto Rican Experience* (pp. 198–212). Totowa, NJ: Littlefield, Adams.

Handlin, O. (1959). *The Newcomers: Negroes and Puerto Ricans in a Changing Metropolis.* Garden City, NY: Anchor Books.

———. (1962). *The Newcomers: Negroes and Puerto Ricans in a Changing Metropolis.* Garden City, NY: Anchor Books.

Harre, R. (2002). "Social Reality and the Myth of Social Structure." *European Journal of Social Theory* 5, 1, 111–23.

Haslip-Viera, G., A. Falcon, and F. M. Rodriguez (Ed.) (2004). *Boricuas in Gotham: Puerto Ricans in the Making of Modern New York City.* Princeton, NJ: Markus Weiner.

Haslip-Viera, G., and S. L. Baver (Ed.) (1996). *Latinos in New York: Communities in Transition.* Notre Dame, IN: University of Notre Dame Press.

Haugaard, M. (2000). "Power, Ideology and Legitimacy." In Goverde, H., P. G. Cerny, M. Haugaard, and H. H. Lentner (pp. 59–76). Thousand Oaks, CA: Sage.

Hayes, L. M. (1983). "And Darkness Closes In: . . . A National Study of Jail Suicides."

Criminal Justice and Behavior 10, 4, 461–84.

Hayward, Clarissa R. (2000). *De-Facing Power.* Cambridge, UK: Cambridge University Press.

Hegel, G. W. F. (1967). *Hegel's Philosophy of Right.* London, UK: Oxford University Press.

Heilbroner, R. L. (1985). *The Nature and Logic of Capitalism.* New York: Norton.

Heine, J. (Ed.) (1983). *Time for Decision: The United States and Puerto Rico.* Lanham, MD: The North-South Publishing.

Heller, Agnes (1974). *The Theory of Need in Marx.* New York: St. Martin's Press.

Hirsch, P., S. Michaels, and R. Friedman (1990). "Clean Models vs. Dirty Hands: Why Economics Is different from Sociology." In S. Zukin and P. DiMaggio, *Structures of Capital: The Social Organization of the Economy* (pp. 39–56). Cambridge, UK: Cambridge University Press.

Hirschmann, Albert O. (1970). *Exit, Voice, and Loyalty.* Cambridge, MA: Harvard University Press.

History Task Force (HTF) (1982). *Sources for the Study of Puerto Rican Migration, 1879–1930.* New York: Centro de Estudios Puertorriquenos.

Hitt, J. "The Newest Indians" (2005). *New York Times,* Aug. 21, Section 6, 36.

Hobbes, Thomas (1986). *Leviathan.* New York: Scribners.

Hoffman, A. R., and C. A. Noriega (2004). *Looking for Latino Regulars on Prime-Time Television: The Fall 2003 Season.* UCLA Chicano Studies Research Center, 193 Haines Hall, Los Angeles, CA 90095-1544: Chicano Studies Research Center.

Holsti, O. R. (1969). *Content Analysis for the Social Sciences and Humanities.* Reading, MA: Addison-Wesley.

Housing Authority (1955). *Annual Report.* New York: New York City Housing Authority.

Hunter, S., and J. Bainbridge (2005). *American Gunfight: The Plot to Kill Harry Truman* and the Shootout That Stopped It. New York: Simon and Schuster.

IPR (1995). *1995 Guide to Puerto Rican and Other Latino Elected Officials in New York City*. New York: Institute for Puerto Rican Policy.

Irvine, W. B. (2006). *On Desire: Why We Want What We Want*. New York: Oxford University Press.

Isaac, J. C. (1987). *Power and Marxist Theory: A Realist View*. Ithaca, NY: Cornell University Press.

——— (1992). "Beyond the Three Faces of Power: A Realist Critique." In T. E. Wartenberg, *Rethinking Power* (pp. 32–55). Albany, NY: SUNY Press.

Jackson, Anthony (1976). *A Place Called Home: A History of Low-Cost Housing in Manhattan*. Cambridge, MA: MIT Press.

Jackson, Peter (1983). "Vito Marcantonio and Ethnic Politics in New York." *Ethnic and Racial Studies* 6, 1.

Janeway, E. (1980). *Powers of the Weak*. New York: Knopf.

Jennings, J. (1977). *Puerto Rican Politics in New York City*. Washington, DC: University Press of America.

——— (1999). "Missing Links in the Study of Puerto Rican Poverty in the United States." In J. Jennings and L. Kushnick (Ed.), *A New Introduction to Poverty: The Role of Race, Power, and Politics* (pp. 89–101). New York: New York University Press.

Jennings, J., and M. Rivera (Ed.) (1984). *Puerto Rican Politics in Urban America*. Westport, CT: Greenwood.

Johnson, J. (1988). *Black Manhattan*. New York: Atheneum.

Jonas, G. (1992). *Dancing: The Pleasure, Power, and Art of Movement*. New York: Harry Abrams.

Jukes, P. (1990). *A Shout in the Street: An Excursion into the Modern City*. Los Angeles: University of California Press.

Katz, M. A. (2004). "The Beats Have No Color Lines: An Exploration of White Consump-

tion of Rap Music." Master of Science in Sociology, Virginia Polytechnic Institute, April 30.

Katz, W. L. (1997). *Black Legacy: A History of New York's African Americans*. New York, NY: Atheneum.

Kerbel, M. R. (1999). *Remote and Controlled: Media Politics in a Cynical Age*. Boulder, CO: Westview.

Kihss, P. (1957). "Gains Made Here by Puerto Ricans." *New York Times*, May 31, 33.

——— (1965). "Newly Increased Inspection of Cells Thwarts Puerto Ricans' Suicide Attempt." *New York Times*, April 8.

Killough, L. (1924). *The Tobacco Products Industry in New York and Its Environs: Present Trends and Probable Future Development*. New York: Regional Plan Association.

Korda, M. (1975). *Power: How to Get It, How to Use It*. New York: Ballantine Books.

Lancaster, Roger N. (1992). *Life is Hard: Machismo, Danger, and the Intimacy of Power in Nicaragua*. Berkeley: University of California Press.

Landale, N. S., and R. S. Oropesa (2002). "White, Black, or Puerto Rican? Racial Self-Identification among Mainland and Island Puerto Ricans." *Social Forces* 81, 1, 231–54.

Landale, N. S., R. S. Oropesa, D. Llanes, and B. K. Gorman (1999). "Does Americanization Have Adverse Effects on Health? Stress, Health Habits, and Infant Health Outcomes among Puerto Ricans." *Social Forces* 78, 2, 613–41.

Landale, N. S., R. S. Oropesa, and Bridget K. Gorman (2000). "Migration and Infant Death: Assimilation or Selective Migration among Puerto Ricans." *American Sociological Review* 65, 888–909.

Lapp, M. (1990). *The Migration Division of Puerto Rico and Puerto Ricans in New York City, 1948–1969*. Johns Hopkins University Ph.D. dissertation.

Lauria, A. (1964). "*Respeto, Relajo*, and Inter-Personal Relations in Puerto Rico." *Anthro-

pological Quarterly* 37, 2, 53–67.

Lawson, R., and M. Naison (1986). *The Tenant Movement in New York City, 1904–1984*. New Brunswick, NJ: Rutgers University Press.

LeBlanc, A. N. (2003). *Random Family: Love, Drugs, Trouble, and Coming of Age in the Bronx*. New York: Scribners.

Lee, T., and K. Ramakrishnan (2002). "What's in a Name? Ethnic Names, Immigrant Acculturation, and Latino Mass Opinion." Boston, MA: American Political Science Association.

Lemann, N. (1991). "The Other Underclass." *Atlantic* 268, 6, 96–110.

Lembcke, J. (1991). "Class Analysis and Studies of the U.S. Working Class: Theoretical, Conceptual, and Methodological Issues." In R. F. Levine, S. G. McNall, and R. Fantasia (Ed.), *Bringing Class Back in Contemporary and Historical Perspectives* (pp. 83–98). Boulder, CO: Westview.

Lemert, C. C. (1997). *Social Things: An Introduction to the Sociological Life*. Lanham, MD: Rowman & Littlefield.

Levine, Rhonda F., S. G. McNall, and R. Fantasia (Ed.) (1991). *Class Analysis and Studies of the U.S. Working Class: Theoretical, Conceptual, and Methodological Issues*. Boulder, CO: Westview.

Levinson, D., and M. Ember (Ed.) (1996). *Encyclopedia of Cultural Anthropology*. New York: Henry Holt.

Lewis, G. K. (1963). *Puerto Rico: Freedom and Power in the Caribbean*. New York, NY: Monthly Review Press.

Lieberson, S. (2000). *A Matter of Taste: How Names, Fashions, and Culture Change*. New Haven, CT: Yale University Press.

Lieberson, and S., K. Mikelson (1995). "Distinctive African-American Names: An Experimental, Historical, and Linguistic Analysis of Innovation." *American Sociological Review* 60, 928–46.

Lipsitz, G. (1998). *The Possessive Investment in Whiteness: How*

White People Profit from Identity Politics. Philadelphia, PA: Temple University Press.

Little, D. (1991). *Varieties of Social Explanation: An Introduction to the Philosophy of Social Science*. Boulder, CO: Westview.

Lloyd, C. (1993). *The Structures of History*. Oxford, UK: Blackwell Oxford.

Lopez, A. (1979). "Vito Marcantonio: An Italian-American's Defense of Puerto Rico and Puerto Ricans." *Caribbean Review* 8, 1 (January).

———— (1997). "Of Rhythms and Borders." In C. F. Delgado and J. E. Munoz, *Everynight Life: Culture and Dance in Latin/o America* (pp. 310–44). Durham, NC: Duke University Press.

"Los anos han pasado provechosamente para todos los oficios menos para los tabaqueros" (1925). *La Prensa*, Feb. 25, 5.

"Los Puertorriquenos de Nueva York piden explicaciones a Sol Bloom" (1925). *La Prensa*, April 29, 2.

"Los Puertorriquenos en Arizona Buscan trabajo (1926). *La Prensa*, Sept. 28.

"Los tabaqueros de Nueva York tendran la ayuda de 700.000 obreros organizados" (1925). *La Prensa*, April 8, 6.

"Los Trabajadores Hispanos son mal pagados en las fabricas de botones" (1925). *La Prensa*, Jan. 22, 1.

"Lowenstein Loses Seat in Congress (1970). *New York Times*, Nov. 4.

Lukes, Steven (1974). *Power: A Radical View*. London, UK: Macmillan.

Machiavelli, Niccolo (1950). *The Prince and the Discourses*. New York: Modern Library.

MacLeod, J. (1987). *Ain't No Makin' It*. Boulder, CO: Westview.

Malanga, S. (2002). "Gotham's Unrepresentative Representatives." *City Journal*, Summer (http://www.city-journal.org/html/12_3_gothams.html).

Mann, A. (1959). *LaGuardia: A Fighter against His Times, 1882–1933*. Chicago, IL:

University of Chicago Press.

"Marcantonio Plot Charged by Mayor" (1949). *New York Times*, Nov. 7.

Marsden, R., and B. Townley (1995). "Power and Postmodernity: Reflections on the Pleasure Dome." *Electronic Journal of Radical Organization Theory* 1, 1 (November). (http://www.mngt.waikato.ac.nz/ejrot/EJROT(newdesign)Vo11_1_front.asp).

Massey, D. (1993). *American Apartheid: Segregation and the Making of the Underclass*. Cambridge, MA: Harvard University Press.

Mastro, D. E., and S. R. Stern (2003). "Representations of Race in Television Commercials: A Content Analysis of Prime-Time Advertising." *Journal of Broadcasting and Electronic Media* 47, 4, 638–47.

Mazelis, F. (2000). "Mexican Immigrants Beaten in New York Suburb." At (http://www.wsws.org/articles/2000/sep2000).

McConville, S., and P. Ong, with D. Houston and J. Rickles (2001). "Examining Residential Segregation Patterns." Lewis Center Research Initiative, University of California.

McGinty, Brian (1991). "Jazz: Red Hot and Cool." In R. J. Maddox (Ed.), *American History: Early Modern Through the 20th Century* (pp. 136–39) Guilford, CT: Dushkin Publisher.

MCPRA (1952). Mayor's Commission on Puerto Rican Affairs. "December 16, 1952 Minutes." *New York City Municipal Archives*.

———— (1953a). Mayor's Commission on Puerto Rican Affairs. "July 23 Minutes." *New York City Municipal Archives*.

———— (1953b). Mayor's Commission on Puerto Rican Affairs. "Interim Report or the MCPRA in New York City: September 1949 to September 1953." *New York City Municipal Archives*.

———— (1954). Mayor's Commission on Puerto Rican Affairs. "November 5, 1954 Minutes." *New York City Municipal Archives*.

Melendez, M. (2003). *We Took the Streets: Fighting for Latino Rights with the Young Lords*. New York: St. Martin's Press.

Merelman, R. M. (1995). *Representing Black Culture: Racial Conflict and Cultural Politics in the United States*. New York: Routledge.

"Mexicans Target of Riot in Bronx: Puerto Ricans Protest Ortiz Verdict—12 Seized" (1966). *New York Times*, Oct. 24, 53.

Miller, M., and C. Werthman (1961). "Public Housing: Tenants and Troubles." *Dissent* 8, 3 (Summer).

Mills, C. W. (1967). *The Sociological Imagination*. Oxford, UK: Oxford University Press.

Mills, C. W., C. Senior, and C. Isales (1948). *The Puerto Ricans of New York City*. New York: Employment and Migration Bureau, Puerto Rico Dept. of Labor.

Mintz, S. W. (1975). "Puerto Rico: An Essay in the Definition of a National Culture." In *Status of Puerto Rico: Selected Background Studies, Prepared for the U.S.–Puerto Rico Commission on the Status of Puerto Rico*. New York: Arno Press.

Miyares, M. (1980). *Models of Political Participation of Hispanic-Americans*. New York: Arno Press.

Moore, J., R. Pinderhughes (Ed.) (1993). *In the Barrios: Latinos and the Underclass Debate*. New York: Russell Sage Foundation.

Morales, J. (1979). "Puerto Rican Poverty and the Migration to Elsewhere; Waltham, Massachusetts: A Case Study." Brandeis University Ph.D. dissertation

Narvaez, A. A. (1970). "City Bodegas Fill Many Roles." *New York Times*, Aug. 3, 33.

National Council of La Raza (2001). "Beyond the Census: Hispanics and an American Agenda." Washington, DC.

Negron-Muntaner, F. (2004). *Boricua Pop: Puerto Ricans and the Latinization of American Culture*. New York: New York University Press.

Neustadt, R. E. (1976). *Presiden-*

tial Power. New York: Wiley and Sons.

New York City Dept. of Commerce (1956). "Puerto Ricans Key Source of Labor in New York Industries." *Highlights,* October.

New York City Planning Commission (1957). *Urban Renewal: Report on West Side Urban Renewal to Mayor Wagner.* New York: City Planning.

"New York City Welfare Department Reports Few Puerto Ricans on Welfare" (1947). *New York Times,* Oct. 17.

"New York's Quota of Strikes" (1914). *New York Times,* Sept. 21, 49.

Nimmo, D., and J.E. Combs. (1990). *Mediated Political Realities.* White Plains, NY: Longman.

Ojeda, F. (1978). *Vito Marcantonio y Puerto Rico: Por Los Trabajadores y Por La Nacion.* Rio Piedras, PR: Ediciones Huracan.

——— (1986). "Puerto Rican Communities in New York." In Oral History Task Force, Centro de Estudios Puertorriquenos, CUNY.

Oliver, P. E., and D. J. Myers (1999). "How Events Enter the Public Sphere: Conflict, Location and Sponsorship in Local Newspaper Coverage of Public Events." *American Journal of Sociology* 105, 1 (July), 38–87.

Olsen, M. E. (Ed.) (1970). *Power in Societies.* London: Macmillan.

Oral History Task Force (1986). *Extended Roots: From Hawaii to New York: Migraciones Puertorriquenas a los Estados Unidos.* New York: Centro de Estudios Puertorriquenos, CUNY.

Ospina, H. C., and N. Caistor, translator (1995). *Salsa! Havana Heat, Bronx Beat.* London, England: Latin American Bureau.

Padilla, E. (1958). *Up from Puerto Rico.* New York: Columbia University Press.

——— (1972). "Race Relations: A Puerto Rican View." In R. K. Yin, *The City in the Seventies* (pp. 16–20) . Itasca, IL: F. E. Peacock Publishers.

——— (Ed.) (1994). *Handbook*

of *Hispanic Cultures in the United States: Sociology.* Houston, TX: Arte Publico Press.

Pantoja, A. (1989). "Puerto Ricans in New York: A Historical and Community Development Perspective." *Centro* 2, 5 (Spring).

——— (2002). *Antonia Pantoja: Memoir of a Visionary.* Houston, TX: Arte Publico Press.

——— (2004). "Puerto Ricans in New York: A Historical and Community Perspective." In G. Haslip-Viera, A. Falcon, and F. M. Rodriguez, Princeton, NJ: Markus Weiner, 227–237.

Parenti, M. (1978). *Power and the Powerless.* New York: St. Martin's Press.

PEW Hispanic Center (2002). *2002 National Survey of Latinos.* Washington, DC.

Perez, R. (1990). "From Assimilation to Annihilation: Puerto Rican Images in U.S. Films." *Centro* 3, 1 (Spring).

Pierson, P. (2004). *Politics in Time: History, Institutions, and Social Analysis.* Princeton, NJ: Princeton University Press.

"Pinero Predicts Influx Reversal in Fall" (1947). *New York Times,* Aug. 10.

Piven, F. F., R. A. Cloward (1993). *Regulating the Poor: The Functions of Public Welfare.* New York: Random House.

"Power 101" (1996). *Entertainment,* Oct. 25, 30–87.

Post, Langdon (1936). *Housing . . . or Else: A Letter to a Banker.* New York: New York City Housing Authority.

Preuse, C. F. (Ed.) (1955). "On a Political Quota System." NYC Municipal Archives, Mayor Wagner Papers, MN 40148, Subject Files 1954–1965.

"Puerto Rican Leader: Gilberto Gerena-Valentine" (1964). *New York Times,* March 2, 18.

"Puerto Ricans Get Campaign Warning: Island Governor Tells Voting for Marcantonio May Cause Misunderstanding (1949). *New York Times,* Oct. 17.

"Puerto Ricans Here as Domestics" (1948). *New York Times,* Feb. 28, 21.

"Puerto Ricans 'In No Man's

Land' Here" (1969). *New York Times,* Sept. 28.

"Puerto Ricans Warned by City" (1968). *New York Times,* Jan. 10.

"Puerto Rico Acts to Cut Migration" (1947). *New York Times,* Aug. 4.

"Puerto Rico Cited In U.N. as Model (1961). *New York Times,* March 30, 1.

"Puerto Rican Group Seizes Church in E. Harlem in Demand for Space" (1969). *New York Times,* Dec. 29.

Ramos-Zayas, A. Y. (2003). *National Performances: The Politics of Class, Race, and Space in Puerto Rican Chicago.* Chicago: University of Chicago Press.

"Record of Strikes 11,092 In 3 Years" (1919). *New York Times,* July 20, 24.

Redner, H. (1991). "What's the Use of Social Science? A Review of Charles E. Lindblom's *Inquiry and Change.*" *Methodus,* Dec., 314–20.

"Relief Given to Puerto Ricans" (1947). *New York Times,* Aug. 26.

"Resident Commissioner Asks for Agency for Would-be Migrants" (1947). *New York Times,* Oct. 30.

Reyes, L., and P. Rubie (1994). *Hispanics in Hollywood: An Encyclopedia of Film and Television.* Westview, CT: Greenwood Press.

Richard, Alfred C. (1993). *Censorship and Hollywood's Hispanic Image: An Interpretative Filmography, 1936–1955.* Westport, CT: Greenwood Press.

Rivera, R. Z. (2001). "Hip-Hop, Puerto Ricans, and Ethnoracial Identities in New York." In A. Lao-Montes, and A. Davila, *Mambo Montage: The Latinization of New York* (pp. 235–61) New York: Columbia University Press.

Rivera-Batiz, F. L. (2004). "Puerto Rican New Yorkers in the 1990s: A Demographic and Socioeconomic Profile." In Haslip-Viera, et al, 107–129.

Roberts, J. S. (1999). *Latin Jazz: The First of the Fusions, 1880s to Today.* New York: Schirmer Books.

Rodriguez, C. (1974). *The Ethnic Queue in the U.S.: The Case of Puerto Ricans.* San Francisco, CA: R & E Research Associates.

———— (2000). *Changing Race: Latinos, the Census, and the History of Ethnicity in the United States.* New York: New York University Press.

Rodriquez, G. (2003). "Race and Ethnicity: Morality Play Stays the Same; Latinos Are Now the No. 1 U.S. Minority but Lack the Historical Claims of Blacks." *Los Angeles Times,* June 22.

Rogler, L. H., R. S. Cooney, and V. Ortiz (1980). "Intergenerational Change in Ethnic Identity in the Puerto Rican Family." *International Migration Review* 14, 2, 193–214.

Rogoff, L. (1997). "Is the Jew White? The Racial Place of the Southern Jew." *American Jewish History,* 85, 3, 195–230.

Rorty, Amelie O. (1992). "Power and Powers: A Dialogue between Buff and Rebuff." In T. E. Wartenberg (Ed.), *Rethinking Power* (pp. 1–13). Albany, NY: SUNY Press.

Rothenberg, M. A. (2004). "Articulating Social Agency in *Our Mutual Friend:* Problems with Performances, Practices, and Political Efficacy." *English Literary History* 71, 719–49.

Rothgeb, J. M. (1993). *Defining Power: Influence and Force in the Contemporary International System.* New York: St. Martin's Press.

Sanchez, J. R. (1986). "Residual Work and Residual Shelter: Housing Puerto Rican Labor in New York City from World War II to 1983." In R. G. Bratt, C. Hartman, and A. Meyerson (Ed.), *Critical Perspectives on Housing* (pp. 202–20). Philadelphia, PA: Temple University Press.

———— (1989). "Housing from the Past." *Centro* 2, 5, 37–45.

———— (1990). *Housing Puerto Ricans in New York City, 1945 to 1984: A Study in Class Powerlessness.* New York University Ph.D. dissertation.

———— (1994). "Puerto Ricans and the Door of Participation in U.S. Politics." In F. Padilla, 259–301.

———— (1996). "Puerto Rican Politics in New York: Beyond 'Secondhand' Theory." In Haslip-Viera, G., S. L. Baver (Ed.) *Latinos in New York: Communities in Transition* (pp. 259–301). Notre Dame, IN: University of Notre Dame Press.

———— (2005). "Latinos Desegregate and Re-Segregate." *Hispanic Encyclopedia.* London: Oxford University Press.

Sanchez-Korral, V. E. (1983). *From Colonia to Community: The History of Puerto Ricans in New York City, 1917–1948.* Westport, CT: Greenwood Press.

———— (2004). "Building the New York Puerto Rican Community, 1945–1965: A Historical Interpretation." In G. Haslip-Viera, et al., 1–18.

Sandis, E. E. (1973). "Characteristics of Puerto Rican Migrants to, and from, the United States." In F. Cordasco and E. Bucchioni (Ed.), *The Puerto Rican Experience: A Sociological Sourcebook.* Totowa, NJ: Littlefield, Adams.

Santiago, A. M., and G. Galster (1995). "Puerto Rican Segregation in the United States: cause or Consequence of Economic Status." *Social Problems* 42, 3, 361–89.

Santiago, A. M., and M. G. Wilder (1991). "Residential Segregation and Links to Minority Poverty: The Case of Latinos in the US." *Social Problems* 38, 701–23.

Savigliano, Marta (1995). *Tango and the Political Economy of Passion.* Boulder, CO: Westview.

Schaffer, A. (1966). *Vito Marcantonio, Radical in Congress.* Syracuse, NY: Syracuse University Press.

Schmitt, R. (1995). *Beyond Separateness: The Social Nature of Human Beings—Their Autonomy, Knowledge, and Power.* Boulder, CO: Westview Press.

Schneider, Anne, and H. Ingram (1995). "Response to Robert C. Lieberman." *American Political Science Review* 89, 443–46.

Sciorra, J. (1996). "Return to the Future: Puerto Rican Vernacular Architecture in New York City." In A. D. King, *Re-Presenting the City: Ethnicity, Capital, and Culture in the 21st-Century Metropolis* (pp. 60–91). New York: New York University Press.

Senior, C. (1965). *The Puerto Ricans: Strangers—Then Neighbors.* Chicago, IL: Quadrangle Books.

Senior, C., and D. O. Watkins (1973). "Toward a Balance Sheet of Puerto Rican Migration." In F. Cordasco and E. Bucchioni (Ed.), *The Puerto Rican Experience: A Sociological Sourcebook.* Totowa, NJ: Littlefield, Adams.

Shefter, Martin (1985). *Political Crisis, Fiscal Crisis: The Collapse and Revival of New York City.* New York: Basic Books.

Shively, W. P. (1998). *The Craft of Political Research.* Upper Saddle River, NJ: Prentice Hall.

Singer, A. (2003). "At Home in the Nation's Capital: Immigrant Trends in Metropolitan Washington." Washington, DC: Brookings Institute.

Skitka, L. J. (2005). "Patriotism or Nationalism? Understanding Post-September 11, 2001, Flag-Display Behavior." *Journal of Applied Social Psychology,* 35, 10, Oct., 1995–2011.

Smith, J. P. (1999). "Race and Ethnicity in the Labor Market: Trends over the Short and Long Run." *National Research Council Conference on Racial Trends,* June.

Sowell, T. (1981). *Markets and Minorities.* New York: Basic Books.

Steele, S. (1990). *The Content of Our Character: A New Vision of Race in America.* New York: St. Martin's Press.

Steele, S. (2002). "The Age of White Guilt." *Harper's Magazine,* 305 (1830), 33–42.

Steiner, Stan (1974). *The Islands: The Worlds of the Puerto Ricans.* New York: Harper & Row.

Stuart, G. (2002). "Integration or Resegregation: Metropolitan Chicago at the Turn of the New Century." Cambridge,

MA: The Civil Rights Project at Harvard.

Suro, R., and A. Singer (2002). "Latino Growth in Metropolitan America: Changing Patterns, New Locations." The PEW Hispanic Center, Washington, DC, July.

"Survey Finds New Jobs in City Exceed Influx of Puerto Ricans" (1954). *New York Times,* Jan. 16, 1.

Susler, J. (1998). "Unreconstructed Revolutionaries: Today's Puerto Rican Political Prisoners/Prisoners of War." In Torres, A., and J. E. Velazquez (Ed.), *The Puerto Rican Movement* (pp. 144–52). Philadelphia, PA: Temple University Press.

Swift, M. (2002). "Still Segregated: After 20 Years of Population Growth, Latinos Concentrated in a Few Cities." *Hartford Courant,* December 29.

Tafoya, S. (2004). *Shades of Belonging.* PEW Hispanic Center Report, Washington, D.C.

Takaki, Ronald T. (1993). *A Different Mirror: A History of Multicultural America.* Boston, MA: Little, Brown.

Taki (1997). "High Life Column." *The Spectator,* June 14.

"Tenth Prisoner Suicide in City This Year Is Under Investigation by Brooklyn Prosecution" (1969). *New York Times,* Sept. 8, 39.

Thomas, L. R. (2002). "Citizens on the Margins: Puerto Rican Migrants in New York City, 1917–1960." University of Pennsylvania Ph.D. dissertation.

"The Puerto Ricans: Behind the Flare-ups" (1967). *New York Times,* July 30, 133.

Tilly, C. (1984). *Statemaking and Social Movements: Essays in History and Theory.* Ann Arbor: University of Michigan Press.

——— (1999). *Durable Inequality.* Berkeley: University of California Press.

"Time 25" (1996). *Time,* 147, 25, June 17, 15–39.

"Time's 25 Most Influential Americans" (1997). *Time,* 149, 16, April 21, 40–66.

Tolchin, M. (1991). "Congress's

Influential Aides Discover Power but Little Glory on Capital Hill." *New York Times,* Nov. 12, A22.

TONY (2005). "25 in '05." *Time Out New York,* Jan. 20–25, 17–28.

Torres, A. (1995). *Between Melting Pot and Mosaic: African Americans and Puerto Ricans in the New York Political Economy.* Philadelphia, PA: Temple University Press.

Torres, A., and J. E. Velazquez (Ed.) (1998). *The Puerto Rican Movement.* Philadelphia, PA: Temple University Press.

Torres-Saillant, S. (2003). "Inventing the Race: Latinos and the Ethnoracial Pentagon." *Latino Studies,* 1,1, 123–51.

Tracey, F. J. (1972). "Suicide and Suicide Prevention in New York City Prisons." *Probation and Parole,* 4, 20–29.

Trolander, Judith A. (1987). *Professionalism and Social Change: From the Settlement House Movement to Neighborhood Centers, 1886 to the Present.* New York: Columbia University Press.

Tuan, Yi-Fu (1977). *Space and Place.* Minneapolis: University of Minnesota Press.

Tucker, R. C. (Ed.) (1972). *The Marx-Engels Reader.* New York: Norton Press.

Turner, V. (1974). *Dramas, Fields, and Metaphors: Symbolic Action in Human Society.* Ithaca, NY: Cornell University Press.

——— (1985). *On the Edge of the Bush: Anthropology as Experience.* Tucson: University of Arizona Press.

U. S. Census Bureau (2000a). "Mapping Census 2000: The Geography of U.S. Diversity—Hispanic or Latino Origin." (Accessed at www.census.gov/population/www/cen2000/atlas.html).

——— (2000b). "The Places People Live: Housing 1999." Washington, DC.

——— (2001). *Census 2000 Fact Sheet.* Washington, DC.

"Utne Visionaries: 120 Voices, 120 Lives" (1995). *Utne,* January/February.

Van Evera, S. (1997). *Guide to Methods for Students of Politi-*

cal Science. Ithaca, NY: Cornell University Press.

Vega, B. (1980). *Memorias de Bernardo Vega.* Rio Piedras: Ediciones Huracan.

Vega, B., and C. A. Iglesias (Ed.) (1984). *Memoirs of Bernardo Vega: A Contribution to the History of the Puerto Rican Community in New York.* New York: Monthly Review Press.

Velilla, M. (1967). *2,000,000 People to Captivate: Greater New York Spanish Market.* New York: Thunder/Book Company.

Wakefield, D. (1959). *Island in the City: The World of Spanish Harlem.* New York: Arno Press.

Wartenberg, T. E. (1990). *The Forms of Power: From Domination to Transformation.* Philadelphia, PA: Temple University Press.

——— (Ed.) (1992). *Rethinking Power.* Albany: State University of New York Press.

Weatherby, W. J., and Roi Ottley (1967). *The Negro in New York: An Informal Social History, 1626–1940.* New York: Praeger.

Whalen, C. T. (2001). *From Puerto Rico to Philadelphia: Puerto Rican Workers and Postwar Economies.* Philadelphia, PA: Temple University Press.

"Who Has Juice?" (1995). *Vibe,* 3, 7, September, 110–121.

Wilkinson, M. J. (2004). "Haciendo Patria: The Puerto Rican Flag in the Art of Juan Sanchez." *Small Axe* 16, 61–83.

Williams, S. (2001). *Emotion and Social Theory.* Thousand Oaks, CA: Sage.

Wilson, W. J. (1987). *The Truly Disadvantaged.* Chicago, IL: University of Chicago Press.

Wolfsfeld, G. (2003). "The Political Contest Model." In S. Cottle, *News, Public Relations, and Power* (pp. 81–95). Thousand Oaks, CA: Sage.

Wright, R. T., and S. H. Decker (1997). "Creating the Illusion of Impending Death: Armed Robbers in Action." *The HFG Review* 2, 1, 10–18.

Wrong, D. H. (1993). "Problems in Defining Power." In M. E.

Olsen and M. N. Marger (Ed.), *Power in Modern Societies.* (pp. 9–17) Boulder, CO: Westview Press.

Young Lords Party (1975). "Palante." In F. Cordasco and E. Bucchioni (Ed.), *The Puerto Rican Experience: A Sociological Sourcebook.* (pp. 231–245). Totowa, NJ: Littlefield, Adams.

Young, Alford (1999). "The (Non)Accumulation of Capital: Explicating the Relationship of Structure and Agency in the Lives of Poor Black Men." *Sociological Theory* 17, 2, 201–27.

Young, H. P. (1998). *Individual Strategy and Social Structure.* Princeton, NJ: Princeton University Press.

Zentella, A. C. (2004). "Commentary: A Nuyorican's View of our History and Languages(s) in New York, 1945–1965". In Haslip-Viera, A. Falcon., and F. M. Rodriquez, (pp. 21–34).

Zimmerman, M. (2003). "Erasure, Imposition, and Crossover of Puerto Ricans and Chicanos in U.S. Film and Music Culture." *Latino Studies* 1, 115–22.

Index

About the Author

José Ramón Sánchez is Associate Professor of Political Science and Chair of Urban Studies at Long Island University, Brooklyn. He is also the Chair of the National Institute for Latino Policy.